INTERCOUNTRY ADOPTION

Contemporary Social Work Studies

Contemporary Social Work Studies is a series disseminating high quality new research and scholarship in the discipline and profession of social work. The series promotes critical engagement with contemporary issues relevant across the social work community and captures the diversity of interests currently evident at national, international and local levels.

CSWS is located in the School of Social Sciences (Social Work Studies Division) at the University of Southampton, UK and is a development from the successful series of books published by Ashgate in association with CEDR (the Centre for Evaluative and Developmental Research) from 1991.

Other titles in this series:

Spirituality and Social Work
Beth R. Crisp
978-0-7546-7734-5

Practice and Research
Ian F. Shaw
978-1-4094-3917-2

Intercountry Adoption

Policies, Practices, and Outcomes

Edited by
JUDITH L. GIBBONS
Saint Louis University, USA
and
KAREN SMITH ROTABI
Virginia Commonwealth University, USA

LONDON AND NEW YORK

First published 2012 by Ashgate Publishing

Published 2016 by Routledge
2 Park Square, Milton Park, Abingdon, Oxon OX14 4RN
711 Third Avenue, New York, NY 10017, USA

Routledge is an imprint of the Taylor & Francis Group, an informa business

British Library Cataloguing in Publication Data
Intercountry adoption : policies, practices, and outcomes.
-- (Contemporary social work studies)
1. Intercountry adoption. 2. Intercountry adoption--Law and legislation. 3. Intercountry adoption--Government policy. 4. Adopted children--Social conditions.
I. Series II. Gibbons, Judith L. III. Rotabi, Karen Smith.
362.7'34'089-dc23

Library of Congress Cataloging-in-Publication Data
Intercountry adoption : policies, practices, and outcomes / [edited] by Judith L. Gibbons and Karen Smith Rotabi.
p. cm. -- (Contemporary social work studies)
Includes bibliographical references and index.
ISBN 978-1-4094-1054-6 (hbk) 1. Intercountry adoption.
I. Gibbons, Judith L. II. Rotabi, Karen Smith.
HV875.5.I547 2011
362.734--dc23

2011052074

ISBN 9781409410546 (hbk)
ISBN 9781472468246 (pbk)

Printed in the United Kingdom
by Henry Ling Limited

Contents

PART II SENDING COUNTRY PERSPECTIVES

PART III OUTCOMES FOR INTERCOUNTRY ADOPTEES

List of Figures and Tables

Figures

Tables

List of Abbreviations

AAAW	Asian Adult Adoptees of Washington (USA)
ADHD	Attention deficit hyperactivity disorder
AFP	Agence France-Presse
AHP	Adoption History Project
AID	Agency for International Development
AKA-SoCal	Association of Korean-Adoptees-Southern California
AKF	Adopterade Koreaners Förening [Association of Adopted Koreans]
AP	Associated Press
ASFA	Adoption and Safe Families Act (USA)
ASK	Adoptee Solidarity Korea
ASP	Adoption service provider
BEIP	Bucharest Early Intervention Project
BKA	Boston Korean Adoptees
CCAA	China Centre for Adoption Affairs (Central Authority in China)
CCAI	Congressional Coalition on Adoption (USA)
CCI	Celebrate Children International
CCR	Center for Constitutional Rights
CIA	Central Intelligence Agency (USA)
CICIG	Comisión Internacional Contra la Impunidad en Guatemala [International Commission against Impunity in Guatemala]
CFR	Code of Federal Regulations (USA)
CNA	Consejo Nacional de Adopciones [National Council for Adoptions] (Guatemala)
COA	Council on Accreditation (USA)
CRC	Convention on the Rights of the Child
CWIG	Child Welfare Information Gateway
CWLA	Child Welfare League of America
CYFS	Child, Youth and Family Services (New Zealand)
DHS	Department of Homeland Security (USA)
EKL	Euro-Korean League
FAS	Fetal alcohol syndrome
GNP	Gross national product
GOA'L	Global Overseas Adoptees' Link
HAC	Hague Adoption Certificate
HCD	Hague Custody Declaration
HCIA	Hague Convention on Intercountry Adoption
HCPIL	Hague Conference on Private International Law

HFI	Holy Family Institute
HIV	Human immunodeficiency virus
IAA	Intercountry Adoption Act of 2000 (USA)
IACHR	Inter-American Commission on Human Rights
ICA	Intercountry or international adoption
IGIAA	Independent Group for International Adoption Analysis
IKAA	International Korean Adoptee Association
ILPEC	Instituto Latinoamericano para la Educación y la Comunicación [Latin American Institute for Education and Communication]
ISS	International Social Service
JCICS	Joint Council on International Children's Services
KAD	Korean adoptee
MBD	Minimal brain dysfunction
MIHWAF	Ministry for Health, Welfare, and Family Affairs (South Korea)
MoWCYA	Ministry of Women's, Children's, and Youth Affairs (Ethiopia)
NAPCR	National Authority for the Protection of Child's Rights (Romania)
NGO	Non-governmental organization
OKA	Overseas Koreans Act
PAP	Prospective adoptive parent
PEAR	Parents for Ethical Adoption Reform
PINA	Protección Integral de la Niñez y Adolescencia [Integrated Protection Law for Children and Adolescents] (Guatemala)
PGN	Procuraduría General de la Nación [Attorney General's Office] (Guatemala)
RAC	Romanian Committee on Adoption
RCC	Revised Criminal Code (Ethiopia)
RFC	Revised Family Code (Ethiopia)
SAFE	Structured Analysis Family Evaluation
SD	Standard deviation
SES	Socio-economic status
TRACK	Truth and Reconciliation for the Adoption Community of Korea
TST	Tuberculin skin test
UNCRC	United Nations Committee on the Rights of the Child
UNHCHR	United Nations Office of the High Commissioner for Human Rights
UNICEF	United Nations Children's Fund
UNDP	United Nations Development Programme
USAID	United States Agency for International Development
USCIS	United States Citizenship and Immigration Services
U.S. DOS	United States Department of State

List of Contributors

The Editors

Judith L. Gibbons (PhD) is Professor of Psychology and International Studies at Saint Louis University, a 2012 Fulbright scholar at the Universidad del Valle de Guatemala, and the editor of the journal *International Perspectives in Psychology: Research Practice Consultation.* She is president-elect of the international organization, Interamerican Society of Psychology, better known by its Spanish acronym, SIP. Dr. Gibbons has published widely in international psychology on adolescent development, including a book co-authored with Deborah Stiles entitled *The Thoughts of Youth: An International Perspective on Adolescents' Ideal Persons.* (Information Age Publishing, 2004). More recently, she has been studying intercountry adoption as seen from the Guatemalan perspective.

Karen Smith Rotabi (MSW, MPH, PhD) is Assistant Professor of Social Work at Virginia Commonwealth University School of Social Work. Dr. Rotabi's research agenda focuses on families impacted by war, including intercountry adoption. She serves as an agency evaluator and a Hague Commissioner for the USA Council on Accreditation in coordination with U.S. Department of State. Her research includes analysis of the Hague Intercountry Adoption Convention and implications for practice, both in the USA and globally. Dr. Rotabi began a focus on intercountry adoption in 2000 while working for Peace Corps training child health education volunteers in Guatemala. Focused on social justice, ethics, and human rights, Rotabi's contributions to knowledge include her website: www.HagueEvaluation.com.

Contributors

Elizabeth Bartholet (JD) is the Morris Wasserstein Public Interest Professor of Law at Harvard Law School, and Faculty Director of the Child Advocacy Program (CAP). She teaches civil rights and family law, specializing in child welfare, adoption and reproductive technology. Before joining the Harvard faculty, she was engaged in civil rights and public interest work, first with the NAACP Legal Defense Fund, and later as founder and director of the Legal Action Center. Her publications include two books and many articles and book chapters on adoption generally, and international adoption specifically, including *Nobody's Children*

(Beacon, 1999), *Family Bonds* (Beacon, 1999), and *International Adoption: The Human Rights Position*, 1; *Global Policy*, 91 (2010). Professor Bartholet has won several awards for her writing and related work in adoption and child welfare, as well as a "Media Achievement Award" in 1994 and the Radcliffe College Humane Recognition Award in 1997.

Kathleen Ja Sook Bergquist (MSW, PhD, JD) is Associate Professor in the School of Social at the University of Nevada, Las Vegas (UNLV). She earned her MSW at Norfolk State University, her PhD in Education at the College of William and Mary, and her JD at the William S. Boyd School of Law at UNLV. Dr. Bergquist is a Korean adoptee and Korean adoptive parent. Her areas of research are intercountry adoption, domestic violence in Asian Pacific American communities, and human trafficking. Her publications and research include co-editing a collection of scholarly works entitled, *International Korean Adoption: A Fifty-Year History of Policy and Practice*, and more recently considering the intersections of intercountry adoption and human trafficking. Kathleen is also an attorney and provides pro bono legal assistance.

Kelley McCreery Bunkers (MA) is an international child protection consultant with 20 years of professional experience working in Ethiopia, Guatemala, El Salvador, and Romania and a Master of Advanced Studies in Child Rights. Her work has focused on developing child-focused social welfare systems, with particular focus on alternative care for children; specifically foster care and domestic adoption. Ms. Bunkers has worked for private foundations, international non-governmental organizations, and UNICEF. Her most recent work is in Ethiopia where she works closely with government and non-governmental organizations in the development of foster care, domestic adoption and the social welfare workforce. Her work with UNICEF in Guatemala and Romania involved developing governmental alternative care programs as well as facilitating the Hague-ratification process. She has published several articles related to child protection systems and adoption reform in Guatemala and Ethiopia. Ms. Bunkers is an advisor for Hague Evaluation, the Better Care Network, and Global Health Promise.

Thomas M. Crea (PhD, LCSW) is Assistant Professor at the Graduate School of Social Work at Boston College. Dr. Crea is a former child therapist and special needs adoption worker and a licensed clinical social worker. He has evaluated local and national projects for children residing in, and adopted from, the U.S. child welfare system. Dr. Crea has served as an investigator on the evaluation of the Family to Family initiative; the evaluation of the Structured Analysis Family Evaluation (SAFE) uniform home study method; the California Long-Range Adoption Study (CLAS); the evaluation of cash transfers for orphans and vulnerable children in rural Zimbabwe; and the evaluation of supervisor training for the Massachusetts Department of Children and Families. His research has been sponsored by the Annie E. Casey Foundation, the Dave Thomas Foundation for Adoption, Catholic Relief Services, the Northeast and Caribbean Implementation Center, and a variety of non-profit organizations.

Monica Dalen (PhD) is Professor of Education at University of Oslo. Her main subjects have been Special Needs Education and International Adoption. In the last 10 years, Dr. Dalen's research has mainly been on international adoptions and she has conducted several large studies in Norway with support from The Norwegian Research Council and Ministry of Children, Equality and Social Inclusion. Monica Dalen has collaborated with a Swedish Research team and they have lately published several articles on cognitive and academic achievement among international adoptees. At the moment Dr. Dalen leads a longitudinal study following a cohort of internationally adopted children from the age at adoption through early childhood and school years. The study is collaborating with a larger study on Norwegian-born children. The two studies are using the same methods and instruments providing a unique opportunity to compare early childhood developmental trajectories in the two groups.

Jonathan Dickens (PhD) is Senior Lecturer in Social Work at the University of East Anglia, England. He is a qualified social worker, specialising in work with children and families and court proceedings. Prior to starting at UEA in 1998 he had spent over three years living and working in Romania, as a social work trainer and consultant. His work there was to assist in the development of social work support services for children and families, and in-country alternatives to residential care. His research interests are in the legal and social policy contexts of social work. He is the author of *Social Work and Social Policy: An Introduction* (Routledge, 2010), and is currently writing a book on social work, law and ethics. His current research is on UK social work decision-making for children on the edge of care.

Patricia Fronek (BSocWk, PhD) joined the faculty of Griffith University, School of Human Services and Social Work and Griffith Health Institute, Australia, in January 2010 after almost 30 years in social work practice. Her work spanned private practice, government and non-governmental organizations in several specialty areas and she was a private practitioner in the intercountry field for almost 15 years. It was this practice experience, gaps in knowledge, and the dominance of narrow perspectives in popular understandings of intercountry adoption that led to her researching the phenomena. Patricia currently serves on the National Intercountry Adoption Advisory Group (NICAAG) for the Australian Attorney-General's Department, is a regular speaker at conferences and publishes her work on intercountry adoptions.

Victor Groza (MWS, PhD) is the Grace F. Brody Professor of Parent-Child Studies at the Mandel School of Applied Social Sciences, Case Western Reserve

University, Cleveland, Ohio. His research in child welfare focuses on two areas: (1) an examination of the institutional care of children, ways to improve the care of children who must reside in institutions, and the negative impact on child development from early trauma due to institutionalization; and (2) family, children and service system issues in domestic, older-child adoption and international adoption. Since 1991, he has been involved in various child welfare technical assistance, research and training projects in Romania, India, Ukraine, Guatemala and Ethiopia. More information about his work can be found on his faculty website, http://msass.case.edu/faculty/vgroza/index.html.

Riitta Högbacka (PhD) is a Visiting Scholar at the University of California, Berkeley, and a Research Fellow in the Department of Social Research (Sociology) at the University of Helsinki, Finland where she also teaches part-time. Her research interests include rural gender studies, family sociology, and globalization. More recently Dr. Högbacka has investigated and written about intercountry adoption from the perspectives of Finnish adoptive parents and South African birth mothers focusing on the hidden hierarchies of adoption and on the possibilities of opening intercountry adoptions. She has published book chapters and articles in Finnish and in English on these topics, and is currently writing a book on the making and unmaking of families in intercountry adoption.

Tobias Hübinette (PhD) has a doctorate in Korean Studies from Stockholm University, and is a researcher at the Multicultural Centre and a lecturer at Södertörn University, Sweden. He is active within the international and multidisciplinary fields of Korean adoption studies, adoption cultural studies and critical adoption studies, and is also building up an extensive archive and library related to Korean adoption and Korean adoptees. He is a member of the history project TRACK (Truth and Reconciliation for the Adoption Community of Korea), and his research also concerns Swedish critical race and whiteness studies.

Kay Johnson (PhD) is Professor of Asian Studies and Politics and Faculty Director of the China Exchange Program at Hampshire College, Massachusetts. Her research and publications focus on the impact of Chinese government policies on women and the family in rural China. Since the early 1990s, she has conducted extensive field research in China on infant abandonment, domestic adoption, and the lives of "hidden" unregistered children as a by-product of China's population control policies. She has also investigated and written about Chinese orphanages and international adoption. She is currently working on a book, *The Circulation of Children under the One Child Policy*, based on the narratives of Chinese parents who have relinquished, adopted and hidden children during this era. She is also a coordinator and participant in the community-based programs of a non-governmental AIDS orphan organization in rural Anhui.

Femmie Juffer (PhD) is Professor of Adoption Studies at the Centre for Child and Family Centre, Leiden University, the Netherlands. The chair for Adoption Studies has been supported by Wereldkinderen since 2000. Dr. Juffer is interested in the life-long consequences of adoption, children's resilience and recovery from adversity, and effects of attachment-based early childhood interventions for families. Together with colleagues she is involved in several longitudinal and meta-analytic studies of adopted children/adolescents/adults. In the *Leiden Longitudinal Adoption Study* internationally adopted children have been followed since the late-1980s, from infancy to young adulthood. Her current projects also include the development of children in institutional care and the adjustment of children adopted from institutions or foster care. She is member of the editorial board of *Adoption Quarterly*.

Trish Maskew (JD) is Adjunct Professor of Law at American University's Washington College of Law, where she teaches Adoption Law, Policy and Practice. Trish previously worked as a program coordinator for an international adoption agency, and as a board member and administrator for the Joint Council on International Children's Services. In late 2002, she founded Ethica, a non-governmental organization dedicated to adoption reform, where she served as President until 2008. Trish went to Cambodia in the summer of 2008 as a consultant to the Permanent Bureau of the Hague Conference on Private Law to assist in the implementation of the Hague Convention. Trish is the author of *Our Own: Adopting and Parenting the Older Child*, and numerous articles on adoption ethics and practice.

Hollee McGinnis (MSW) is a prominent speaker, writer, and community organizer on intercountry and transracial adoptions. She was formerly the Policy and Operations Director at the Evan B. Donaldson Adoption Institute, and is currently pursuing a doctorate in social work at Washington University in St. Louis. She received her masters of science from Columbia University School of Social Work and completed a post-masters' clinical social work fellowship at the Yale University Child Study Center. In 1996, she founded Also-Known-As, Inc., a non-profit adult intercountry adoptee organization and in 2008 was recognized with a Congressional Angel in Adoption award.

Benyam Dawit Mezmur (LLB, LLM, LLD), is a researcher from Ethiopia currently based at the Community Law Centre, University of the Western Cape (UWC) in Cape Town, South Africa. At present, he is the lecturer of the LLM module on Children's Rights and the Law at UWC and a Mellon Foundation Research Fellow at the Community Law Centre. He is also an Assistant Professor (part-time) at the Addis Ababa University in Ethiopia. In addition, Mr. Mezmur is the Vice-Chair (2nd) of the African Committee of Experts on the Rights and Welfare of the Child of the African Union, which is the treaty body with the mandate to monitor the implementation of the African Charter on the Rights and

Welfare of the Child in 46 African State Parties. He has published widely on issues pertaining to children's rights, and his book on intercountry adoption in the context of Africa will be published by Intersentia Publishers soon.

Laurie C. Miller (MD) is Professor of Pediatrics at Tufts University School of Medicine and founded the International Adoption Clinic at Tufts Medical Center in 1988. She has served as a pediatric consultant in more than 10 countries. She oversaw an NIH-funded program to improve outcomes for orphanage residents in Russia for many years. She established "Big Sisters" projects in Baby Homes in Russia, Ukraine, and India. Dr. Miller serves on the NIH Study Section for Brain Disorders in the Developing World. She currently is the Principal Investigator of a longitudinal project to monitor and improve the health and nutritional status of impoverished children in Nepal. She has published over 80 peer-reviewed articles and 30 chapters related to pediatrics and international adoption, as well as two books (Handbook of International Adoption Medicine, Oxford University Press, and Encyclopedia of Adoption [with C. Adamec], Facts on File). She also is a board-certified pediatric rheumatologist and directs the pediatric rheumatology training program at Tufts Medical Center.

Carmen Mónico (BS, MS, MSW) is completing her PhD at the School of Social Work at the Virginia Commonwealth University while doing an academic exchange with the Women's Institute at the Universidad of San Carlos de Guatemala. She has been a Child Welfare Education and Support Program student (2008-2009), a fellow from the Council of Social Work Education's Minority Fellowship Program (2009-2011) and is an Ambassadorial Research Scholar from the Rotary Foundation (2011-2012). She has written on birth parents searching for their forcibly disappeared children during and after El Salvador's civil war, and is conducting her dissertation research on child abduction, child protection and intercountry adoption from the perspective of Guatemalan birthmothers. She has published extensively on civic engagement and social accountability as a World Bank consultant, worked on U.S. refugee and foreign policy issues, and managed national and local organizations and programs.

Dana Naughton (LCSW) is a PhD candidate in a dual title doctoral program at Pennsylvania State University where she is focusing on Adult Education and Comparative and International Education. Prior to attending Penn State, Ms. Naughton worked as a social work clinician and administrator for nearly 25 years in health, mental health and international social welfare, including intercountry adoption. She has worked for the U.S. Peace Corps, Johns Hopkins University, International Social Service, and the University of California at San Diego among other institutions. Her research interests meet at the intersection of adult education and social work: learning through trauma and terror, the learning experiences of adoptive parents, learning through caregiving and work with immigrant, refugee and asylum populations.

Cristina Nedelcu (MSSA, LISW) is a senior manager of training and professional development and manager of the Ohio University Partnership Program at the North Central Regional Training Center-Cuyahoga County Department of Children and Family Services. She is also a certified Child Welfare trainer with the Ohio Child Welfare Training Program and a doctoral student at Case Western Reserve University, Mandel School of Applied Social Sciences in Cleveland, Ohio. Cristina has 20 years' experience of working in child welfare in various capacities both in Romania and the United States. Cristina co-authored journal articles on Indian and Norwegian adoptions, on the developmental stages of young adulthood for children who exited the Child Welfare system and authored an encyclopedia entry on Romanian adoptions in the *Praeger Handbook of Adoption*. Cristina emigrated from Romania to the United States in 1994.

Mary Katherine O'Connor (PhD) is Professor of Social Work at Virginia Commonwealth University where she teaches in the MSW and PhD programs. She was a Peace Corps Volunteer and Fulbright Scholar in Brazil and continues those connections through Partners of the Americas as a Board Member of Virginia Partners and their partner state, Santa Catarina, Brazil. She has more than 30 years of consultative work in Brazil related to the development of systems of protection for children and families including child protection, adoption, and domestic violence. She is the sole author or co-author of six books and has published over 50 book chapters and refereed journal articles in English and Portuguese. Her research and scholarship focuses on child welfare and family violence practice issues including public child welfare practice, services to street children, organization assessment and management as well as qualitative research method development.

Jesús Palacios (PhD) is Professor of Developmental and Educational Psychology at the University of Seville, Spain. His areas of expertise include child abuse and neglect, foster care and adoption. In the adoption field, his work involves teaching, research, policy consultancy and the development of tools for professional intervention (prospective adopters' preparation and suitability assessment through the home study). His studies include both domestic and intercountry adoption, with both cross-sectional and longitudinal designs. The process of recovery following initial adversity is one of his main research interests. Together with David Brodzinsky, he has edited *Psychological Issues in Adoption: Research and Practice* (Praeger, 2005) and published a review of adoption research in the *International Journal of Behavioral Development* (2010). He is the organizer of the 4th International Conference on Adoption Research, to be held in 2013.

Jini L. Roby (JD, MSW, MS) was formerly an adoption social worker, founder and director of an agency to prevent and treat child abuse, and a court-appointed attorney for children in the public child welfare system in the United States. Currently she is professor of social work at Brigham Young University, where she researches and teaches about children at risk, including those involved in intercountry adoption. She was the principal drafter of the adoption laws in the Republic of Marshall Islands, and served as a government consultant between 2000-2004. She served in 2009 as a consultant to Cambodia to help establish the nation's child welfare infrastructure, regulations and procedures. She has served as a child welfare consultant for UNICEF in Guatemala, Cambodia, and Ethiopia; and has conducted child welfare research in the USA, Pacific, Africa and Asia. Her work is widely published and utilized by governments and NGOs.

Peter Selman (BA, DPSA, PhD) is Visiting Fellow in the School of Geography, Politics & Sociology at the Newcastle University, UK. He is Chair of NICA (*Network for Intercountry Adoption*) and a member of the Board of Trustees and Research Advisory Group of BAAF (*British Agencies for Adoption & Fostering).* He is editor of *Intercountry Adoption; Development, Trends and Perspectives* (BAAF, 2000) and has written many articles and chapters on adoption policy. His main areas of research interest are child adoption, teenage pregnancy, and demographic change. In recent years he has focused on the demography of child adoption with a special emphasis on intercountry adoption. He has presented many papers on this topic at international conferences and has acted as research consultant to international organizations such as the United Nations Population Division, the Hague Conference on Private International Law and the Innocenti Research Centre in Florence.

Rhoda Scherman (PhD) is a Senior Lecturer in the Department of Psychology, and the Head of Research for the School of Public Health and Psychosocial Studies at Auckland University of Technology. Originally from the USA, she immigrated to New Zealand in 1997 in order to complete her Masters and PhD at the University of Auckland, where she could specialise in adoption-related research due to New Zealand's unique and progressive adoption practices. Dr. Scherman continues to research and supervise in the area of adoption broadly, with particular interest in intercountry adoption, openness in adoption practices, developmental outcomes for adopted persons, ethnic and bicultural identity development, adjustment of adult adoptees, adoptive fatherhood, and school experiences of post-institutionalised adopted children. Dr. Scherman sits on the board of *Inter-Country Adoption New Zealand*, and was one of the founding trustees of *Adoption, Counseling, Education and Research Trust.*

David Smolin (JD) is Harwell G. Davis Professor of Constitutional Law, and Director, Center for Biotechnology, Law, and Ethics, at Cumberland Law School, Samford University. He has published over 35 articles, been the primary author/co-author of *amicus curiae* briefs in significant United States Supreme Court cases, and submitted testimony before two U.S. Congressional Committees and legislative committees in five states. His scholarly articles on adoption are available at http://works.bepress.com/david_smolin/. On adoption issues he has written for the *New York Times* and frequently is a media source. He has made presentations on adoption in multiple forums, including the Korean Women's Development Institute in Seoul, Korea; the Second International Symposium on Korean Adoption Studies in Seoul, Korea; and at the Hague Special Commission on the Practical Operation of the Hague Adoption Convention. He works with Desiree Smolin on analysis and reform of adoption systems and practices, including contributing to her blog, http://fleasbiting.blogspot.com/.

Wendy Tieman (PhD) is an Assistant Professor at the Centre for Child and Family Studies, Leiden University, the Netherlands. Her PhD study focused on the mental health of young adult international adoptees, and was part of the *Sophia Longitudinal Adoption Study* started by Dr Frank Verhulst. Currently Dr. Tieman is involved in several adoption research projects: the development of adopted children from China and India, special needs adoptions, and the development of adult international adoptees compared to adult domestic adoptees. With her colleagues Femmie Juffer and Marinus van IJzendoorn she has started a new follow-up of the *Sophia Longitudinal Adoption Study* in cooperation with Jan van der Ende and Frank Verhulst (Erasmus MC-Sophia, Rotterdam, the Netherlands). She is a member of the editorial board of *Adoption Quarterly.*

Marinus H. van IJzendoorn (PhD) is Professor at the Centre for Child and Family Studies, Leiden University, the Netherlands. His interests are attachment and emotion regulation across the life-span, in typical (family, day care) and extreme social conditions (orphanages, child abuse and neglect). Current emphasis is on the role of parenting/caregiving in child development, from the perspective of gene by environment interaction and differential susceptibility. With his colleague Femmie Juffer, he is involved in meta-analyses on adoption and foster care. He is also involved in bio-behavioral interventions with video feedback and with intranasal administration of oxytocin. Personal website: marinusvanijzendoorn.com.

Acknowledgments

We would like to acknowledge the capable and conscientious assistance of Wells Ling who did meticulous stylistic editing for this book. Also, our contributors obligingly updated their chapters at the very end of this process to reflect the most recent information and knowledge about intercountry adoptions in an ever-changing environment. For their diligence in scholarship and thoughtful discourse, they are very much appreciated.

Dedications

For Raymond, who not only endured the loss of my attention, but also cooked for the editors while they were working on this book. And for Monica and Katerin, my "ahijadas," talented, strong, and brave as they construct their futures.

Judith L. Gibbons

For my parents Michael and Irma Smith who not only believed in me, but committed to my education because, as my father says, "you never want to be bored or lonely." Engaging in intercountry adoption is never boring. Then there is my husband who is an amazing companion also willing to give up my time and my attention during our first year of marriage. And, with Paul Martin I am never bored or lonely.

Karen Smith Rotabi

Foreword

Intercountry adoption is a contested arena. While competing discourses characterize this controversial field, there is no doubt that its practice primarily affects the lives of birth families and their children followed by that of adoptive and prospective adoptive parents across the globe. Perhaps the most powerful critiques concerning the impact of intercountry adoptions emanate from adoptees themselves. As the doors of source countries open and close and the numbers of children adopted internationally are declining, debates concerning intercountry adoption are gaining momentum forcing the attention of governments. The views of adoptees and birth parents can now be heard while at the same time the demand from prospective adopters is not diminishing nor is the influence of intercountry adoption proponents on the practice.

Social workers are at the center of these controversies and subjected to competing pressures whether their practice is in policy making, child relinquishment, assessment or family support services. An understanding of these tensions and a critical perspective are central to social work, not only in terms of competent and safe practices but perhaps more importantly to question assumptions and to ensure social work values and ethics are not subsumed by singular perspectives and the economic and political priorities that weigh heavily on practice. Knowledge concerning intercountry adoption has exploded in the last two decades. Consequently, social workers and students are compelled to look beyond adopter subjectivities to include the multiple and competing influences on intercountry adoption that include abuses, structural inequalities, disadvantage and vested interests.

A range of perspectives informed by research and at times divergent philosophical positions comprise this timely book. Intercountry adoption scholars in the fields of social work, psychology, law, education, cultural studies and demography offer new knowledge, contemporary debates and critical perspectives on policies, practices, birth parent and adoptee experiences, and developmental outcomes. Intercountry adoption is truly a multidisciplinary field. Yet, it is one where social workers can, should, and are increasingly exercising leadership and influencing policies, practices, and current and future directions. Debates and critical perspectives found within this book provide social workers and students with an understanding of the issues dominating intercountry adoption today. This edited volume is exciting, in that, its scope is not limited to receiving countries. Rather, issues of human rights abuses and child trafficking and perspectives from Cambodia, El Salvador, the Marshall Islands, Romania, Guatemala, China, South Korea, South Africa and Ethiopia provide a more complex picture than popular, sentimentalized notions of child rescue often portray. A unique and compelling feature is the debate between the prominent legal scholars, David Smolin and Elizabeth Bartholet, seeking intercountry adoption reform and the promotion of the practice respectively. Their dialog showcases the disparate positions influential in intercountry adoption enabling critical evaluation and the unpacking of the many assumptions prevalent in intercountry adoption discourse.

The focus on policy, international agreements and politicking, pertinent to social work's interests in social policy, planning and development, sets this book apart from its predecessors. The authors highlight an urgent need for reform that is currently inhibited by the forces of the free market that regrettably prevails in many sending and receiving countries despite earnest international attempts to mediate its negative consequences. The academic work published in this volume also probes inadequacies in existing approaches to the welfare of children, families and communities; the ambiguity of international conventions and inadequate social welfare structures; the operation of protective legal mechanisms; and political instability in source countries such as Guatemala.

This book embraces difficult questions concerning the best interests of children, offering both pragmatism and radicalism in addition to traditional perspectives on intercountry adoption. The importance of these scholarly contributions for social work in intercountry adoptions cannot be overstated. The critical lens for understanding intercountry adoption that these works encourage is much needed. Values and ethics such as social justice and respect for human rights are deeply embedded in the practice of social work. Intercountry adoption must be critically examined from this value base, despite the challenges of doing so. Critically informed social workers and students must extend their understandings of intercountry adoption beyond sentimentality and work towards educating and guiding clients, policy makers and governments to a fuller understanding of intercountry adoption as the complex phenomenon it is. This book will assist in this process.

Patricia Fronek

Introduction

Judith L. Gibbons and Karen Smith Rotabi

Dilemmas and decisions in the field of adoption touch on the fundamentals of humanity. (Bos, 2007, p. 18)

In today's world, social workers find themselves at the center of controversies over intercountry adoption (ICA). Adoption across borders represents a significant component of international migration; in recent years, up to 45,000 children have crossed borders annually as part of the intercountry adoption boom. Proponents have touted intercountry adoption as a natural intervention for promoting child welfare. However, in cases of fraud, economic incentives, child sales, and abduction, intercountry adoption has been denounced as child trafficking. The debate on intercountry adoption has been framed in terms of three perspectives: proponents who advocate intercountry adoption, abolitionists who argue for its elimination, and pragmatists who look for ways to improve both the conditions in sending countries and the procedures for intercountry transfer of children (Masson, 2001). All three perspectives are represented in this book.

Social workers play critical roles in intercountry adoption, arguably the most controversial practice area for the profession. Social workers are often involved in family support services or child relinquishment in sending countries, and in evaluating potential adoptive homes, processing applications, and providing support for adoptive families in receiving countries; social workers serve as brokers and policy makers with regard to the processes, procedures, and regulations that govern intercountry adoption. Their voice is essential in shaping practical and ethical policies of the future.

This is a critical juncture for intercountry adoption as *The Hague Convention on Protection of Children and Co-operation in Respect of Intercountry Adoption* comes into effect in many countries. The Convention is designed to promote the best interests of the child and prevent sales, abduction and trafficking of children. This is also an important time for evaluating the outcomes of intercountry adoption as substantial evidence is emerging on the physical, emotional, and cognitive development of internationally adopted children and on the identity development and challenges faced by adopted adolescents and young adults.

This volume consists of critical reviews of current issues with respect to intercountry adoption, written by scholars from the fields of social work, psychology, law, and education. Several of the authors have updated and expanded chapters based on their articles in a special issue of the journal *International Social Work*, 52(5) published by © Sage in September 2009. The major goal of this book is to present current information on the policies, practices, and outcomes of intercountry adoption that can inform the practice of social work. We are pleased that this book is a part of the Ashgate *Contemporary Social Work Studies* series headed by Lucy Jordan and Patrick O'Leary and formerly edited (when the book was contracted) by Robin Lovelock.

Intercountry Adoption boasts 25 chapters covering five domains (1) policy and regulations, (2) sending country perspectives, (3) outcomes for intercountry adoptees, (4) a debate between two attorneys with opposing views, and (5) pragmatists' guides for improving intercountry adoption practices. Receiving countries' perspectives are well-represented in Part 3 on outcomes for intercountry adoptees, as well as in Chapters 3, 6, 20, 21, and 22. Thus, issues related to policy, regulation, adoptive family assessment, adoptee adjustment, adoption breakdown prevention, and openness are addressed based on the extensive research literature from receiving countries.

The part on policy and regulations begins with an essential analysis by Peter Selman of the demographics of intercountry adoption. Which countries make up the primary countries of origin and which are the primary receiving countries? How do the numbers change from year to year and what accounts for the steady decline in intercountry adoption in recent years? Jonathan Dickens, in Chapter 2, describes three policy approaches to intercountry adoption and concludes with the abolitionist stance that intercountry adoption should be halted for the greater good. Because intercountry adoption has often been advocated as a child rescue strategy following disasters, Chapter 3 by Kathleen Ja Sook Bergquist provides an essential analysis of the implications of the Hague Convention for humanitarian child rescue in environments of chaos. The human rights approach toward intercountry adoption is addressed in Chapter 4 by Jini L. Roby and Trish Maskew through their examination of the legal reform movements in two countries of origin, the Marshall Islands and Cambodia. In Chapter 5, Karen Smith Rotabi reports on the history of fraud and corruption in ICA, including child sales and trafficking, using past events in Vietnam, Cambodia, and Guatemala to illustrate the tactics and strategies used by unscrupulous entrepreneurs. To finish off this part, Karen Smith Rotabi and Mary Katherine O'Connor provide a policy analysis of different approaches to child welfare in the USA and other countries that have contributed to the creation of a marketplace for children.

There is a gap in knowledge from countries of origin and receiving countries, with more information and a greater number of research studies coming from the wealthier receiving countries. The second part of this book attempts to offset this imbalance by providing accounts of the situations in countries of origin. In Chapter 7, Cristina Nedelcu and Victor Groza provide a history of child welfare in Romania, including its involvement in ICA and recent advances in deinstitutionalization and alternative care. Kay Johnson in Chapter 8 counters two current discourses in ICA (the narrative of Chinese cultural traditions that devalue girls and the narrative of trafficking and corruption in ICA). She makes the case that relinquishment of children in China is primarily the result of oppressive state policies. Kelley McCreery Bunkers and Victor Groza describe the changes that Guatemalan child welfare policies have undergone before and after the ratification of the Hague Convention in Chapter 9. Ethiopia is a nation at the crossroads of policies with respect to ICA and the situation there is reviewed in Chapter 10 by Kelley McCreery Bunkers, Karen Smith Rotabi, and Benyam Dawit Mezmur, who note serious practice irregularities in that nation. Based on her research with birth mothers in South Africa, Riitta Högbacka writes in Chapter 11 about the conditions that compel relinquishment. She documents mothers' lack of options and their misunderstandings of the adoption process. In Chapter 12, Dana Naughton explores the relatively unknown territory of the USA outgoing adoptions, children relinquished from the USA to other countries.

The outcomes for intercountry adoptees are essential to understand in order to create effective policies and processes. In the first chapter of Part 3 (Chapter 13) Femmie Juffer and Marinus H. van IJzendoorn review the large number of meta-analytic studies they have done on the physical, emotional, and cognitive development of intercountry adoptees. They document the extensive gains made by adoptees in all domains. Laurie C. Miller in Chapter 14 reports on the medical problems of internationally adopted children, and makes recommendations for medical tests that should be conducted at arrival and at later dates. The cognitive and educational outcomes of adoptees as revealed in the extensive population studies from the Nordic countries are reported by Monica Dalen in Chapter 15. In Chapter 16, Femmie Juffer and Wendy Tieman report on their studies on children's relation with their birth culture. To close this section, Tobias Hübinette reports on his studies on the often-ignored issue of the racism faced by many international adoptees.

Part 4 of the book is structured in a unique format—a debate between Elizabeth Bartholet who is an advocate of intercounty adoption as an effective child care intervention, and David Smolin who has severely critiqued intercountry adoption as child trafficking. The debate highlights the sharp contrasts in the critical and compelling issues for intercountry adoption, especially with respect to implementation of the Hague Convention. This particular chapter illustrates the tensions for all disciplines involved in social interventions for orphaned and vulnerable children.

The fifth and final part of the book is comprised of pragmatic perspectives. Can the criticisms of intercountry adoption be answered? How can children's best interests be protected? Judith L. Gibbons and Karen Smith Rotabi, in Chapter 19, review the limitations and loopholes of the Hague Convention and how the Convention might best be implemented in both countries of origin and receiving countries. In Chapter 20, Thomas M. Crea characterizes the best practices for home studies for potential adoptive families. The problem of adoption breakdown and how it might be prevented is addressed in Chapter 21 by Jesús Palacios. In Chapter 22, Rhoda Scherman discusses the emerging issue of openness in intercountry adoption, using New Zealand and its practices as based in Maori traditions as a case study. Hollee McGinnis, in Chapter 23, writes about the Korean

Adult adoptee movement as adoptees themselves are starting to speak out about ICA from their own perspective. In Chapter 24, Carmen Mónico and Karen Smith Rotabi present a process for reconciliation for children who disappeared during the war in El Salvador. The Pro-Búsqueda process might serve as a model for other situations in which stolen children are adopted nationally and internationally.

We hope that this book will be useful to a broad range of scholars and graduate students in social work, psychology, counseling, education, cultural studies and law with interests in child welfare. In addition, the book addresses issues of importance to practitioners and policy makers working in the field of intercountry adoption as they strive to implement good practices. Finally, we hope that individuals personally affected by intercountry adoption, including adoptees, adoptive parents, and their families, find value in these chapters.

The debates within the delimited scope of ICA reflect broader issues about how to promote children's well-being. They touch upon the profound challenges facing humanity in the context of globalization. How can regulations and policies best be converted into practice? What are effective courses of action that honor human rights and protect vulnerable individuals? Do the well-being and positive outcomes of a few children trump the interests of those who are left behind? How can traditional understandings and practices be reconciled with contemporary understandings of individual rights? Although we cannot answer these important questions, in this book we attempt to bring them into clearer focus and provide a diversity of perspectives.

PART I
Policy and Regulations

Chapter 1
The Rise and Fall of Intercountry Adoption in the 21st Century: Global Trends from 2001 to 2010[1]

Peter Selman

This chapter focuses on the remarkable changes in the number of intercountry adoptions (ICAs) in the first decade of the new millennium. In the 50 years following the initiation of transracial intercountry adoption from Korea in 1953, global numbers of children moving for ICA had steadily increased to an estimated total worldwide of over 45,000 a year in 2004 (Selman, 2006). At that stage there seemed to be an assumption that growth would continue, and the number of applicants in receiving states continued to rise. However, the last six years have witnessed a reversal of growth, and by 2009 global estimates were lower than in 1998 (Table 1.1).

Since 2004, numbers have fallen in most receiving countries, an exception being Italy where the 2010 total of 4,130 was 21 percent higher than in 2004 (see Figures 1.1 and 1.2). The total number of adoptions to the USA in fiscal year 2011[2] was 9,320 (US Department of State 2011e), less than half the highest recorded number of 22,728 in 2004 and the lowest annual total since 1995.

The chapter will review trends in receiving states and states of origin from 2001 through 2010, with a detailed study of selected states of origin. The global and regional totals cited in the chapter are based on an aggregation of data from 23 receiving states. Problems of data are discussed elsewhere (Selman, 2002, 2006). The chapter ends with a consideration of the implications of the current changes.

Intercountry Adoption in the 21st Century

The fall in adoptions since 2004 has brought global numbers to below the level of 1998 (see Table 1.1). Figure 1.1 shows trends from 2001 to 2010 for 23

1 This chapter is based, in part, on: Selman, P. (2009). The rise and fall of international adoption in the 21st century. *International Social Work,* 52, 575-94. © Sage.

2 USA statistics on ICA are recorded by fiscal year, which begins on October 1 and ends on September 30. Calendar Year totals 2005-2009 were provided for the 2010 Hague Special Commission and will be referred to where relevant.

Table 1.1 Intercountry Adoption to Selected Receiving Countries 1998-2010: By Rank in 2004—Peak Year in Bold

Country	1998	2001	2003	2004	2006	2008	2009	2010[d]
USA (FY)[a]	15,774	19,237	21,616	**22,884**	20,679	17,438	12,753	12,149[d]
Spain	1,487	3,428	3,951	**5,541**	4,472	3,156	3,006	2,891
France	3,769	3,094	3,995	**4,079**	3,977	3,271	3,017	3,504
Italy	2,374	1,797	2,772	3,402	3,188	3,977	3,964	**4,130**
Canada	**2,222**	1,874	2,180	1,955	1,535	1,916	2,129	1,946
5 top States	**25,626**	**29,430**	**34,514**	**37,861**	**33,851**	**29,758**	**24,869**	**24,620**
Netherlands	825	1,122	1,154	**1,307**	816	767	682	705
Sweden	928	1,044	1,046	**1,109**	879	793	912	729
Norway	643	713	**714**	706	448	304	347	343
Denmark	624	**631**	523	528	447	395	496	419
Australia	245	289	278	**370**	421	270	269	222
European States	**13,231**	**14,364**	**16,930**	**19,512**	**16,629**	**14,983**	**14,583**	**14,642**
Total to all states[b] (max 23)	**31,875 (22)**	**36,391 (23)**	**41,540 (23)**	**45,298 (23)**	**39,460 (22)[c]**	**34,785 (23)**	**29,867 (23)**	**29,095 (23)**
% to top 5	80%	81%	83%	84%	85%	86%	83%	85%
% to USA	49%	53%	52%	51%	52%	50%	43%	42%
% to Europe	41%	39%	41%	43%	42%	43%	49%	50%

Notes: a) U.S. Department of State publishes data on a financial year basis (October-September). Calendar year data for 2005-2009 were sent to the 2010 Hague Special Commission and will be referred to where appropriate, but have some inconsistencies not resolved at time of writing, b) 13 other countries are included in the overall totals: Belgium, Cyprus, Finland, Germany, Iceland, Ireland, Israel, Luxembourg, Malta, New Zealand, Switzerland and the UK, with the addition of Andorra from 2001. c) Data for Cyprus 2006 not available; d) 2010 data; US data include 1,090 emergency visas for Haiti (see Table 1.8), without these the global total is 28,005 and the US share falls to 40 percent; Swedish data are for authorised organisations only.

Source: Statistics provided by Central Authorities of the 23 receiving states.

receiving states (global), the top five, the USA, and 18 European states. Until 2008, the pattern was similar for each grouping, but in the last three years the decline has been greatest in the United States, while numbers have risen in Italy. As a result there are now more adoptions to Europe than to the USA.

Figure 1.2 shows the changes between 2001 and 2010 in the five receiving states taking most children after the USA: Spain, France, Italy, Canada, and the Netherlands. In Spain, there was a very sharp rise from 2001 to 2004, followed by an equally rapid decline. Only Italy showed an overall increase in the nine years.

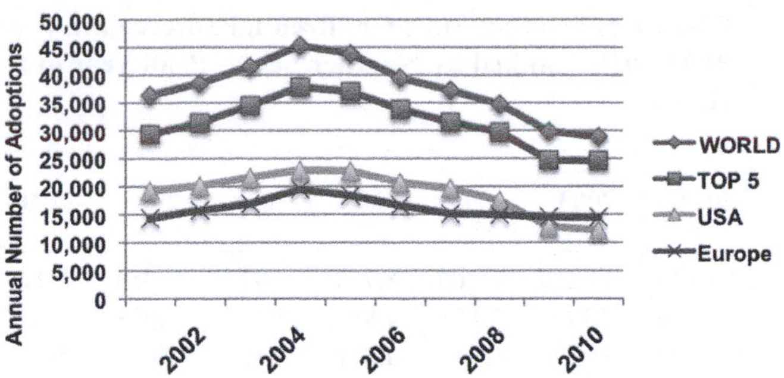

Figure 1.1 Trends in Intercountry Adoption to 23 Receiving States

Trends in ICA in Receiving States 1998-2010

Table 1.1 shows the rise and fall in the number of children received by 23 countries between 1998 and 2010. Between 1998 and 2004 the number of ICAs worldwide increased by 43 percent, with Spain experiencing a rise of 273 percent and Ireland a rise of 171 percent. Between 1998 and 2001 there was a 15 percent rise, but much variation among countries, with Canada, France, and Italy taking fewer children each year, while the numbers to Spain doubled and those to the Netherlands increased by a third. In the following three years there was an increase in all five countries (Figure 1.2).

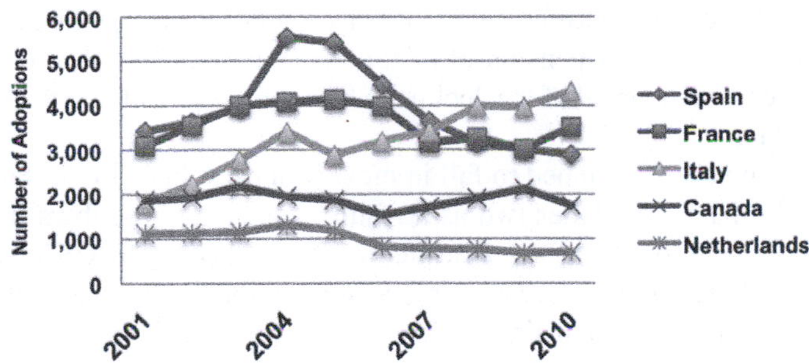

Figure 1.2 Five States Receiving Most Children After the USA

Between 2001 and 2004, overall numbers rose by 25 percent, but Ireland, Italy, and Spain experienced much more rapid growth, while numbers fell by 16 percent in Israel and Denmark (Selman, 2009d).

This steady increase in the global number of ICAs was reversed in 2005, and overall there was an estimated decline of 23 percent from 2004 to 2008. The largest falls were in the Nordic countries, the Netherlands, and Spain, but numbers rose in

Table 1.2 Countries Sending Most Children for Intercountry Adoption 2003-2010, Ranked by Number Sent—Peak Year in Bold—and Ratio

	2003-10	2003	2005	2007	2008	2009	2010	Ratio (Peak Year)
China	75,149	11,229	14,496	8,744	5,972	5,085	5,471	0.83
Russia	47,856	7,743	7,480	4,880	4,140	4,033	3,387	6.2
Guatemala	24,099	2,677	3,857	4,851	4,186	799	58	10.8
Ethiopia	22,221	854	1,778	3,033	3,896	4,565	4,396	1.5
South Korea	13,197	2,287	2,101	1,264	1,250	1,125	1,013	4.8
Colombia	13,059	1,750	1,470	1,636	1,617	1,413	1,798	2.1
Ukraine	12,903	2,049	1,982	1,614	1,577	1,516	1,093	5.0
Haiti	10,258	1,055	958	783	1,368	1,238	2,601	9.9
Vietnam	10,177	936	1,190	1,695	1,739	1,506	1,242	1.2
India	7,075	1,172	857	1,003	759	725	613	0.05
Kazakhstan	5,977	860	823	779	723	659	513	6.0
Philippines	4,066	406	499	574	600	583	515	0.27
Brazil	3,747	470	473	485	485	461	377	0.14
Thailand	3,319	490	465	442	377	328	298	0.46
Poland	3,072	346	409	381	408	402	325	1.12

Source: Statistics for 23 Receiving Countries; Korean figures are from the Ministry of Health & Welfare.

Italy. The global decline accelerated in 2009 as a consequence of the large fall for the USA following the suspension of adoptions from Guatemala and Liberia. In contrast there was a reversal of the decline in Denmark, Finland, Norway, Sweden, and Switzerland.

In 2010, numbers continued to fall in most countries, but rose in Italy, France and the Netherlands, the latter two as a result of increased numbers from Haiti. Preliminary figures for 2011 show a further fall in numbers to the USA, while Italy has maintained the 2010 level. The number of adoptions in France in 2011 fell to 1,995, the lowest annual total since 1985.

States of Origin in the 21st Century

The data presented in the tables below are estimates based on children received by 23 receiving countries. The accuracy of such estimates is discussed by Kane (1993) and Selman (2002, 2006). Table 1.2 shows the changes in the numbers from the 15 countries sending most children worldwide between 2003 and 2010. In contrast to most receiving states, the pattern of change over this period varies greatly among states of origin. Figure 1.3 shows the trends in total adoptions for the four countries (China, Russia, Guatemala and Ethiopia) sending most children

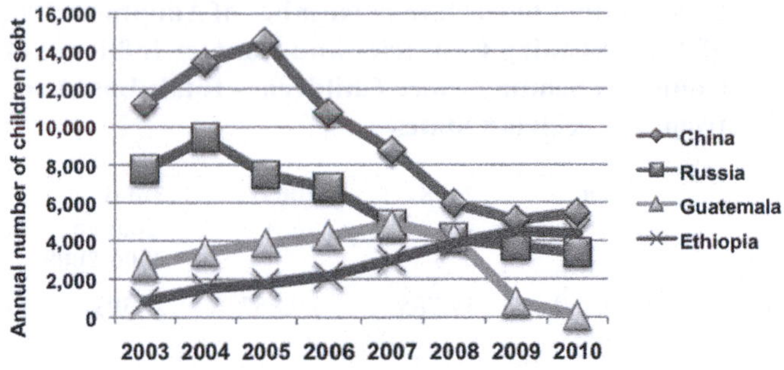

Figure 1.3 Countries Sending Most Children 2003-2010

during this period. Adoptions from China peaked in 2005 (Table 1.5); those from Russia in 2004 (Table 1.9); those from Guatemala in 2007 (Table 1.7). Adoptions from Ethiopia rose annually until 2009, but fell slightly in 2010 (Table 1.11).

The reduction in the number of children sent by China and Russia would have had even more impact if it were not for the large rise in numbers from Ethiopia and the continuing growth until 2007-2008 in the number of children sent by Vietnam and Guatemala (Selman 2009d).

However, in 2009 there was a huge fall in the number of children adopted from Guatemala and a significant reduction in the number of children adopted from Vietnam. The number of children sent by China, Russia, and Korea declined further. Table 1.3 shows the contribution to the decline from 2006 to 2009 of three key states of origin and the counter effect of three countries that experienced an increase over the same period.

There are well over 100 countries involved in sending children for ICA and it is impossible to review trends in all of those. However, the past ten years have indicated some clear changes in movements between continents. In 1997, 67 percent of children adopted in Spain came from Latin America. By 2000, this had fallen to 21 percent and Eastern Europe had become the main source accounting for 47 percent. By 2005 the growth of adoption from China meant that Asia was the main source at 53 percent, but as China reduced the number sent this fell back to 24 percent in 2009 and Europe was again the main source. The contribution of Africa alone showed growth throughout the period—to 26 percent of all adoptions to Spain by 2009.

On a global level the proportion of adoptions from Asia fell from 46 percent in 2005 to 35 percent in 2009 and 2010, the proportion from Europe from 30 percent to 20 percent. The proportion from Africa rose from 5 percent in 2003 to 22 percent in 2009/10. The next four sections will look at trends in four continents with some brief case studies.

Table 1.3 Contribution to Decline in Number of Adoptions 2006-2009 of 3 Key Sending Countries and Counter Influence of 3 Countries Sending More Children—Totals Based on Data from 23 Receiving States

Country	2006	2008	2009	Total Change 2006-2009	% Change 2006-2009
Total sent to 23 receiving states	39,460	34,785	29,867	-9,593	-24%
Countries sending fewer children					
China[a]	10,745	5,972	5,085	-5,660	-53%
Guatemala[b]	4,232	4,185	799	-3,433	-81%
Russia	6,766	4,135	4,003	-2,763	-41%
Total for 3 countries	21,743		9,887	-11,856	-55%
Countries sending more children					
Ethiopia	2,172	3,896	4,565	+2,393	+110%
Ukraine	1,046	1,577	1,516	+470	+45%
Philippines	476	600	583	+107	+ 22%
Total for 3 countries	3,694		6,664	+2,970	+80%

Source: Numbers calculated from data on states of origin in statistics provided by the receiving states listed in Table 1.

Note: a) Adoptions to 17 countries recognised by China, b) Adoptions from Guatemala peaked at 4,851 in 2007—see Table 1.7

Intercountry Adoption from Asia in the 21st century[3] For many years Asian countries were the main source of children for ICA in both Europe and the USA (Selman, 2010d). Adoption from Korea dates back to the 1950s and the Korean War.[4] In the USA, in particular, Korea dominated the scene, accounting for over 50 percent of children adopted from abroad in the years 1972 to 1987 (Altstein and Simon, 1991). By then, nearly 111,000 children had been adopted worldwide from Korea and by 2010, the total had risen to over 165,000 despite a sharp decline in annual totals after the Seoul Olympics in 1988. The number of adoptions from Korea, as reported by their Ministry of Health and Welfare, fell steadily after 2004 to 1,103 in 2010, and in 2008 the government set a goal of eliminating foreign adoptions altogether by 2012 (Onishi, 2008).

Adoptions from the Philippines started in the 1960s; from India and Vietnam in the 1970s. Kane (1993) lists three Asian countries—Korea, India, and Sri Lanka—in the top 5 states sending children for ICA in the 1980s. In the mid-1990s

3 For a more detailed discussion of Asia see Selman (2010d)

4 For more discussion on Korea see Bergquist, Vonk, Kim, and Feit (2007), Hübinette (2006), Selman (2007, 2009a).

Table 1.4 Adoptions from Asia 2003-2010 by Number Sent in 2003: Decline from Peak Year (in bold) to 2010—or Increase from 2003 to Peak. Peak Year Ratio (per 1,000 live births)

	2003	2005	2007	2008	2009	2010	Rise 2003 to peak	Decline From peak year	Ratio in Peak year
China	11,229	**14,496**	8,744	5,972	5,085	5,471	**29%**	**-62%**	**0.8**
China[a] (CCAA)		**14,221**	7,858	5,531	5,294			**-63 %**	**0.8**
Korea	**2,287**	2,101	1,264	1,250	1,125	1,013		**-56 %**	**4.7**
India[b]	**1,173**	873	1,003	759	725	613		**-48%**	**0.05**
Vietnam	936	1,198	1,695	**1,739**	1,506	1,242	**86%**	**-28%**	**1.16**
Thailand	**490**	465	442	371	328	298		**-39 %**	**0.46**
Philippines	406	503	574	**600**	583	515	**48%**	**-14%**	**0.27**
Cambodia[c]	**308**	110	207	215	77	95		**-69%**	**2.2**
Taiwan	222	242	252	365	374	**420**	**90%**		**2.0**
Nepal[d]	194	184	255	**405**	20	171	**109%**	**-58%**	**0.53**
All Asia[e]	**17,475**	**20,369**	**14,660**	**12,003**	**10,423**	**10,075**	**16%**	**-50%**	

Source: Data for Korea are provided by the Korean Ministry of Health and Welfare. Numbers for the other eight countries are calculated from data on countries of origin in statistics provided by the receiving states listed in Table 1. US FY data used throughout.

Note: a) CCAA data for China is available only from 2005-2009, b) Data for India from CARA vary slightly from those in the table, c) Total for Cambodia had been 655 in 2000, d) Peak year for Nepal is 2006, when there were 410 adoptions, e) Totals are based on adoptions recorded by receiving states and exclude adoptions from the five central Asian republics.

China entered the ICA arena and is now the most important Asian State of origin. Between 2001 and 2007, China was the origin of more than half the children sent from Asian countries, but India, Korea, and Vietnam continued to send significant numbers.

Table 1.4 shows annual totals for the nine Asian countries sending most children in 2003. By 2009, some—China, Korea, Cambodia, and India—were sending substantially fewer; but adoptions from Taiwan and Vietnam rose rapidly after 2004, and the Philippines has shown steady growth.

In China the number of children sent for adoption fell by over 60 percent between 2005 and 2009 (Table 1.5), suggesting that intercountry adoption from China may cease in the next decade—or be restricted to children with special needs. By the end of 2009 there had been over 125,000 ICAs from China, but the recent decline suggests that China may not pass the total of 165,000, achieved by South Korea. Some fear that the decline in adoptions from China when demand remains high is already leading to child buying or trafficking (Meier and Zhang, 2008). Table 1.5 shows data for China, 2005-2009, as submitted by the Central Authority to the 2010 Hague Special Commission. Nearly half the children sent

Table 1.5 Intercountry Adoptions from China 2005-2009. Ten Countries Receiving Most Children in 2005; Reduction in Numbers 2005-2009. Data Provided by CCAA for Hague Special Commission of June 2010

Country	2005	2006	2007	2008	2009	Change 2005 -2009	% Special Needs in 2009
USA	7,933	6,138	4,736	3,515	3,029	**- 62%**	**61%**
Spain	2,608	1,909	1,269	738	817	**- 79%**	**9%**
Canada	928	748	496	294	379	**- 61%**	**40%**
NL	667	367	330	297	297	**- 57%**	**66%**
France	439	331	178	139	95	**- 71%**	**34%**
Sweden	432	335	248	198	255	**- 41%**	**69%**
Norway	284	204	136	78	104	**- 37%**	**28%**
Denmark	230	163	111	76	73	**- 32%**	**38%**
Belgium	196	147	111	45	78	**- 40%**	**54%**
Australia	138	112	93	57	55	**- 40%**	**5%**
Total	**14,221**	**10,648**	**7,858**	**5,531**	**5,294**	**- 63%**	**49%**

Source: CCAA submission to Hague Special Commission—available at: http://hcch.e-vision.nl/upload/wop/adop2010pd05_cn.pdf. Figures do not include adoptions from Hong Kong SAR (30 in 2005; 19 in 2009), which were submitted separately.

in 2009 had ‘special needs’; the proportion aged 5 and over had risen from 1.4 percent in 2005 to 10.9 percent in 2009; and the proportion of girls had fallen from 95 percent to 74 percent.[5]

Figure 1.4 shows the very different trajectories in four other Asian countries—Korea, India, Vietnam and the Philippines—between 2003 and 2010.

Since 2007 Vietnam has been the second most important source of children for intercountry adoption from Asia after China (see Figure 1.4 and Table 1.4). Since the end of the Vietnam War in 1975, many children have been sent for intercountry adoption. It is said that over 2,000 were air-lifted to the USA in the last days of the war (see Chapter 3). Between 1994 and 2008, over 20,000 children were sent for adoption, the majority to France and the USA. Annual numbers peaked at 1,739 in 2008, but there were growing concerns about irregularities, and Vietnam now requires a bi-lateral agreement. In 2008, only six countries received children from Vietnam, most going to France, Italy, and the USA (Selman, 2012, p. 10). However, concerns over adoption from Vietnam continue and a Report by ISS for UNICEF concluded that “it will nonetheless require not only far-reaching

5 For a detailed consideration of issues of gender in adoption from China see Johnson (2004) and Smolin (2011)

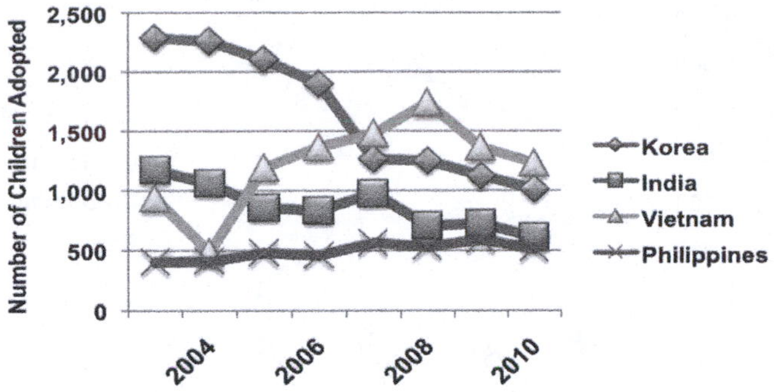

Figure 1.4 Number of Children Sent by 4 Asian States of Origin 2003-2010

legislative changes, which Vietnam already envisages, but also a fundamental change in outlook, including in particular a total divorce between 'humanitarian aid' or other financial contributions and the ICA of those of its children who may require this measure" (International Social Service, 2009, p. 10). The USA has now suspended adoptions from Vietnam: only nine visas were issued in FY 2010 and none in 2011. In February 2012 Vietnam's ratification of the Hague Convention came into force but the US suspension continued.

Other Asian countries causing concern include Nepal, which has been the subject of a report by UNICEF and Terre Des Hommes (2008), which found that "the majority of children surveyed have living relatives from whom they have been separated" (p. viii) and that "children who still have parents are routinely declared 'orphans' or 'abandoned' when adopters show interest in them" (p. 30). A special report from the Hague Conference (Degeling, 2010a) endorsed the findings of this earlier study by UNICEF, and recommended that Nepal should develop their child protection system and support measures for family preservation and alternatives to parental care with better regulation of children's homes. Before Nepal can ratify the Hague Convention, a new law will be needed that eliminates financial gain from the process. The Nepalese Government had suspended intercountry adoptions in 2007 and 2008 due to a range of concerns, but lifted the suspension in late 2008. The number of children sent fell sharply in 2009 but recovered slowly in 2010 (see Table 1.4). Although the number of adoptions from India remains low in relation to population size and the number of births (Table 1.4) there has been a continuing concern over child trafficking (Rollings, 2008; Selman, 2010b) and corrupt agencies (Dohle, 2008). Smolin (2005) speaks of the "two faces of intercountry adoption" in India.

Intercountry Adoption from Latin America and the Caribbean Adoption from Latin America dates back to the 1970s when Colombia began to send children to the USA, becoming the second most important source of children after Korea from 1975. By 1980, El Salvador and Mexico also featured in the top six states sending children to the USA. In Kane's study of ICA in the 1980s, six of the

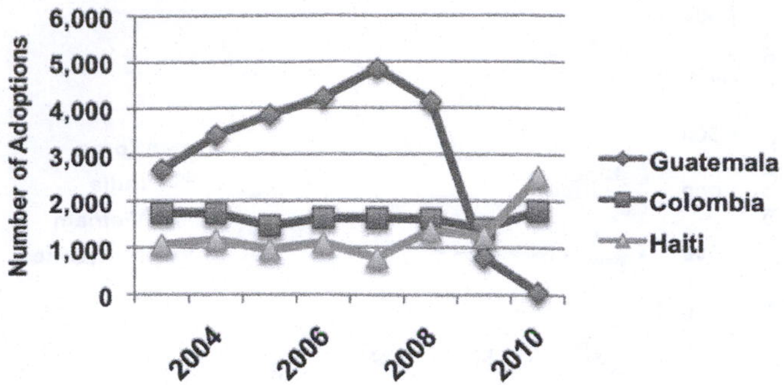

Figure 1.5 Trends in Number of Children Sent by Three Latin American Countries Sending Most Children Between 2004-2010

top ten sending countries (which together accounted for 90 percent of adoptions in that decade) were in Latin America (Selman, 2009a). By 2006, only two of those—Guatemala and Colombia—remained in the top ten, although Haiti had become a new major source (see Table 1.8).

Figure 1.5 shows the pattern of adoption in these three states between 2003 and 2010. Guatemala was of most significance until 2008. Figures submitted by Guatemala to the 2005 Hague Special Commission show a rise in transnational adoptions from 1,347 in 1998 to 3,572 in 2004 (see Chapter 9). Estimates based on adoptions recorded by 18 receiving states (Table 1.7) indicate a continued rise through 2007, which is reversed from 2008 with a sharp fall to under 1,000 in 2009 and less than 100 in 2010.

Table 1.6 shows annual totals from 2003 to 2010 for nine countries from Central and South America and the Caribbean, with the adoption ratio (adoptions per 1,000 live births) for the peak year.

In 2007, Guatemala had the highest ratio of all sending countries, with one out of every 100 live births leading to an overseas adoption, a level exceeded only by Korea in the 1980s, Romania in 1990-1991, and Bulgaria in 2002-2003. In 1999, 68 percent of the children sent by Guatemala went to the USA, but Canada, France, Spain, and the Netherlands also received significant numbers (Table 1.7). By 2004, over 95 percent went to the USA while Canada, Norway, Sweden, the Netherlands, and many other countries had stopped ICAs because of persistent scandals. In 2008 the USA received 98 percent of the estimated total of 4,850 and only Italy, Israel, and the UK[6] received more than 10 children. In January 2008 the USA imposed a moratorium on new adoptions from Guatemala, while Guatemala sought to resolve the many flaws apparent in its system. This had a huge impact in fiscal year 2009 when the number of orphan visas issued for Guatemala fell to 773 (from 4,123 in 2008). In 2010, only 51 visas were issued; in 2011 only 32.

6 The UK has now imposed a moratorium on all adoptions from Guatemala.

Table 1.6 Adoptions from Central and South America and Caribbean to 23 Receiving States 2003-2010. 10 Countries Ranked by Number of Children Sent in 2003; Peak Year in Bold; Ratio in Peak Year

	2003	2004	2005	2006	2007	2008	2009	2010	Ratio in peak year
Guatemala[b]	2,677	3,424	3,857	4,232	**4,851**	4,186	799	58	**10.8**
Colombia	1,750	1,741	1,466	1,639	1,636	1,617	1,413	**1,798**	**2.1**
Haiti	1,055	1,159	958	1,096	783	1,368	1,238	**2,601**	**9.9**
Brazil	470	478	473	**518**	485	485	461	377	**0.14**
Bolivia	**273**	260	250	152	148	79	88	71	**1.07**
Peru	118	91	163	**182**	168	121	132	169	**0.32**
Chile	**100**	93	85	89	80	44	77	74	**0.43**
Mexico	79	145	149	158	**181**	102	145	117	**0.09**
Jamaica	79	75	**85**	69	66	38	84	77	**1.67**
El Salvador	40	45	46	**48**	45	43	42	19	**0.31**

Source: Numbers calculated from data on adoptions from the 10 countries in statistics provided by the 23 receiving states listed in Table 1.

Note: a) Ratio = number of adoptions per 1,000 live births. b) More than 95 percent of adoptions from Guatemala are to the USA. Following the country's decision in 2008 to halt all but pending adoptions, the number of orphan visas issued for Guatemala by the US fell sharply to 773 in FY 2009 and 51 in FY 2010—see Table 1.7.

In contrast only 12 percent of adoptions from Brazil in 2007 were to the USA, and over two thirds went to Italy. Numbers fell from 2008 and Brazil has indicated that it will limit adoptions further as there is no Hague-accredited USA Agency in the country. Brazil has reduced the number of intercountry adoptions from over 1,600 in 1993 (Fonseca, 2002) to less than 400 in 2010, and now only sends children over age five or younger ones with special needs or who are in sibling groups. Many other countries in the region—e.g., Bolivia, Colombia, and El Salvador—send children primarily to Europe (Selman 2009c, 2010a).

Elsewhere in South and Central America the number of children sent for adoption is well below the level found in the 1990s. In the USA, in 1990 13 of the top 20 sending countries were in the Caribbean and Central or South America. By 2006, only four of those—Guatemala, Colombia, Haiti and Mexico—remained in the top 20 and five (Chile, Costa Rica, Cuba, Honduras, and Paraguay) sent few or no children to the USA (Selman, 2009b). In 1991, Chile sent 302 children to the USA; in 2007 it sent none to the USA, but 60 to Italy. The children sent now are largely over the age of five and many are from ethnic minority groups. Argentina has outlawed ICA, given its tragic history in that country, and now only classifies itself as a receiving state.

Table 1.7 Adoption from Guatemala 1999 to 2010—States Receiving 20+ Children in at Least One Year. Ranked by Number Received in 2001

	1999	2001	2003	2005	2006	2007	2008	2009	2010
USA FY	1,002	1,609	2,328	3,783	4,135	4,728	4,123	773	51
USA (Hague)[a]	–	–	–	**3,890**	**4,275**	**4,849**	**3,235**	**329**	–
France	186	187	247	5	0	0	0	0	0
Spain	70	46	8	0	6	8	4	6	0
Netherlands	41	45	4	1	1	3	0	0	0
Canada	74	22	0	0	1	4	4	2	2
Israel	4	16	4	17	21	31	24	6	2
UK[b]	15	13	29	21	30	46	0	0	0
Italy	22	8	8	13	14	14	9	10	3
Total[c]	**1,457**	**2,010**	**2,677**	**3,872**	**4,230**	**4,851**	**4,185**	**799**	**58**
% to USA	**68.8**	**80.1**	**87.0**	**97.7**	**97.5**	**97.8**	**98.6**	**96.9**	**87.9**

Source: Numbers calculated from data on adoptions from Guatemala in statistics provided by the 23 receiving states listed in Table 1.

Note: a) US calendar year data submitted to Hague Special Commission, b) The UK no longer permits adoptions from Guatemala, c) Totals include smaller numbers of adoptions from Denmark, Ireland, Norway, Sweden and Switzerland. There were also adoptions to Austria which are not included due to lack of accurate data.

But it is Haiti that has become the greatest concern of all Latin American countries, especially in the aftermath of the earthquake of 12 January, 2010 (Rotabi and Bergquist, 2010). The number of adoptions from Haiti had been fluctuating around 1,000 from 2003 to 2007, but rose significantly in 2008-2009. Adoption from Haiti has been dominated by the movement of children to four countries, France, the USA, Canada, and the Netherlands, with France accounting for about 50 percent in most years (Table 1.8).

Following the earthquake there was a huge concern for the victims and not least for the thousands of children said to have been orphaned. Similar concern had been felt following the Asian Tsunami of December 2004 (McGinnis, 2005). UNICEF and the Hague Conference warned against seeing these children as adoptable (Adams, 2010), but several countries sought to fast track adoptions 'in progress' even where this process was incomplete. By the end of February, emergency airlifts to Canada had brought 179 children who were already matched with parents (Hilborn, 2010).

The pattern of adoption in the aftermath of the earthquake has been critically examined by International Social Services (ISS) in a report entitled "Expediting intercountry adoptions in the aftermath of a natural disaster" (Dambach and \

Table 1.8 Adoption from Haiti 2003 to 2010 (with ISS Estimates if Data Incomplete or not Available)—Countries Ranked by Number Received in 2009 with Peak Year in Bold

	Haiti 2003-2010							
	2003	**2004**	**2005**	**2006**	**2007**	**2008**	**2009**	**2010**
France	542	507	475	571	403	731	651	**992**
USA	250	356	231	309	190	302	330	**1,223**[a]
Canada	149	159	115	123	89	148	141	**172**
Netherlands	69	42	51	41	28	91	60	**108**
Germany[b]	n/a	35	37	23	31	61	30	**(62)**
Spain	17	**36**	24	15	22	27	13	0
Top Six with ISS estimates[c]	**1,027**	**1,135**	**933**	**1,082**	**763**	**1,360**	**1,225**	**2,495 (2,557)**
Switzerland	9	7	7	10	**16**	4	9	**16**
Luxembourg	0	0	1	1	2	1	3	**(14)**
Belgium	12	6	4	1	0	3	1	**14**
Italy	6	9	**13**	2	2	0	0	0
Denmark	1	**2**	0	0	0	0	0	0
Total	**1,055**	**1,159**	**958**	**1,096**	**783**	**1,368**	**1,238**	**2,525**
Total with ISS estimates[c]								**(2,601)**

Note: a) US Fiscal year data—includes 1,090 children admitted as part of the Special Humanitarian Parole Program for Haitian Orphans—US Department of State (2010b) b) Figures for Germany are taken from the ISS Report (p.13)—the German Federal CA notes that these are "approximate" and may be reported in different year from the adoption's registration. c) ISS estimates for January-February 2010 (in brackets) from Dambach C. and Baglietto C. Haiti: *"Expediting" Intercountry Adoptions in the Aftermath of a Natural Disaster* (ISS 2010). See also Selman (2011).

Baglietto, 2010). Data for 2010 (Table 1.8) have confirmed the ISS prediction of a significant increase in the number of children going to France and to the USA, where over 1,000 were admitted on 'emergency visas.' The total number of adoptions from Haiti to all countries doubled in 2010, with most of the children placed in the two months after the earthquake. In 2011 there were very few intercountry adoptions from Haiti—33 to the United States (U.S. Department of State 2011e) and 34 to France (Selman, 2011).

Finally, it is worth noting that the United States now *sends* more children for intercountry adoption than many countries of Latin America (see Chapter 12). Between 2004 and 2009 the number rose from 126 to 315, the majority going

Table 1.9 Intercountry Adoptions from 10 Eastern European Countries to 23 Receiving States 2003-2010; Ranked by Number Sent in 2003

	2003	2004	2006	2007	2008	2009	2010	Ratio in Peak Year
Russia	7,743	**9,417**	6,776	4,880	4,140	4,033	3,387	**7.7**
Ukraine	**2,049**	2,017	1,046	1,619	1,583	1,508	1,798	**5.0**
Bulgaria[a]	**963**	393	109	103	132	226	245	**15.5**
Belarus	**656**	627	34	14	5	27	99	**7.5**
Romania[a]	**473**	287	0	0	0	0	0	**2.0**
Poland[b]	346	406	393	380	**407**	401	322	**1.1**
Lithuania[b]	85	103	109	**150**	121	123	103	**5.0**
Hungary[b]	69	70	100	**139**	115	120	137	**1.2**
Latvia[b]	65	124	**141**	100	89	128	120	**6.7**
Slovakia[b]	42	**75**	28	47	46	49	43	**1.5**
All European States of origin[c]	**13,058**	**13,949**	**9,043**	**7,734**	**7,007**	**6,818**	**5,783**	
Europe as % of all adoptions	**31.4%**	**30.8%**	**22.8%**	**20.6%**	**20.1%**	**22.8%**	**20.1%**	

Note: a) Bulgaria and Romania joined the EU on January 1st 2007, b) These 5 countries joined the EU in May 2004 with Estonia, the Czech Republic and Slovenia, c) 13 listed states plus Albania, Armenia, Azerbaijan, Bosnia, Croatia, Georgia, Macedonia, Montenegro, Serbia and Turkey. Kazakhstan and other EurAsian countries not included.

to Canada, but a significant minority (20 percent in 2006-8) to the Netherlands, where most are reported to be young African American infants and many are said to be adopted by same-sex couples (Selman, 2012, p. 14).

Intercountry Adoption from Europe During the period 1948-1962, USA parents adopted nearly 20,000 children from abroad (Altstein and Simon, 1991, p. 14). Many of them came from European countries—3,116 from Greece, influenced also by the Greek Civil War; 1,845 from Germany; and 744 from Austria (Selman, 2009c). As late as 1967, there were more children arriving in the USA from Germany than from Korea. England and Italy featured alongside these two countries in the top five states of origin for that year. But by the 1980s there were very few intercountry adoptions from Europe.

It is only in the last 20 years that Europe has once again become a significant source of children for adoption in the USA, initially with adoptions from Romania, from 1990/1991, and later from other Eastern European countries, such as Russia, Bulgaria, and the Ukraine (Selman, 2009c). At the turn of the century,

Eastern Europe continued to be a major source for children worldwide, but all that changed when Romania and Bulgaria reduced their numbers sharply as they sought membership in the European Union (see Chapter 7).

The number of children sent by Bulgaria fell from 963 in 2003, when it had the highest ratio of adoptions to live births of all sending countries (15.5) to 103 in 2007, but has risen again since then to 245 in 2010 (see Table 1.9). The most striking change was in Romania, which had accounted for about a third of all intercountry adoptions between January 1990 and July 1991 (Defence for Children International, 1991: UNICEF, 1999) but finally ended all intercountry adoptions to non-relatives in 2005 (Selman 2009a). The number of adoptions from Romania had fallen from over 2,000 in 1999 and 2000, when the ratio would have been higher than 10 per 1,000 births (Selman, 2009c).

Other countries such as Belarus and Russia also send fewer children. The number of children from Belarus fell from 636 in 2003 (when there were nearly eight adoptions per 1,000 live births) to five in 2008, but in 2010 nearly a hundred, mainly older, children went to Italy; the number from Russia fell from over 9,000 in 2004 to 3,387 in 2010 (Selman 2012, p. 11). There had been growing concerns in the Russian media over the fate of children sent for adoption, following reports of the murder of children by their adoptive parents in the USA (Khabbibullina, 2006) and the case of the five-year-old girl adopted by a pedophile for purposes of sexual exploitation (Smolin, 2007a). In 2006, Russia announced that it intended to re-accredit all foreign agencies involved in the placement of children, and in 2009 released a new list of USA agencies with which they will no longer work. Four years later Russia announced that it had suspended the adoption of Russian children by American families after Artyom Savelyev, a 7-year-old adopted Russian boy, was rejected by his American mother and sent back alone to Russia (Abrams, 2010; Rotabi and Heine, 2010). The incident caused widespread outrage in Russia.

Although most countries of Central and Eastern Europe have reduced numbers, the exceptions are five of the countries which joined the EU in 2004—Estonia, Hungary, Latvia, Lithuania, and Poland, all of which sent more children for ICA in 2009 than in 2003 (Selman 2009c). Today the adoption ratios in Latvia and Lithuania are comparable to those found in Russia and Belarus five years ago.

Intercountry adoption is a much debated issue in Europe with big divisions between strong opponents (see Cantwell, 2003; Post, 2007; United Adoptees International, 2010) and those who would like to see ICA become easier, especially between European states (Cavada et al., 2008; De Luca, 2009). For more detailed discussion on issues in the EU and the European Parliament see Selman (2009c; 2010b) and ChildONEurope (2009).

Intercountry Adoption from Africa In the 1980s and 1990s there were few intercountry adoptions from Africa. Only two countries—Ethiopia and Madagascar—featured in the top 25 sending countries in the 1980s according to Kane (1993). The numbers sent by these two countries to France increased in

Table 1.10 Adoptions from Africa 2004-2010; 12 Countries Sending Most Children in this Period—Peak Year in Bold—and Ratio in Peak Year

	2004-10	2004	2006	2007	2008	2009	2010	Ratio in peak year
All Africa[a]	**33,249**	2,977	3,858	4,672	5,607	**6,393**	6,346	
Ethiopia	**21,367**	1,527	2,172	3,033	3,896	**4,565**	4,396	**1.5**
South Africa	**1,580**	242	206	202	230	**283**	190	**0.26**
Liberia[b]	**1,320**	87	**369**	334	249	36	52	**2.01**
Nigeria	**1,046**	94	104	81	223	184	**259**	**0.04**
Madagascar	**936**	**335**	137	71	15	36	55	**0.47**
Mali	**889**	82	126	158	107	**191**	132	**0.33**
Burkina Faso	**590**	93	**107**	97	82	54	79	**0.12**
Congo D.R.	**583**	12	62	68	62	149	**188**	**0.06**
Ghana	**530**	32	34	57	116	116	**129**	**0.18**
Ivory Coast	**446**	26	36	65	76	100	**105**	**0.15**
Morocco	**415**	65	55	38	59	70	**90**	**0.14**
Cameroon	**406**	53	53	47	48	**87**	72	**0.13**

Note: a) In 2010 adoptions from Africa were 22 percent of global total, b) Adoptions from Liberia—mostly to the USA—rose rapidly until 2006, but subsequently declined amidst concern over irregularities.

Source: Numbers calculated from data on adoptions in statistics provided by the 23 receiving states listed in Table 1.1.

the 1990s—Ethiopia from 70 in 1991 to 217 in 2003; Madagascar from 104 to 325 over the same period. After 2003 the number of children sent by Madagascar fell steadily, but numbers from Ethiopia rose, doubling in France and increasing very rapidly in the USA and Spain, which had become the main destinations for Ethiopian children by 2007 (Table 1.11).

Table 1.10 shows the changes in 12 African States of origin, sending most children for intercountry adoption between 2004 and 2010, during which time the total number sent by all African states has more than doubled. Only Madagascar has reduced numbers significantly over this period. Adoptions from Liberia have been almost entirely to the USA. These rose sharply for some years, but have now fallen to a low level due to many problems. The rapid growth in Ethiopia (Table 1.11) is partly due to an increase in the number of children sent to the USA, which some attribute to the publicity around the adoption of an Ethiopian child by film-stars Angelina Jolie and Brad Pitt (Mezmur, 2009a).

Table 1.11 Adoptions from Ethiopia 1998-2010: Countries Ranked by Number of Children Received in 2009. Peak Year for Each Country in Bold

Country	1998	2003	2004	2006	2007	2008	2009	2010
USA FY	96	135	289	732	1,255	1,725	2,225	**2,513**
Spain	0	107	220	304	481	629	**722**	508
France	155	217	390	408	417	**484**	445	352
Italy	9	47	193	227	256	338	**346**	274
Canada	10	14	34	61	135	**183**	170	112
Belgium	46	52	62	88	124	**144**	143	120
Denmark	26	40	41	38	39	92	**125**	117
Germany	20	19	20	33	29	47	72	**97**
Switzerland	13	58	43	54	56	47	49	**76**
Norway	46	46	**47**	27	33	26	43	38
NL	18	39	72	48	**68**	50	39	23
Australia	37	39	45	**70**	47	35	38	33
TOTAL to all states[ab]	**501**	**854**	**1,527**	**2,172**	**3,033**	**3,896**	**4,565**	**4,396**

Note: a) The total includes other countries which have received children from Ethiopia in this period: e.g., Finland, Ireland, Malta, Sweden, Switzerland and the UK. b) Adoptions to Austria (34 between 2005-2009 in Hague Return) are not included, as statistics are unreliable. The Austrian agency (Families for You), which received over 70 children between 2004 and 2006, has been removed from the approved list.

Ethiopia has clearly been of greatest significance in global terms (see Chapter 10). The estimated number of children sent for ICA has risen from 500 in 1998 to more than 4,500 in 2009. Over 80 percent go to four countries—the USA, Spain, France, and Italy. But the adoption ratio remains modest and if Ethiopia were to send children on the scale of Korea or the Ukraine in 2003, the total number would be over 15,000 a year.

In March 2011, Ethiopia announced a plan to reduce the number of adoptions processed each day from 50 to 5 (Heinlein, 2011b). If implemented this could reduce the annual total of intercountry adoptions by 90 percent and bring global levels back to those found in the mid-1990s. It would also be likely to lead to pressure on other African countries, especially Nigeria and the Democratic Republic of the Congo, which have had increasing numbers over the past five years but currently have low adoption ratios and the potential to send as many children as Ethiopia has sent in recent years.

Much has been made of the huge number of 'AIDS orphans' in Ethiopia and other African countries, but most of them are cared for by their extended family and the priority is to give support to grandparents and other caring relatives. Fears that Africa might be seen as a new source of children to replace those formerly received from China and Russia were fuelled by the arrest in October 2007 of seven French aid workers who were attempting to fly out 103 children from the impoverished country of Chad, which borders on the Darfur region of Sudan, (Duval Smith and Rolley 2007; see Chapter 3). This episode raised again the unacceptability of ICA as a rescue mission at times of crisis when so many children are separated from their families (McGinnis, 2005; Mezmur 2009a). The organization involved, Zoe's Ark, which was set up to help Tsunami victims in 2005 (BBC News, 2007), has been condemned by the French Government. The episode was reminiscent of the Italian 'adoptions' from Rwanda in 2000 (BBC News, 2000, 2001), and is replicated in some of the activities surrounding the removal of children from Haiti after the earthquake. For further insights into issues raised by the accelerating number of adoptions from Africa, see the series of articles by Mezmur (2009a, 2009b, 2010) and an article by Högbacka (2011) on birth mothers in South Africa (see Chapter 11).

Why Are Numbers Falling After a Decade Of Growth?

The rise in intercountry adoptions to 2004 seems in many ways to have been driven by an increasing 'demand' for children, fuelled by the apparent steady increase in the number of children available in China, Russia, and Guatemala and the opening up of possibilities for adoption by single individuals. The subsequent decline seems to be more influenced by the 'supply; of children from key states of origin (Tables 1.2 and 1.3). A reduction in numbers from individual countries has been found in the past, notably in Latin American and Asian countries in the 1980s. The reduction in the number of children received in the Netherlands—from 1,704 in 1980 to 574 in 1993—was seen as reflecting a fall in demand, as the problems associated with ICA became apparent (Hoksbergen, 1991a, 2000). Similar falls were recorded in Sweden, where the number of overseas adoptions was the equivalent of two for every 100 births in 1979 (Andersson, 1986). By the end of the 1980s, global numbers seemed to have peaked and Altstein and Simon (1991) predicted a continuing decline despite the temporary rise as a result of the situation in post-Ceausescu Romania. In reality, the years from 1988 to 1992, when numbers fell in the USA and many other countries, proved to be a period of transition to the huge acceleration in ICA from 1993 to 2004, fuelled by the increased demand created by the Romanian surge, the rise in adoptions from Guatemala to the USA (from 257 in 1990 to 4,851 in 2007), and the new potential of children from China and Russia.

Although the impact of the decline in adoptions from China after 2005 has been most dramatic, in some countries the reduction in numbers can be traced back to the first years of the 21st century. The rapid reduction in numbers from Romania and Bulgaria described earlier was no doubt influenced in part by pressures from the EU as the two countries sought membership, but the equally dramatic decline in Belarus and the steady reduction in Russia seem to reflect a reaction in all of those countries to the poorly controlled adoption practices, reflected in a series of scandals and increasing opposition from citizens of those countries as previously discussed.

The reversal in China reflects a steady decline in the number of healthy infants in orphanages (see Chapter 8) and a reaction to the Hunan scandal (Meier and Zhang 2008). Concern had also been building in China about the growing number of applications from single women (many in same-sex relationships). The reduction in the number of children sent, dates from 2006 when the CCAA announced new guidelines including a requirement that prospective adopters must be a heterosexual couple who have been married for at least two years (Bellock and Yardley, 2006; Hilborn, 2007). This effectively ended adoption by single women, who accounted for up to a third of USA adopters in the late 1990s (Selman 2009a).[7]

Although China has taken a pragmatic stance seeing short-term value in placing children from overcrowded institutions and deriving valuable revenue from the fee ($3,000-$5,000) charged to all adopters, many observers also note that the child welfare system is now much improved, that there is clearly a large interest in domestic adoption, and that China is becoming aware of the negative image that continuing intercountry adoption can create. However, the rise in the number of older children with special needs who are now being placed suggests that China may now see a new role for ICA, which is similar to the patterns seen in Brazil and some Eastern European countries.

Similar considerations have led the Korean government to move towards a long-promised ending of ICA after 55 years, during which time the country has transformed from a war-torn and developing nation with a population problem to one of the richest countries of the world with one of the lowest fertility rates. It was only in 2008 that the number of in-country adoptions exceeded the number of inter-country. In Korea unlike China, the demand for an end is led, in part, by returning adoptees (e.g., Hübinette 2007b; Trenka, 2003, 2009) but there can be little doubt that similar calls will arise from Chinese adopted 'girls' if ICA continues when they reach adulthood. In 2010 the annual number of children sent fell to 1,000, the lowest level since 1968 and in 2011 the Korean government announced plans to end its intercountry adoption program by 2012, through legislation drafted by adoptees and birthmothers (Dobbs, 2011; Tae Hoon, 2011).

The Future of Intercountry Adoption

Faced with the clear evidence of declining numbers and the growing criticism of a system so open to abuse (Post, 2007; Smolin, 2004, 2005, 2007a, 2010) many feel that this may indeed be the "beginning of the end of wide-scale ICA" which Altstein and Simon (1991, p. 191) predicted more than 15 years ago. The situation of the many childless couples in the high-resource countries of the West hoping for a child seems likely to worsen, so that many of those 'approved' will face a long

7 In March 2011 the CCAA changed its name to CCWAA (China Centre for Children's Welfare and Adoption Affairs) and announced that single women may apply to adopt special focus children listed on their Special Needs System.

wait and may never receive a child, or are offered a child who is very different from the one they had expected. In France, there have been newspaper reports of as many as 25,000 families, approved for intercountry adoption, while the number of adoptions a year has fallen from 4,136 in 2005 to 3,017 in 2009. Similar reports are found in Spain, the Netherlands, and the Nordic countries (Selman, Moretti, and Brogi, 2009). The USA is facing a major shortfall in the number of children available as the moratorium on adoptions from Guatemala and Vietnam continues. In Europe there has been pressure on Romania to open up for intercountry adoption and there is now a substantial lobby group within the European Parliament calling for a new European adoption procedure which would make adoption between EU countries much easier (Selman, 2010b). Cantwell (2003) argues that many of the children now being placed are not really 'available for adoption' in the terms of the Hague Convention and Mezmur (2009b) has questioned how people define adoption as a 'last resort.'

The global economic crisis may lead to a reduction in demand or could result in an acceleration of 'market forces' and an increased risk of trafficking. Smolin has pointed to the continuing evidence of "child trafficking" as a reason why ICA should end unless reformed and has suggested that history may "label … the entire enterprise as a neo-colonialist mistake" (Smolin, 2004, p. 325) just as it is now widely accepted that in the case of the 'shipment' of poor children from England to Australia and Canada " … a damning verdict is inescapable" (Parker, 2008, p. 293) and that apologies have rightly been given the 'stolen generation' of aboriginal children in Australia.

Negative judgments and over-generalizations would be hurtful to the many thousands of people who have adopted children from overseas and to many adoptees who recognize the positives in their experience, knowing that without such intervention they may well have not have survived. The counter argument that ICA can be 'a global gift' (Triseliotis, 2000) is particularly compelling in the cases of the many children with special needs who are now being adopted, and is backed by the growing body of research that indicates the potential of a new family for reversing the impact of early deprivation (Juffer and van IJzendoorn, 2009; see Chapter 13).

Some advocates of ICA (e.g., Wallace, 2003), while acknowledging a need for reform, argue for an increase in the number of international adoptions as a key part of helping children in a globalized world, a view propounded by Mark Zappala and Chuck Johnson (2009) in an issue of *Adoption Advocate* and by Elisabeth Bartholet (2010/2011) and Richard Carlson (2011) and others in a special edition of the *New York Law School Review*. In the USA a new campaign, *Both Ends Burning* has been launched by football star Craig Juntunen, who has adopted three children from Haiti (Juntunen, 2009), "to create a solution to a tragic, worldwide crisis—a global slowdown in the international adoption system." The campaign seeks to encourage intercountry adoption by simplifying procedures and highlighting the extent of need worldwide.

Even if we feel hesitant to accept Smolin's verdict, rooted in a personal experience of adopting children abducted from their birth parents, we must recognize that "in a perfect world, without the gross inequalities which still reign on this planet at the beginning of the new millennium, wide scale ICA would not exist" (Van Loon, 2000, p. 1), and remember Altstein's observation that 'one overriding question exists in relation to ICA. Is it moral and humane to remove a child from his native society to be reared in a culture other than his own?" (Altstein, 1984, p. 202) and Hoksbergen's hope that "culture and economic circumstances in all Third-World Countries change to the extent that it will be the exception when a child's only chance for a satisfactory upbringing exists with a family thousands of miles from its birthplace" (Hoksbergen, 1991a, p. 156). Until such time the imperative is to seek to ensure that intercountry adoptions are only carried out within the vision of the Hague Convention, with full consideration of the principle of the *best interests of the child*, and a determination to press for more open adoptions in which a child can retain links with and pride in her country of origin and, where possible, her birth family. Above all we must ensure that the focus is always on the rights of the child, not the right to a child (Mezmur, 2009b).

Chapter 2
Social Policy Approaches and Social Work Dilemmas in Intercountry Adoption

Jonathan Dickens[1]

This chapter proposes a social policy framework for thinking about intercountry adoption (ICA), drawing on theories of welfare regimes and globalization. Typologies of fundamental welfare approaches, or 'regimes', originated in analyses of nation-state policies, but nowadays have additional value as models for understanding globalization. The framework shows how ICA interacts with national child and family welfare policies in receiving and sending countries; and beyond that, how it links with wider, global social policy. Looking at ICA in this way highlights the tensions and ambiguities of its policy contexts and consequences, and the possibilities of a more radical approach. Romania's ban on ICA is discussed as an example. The model also sheds light on the dilemmas that ICA raises for social work policy and practice under the different welfare approaches.

Welfare Regimes

Esping-Andersen's typology of welfare state regimes in developed capitalist countries (1990) has become a much-used starting point for international social policy comparisons and analysis. A fundamental challenge for western, democratic nation-states with capitalist economies, is to balance the role and responsibilities of the state for ensuring the well-being of its citizens with two other requirements: upholding private and family life, and promoting the effective working of the free market economy. Esping-Andersen identified three archetypal approaches to this challenge: liberal or neo-liberal, conservative corporatist and social democratic. The model has frequently been used and adapted by other researchers and commentators (summarized by Abrahamson, 1999). Gough and Wood (2004) use it as a springboard to build a typology for non-industrialized, developing countries. In fact, the underlying ideas have long historical roots, with their origins in the great political philosophies of libertarianism, utilitarianism and egalitarianism.

---

1 This chapter is based on Dickens, J. (2009). Social policy approaches to intercountry adoption. *International Social Work*, 52, 595-607. © Sage.

Table 2.1 Welfare Regimes and Intercountry Adoption

	Neo-liberal	Conservative corporatist	Social democratic	Radical
Core value	Liberty	Stability	Equality	Transformation
Political philosophy	Libertarianism	Utilitarianism	Egalitarianism	Marxism
State & society	'Laissez faire'—belief in individual freedom and the market place. 'Small state, strong state.'	State's role to uphold the status quo but mitigate worst effects of capitalism.	Active role for state in ensuring welfare of all citizens.	A critical view—state largely serves the interests of capitalism, but can also challenge it.
State's role in welfare	Minimalist—individuals and families should provide and/or purchase.	Significant but limited—collaborates with private and voluntary sectors.	Positive role in planning and providing services, for high quality and equality.	Greater role for state, to create equality: but argues that state welfare sustains inequality too.
Approach to social problems	Failings of individuals, families or communities.	Failings of individuals or families, or welfare system failings.	Problems caused by inequalities of power and resources.	The exploitive relations of capitalism, especially shown in inequalities of social class, race and gender: but state welfare is also seen to mask these differences.

Key roles of social work	Notions of rescue and control dominate work in poorer communities; more of a personal service role with wealthier clients.	Key notions of treatment and reintegration. Positive help for better-off clients, but firmer intervention with poorer people, and escalating sanctions for non-compliance.	Key notions of partnership and empowerment, listening to service users; but reformist not revolutionary.	Campaigning, consciousness-raising, advocacy, working with and on behalf of poorer individuals and communities.
Implications for ICA	Would support ICA, allow profit-making agencies, light touch regulatory regime.	May support ICA, depending on domestic politics (e.g., middle class demand). Key delivery role for non-state agencies, state has regulatory role.	Likely to support ICA, for altruistic reasons and to compensate for low numbers of in-country adoptions.	Opposed to ICA, not just because of its corruption and deceit, but its fundamental basis on inequalities of wealth and opportunity.
Primary risk to social work in ICA	Professional assessments being distorted by (explicit or implicit) financial considerations.	Over-proceduralization, the human face of need hidden by state policies, inter-agency arrangements, bureaucracy.	Hearing only the loudest voices, those of the articulate and powerful, the home market.	ICA banned, but new risks of over-politicization, the human face of need hidden by inflexible policies and political objectives.

Source: Adapted from Dickens (2010, p. 45).

The endurance of this elemental three-way split makes it a powerful framework for looking at national and global social policy, and particularly useful for ICA.

Like all models, Esping-Andersen's framework is a simplification of a complex reality, a caricature rather than a photograph. The main features of each approach are summarized in Table 2.1 (based on Dickens, 2010), along with a fourth, and radical perspective, with implications for social work policy and practice. It is important to stress here that Esping-Andersen's three approaches do not exist anywhere in their pure form: rather, reality is marked by on-going conflict, overlap and ambiguity. Having said that, the USA can be seen as an exemplar of the neo-liberal approach, France and Germany as typical of the conservative corporatist approach, and the Scandinavian countries as the leading examples of the social democratic approach. The current UK approach draws explicitly on all three approaches (Levitas, 2005). In any country, however, there is range of views. For politicians and policy makers the most effective strategy is to support policies that, on the surface, appeal to all perspectives—and ICA is a prime example of that.

Welfare Regimes and Social Services for Children

The liberal or neo-liberal approach holds that the welfare needs of an individual or family are best met by purchasing the services they need from the free market economy (e.g., private health care, pensions, and childcare). Charities might provide services for those who cannot afford to pay. The state has a minimal role to ensure legality and protect the most vulnerable; otherwise it keeps out of the welfare business. When intervention is needed, the state tends to act decisively and rather punitively. For example, state payments to people who are out of work will be modest, means-tested, and with tough employment rules. This approach obliges individuals and families to take maximum responsibility for their own well-being. In some activities, such as adoption, unadulterated market principles may not be judged appropriate, and legislation would prohibit the direct purchase of children, whilst still allowing payment for 'reasonable' fees and expenses. So, this approach would give a major role to independent adoption agencies, run either for profit or on a not-for-profit basis, and also for private, non-agency adoptions, arranged directly between the adopters and the birth parent(s), perhaps with the help of an intermediary. In keeping with the market place ideology, there is an emphasis on choice—prospective adopters, and birth parent(s), would be free to choose an agency, and even to select one another. This leads to a highly competitive market for healthy babies, exemplified by online profiles of prospective adopters (effectively, advertisements) hoping that a birth parent will choose them. There would also be state-run child protection services to monitor the most risky cases of children living with their birth families. Children at gravest risk are likely to be removed from their families by the statutory agencies. There is a mistrust of state care, so there will be tight timescales and legal provisions to ensure that the children, especially the young ones, are moved out of care as quickly as possible, either back to their birth families or on to adoption.

The conservative corporatist state places the greatest value on social cohesion and aims to mitigate the worst effects of capitalism without undermining the smooth running of the economy. Its aim is to facilitate the smooth running of the economy (rather than the neo-liberal approach which, in its pure form, leaves this to market forces). It is conservative in the sense that it seeks to uphold traditional social values and family roles, and corporatist in that it seeks to work with the private and voluntary sectors in coordinating welfare services. It aims to preserve existing social structures and differentials, holding that these serve the interests of society as a whole—so, for example, higher wage earners will pay more in social insurance contributions, but then benefit from higher payments when they need them. This 'buys-in' the support of the middle classes, crucial to social stability. The echo of utilitarianism is the emphasis on the overall good of society. A word that captures the essence of the model is 'integration.' It aims to integrate people who have become socially excluded back into mainstream society, and to do this by integrating the work of state and non-governmental agencies. The state is likely to have a planning and funding role for welfare services, whilst independent agencies are more likely to be delivering the services. So, one would expect to see a prominent role for private and voluntary sector child welfare services and adoption agencies, perhaps linked with churches or other traditional providers of welfare support. When people do fall though the welfare net, this may be attributed to their own failings, as in the neo-liberal model (and those who do not comply with the help on offer can expect increasingly strict sanctions), but also it may be understood as a failure of service planning and delivery, of agencies not targeting their intervention effectively. So in distinction from the neo-liberal approach, one would expect the state to be playing a more active role in working with independent organizations, for example through joint planning, commissioning services and issuing detailed regulations to ensure quality provision, not just minimal standards.

The social democratic state sets its greatest value on social equality, and aims to intervene actively in social and economic life to ensure this. It will have redistributionist tax policies, to shift resources in favor of the least well-off. The state itself will be a primary provider of welfare services, which are seen as non-stigmatizing, high quality services of first resort for all citizens (rather than residual services of last resort for the poorest people, as in the neo-liberal approach). It is a reformative rather than a revolutionary approach, however, and although it emphasizes equality and empowerment, this is firmly within a capitalist economy and democratic political system. So, in terms of social services for children and families, one would expect to see a wide range of support services for parents, day care facilities and after school activities. The priority would be to keep families together, or to reunite them if they are separated; but at the same time, there would be a more positive view of out-of-home care than in the neo-liberal or conservative approaches, seeing it as a service that can itself help children and support families. In this sense there would be a greater willingness to use care than in the other models. However, there would be a reluctance to institute legal proceedings to make separation permanent, so one would expect fewer children to be available for adoption, and children are more likely to stay in care longer (Thoburn, 2007).

Globalization and Welfare Regimes

Globalization raises the fundamental social policy questions to a new international level (Deacon, 2000, 2007). There are hotly contested debates about the characteristics of globalization, its costs and benefits, what it is, what it could be, and what it should be (Midgley, 2007). There are new arguments about the proper roles of the state, family, market and not-for-profit sector in generating economic growth and ensuring social welfare, but beneath them are the older themes of neo-liberalism, conservative corporatism and social democracy.

Proponents of the first position hold, broadly, that globalization should proceed along the lines of free market capitalism, with only minimalist, safety-net provision by national governments for the very poorest. The second perspective is that governments and international agencies should work together to regulate the worst excesses of global markets, to 'socialize' global policy. The third position is that globalization should prioritize social justice and welfare for the poor in developed and developing countries alike. As with the nation-state level of this framework, there are overlaps and ambiguities among the perspectives, and competing views within and between different organizations. For all that, the dominant ideological and economic model for the last 30 years has been the neo-liberal which, despite being exposed by the 2007-2009 global economic crisis, continues to shape the parameters for the others.

Globalization and Intercountry Adoption

So, the old national policy debates have acquired an international dimension, and the focus here is how this framework can shed light on ICA. This section looks in turn at receiving countries, sending countries and international regulation. The following section goes on to describe a more radical perspective on social policy, and considers Romania's ban on ICA as an example.

Receiving Countries

ICA has been characterized as a demand-led market (e.g., Chou and Browne, 2008; Högbacka, 2008; Kapstein, 2003; Selman, 2002, 2006). The number of would-be adopters has risen for various reasons, including delayed child bearing of many couples, and more single people and same-sex couples who wish to adopt. Domestic supply is not able to meet the demand, in terms of 'quality' or quantity. A neo-liberal welfare state will have children available for domestic adoption, the ones removed from their birth families by state agencies, and babies being relinquished by their birth mothers. Children in the former group may be older and troubled, and the number in the latter group insufficient. For those with enough money, the archetypal liberal response is to 'go to market'—if you want a healthy baby and they are not readily available in one's own country, look elsewhere. In this regard, it is significant that the USA, which fits the stereotype of a neo-liberal welfare state, has been such a large importer of children. In the year ending September 30, 2010, there were just over 11,000 ICAs, but this had risen from just over 7000 in 1990 to a high point of 22,990 in 2004 (Smolin, 2010; U.S. Department of State, 2010a; see also Selman Chapter 1). Certainly the recent trend is downwards, and there are far fewer ICAs than domestic adoptions, but even so the market dynamic means that harder-to-place children are more likely to be left in care. There were 55,684 children adopted from public care in the USA in the year ending 30 September 2009, and 114,556 waiting to be adopted (over a third of these were in pre-adoptive homes or kinship placements). Sixty percent of the waiting children had been waiting for more than two years (U.S. Department of Health and Human Services, 2010).

There are further consequences of the neo-liberal approach, which reach beyond the specifics of adoption. The involvement of the wealthy and middle classes is essential to ensuring the maintenance of high quality public services in any country. The ease with which such families can meet their individual welfare needs in a foreign country may reduce the stake that they feel in ensuring that welfare services in their own country are of high quality. It thereby contributes to the residualization of state welfare, as state expenditures on services such as health, education and social protection are cut back in the drive to achieve global economic competitiveness. So state services for children and families in the wealthier countries are vulnerable to neo-liberal globalization, as much as in the poorer countries, and ICA plays a part in that.

The dynamic is different under a social democratic system, but the end result is similar—look abroad. In the past this may have been inspired by a humanitarian commitment, but Yngvesson (2002) holds that motives have changed since the 1960s and 1970s, and are now more about responding to infertility than social justice. There are very few domestic adoptions, so the majority of adoptions are intercountry—as high as 98 percent in Sweden and Norway in 2003 (Chou and Browne, 2008). Whilst the USA is by far the largest importer of children in raw numbers, when one looks at the rate of children adopted from abroad compared to the receiving country's birth rate it is the social democratic countries that are the largest importers (Selman, 2002, 2006). So despite the different ideological positions, ICA is accepted in both systems.

From the conservative point of view, one would expect the state to support ICA if this serves the needs of the economy, the wishes of the middle classes, and the more general stability of society. Western countries with sub-replacement birth rates might well need a population boost from ICA. At the same time, however, such countries are likely to have children of their own in state care, and a culture and relative ease of adopting children from abroad may detract attention from them. Chou and Browne's (2008) study of 25 European countries shows a positive correlation between rates of ICA and rates of institutional care for children aged under three, in receiving as well as sending countries.

Sending Countries

The principal sending countries are not western states with capitalist economies, so the three-part model cannot simply be transposed on to them. Its value here is to show how ICA reflects the dominant neo-liberal characteristics of contemporary globalization, and how it distorts the development of in-country welfare services. Markets and money are the key factors.

In terms of markets, we have to look at the supply-side as well as the demand. Here, a significant point is that children for ICA tend not to come from the very poorest countries, notably those of sub-Saharan Africa. Indeed, Korea, now a relatively wealthy country, is still one of the world's top exporters (Selman, 2006; U.S. Department of State, 2010a). Korea's situation may be understood in terms of its long history of sending children to the USA for adoption, the activity of ICA agencies with their own interest in organizational survival (Sarri, Baik and Bombyk, 1998), its strong traditions about family bloodlines and its welfare regime, recently characterized as residualist (Park, 2008). The point is that ICA goes where there are favorable cultural traditions and legal conditions (including lack of effective measures to tackle malpractice), and a reliable supply chain. The very poorest countries may not meet these market-oriented requirements, so business goes elsewhere. Having said that, sending nations are certainly among the poorer countries, with some of their populations in very great need—and so money comes into play. The potential for illegal payments to birth parents, bribery and extortion is well-known (Graff, 2008; Kapstein, 2003), but there are also possibilities for financial gain legally, which can have a corrosive impact on domestic services. An example is getting a job with one of the ICA agencies. Dickens (2002) shows how jobs in ICA were an attractive option for many Romanian social workers in the 1990s—the pay was better than in the local authority services, the facilities and working conditions tended to be better, and there was the possibility of foreign travel. It is a reasonable choice for the individuals concerned, but the wider result is the weakening of domestic services.

The power of foreign money also has an impact on public commitment to domestic services. In situations of economic hardship, and in cultures where extra payments or 'gifts' for services are widespread (never mind more extreme forms of corruption), the purchasing power of wealthy foreigners is overwhelming. Attempts to incorporate foreigners' payments into the domestic system, say by requiring a donation to an orphanage or to support in-country services, tend to compound the problem because potential domestic adopters are less lucrative for the agencies. This makes it likely that international adopters will be selected over in-country candidates, or over efforts to support birth families (Dickens, 2002; Post, 2007; Smolin, 2007b). As Smolin (2007b) puts it:

> Rather than contributing positively to an effective family or child welfare system, intercountry adoption has the potential to distort whatever system is already in place. The monetary incentives to place children internationally can in practice totally overwhelm the appropriate priorities of a social welfare and services system. (p. 451)

Regulation of Intercountry Adoption

Law and policy on ICA is the responsibility of individual nation-states, but within an international framework shaped primarily by the 1993 Hague Convention (HCIA). The strength of the Hague Convention is that it appeals, in some ways, to supporters of all three perspectives; its weakness is that it does not fully satisfy any of them. Like any international treaty, it has to be ambiguous if it is to be adopted worldwide. It fits best into the conservative corporatist mould, in that it gives the fundamental regulatory responsibility to the state, and a vital role to non-state agencies to deliver services; but it relies on nation-states to implement and enforce it, which may be unwilling or unable to do so effectively. It appeals to neo-liberals because it permits ICA and secures a place for for-profit agencies and private (non-agency) adoptions. Neo-liberals criticize it, though, as unduly restrictive, adding to cost and delay, and making it harder for children to be adopted (e.g., Bartholet, 2007; Varnis, 2001). Social democrats appreciate that at least it brings some regulation, but are suspicious that it is weak and allows market-place behavior to continue. Lammerant and Hofstetter (2007), for example, discussing the different arrangements for the Convention in six European countries, highlight the dangers of competitive, market-place relations among accredited agencies. Ethica, a USA campaign group for ethical adoption practices, criticizes regulations relating to payments for increasing the dangers of children being bought and sold (Ethica, 2006). To pick up on the themes of conflict and ambiguity, there is a significant difference between the Hague Convention and the 1989 UN Convention on the Rights of the Child (CRC). The Hague Convention states that ICA 'may offer the advantage of a permanent family to a child for whom a suitable *family* cannot be found in his or her State of origin' (emphasis added). The CRC, meanwhile, recognizes that ICA may be appropriate in certain cases, but only if the child cannot be cared for 'in any suitable manner' in his/her country of origin (Article 21). This could conceivably include a wide range of alternatives, such as small 'family-type' homes, child-headed households, and informal community-based solutions. Such options may be more suitable than ICA for many children who do not live with their birth families, given that very few separated children are abandoned or orphaned healthy babies (Graff, 2008; Saclier, 2000).

There is tension between the two approaches and the Hague Convention appears to be in the ascendancy, but there are efforts to gloss over the differences. Ambiguity is the key diplomatic skill. This is apparent in the Position Statement of the United Nations Children's Fund (UNICEF) on ICA. UNICEF looks to the CRC as its touchstone and has an ambivalent position on ICA. It says that it supports the Hague Convention but considers ICA 'one of a *range* of care options which may be open to children, and for *individual* children who cannot be placed in a permanent family setting in their countries of origin, it *may* indeed be the best solution' (UNICEF, emphasis added). The sentence hints at UNICEF's unease about ICA: whilst it may be an attractive option for some individual children, the problem is its effects on all the other children, in sending and receiving countries, who will not get the services and support they need because of the way ICA distorts the domestic welfare system.

A Radical Perspective

The discussion so far has shown how ICA chimes with aspects of all three welfare models, but also raises problems for each of them. All three are, in a sense, 'conservative' because they each seek, in their own way, to support the market economy and preserve the status quo. But social policy offers other perspectives, that call for a truly transformative approach to ending poverty, tackling exclusion and securing people's rights (e.g., Ferguson, Lavalette and Mooney, 2002). This approach calls for much more assertive action from the state, but at the same time it is skeptical about the state's role in welfare, seeing it mainly as a smokescreen that hides, and even sustains, the exploitive relations of capitalism. States can and should provide welfare services to help people, for sure: but such provision largely serves the needs of the capitalist economy. One way that it does this is by producing sufficient numbers of people educated to different levels to give a flexible workforce and a diverse market for goods; another is that it can lull people into accepting the way things are, into believing that people in need are there because of their personal inadequacies, rather than because of a whole economic and social system that runs on a relatively few rich people living comfortable lives at the expense of the many. Whilst its philosophical roots are in Marxism, a radical approach does not require a communist political system to make a valuable contribution to policy analysis and change. It is a powerful diagnostic tool for assessing the impact of welfare policies in nation states and at a global level, and is especially illuminating for ICA. It unmasks the hidden realities behind moving pictures of abandoned babies and happy adopters, and behind the equally well-known stories of corruption and deceit. It reveals birth parents and children without adequate support, desperate poverty, fundamental inequalities of wealth and opportunity, and the divisive and disruptive effects of ICA on domestic welfare services in sending and receiving countries alike. Given all this, ending ICA would be a step towards a fairer world for all children. Romania provides an interesting and challenging glimpse of the benefits of this radical step.

Romania's Ban on ICA

The history of ICA and child welfare reform in Romania over the 1990s is well-known (Dickens, 1999, 2002; Dickens and Groza, 2004, see also Chapter

7). Following the overthrow of the communist dictator, Nicolae Ceauşescu, in December 1989, there was an explosion of ICAs from Romania. A moratorium in summer 1991 was an attempt to regain control of the situation. ICA resumed in 1992, and despite legislation professing the priority of family support services and domestic adoption, the number of ICAs far exceeded domestic ones over the 1990s (Independent Group for International Adoption Analysis [IGIAA], 2002). In 2001, the Romanian government introduced another moratorium, which was subsequently extended and then incorporated into a permanent ban from January 2005 (except for adoption by grandparents who live abroad). There are three policy aspects to draw out: the economic challenges for in-country services; the complex international context; and the progress of domestic services since 2001.

Romania's transition from a state-controlled to market economy in the 1990s led to rising unemployment and falling wages. The economic collapse and the rising levels of need left many families struggling to cope, and the Romanian government struggling to develop in-country welfare services. In 1997, it introduced a 'points' system that required international adoption agencies to give money to support domestic services. The more points an agency gained, the more children it could take for ICA (Ambrose and Coburn, 2001; Dickens, 2002). The idea of securing payments from rich foreigners to fund domestic welfare improvements has some attraction for all three welfare perspectives: it may be seen as an example of market-place pricing behavior (selling an asset for the best price), but could also appeal to corporatists (government-agency collaboration) and social democrats (redistribution). Inevitably, it is also very controversial (see Hague Conference on Private International Law, 2008b, paras 239-48). Such policies only secure a relatively small amount of money, are prone to corruption and have the distorting effects mentioned earlier. In Romania's case the scheme undermined the professed aim of making ICA a last resort, as shown by a significant increase in ICA after 1997 (IGIAA, 2002).

The international context also exposes the conflicts and complex overlaps of the three welfare approaches. Romania was under considerable pressure from the European Union (typifying the conservative corporatist approach) to reform its child welfare system and end ICA, as a condition of being allowed to join (Bainham, 2003). Yet at the same time, it was under pressure to continue ICA from the USA (representing the neo-liberal view), and also from other receiving countries, even within the EU, notably France and Italy (Post, 2007). The cracks in the EU position demonstrate one of the dilemmas of conservative corporatism, to balance regulation and middle class demand. Even though the ban has been in force since 2001, the issue is still controversial, with calls to lift it from the USA (U.S. House of Representatives, 2006a) and within the EU (Bartholet, 2007).

Along with legislation to end ICA, major reform of Romanian law to protect children and promote their rights was passed in 2004, coming into force on 1 January, 2005. Its philosophy is that parents, extended families and communities have primary responsibility for raising children, and the state's role is complementary, but with duties and powers to protect children from harm (Article

5 of Law 272/2004). There are echoes here of the neo-liberal approach, but there are also positive provisions to support families, such as a requirement that social workers be employed in maternity hospitals to prevent abandonment (Article 9).

There is evidence of considerable development in domestic child welfare services since 2001. One cannot attribute this exclusively to the ending of ICA because many factors are at play, including the cumulative impact of all the work that has gone on since 1989; but since the moratorium there has been an accelerated pace of change. Official figures give following picture in December 2010 (National Authority for the Protection of Child's Rights [NAPCR], 2010). The number of children living in institutional care had fallen from 57,000 in 2001 (NAPCR, 2006) to 23,600. The range of preventive services had grown significantly, and over 46,000 children were receiving help. The number of infant abandonments had fallen. When separation does occur, children are more likely to placed with extended family or friends (22,000 children) or in foster family care (20,000 children).

Clearly, numbers alone do not tell the whole story and a crucial factor is the quality of the in-country services. There is still room for improvement, as the Romanian authorities have acknowledged (NAPCR, 2006), and as noted by the UN Committee on the Rights of the Child (2009) in its Concluding Observations on Romania's most recent periodic reports. Amongst other recommendations, the Committee calls on the Romanian government to ensure an adequate budget for local social services, clearer strategies for supporting families, better monitoring of services and outcomes generally, and in particular, better planning and supervision for children in foster, kinship, and institutional care (UN Committee on the Rights of the Child, 2009).

The Committee also calls for the lifting of the ban on ICA (paras 53-6), but offers no explanation for this, except to say that doing so will ensure 'full implementation' of Article 21 of the CRC. This is misleading however, because there is nothing in the CRC (or the Hague Convention, for that matter) that *requires* a nation to give up children for ICA. The recommendation is strikingly unconvincing, and an intriguing example of diplomatic ambiguity in calling for the end of the ban, but without strongly advancing any arguments to do so.

It is important to appreciate that Romania has been badly hit by the global economic crisis of 2007-2009 (Stanculescu and Grigoras, 2009), and is once again facing increasing levels of need with fewer resources. In this context, Romania needs consistent support from international agencies to preserve, and if possible continue, the progress it has made in developing its own services for children and families. It does not need the international community to criticize from the sidelines or once again take Romanian children to satisfy the needs of its own middle classes.

As long as ICA continued, developing in-country options was like trying to fill a bath with the plug out. Romania's bold step in ending ICA has removed those powerful distortions and, despite the on-going difficulties, increased its chances of building an effective in-country child and family welfare system.

Social Work Dilemmas

This section focuses on the challenges for social work policy and practice that ICA brings under each of the four perspectives, as highlighted on the bottom row of Table 2.1. It is important to clarify, though, that the risks identified in Table 2.1 are not confined strictly to the perspective under which they are shown. In keeping with the theme of overlaps and ambiguities, social work under all of the regimes is liable to the risks of distortion by money, by bureaucracy, by the loudest voices, and by politics. However, each of those four risks is more obvious in one of the regimes, more characteristic of it. The table shows them as it does for model-building purposes, and it should not be misunderstood as a definitive description. Rather, it is a working tool to help identify the underlying tendencies and tensions in a complex terrain.

A primary feature of the neo-liberal approach is the belief in free markets, and this creates the primary risk to social work, that it will be distorted by the lure of money. This is not necessarily in the sense of criminal behavior, of social workers in receiving countries taking bribes for favorable home studies of prospective adopters, or offering payments to children's homes or poor birth mothers in sending countries. Even without that sort of behavior, money shapes relationships and compromises the independence of all parties. If prospective adopters are paying a large sum of money for their home study, the danger is that it is hard to raise problems or say 'no.' If the adoption agency offers 'donations' to the children's homes or 'living expenses' to the birth mother, the danger is that it is very hard for those people to make a different choice.

A primary feature of the conservative corporatist approach is its rather bureaucratic, regulatory ethos, and this creates the primary risk to social work, that it will be overwhelmed by procedures, conventions, contracts and clauses. So the emphasis will be on procedural compliance—is the agency approved, has the family filed the correct papers, is the child legally 'abandoned'? The danger is that questions of 'have I performed it right?' displace 'is it ethically right?'

A primary feature of the social democratic approach is that it values partnership with service users and empowerment, but the risk for social work here is that the more socially powerful, articulate groups tend to shout loudest and get heard most. That, of course, means the prospective adopters in the receiving country. Certainly those people are needy (for a child) and it is likely that most would have positive qualities to bring up a child; but the danger is that their neediness and their offer drown out the needs and the strengths of birth families, communities, and prospective substitute carers in the poorer countries.

Finally, it must be acknowledged that the radical approach has its risks too. Changing a whole social system, a whole way of doing welfare business, is a big job. It needs workers who are very focused, argue hard, hold their ground. Radicals are rarely the easiest people to work with, and the danger is that the needs of prospective adopters and of some, individual, children might be overruled rather brusquely in the quest for a better world. The answer is that radicals have to have something ready to replace what they are breaking down. So in receiving countries there should be campaigns to recruit and support more people to adopt or foster children and young people from their own country who are 'hard to place'; and there should be more and better-developed schemes to enable them to support children, families and communities in poorer countries. And in the sending countries, of course, there need to be better family support services, family foster care, community fostering, in-country adoption, and new, smaller and better-run children's homes. All of that is a big task for radicals, and they need the help of neo-liberals (who prize self-reliance and a nation's ability to care for its own people), conservative corporatists (who prize social integration and inter-agency collaboration) and social democrats (who prize empowerment of poor communities and high quality social services).

Conclusion

This chapter has shown how ICA can be understood in terms of the interplay of the three dominant tendencies of state welfare and globalization, and the tensions within as well as between them. It has also highlighted the potential of a radical perspective. This offers a fresh way of approaching things, although not just as a fourth position along a spectrum. It raises sharp questions about the main three's support of ICA, but also suggests new possibilities for them.

A refreshed social democratic approach would apply its own principles of family support and empowerment more vigorously in sending countries. A revitalized conservative corporatism would use its integrative and inter-agency approach to prioritize supportive services for families. Even the neo-liberal approach contains the seeds of its own opposition to ICA. At the heart of neo-liberalism are fundamental human rights and freedoms, including respect for private and family life, and protection from any interference that is not necessary, legal, and proportionate (see especially Bainham, 2003). These principles can be threatened by ICA, and a neo-liberalism true to its roots would fight to uphold them.

The overall message is that even though ICA may offer immediate benefits for *some* children, it is essential to end it in the longer-term interests of *all* children. Given the demand for ICA and the challenges faced by families and governments in sending countries, it would be unrealistic to expect a ban by itself to yield instant, unequivocal results. Rather, ending ICA should be seen as a necessary, but not sufficient condition for a more equitable globalization for children and families around the world.

Chapter 3
Implications of the Hague Convention on the Humanitarian Evacuation and 'Rescue' of Children[1]

Kathleen Ja Sook Bergquist

In this chapter, I examine the history of humanitarian evacuation and 'rescue' of children as a form of child welfare practice, the legal and political context of such 'rescue,' and, international responses pre- and post- the Hague Convention on the Protection of Children and Co-operation in Respect of Intercountry Adoption (the Hague Convention). The chapter posits that the Hague Convention does not fully protect children from the well-intended, but legally impermissible, humanitarian impulses of child evacuations.

History of Humanitarian Evacuation and 'Rescue' of Children as a Form of Child Welfare Practice

The notion of 'rescuing' children across borders in the wake of armed conflict and natural disasters began in earnest following World War II. Displaced children from affected European countries and Japan were sent to adoptive homes in Great Britain, the United States, and several Scandinavian countries (O'Keefe, 2007; Thompson, 2004). The USA involvement in armed conflicts overseas both contributed to and raised awareness of the need for intercountry adoption (Adoption History Project, 2007). Following the Korean and Vietnam Wars, concern about 'hatred or discrimination' towards children fathered by USA soldiers fueled notions that "Amerasian" children would be better off in their fathers' homeland (Adoption History Project [AHP], 2007). Haunting images of displaced children were televised into homes across America, inspiring humanitarian responses from largely Christian-based organizations and families (Carlberg, 2006). Similarly, natural disasters in Asia, HIV-AIDS and famine crises in Africa, sociopolitical upheaval and poverty in Eastern European and South American nations, and restrictive family planning policies in China have resulted in calls for the significant

1 This chapter is based, in part, on Bergquist, K. (2009). Operation Babylift or Babyabduction? Implications of the Hague Convention on the humanitarian evacuation and 'rescue' of children. *International Social Work*, 52, 621-33. © Sage.

movement of children to adoptive homes in developed countries (McKinney, 2007; O'Keefe, 2007; Roby and Shaw, 2006). This chapter specifically examines responses to perceived child welfare emergencies in Vietnam during the mid-1970s, in present day war-torn Sudan, and post-earthquake Haiti.

Operation Babylift: Vietnam

Operation Babylift (Babylift) was heralded by some as a heroic humanitarian effort. However, critics rebuked it as a "media relations effort ... to give Americans a positive spin on its role in the war" (Drennan, 2007, para 2), or a well-intended, albeit misguided, attempt to rescue children who were either not orphans or would be better off remaining in Vietnam (AHP, 2007; U.S. Agency for International Development [USAID], 1975).

Operation Babylift was, and still is, the largest mass overseas evacuation of children (Williams, 2003). Responding to pressure from humanitarian organizations working in Vietnam, President Ford allocated $2 million for 30 flights to airlift infants and children out of Saigon (Martin, 2000b). Although reports vary, 2,500-3,000 children were evacuated with the majority flown to the United States and the remainder to Canada, Australia, and Europe (USAID, 1975; Martin, 2000b). Tragically the first flight crashed, killing 180 of its passengers (McDonald, 2002). Despite the devastating loss, a fleet of military and commercial transport planes evacuated children until April 26, 1975 (Martin, 2000a).

Would-be adoptive parents responded enthusiastically to the children's arrival. Record numbers of inquiries were received by agencies. New South Wales, Australia had only 14 children available for adoption but reportedly received 600 applications (Martin, 2000b). Friends for Children solicited donations in the *New York Times* and advised readers that, "We've been besieged by thousands of generous people anxious to offer their homes and their hearts" (AHP, 2007).

Controversy and criticism resulted in lawsuits and public condemnation. Operation Babylift was characterized as a "successful propaganda effort," (Emerson, 1978, para. 3) putting into question USA motivations (Zigler, 1976). A contingent of ethics and religion professors denounced Babylift as immoral, raising concerns that the children may not be orphans and asserting that they would be better off remaining in Vietnam (AHP, 2007).

Tran Tuong Nhu, a Vietnamese American who helped care for the newly arrived children, was startled to learn that many of the 'orphans' had living parents (Dolgin, Dolgin and Franco, 2002). When her concerns went unaddressed by adoption agencies and federal government officials, a class action lawsuit was filed (*Nguyen Da Yen, et al. v. Kissinger*) asserting that the children were being unconstitutionally detained. However because of questions as to whether the plaintiffs could be designated as a class, a protracted appeal process, and the likelihood of reunion with birth families diminished, the best interests of the children were deemed to remain with their American families (Center for Constitutional Rights [CCR], n.d.). Nonetheless, lawsuits were filed by family members. Over 30 years later, debate and controversy surround Operation Babylift, especially in light of the implementation of the Hague Convention's protocol to protect children in intercountry adoption.

Tsunami 'Orphans': Asia and Africa

An estimated 1.5 million children were affected by the 2004 Great Sumatra-Andaman earthquake and tsunami in India, Indonesia, Malaysia, Maldives, Myanmar, Somalia, Sri Lanka, and Thailand, leaving thousands orphaned (Thomas, 2006; United Nations Children's Fund [UNICEF], 2007b). The immediacy by which information of natural disasters is disseminated via the Internet and international media fueled global response to the Tsunami with adoption agencies and embassies besieged by inquiries from would-be adoptive parents. The USA government issued a notice that children in affected areas would not be available for adoption, citing the difficulty in determining whether they were truly orphans (Kapstein, 2005). Initially France announced, but later retracted, that it would put in place "special mechanisms" to streamline Tsunami-affected orphans (Agence France-Presse [AFP], 2005; Associated Press [AP], 2005). Governmental officials and adoption agencies throughout Europe and North America imposed similar moratoriums, while applauding the humanitarian inclinations of well-meaning families. Germany and Austria urged those interested in adopting to respond instead through relief or sponsorship programs. Nonetheless, there were calls for governments to ease restrictions and to 'put special measures in place' in order to better facilitate intercountry adoptions (AP, 2005).

Meanwhile, despite the offers to take in their children, the affected countries were quick to impose restrictions to prevent exploitation and preserve families. Sri Lanka and Indonesia banned intercountry adoption altogether in the short term, allowing families to reunite as their governments began the slow work of assessing loss and planning for reconstruction (AP, 2005). However, Indonesia approved adoptions only for Aceh residents and Thailand placed a temporary moratorium on intercountry adoption, but announced an intention to 'fast-track' in-country adoptions (Hariyadi, 2005).

The chaos of natural and manmade disasters creates opportunity for displaced children to be exploited, as reflected in the restrictions on the immediate movement of children. According to UNICEF it is a race against time to get children registered and into a safe environment, often taking weeks and even months to reach remote villages. Nonetheless, children have been sold, recruited by guerilla armies, and adults have claimed children that are not theirs (Sindelar, 2005; Terzieff, 2005).

The Joint Council on International Children's Services (JCICS) proffered considerations, which reflect the ideals embodied by the Hague Convention, as to why it may be commendable, but not advisable or even feasible, to make children available for intercountry adoption following the Tsunami. JCICS pointed to the difficulty in determining the adoptability of a child, the need to prioritize placement with extended family and/or within community of origin, the necessity to follow the legal procedures for relinquishment and adoption, and the possibility that adoption may be impermissible by local law or custom. Kapstein (2005) asserts that the USA and other industrial states' refusal to allow intercountry adoptions following the Tsunami resulted from a resolve to uphold the Hague Convention. Additionally, the Child Welfare League of America (CWLA, 2005) pointed out that India, Sri Lanka, and Thailand are all parties to the Hague Convention and cautioned that intercounty adoption should be a "last resort" in order to preserve families of origin, language, culture, and religion (para. 4).

Zoe's Ark: Sudan/Chad

In 2007, L'Arché de Zoe (Zoe's Ark), a French non-profit organization, announced its plan to evacuate 10,000 'orphans' from war-torn Darfur in the western region of Sudan. Although French officials warned that the group's intentions were legally impermissible because the children's status as orphans was in question and adoption in Sudan and Chad is prohibited under Muslim tradition, the group attempted to airlift 103 children out of the Chadian city of Abéché (Charlton and von Derschau, 2007; 'Children Taken, 2008; France 24, 2007b; Profile: Zoe's Ark, 2007). On notice from the French government, Chadian officials arrested the workers for abducting children who were "neither orphans, nor from Darfur" (Huizinga, 2007, para. 9). Meanwhile, families in France and Denmark had paid between 2,800 and 6,000 euros each to 'host' the children while asylum was sought (France 24, 2007a; "L'Arché de Zoe").

The group's actions and intentions were reportedly shrouded in mistruths and deception from the moment it began work in Sudan. Although the group's original stated objective was to have the children adopted, they later insisted, "These children were not intended for adoption. Our motives were simple: we just wanted to rescue them from death," (French held, 2007). Some of the children reported they were lured away with candy, while the parents of others were told that their children were being taken to Abéché for school (AP, 2007; Rosnoblet, 2007). The subsequent trial and disposition of the Zoe's Ark workers brought widespread attention to the legal implications of 'rescuing' children across international borders. A Chadian court sentenced the group to eight years of hard labor and $9 million USD in damages, however the workers were later pardoned after being extradited to France, a move largely viewed as quid pro quo for France's military support (France 24, 2008; "France-Chad," 1978; Heilmann, 2008; Ngarmbassa, 2007).

Throughout, Zoe's Ark maintained that its actions were not only permissible under international law but "morally imposed," citing the UNHR and the CRC ("L'Arche de Zoé"). Breteau, the group's founder, sought an acquittal asserting that, "Evacuating children in danger is provided for under the Geneva Convention, and those who evacuate them can face no criminal liability" (AP, 2007). A 2011 trial has since been set for Breteau to face charges in France for "swindle," the result of complaints from Zoe's Ark volunteers; the illegal exercise of the profession of an intermediary in adoption; and aiding in the illegal stay of foreign minors in France which could carry penalties up to 10 years in prison and a fine of 750,000 euros (AFP, 2009, 2010a, 2010b).

Evacuation of Haitian Earthquake 'Orphans'

The devastation that followed the January 12, 2010 earthquake in Haiti raised again not only worldwide humanitarian impulses to rescue children, but also calls for caution and measured responses from child welfare advocates and aid organizations (Rotabi and Bergquist, 2010). According to UNICEF (2010) the earthquake affected three million people, of which half were children. Prior to the earthquake there were an estimated 380,000 orphans in Haiti, however only 14 percent or 50,000 were orphans with no living parents (Balsari, Lemery, Williams, and Nelson, 2010; UNICEF, 2008a; USAID, 2010). While there were many individual appeals to 'rescue' children from Haiti, there were two very public efforts to remove children; both circumventing the protections of the Hague Convention.

Less than a week after the earthquake, on January 18, the Department of Homeland Security (DHS) announced a temporary humanitarian parole policy to allow Haitian children to enter the United States who were, prior to January 12 (emphasis added):

- Legally *confirmed* as orphans eligible for intercountry adoption by the Government of Haiti, *were in the process* of being adopted by Americans, *or*
- Identified by an adoption service provider or facilitator as *eligible* for intercountry adoption and were *matched* to prospective American adoptive parents

Additionally, the parole applied to "urgent humanitarian reasons or other emergencies," which paved the way for unaccompanied children to receive medical care (DHS, 2010; Yanez, 2010). Concerns were raised that the standard of proof was too low, leading to the submission of unofficial documents such as, "emails, letters, or photographs showing that the child had some connection to a family in the United States" (Thompson, 2010b). The humanitarian parole provided a three-month window for the evacuation of 1,200 Haitian children to the United States; a more than three-fold increase from the 330 adoptions in 2009 (AP, 2010a; JCICS, 2010; U.S. Department of State [U.S. DOS], n.d.b).

At least two airlifts of children from orphanages out of Haiti were attempted within the first week following the earthquake. Before the announcement of the Humanitarian Parole policy, 26 children from Haiti's Angel House Orphanage were evacuated on two private jets to Florida (Goldberg, 2010; Laughlin, 2010a). "Acting without hesitation" before the "slowdown of bureaucratic protocol set in" was reportedly critical in getting the children out (26 Orphans, 2010; Laughlin,

2010a). The children were described as being "at one point or another of the long process of being adopted" (Goldberg, 2010). However, an Angel House representative reported that at least three of the children had not been matched and that "Most if not all of the adoption files have been lost in the earthquake. Many of the adoption case workers and attorneys have either been killed or severely injured" (Ingle, 2010; Laughlin, 2010b; Osborne, 2010).

The day after the humanitarian parole was officially instituted, Pennsylvania Governor Ed Rendell and USA Representative Jason Altmire delivered 54 children from the BRESMA (Brebis de Saint-Michel de L'Attalaye) Orphanage in Port-au-Prince to Pittsburgh (Gurman and Schmitz, 2010; McKinley, Jr. and Hamill, 2010). The media heralded the McMurtie sisters who, upon receiving clearance to evacuate 28 of the 54 children, refused to leave without all of the children (Templeton, et al., 2010). Of the 54 "orphans," 19 had not "cleared all the hurdles of adoption" and an additional seven had not yet been matched with prospective adoptive parents, clearly not falling within the criteria of the humanitarian parole exception. Upon arriving in Pittsburgh, the majority of the children went to pre-adoptive homes, while 18 children were placed at the Holy Family Institute (HFI), a residential care facility (Thompson, 2010a). An undated update from HFI reports that 12 of the children who did not meet the criteria of the Humanitarian Parole remain in their care "until adoptions for these children can be finalized" (Yankoski, 2010). A more recent report indicates that up to 20 of the 35 children not placed at HFI are lingering in foster care after would-be parents withdrew their petitions to adopt and in some cases state courts have "balked" at finalizing adoptions due to insufficient documentation (Thompson, 2010b).

These two airlifts expose and reinforce the relative ease with which sheer USA determination, or sense of entitlement, can negate legislation or policies intended to protect children from genuine, but perhaps misguided attempts to 'rescue' children. The result in both cases appears to be children in legal limbo, with greatly diminished chances of reunification with family in Haiti, which seemingly could take years (Roche, 2010; Thompson, 2010a).

Similar to the Zoe's Ark incident in Chad, a Baptist church group attempted to take 33 children from Port-au-Prince to the Dominican Republic on January 29, 2010 (Bajak and Dodds, 2010). The Haitian Orphan Rescue Mission (Rescue Mission), led by Laura Silsby, was stopped at the border "without proper authorization" (Gaskell, 2010). The group's stated intention was to temporarily house orphans in a hotel until they were able to raise funds to build an orphanage (Bajak, 2010; Millman, Ball, and Schoofs, 2010; Sheridan, 2010). The Haitian authorities took the children to the SOS Children's Village in Port-au-Prince while the workers were arrested and charged with kidnapping and criminal association, which carry sentences of up to nine years and three years respectively (Millman et al., 2010). Within three weeks of their arrest, all except for Silsby and Charisa Coulter, were released provisionally and permitted to leave Haiti (Mazzei, Reyes, and Burnett, 2010; Miller Llana, 2010). Coulter was released on March 8 when all charges were dropped against her and the other workers, while Silsby was convicted on the lesser charge of arranging illegal travel and sentenced with time served and released on May 18, 2010 (AP, 2010a; AP, 2010c). The judge determined that because parents knowingly released their children, the group could not be charged with kidnapping (AP, 2010b). Ultimately, the group's original position, that the children were abandoned or orphaned, was unsubstantiated. Most of the children had living relatives who simply felt ill-equipped to care for the children, believing they could visit and/or recover the children when their housing and employment stabilized (Bajak, 2010). Additionally, at least three of the "parents" who provided consent were not in fact parents (Millman, 2010). It was reported in March 2010 that all but one of the 33 children were returned home to at least one parent (Cook and Snider, 2010).

Legal and Political Context of 'Rescuing' Children

The evacuating of children outside their families of origin, in times of perceived emergency, creates both a need for heightened protections and a call for lowered barriers. The tensions between humanitarian impulses to rescue and international and domestic protective protocols result in attempts to circumvent legal processes. Operation Babylift and the failed evacuations by Zoe's Ark and the Rescue Mission all stand as examples.

As intercountry adoption has become more prevalent, concerns about the welfare of children spawned multilateral instruments to promote the "best interests" of children (McKinney, 2007). The 1986 UN Declaration on the Social and Legal Principles Relating to the Protection and the Welfare of Children (the UN Declaration), the 1989 UN Convention on the Rights of the Child [CRC] (UNICEF, n.d.), and the 1993 Hague Convention on the Protection of Children and Co-operation in Respect of Intercountry Adoption (the Hague Convention) established rights and assurances for children. The UN Declaration and the CRC positioned intercountry adoption as an option of last resort (Bartholet, 1993b). The UN declared in Article 17 that intercountry adoption "may be considered as an alternative means of providing the child with a family," while the CRC further conditioned that the foreign placement of children be in the absence of "suitable [alternatives] ... in the child's country of origin" (Office of the High Commissioner for Human Rights [UNHCHR] ; UNICEF, 1999). However, the Hague Convention is viewed by many as an institutionalization of a global child welfare practice (Shiu, 2001). The Convention was approved by 66 nations in 1993. The United States became a signatory in 1994 and ratified 14 years later (Hague Conference on Private International Law [HCPIL], 2011a). Today, over eighty nations have signed the international agreement.

Additionally, each nation has federal legislation and policies that regulate intercountry adoption. In the USA, the federal government impacts adoptive families primarily in two arenas: immigration and the interpretation of international conventions. First, although the authority to approve foreign adoption lies with the states, the USA Citizenship and Immigration Services (USCIS) makes an administrative judgment about a child's adoptability and thereby ability to legally enter the USA. Second, international child welfare laws or conventions are implemented through federal legislation. The Intercountry Adoption Act of 2000 (IAA) designated the Department of State as the Central Authority to monitor and regulate intercountry adoption (USCIS). The IAA mandated the development of both an accreditation process for adoption agencies and a certification process that would provide "conclusive evidence of the relationship between the adopted child and the adoptive parent(s)" (USCIS, 2001). Also, the Immigration and Nationality Act was amended to expand the definition of "child" to reflect the Hague Convention.

In the USA, individual states have exclusive jurisdiction over family law and child welfare, to include adoption (Child Welfare Information Gateway [CWIG], 2010). In domestic adoptions, state regulations control how parental rights are terminated, whether a child is adoption-eligible, home study criteria, eligibility requirements for adoptive parents, and the process of finalizing adoption (CWIG, 2010). Although federal and international laws may control certain aspects of the process for foreign-born children, pre- and post-adoption services are typically managed by agencies in the adoptive parents' state of residence. Intercountry adoptions are facilitated by both non-profit and for-profit private agencies, and if a placement is disrupted, local state or county child welfare agencies will intervene and make placement determinations. Additionally, most children enter the USA on orphan visas and their adoptions are finalized in their parents' state of residence. However, more recently sending countries have been requiring that the adoption be finalized under their national law (i.e., China and Russia; U.S. DOS, n.d.b).

Pre- and Post-Hague Convention International Responses

Operation Babylift, the aborted "rescues" in Chad and Haiti, and the Haitian children left in a legal holding pattern in the United States reflect both the need for and failures of international laws to protect children. The Hague Convention established safeguards to ensure the best interests of the child, establish a system of co-operation among Contracting States, and secure the recognition of adoptions made in accordance with the Convention.

Chapter 2 of the Convention details the responsibilities of the State of origin and the receiving State. The State of origin is charged with establishing that the child is adoptable and that informed consent has been freely given without inducement and, to the degree possible, the child's wishes have been taken into consideration. Additionally, the receiving State must ensure that would-be adoptive parents are "eligible and suited to adopt," have been appropriately counseled, and that the child will be eligible for entry and permanent residence (HCPIL, 2011a). A cornerstone of the Convention is the requirement that each State establish a

Central Authority (CA) with which member States will cooperate and which will provide oversight of all aspects of the adoption process.

Despite the procedural safeguards, the ability of the Convention—or perhaps any international agreement—in addressing violations of its proscriptions is questionable at best. Litigation arising resulting from Operation Babylift, Zoe's Ark, and the Rescue Mission, wherein some of the basic procedural protections addressed by the Convention were purportedly violated, are instructive.

Pre-Hague Convention Response

At the heart of the legal controversy surrounding Operation Babylift was the presumption, currently reflected in the Convention, that a child must first be determined to be adoptable. The central case that tested the legal viability of the Babylift was *Nguyen Da Yen et al. v. Kissinger* (1975), a class action suit that charged the children were not validly released into the custody of adoption agencies. The habeas corpus suit contended that the children were impermissibly detained, violating their Fifth Amendment right to due process and liberty (CCR, n.d.). The federal district court ordered INS to "determine whether they are eligible for adoption, and develop a plan for repatriating those whose parents wish their return" (CCR, n.d.). The opinion was notable in its recognition that some of the 'orphans' may have been removed in violation of international and Vietnamese law and unlawfully detained (Buser, 1993; CCR, n.d.). The Court explained that the intention of the Babylift was to evacuate only children who were "adoptable under Vietnamese law, legally in the custody of the American private agencies, and who satisfied the criteria for admission in the United States" (*Nguyen et al. v. Kissinger*, 1975, p. 1197). The Court found that some of the children arrived with accompanying documentation that was on its face insufficient to establish orphan status, but conceded that given the urgency of the airlift, the INS permissibly could allow entry under discretionary parole until immigration status could be determined.

The plaintiffs argued that: Vietnamese custom excludes western notions of adoption and includes the use of orphanages as institutions for temporary safekeeping; and that some of the children had living parents, were released with the assumption they would be reunited with their parents in the United States, or parents "consented" out of fear for the well-being of their child. Ultimately, the Court found that the action could not be maintained as a class action, explaining that the facts in each child's case would be different, and found no risk in separate adjudications. Accordingly, in subsequent separate actions the Ohio Supreme Court affirmed a finding of an invalid consent under Ohio and Vietnamese law due to duress where an illiterate mother was pressured to sign a release (*Hua v. Scott*, 1980) and in Connecticut (*Hao Thi Popp v. Richard*, 1980) it was held that the trial court lacked jurisdiction to terminate the mother's parental rights. In *Huynh Thi Anh v. Levi* (1978) the Court found that treaties do not create a private right of action and that there is no "law of nations" or private international law that imbues a presumptive right to grandparents over foster parents (p. 609).

The Babylift cases illustrate unsuccessful attempts to grasp at a theory of law that the courts would recognize, while racing against time, a factor that is particularly salient in child custody cases.

Post-Hague Convention Response

Unlike the Babylift cases, the charges levied against Zoe's Ark and the Rescue Mission were criminal, not civil. Although many of the facts and circumstances of events in the Chadian and Haitian cases were dissimilar to the Babylift cases, they all involve an assertion that "consent" was invalid, if solicited at all, and that the children were not in fact orphans (Bajak, 2010; Goodman, 2007).

French Secretary Yade (2007) reported that she had cautioned Zoe's Ark that their intentions were "illegal and irresponsible." Additionally, UNICEF (Veneman, 2007), condemned the group, stating that "It is unacceptable to see children taken out of their home countries without complying with national and international laws." Similarly in Haiti, the Consul General for the Dominican Republic reportedly advised Silsby that she did not have the necessary documentation to take the children and that she could be arrested if she attempted to do so (Millman et al., 2010).

In both the Zoe's Ark and Rescue Mission cases, the children involved were not from Hague countries. Neither Chad nor Sudan is a party to the Hague, although France ratified it in 1998 (HCPIL, 2011a). Similarly, Haiti was not a signatory at the time of the earthquake, although it recently became a signatory on March 2, 2011, while the USA and the Dominican Republic are both member States. One of the major critiques of the Convention is that it is not binding on non-members, and member States may continue to facilitate adoptions with non-members (O'Keefe, 2007). However, these cases illustrate a more fundamental challenge in determining when and whether the Hague applies. For example, Zoe's Ark denied any intention to bring children to France for purposes of adoption, asserting that it merely intended to provide foster homes while awaiting applications for asylum (Crumley, 2007). Zoe's Ark's actions embody the very unmonitored, and arguably unethical, practice that the Hague is intended to prevent. That is, the group had no authority to find adoptive placements for the children, had not sought any legally cognizable form of consent from parents, and presumably had not conducted background checks or home studies on would-be adoptive parents. Nonetheless, France did not characterize this case as a violation of the Convention. Despite the fact that Chad is not a member, France appears to have the authority and responsibility to levy consequences under the Hague. As the Court pointed out in *Huynh Thi Anh v. Levi* (1978), the appropriate lexi fori for the group to be tried was Chad, although France's request for extradition was later granted (French Aid, 2008).

Similarly, because Haiti has not ratified the Hague Convention processing of adoptions from Haiti did not change when the Hague entered into force in the USA in 2008 (U.S. DOS, n.d.b). Thus, intercountry adoptions are governed largely by Haitian courts and adoptions must be finalized in-country. In the Silsby case the court's time-served sentence seemed to be largely symbolic and did not fully address the heart of the matter, the issue of consent. That is, while the parents or family members of the children may have sought to protect their children by allowing them to be cared for by the Rescue Mission, that consent could not under rigorous legal analysis rise to the standard necessary to permanently relinquish parental rights. This case serves not as a deterrent to future would-be traffickers, or well-intended but misguided humanitarians, but rather has lowered the bar—placing the burden on the parents to show that their consent was temporary rather than permanent. So, while the families in this case were fortunate that Silsby was not successful in removing the children to the Dominican Republic, making it possible for them to reunite with their children, the parents of the children who were airlifted to the United States face enormous legal and financial barriers.

As a member State, the USA has been complicit in violating the spirit and intent of the Hague Convention. The USA has allowed its own humanitarian parole policy, that was grounded in the protections of the Hague, to be rendered ineffective and subject to political will by allowing children to be evacuated from Haiti who were neither legally confirmed to be orphans and/or in the process of being adopted or matched to adoptive parents. Following the issuing of the humanitarian parole, there were incidences reported wherein children that were in orphanages "not affected by the quake or licensed to handle adoptions" were released for evacuation (Thompson, 2010a).

Additionally, several legislators, including Senators Landrieu and Inhofe, are supporting the Families for Orphans Act which seeks to create a State Department Office of Orphan Policy, Diplomacy, and Development, pointing to Haiti as proof that: "Had this office been in place prior to the earthquake, the USA would have been in a better position to provide temporary and permanent homes for the tens of thousands of orphaned children" (Landrieu and Inhofe, 2010, para. 11).

Conclusion

Several commentators have noted the absence of any real teeth to the Hague for purposes of enforcement. Non-party states are not prohibited from facilitating intercountry adoption, while the possible harm to children if there were prohibitions are argued to be unjustifiable (see for example, Carlberg, 2006; JCICS, 2010; Kimball, 2005). Others suggest that tasking a Central Authority with creating structures to both oversee the processes of intercountry adoption and to ensure enforcement without a non-partisan oversight will encourage corruption (Calberg, 2006; Kimball, 2005). Perhaps the action or inaction of France and the

United States exemplifies this concern. That is, the French government's response to an NGO that had publicly stated its intention to bring 10,000 children out of Sudan for adoption was ineffective ("L'Arche de Zoé"). Similarly, while the post-Hague response to calls in the United States for evacuating children have been more measured, intending to allow affected families to reunite, the political will to uphold the protections of the Hague in the face of moral fervor and rhetoric about 'saving children' is clearly lacking.

Chapter 4

Human Rights Considerations in Intercountry Adoption: The Children and Families of Cambodia and Marshall Islands

Jini L. Roby and Trish Maskew[1]

Intercountry adoption is often viewed as an act of international charity, with families in wealthy receiving countries accepting orphaned children from poor countries of origin into their homes as permanent members of the family (Freundlich, 1998; Sargent, 2003). The adoptive family thus gets its wish for more children, and needy children are provided with a permanent family through the professional assistance of an altruistic adoption agency—an idyllic scenario in which everyone's needs and wishes are fulfilled (Bartholet, 2007). However, this simplistic and benevolent view has been challenged by recent developments and raised awareness about the complexity of the issues, leading to a burgeoning discourse on human rights in the intercountry adoption process (Oreskovic and Maskew, 2008).

In this chapter, we examine major human rights concepts as they relate to intercountry adoption, and how they play out on the ground. First we will review the state of the academic discourse on human rights and intercountry adoption. Next, we will highlight the most pertinent human rights concepts implicated in intercountry adoptions and link them to the provisions of various human rights instruments. We will then discuss adoption-related human rights challenges in two case studies—Cambodia and the Republic of Marshall Islands—and review selected solutions that have been applied or proposed in their specific social and cultural contexts.

Discourse on Human Rights as Applied to Intercountry Adoption

Human rights discourse in the literature regarding intercountry adoption has been brewing for several decades (e.g., Melone, 1976); however, the discussion took

1 This chapter is based, in part, on Roby, J.L. and Ife, J. (2009). Human rights, politics and intercountry adoption: An examination of two sending countries. *International Social Work*, 52, 661-71. © Sage.

on greater urgency in the mid-1990s. In the absence of unified agreement on the definition of human rights as applied to the intercountry adoption context—whose human rights are implicated or how these rights should be considered within the intercountry adoption process—conceptualization of common themes and analyses are still in their infancy.

Many intercountry adoption human rights discussions focus on the rights of the child. Dillon (2003), for example, argues that leading international instruments guiding intercountry adoption do not go far enough in providing a child's right to a permanent family, particularly when children languish in institutions. Bartholet argues that a child's right to a family should override all other concerns, particularly the interests of the group (2000) or a low-resource country's sovereign right to refuse adoption, and that more autonomy should be given to private entities conducting such adoptions (2007). Oreskovic and Maskew (2008) have countered that there is insufficient evidence of how many children are truly without parental care, whether the current ICA legal regime assists those most in need, and whether the right of children to be raised by their biological families is being abused. Smolin (2004) and Maskew (2004) have criticized dynamics in intercountry adoption that resemble child trafficking, such as child-buying and exploitation of poor birth families. Roby (2007) traces the development of the child's rights in the intercountry adoption experience, and points out gaps in protection.

Some authors have focused on the human rights of birth parents, particularly birth mothers. Herrmann and Kasper (1992) stress that care must be taken to avoid exploitation of poor women in developing countries when carrying out adoptions. Perry (1998, 2006) has applied a gendered power construct to intercountry adoptions, as well as one of racial power inequality. Roby and Matsumura (2002), have reported that 83 percent of the birth mothers they interviewed in the Marshall Islands relinquished their children under a misunderstanding regarding the permanency of intercountry adoption—a flagrant violation of their right to give informed consent. Manley (2006) has characterized birthmothers as the "forgotten members of the adoption triad" (p. 627).

At the macro level, Melone (1976), Freundlich (1998) and others (Hollingsworth, 2003; Triseliotis, Shireman, and Hundleby, 1997) have cautioned that intercountry adoption may be a form of exploitation of poor countries by wealthy receiving countries. Breuning and Ishiyama (2009) have found a statistically significant correlation between the trade relationship of the countries of origin and receiving countries and intercountry adoption policy. Bergquist (2009) has questioned the motives of a powerful country in 'rescuing' the children of a country experiencing a natural disaster or political crisis (see Chapter 3). Roby and Ife (2009) examine human rights violations in context of political dynamics that influence national adoption policies in the countries of origin.

Human rights concepts, coupled with scientific research related to the harmful effects of institutional care and the benefits of family-based care (Nelson, et al., 2007; Ryan and Groza, 2004), have contributed to the development of international instruments related to the care of children including intercountry adoption as one option on the continuum of care. In the next section, we review human rights protected under leading international instruments.

Human Rights Concepts Embodied in Relevant International Instruments

Several widely ratified international instruments address human rights in intercountry adoption. A brief summary of the leading instruments follows. While one should use caution when utilizing these international instruments in the effort to define and apply human rights (Dillon, 2003), it often becomes necessary to rely on them in the absence of other agreed upon standards (Roby and Ife, 2009).

The United Nations Convention on the Rights of the Child (CRC):

Concluded in 1990 and ratified by all but two members of the United Nations (Somalia and the USA), the CRC is the most widely agreed upon instrument articulating the rights of children (United Nations Treaty Collection, 2011a). Among other rights, the CRC affords children involved in intercountry adoption the right:

- to grow up in a family environment (preamble 6);
- to identity, name and family relationships without undue interference (Art. 8);
- to know and be cared for by their parents (Art. 7);
- to not be separated from their family without judicial review (Art. 9), and when separation is necessary to serve the child's best interest, to be cared for in a suitable alternative care environment including foster care, Islamic *kafala*, and adoption (Art. 20), with priority given to domestic placements (Art. 21);
- to a determination of child's best interest as the paramount consideration (Art. 21);
- to the services of competent authorities in the adoption process (Art. 21);
- to safeguards and standards equivalent to national adoption (Art. 21);
- to not be the subject of improper financial gain (Art. 21); and
- to an opportunity to express their view in administrative or judicial matters concerning themselves and to have these given proper weight (Art. 12).

The CRC Optional Protocol on the Sale of Children, Child Prostitution and Child Pornography ("Protocol on Sale of Children")

This instrument, concluded in 2002, has been ratified by 143 countries including the USA. Specific to intercountry adoption, the instrument furthers the purposes of several articles of the CRC including Article 21—the major source of substantive rights for children involved in intercountry adoption (United Nations Treaty

Collection, 2011b). It defines 'sale of children' as "any act or transaction whereby a child is transferred by any person or group of persons to another for remuneration or any other consideration" (Art 2.a), and mandates signatory States to criminalize the improper inducement of consent for the adoption (Art. 3.1.a.ii).

Hague Convention on Protection of Children and Cooperation in Respect of Intercountry Adoption ("the Hague Convention")

This convention, concluded in 1993, has been ratified by over 80 countries, both members and non-members of the Hague Conference on Private International Law. The Convention has the dual purpose of protecting participants in the adoption process and creating a framework for cooperation between sending and receiving countries. For children involved in intercountry adoption, the Hague Convention reinforces many of the rights provided under the CRC, as well as additional procedural rights such as the right:

- to a best interest determination (Art. 4a);
- to a determination of adoptability, based on legal availability, consideration of the child's ethnic, religious, and cultural background, family and social environment, and any special needs (Art. 16);
- to a determination on the availability of domestic placements before intercountry adoption is considered—known as the "subsidiarity principle" (Art. 4b);
- if of appropriate age and maturity, to be counseled and duly informed of the effects of adoption, to express his or her opinion about the adoption, and to give informed and voluntary consent in writing without inducement (Art. 4d); and
- to enjoy the full legal rights as a child of the adoptive parents (Art. 26)

The Hague Convention also provides procedural rights to parents and guardians whose consent is necessary in intercountry adoption. These include the right:

- to be counseled before giving consent, particularly as to the legal impact on the parent-child relationship, (Art. 4c(1));
- to give free and informed consent in writing (Art. 4c(2)),without inducement of payment or compensation of any kind (Art. 4c(3));
- of the mother not to give consent before the child is born (Art. 4c(4));

Case Studies: Cambodia and the Marshall Islands

In this section we examine the experiences of two sending countries: Cambodia and the Republic of Marshall Islands (RMI) in relation to human rights issues in intercountry adoption. We were each involved in the legislative process in these two countries and observed first hand much of what is reported here. These case studies provide comparisons and contrasts of how market forces, when left unregulated, violated fundamental human rights, demonstrate the struggle to cope with such forces, and describe the attempts made to incorporate human rights standards into their national policies.

Cambodia

Cambodia is a small southeast Asian country with about 14.7 million inhabitants (Central Intelligence Agency, 2011). It is impossible to separate a discussion of Cambodian adoption from the historical and political context of the country at large. Following a period of war, genocide, and extended internal conflict, Cambodia has enjoyed fewer than 15 years of relative peace and stability (January, 2007). The wounds of the recent history are still fresh, and many Cambodians live a hardscrabble existence. Much of the educated class was eliminated during the Pol Pot regime, and the effect of those years is still evident in governmental and educational structures as they struggle with the overwhelming challenges to establish a functional political infrastructure, educate their citizenry, and push forward with economic development.

Cambodian adoptions have been plagued by allegations of human rights abuses from their inception (Schuster Institute for Investigative Journalism, n.d.). Intercountry adoption began in Cambodia in the early 1990s with a handful of children being adopted into the USA each year, followed by rising numbers in the mid-1990s (Australian Intercountry Adoption Network, n.d.). In 2000, concerns about irregularities and lax procedures led to a shutdown of international adoptions to allow Cambodia to enact new rules governing adoptions. In March 2001, the Cambodian government issued a sub-decree, a document similar to a governmental agency policy, on intercountry adoption. With the new sub-decree, which outlined a brief and simple adoption proceeding for children as young as three months old, the number of families seeking to adopt children from Cambodia rapidly escalated. This rise coincided with two important developments—the closure or slowdown of other countries popular with adopting families, and an increase in the number of adoption 'facilitators' operating orphanages and adoption programs.

Within a few months of the announcement of the sub-decree, hundreds of applications poured into Cambodia, which quickly developed a reputation for fast adoptions of very young infants. The rapid increase in demand, coupled with the absence of appropriate government oversight and endemic corruption, led to rumors of profiteering and illegal adoption. In September 2001, two birth mothers approached a human rights organization seeking assistance because they had been prevented from retrieving children they had temporary placed in the custody of an orphanage. One of the children was found in the custody of a facilitator operating an orphanage and international adoption program. The child had been given a new identity and false paperwork had been prepared. He had already been adopted by American parents in Cambodia, and was days away from obtaining a visa to enter the USA (Detailed summary of Cambodian adoption contained in Oreskovic and Maskew, 2008). The USA government closed adoption from Cambodia in December, 2001 with several other countries following suit in rapid succession. Subsequent investigations detailed numerous human rights abuses. An investigation by the USA government found evidence of a network of "child-finders" who moved children through the system, with each person in the chain being paid for their services. Payments to birth families were documented (Cross, 2005). Moreover, high ranking officials were implicated in the schemes (Oreskovic and Maskew, 2008).

Though many considered it likely, given the country's history, that there were tens of thousands of orphaned children needing adoptive parents in Cambodia and that closing adoptions would cause the number of children in institutions to skyrocket, subsequent investigations proved that supposition untrue. Statistics compiled by USAID in 2005 revealed that the orphanage population of infants and toddlers did not increase between closure of intercountry adoptions in 2001 and 2005. The survey found only 329 children under the age of three in care in 2005; male children over the age of nine were the largest group in care (USAID, 2005). In the years since, the government of Cambodia has compiled statistics on the number of children in institutions, finding that there are fewer than 600 children under the age of six in care in Cambodia at any given time, many of these being severely disabled. These numbers contrast starkly with the hundreds of infants that were leaving Cambodia through adoption in 2001. One news article revealed that on the day of their orphanage visit in the fall of 2001, one institution housed 157 children under the age of one, almost two thirds of them female (Corbett, 2002). The adoption population bore little resemblance to the general orphanage population in Cambodia, leading to a conclusion that unregulated adoption practice had increased the number of children coming into care, often through nefarious means.

Throughout the last decade, the Cambodian government, assisted by other countries and inter-governmental and non-governmental partners, has made numerous efforts to promulgate and implement new laws and regulations for intercountry adoption. Numerous obstacles stood in the way of success. In the aftermath of the Khmer Rouge, the governmental and legal structures of Cambodia were decimated. The country did not pass its Civil Code until 2007, and was still working on its implementation in 2008. A Criminal Code had not yet been passed. Without such basic frameworks, writing a new adoption law was not a legislative priority; moreover, the country lacked a reliable judicial and regulatory structure in which to anchor such a law. While the new intercountry law was being drafted, Cambodia became a signatory to the Hague Convention, and the Convention entered into force in 2007. However, several countries objected to Cambodia's accession because of persistent concerns about the status of the law and regulations, their implementation, and mechanisms to curb human rights abuses (Hague Conference on Private International Law, 2011c).

Cambodia also lacked basic social welfare mechanisms, or, until late 2011, a system of child welfare that could provide assistance to families or determine when a child is eligible for adoption. Births are often not recorded, and families in crisis have almost no social services available. Statistics show that the number of children entering institutions rises rapidly at the age of six—because many parents make use of institutions to obtain education for their children. These children are not being permanently relinquished, nor are they without parental care. Their presence in an orphanage alone is not sufficient to determine their adoptability. Procedures for parents to permanently relinquish children, or to consent to adoption, are still being developed. Thus, in order to adequately determine a child's status, some basic structure must be implemented.

Perhaps the largest obstacle, and possibly the most intractable, is Cambodia's culture of corruption. Bribes, both large and small, are commonplace and accepted in virtually every transaction. Civil servants are so poorly paid that most consider it reasonable for a clerk, a policeman, or a village official to demand payment. Yet in some case, higher ranking officials benefit far more than the lowest paid civil servants.

Incremental progress is occurring. An adoption law was finally passed by the Cambodian legislature in 2009, and various assistance efforts have resulted in the development of procedures and forms necessary to implement portions of the law. However, basic enforcement mechanisms that could serve as a curb on potential nefarious activity do not yet exist. With corruption being so endemic, preventing the kind of illegal activity that occurred in 2001 will require numerous protective mechanisms, and more importantly, a commitment on the part of the Cambodian government to put the rights of children and families ahead of other concerns. Thus, while the international community has assisted Cambodia in developing the basic laws and tools to implement an adoption system that protects the rights of children and families, it will be incumbent on Cambodia itself to implement them in the way that does so.

Marshall Islands

The Republic of Marshall Islands (RMI) is a small Micronesian nation consisting of 29 atolls in Central Pacific with 66,000 inhabitants (Central Intelligence Agency, 2011). Named after a British explorer, the country has been controlled for the past several hundred years by Germany, Japan and the USA until the nation gained independence from the USA in 1986. Due to the destruction and dislocation of island communities caused by atomic bomb testing by the USA during World War II (1939-1945), the two countries entered into the Compact of Free Association, a major compensation and aid package providing 70 percent of the RMI national budget. Under the Compact, Marshallese citizens can enter the USA without a visa, excluding for purposes of permanent immigration—an important provision that contributed, ironically, to human rights abuses in intercountry adoptions (Roby and Matsumura, 2002).

Adoption of Marshallese children by American families began informally and benignly. In the early 1990s, USA military families living in the RMI befriended local families and took in their children to raise. This was culturally compatible since the Marshallese have practiced kin-based informal adoptions for millennia; the adopted child belongs to both families and often returns to care for their biological parents in their old age. Hence, the concept of termination of parental rights was never instituted (Walsh, 1999). Upon completion of their military post, the American families simply took their 'adopted' children back to the USA under the Compact of Free Association, presumably to complete the adoption in state courts. No suitability evaluations were conducted of the adoptive families, no legal proceedings were held to examine the child's availability for adoption, and no professional or legal procedures were adhered to.

By mid-1990s word of healthy infants from the RMI and the ease of the process spread like wild fire in the USA adoption community (Walsh, 1999). Since there were no legal parameters, a wide range of adoption ethics were employed. While some USA adoption agencies meticulously applied the same high standards that they would adhere to back at home, others saw it as a free-for-all. Local 'finders' were rumored to be scouring maternity wards offering wads of cash to new mothers, and others going door to door asking grandmothers for their 'extra' grandchildren. Government leaders, teachers and even religious leaders were reportedly receiving 'commissions' for adoption referrals. In addition, pregnant women were brought to the USA to relinquish their children, most of them without understanding the legal implications of such actions (Roby and Matsumura, 2002).

In response, the Marshallese High Court developed a set of procedures to facilitate adoptions by agencies licensed in their state, supported by a number of basic documents including a home study of the adoptive family, birth and marriage certificates, and a consent document from the birth parents. Between 1996-1999, 600 children were adopted in the Marshallese court, constituting one percent of all Marshallese children, the highest *per capita* rate in the world (Walsh, 1999). However, children continued to be taken out of the RMI without documentation during this period and there is still no record of their numbers and what the ultimate outcomes were, although anecdotes abound of families unable to adopt these children in their state courts and of the inability to obtain USA citizenship (Roby, Wyatt, and Pettys, 2005).

In September 1999, in the midst of accusatory headlines the RMI Nitijela (national parliament) imposed a moratorium on international adoptions, pending passage of legislation. However, one effect of this moratorium was to push intercountry adoptions 'underground', as adoption agencies and facilitators accelerated their efforts to lure women with young children or pregnant women to the USA for relinquishments. A study conducted in 2000 showed that 83 percent of birthmothers reported that at the time of relinquishment they did not understand the finality of adoption (Roby and Matsumura, 2002).

The legislative process was arduous. Started in early 2000, the legislative effort at times seemed at a hopeless impasse as relentless debates raged for nearly three years, with opponents regarding intercountry adoption as a national shame and supporters viewing it as a legitimate option for some children. In addition, the policy foundation was fragile since the RMI had ratified the CRC but not the Hague Convention, and no infrastructure or resources were in place to monitor intercountry adoptions. In the end, the USA, the only receiving country from the RMI, raised concerns and made intercountry adoption a focal point of the renewed Compact (effective through 2023). Thus, the Adoption Act was passed in late 2002 (Marshall Islands Public Law 2002-64; codified as Marshall Islands Revised Code [MIRC], §26-806), and the visa-free provision of the Compact was amended to exclude women and children entering the U.S. for purposes of adoption (U.S. Department of State, n.d.b). These laws became enforceable in 2003 and 2004 respectively.

Human Rights Considerations: Going Forward

In the foregoing section we presented case studies of two sending countries where children and families were subjected to human rights violations in the intercountry adoption process. In this section we discuss particular aspects of such violations and the remedies proposed or utilized. Cambodia acceded to the CRC in 1992, to the Optional Protocol on the Sale of Children in 2002, and to the Hague Convention in 2007. The RMI ratified the CRC in 1993 but has never ratified the Optional Protocol on the Sale of Children or the Hague Convention; however, the Marshallese legislation was drafted to provide protections similar to the Hague Convention. Cambodia passed comprehensive adoption legislation in 2009 but implementation is still not in full effect. The RMI passed the Adoption Act in 2002 and it has been implemented since 2003.

Adoptability of the Child

In both countries, parents often gave consent without full knowledge of the legal implications of adoption, or did so under fraudulent misrepresentation or as a result of financial inducement. In Cambodia, child finders and adoption mediators often took children from intact families and presented them as orphans in order to obtain entry into the receiving countries. Evidence suggests that fictional names, dates and status of parents were fabricated to expedite adoptions. In both countries older children were not given counseling or the opportunity to form and express their opinions about the adoption.

Legislative efforts have addressed human rights considerations in both countries. Under the RMI law, parents are provided with counseling with an emphasis on understanding the irrevocability and permanency of adoption. Solicitation of children for adoption, fraudulent misrepresentation of adoption, and financial inducements constitute criminal offenses under the Adoption Act; and a facilitator was jailed as an example of serious government intent. Although Lauryn Galindo was imprisoned in the USA under U.S. law for her Cambodian adoption activities prior to 2001 (Pound Pup Legacy, n.d.; see Chapter 5), adoptions of Cambodian children continued in virtually the same manner to several countries for years thereafter without any reform of the Cambodian system. While the language of the new law contains many provisions to protect children and families, it remains to be seen how effective it will prove in practice. Neither country is fully equipped to prepare older children in terms of psycho-social aspects of adoption, a dimension of adoptability that needs more attention around the world (International Social Service, n.d.). However, as both governments take responsibility to bring their laws into practice, the full range of protections in this arena is possible.

Subsidiarity Principle

The subsidiarity principle (see Chapter 20) was completely ignored in both countries, as children targeted for intercountry adoptions were not provided with services to remain with their families, in the extended family network, or in their community or country. In fact, when intercountry adoption activities began, neither country had a child welfare policy and scrambled to regulate it as the only form of government-sponsored child welfare option, which was influenced more by foreign money than the true needs of the children and families.

Since the reform in the RMI, the Central Adoption Authority is tasked under the Adoption Act with the duty to refer birth families for family preservation services, but resources are scarce. Also under the Adoption Act, extended family members are invited to participate in pre-decision family group conferencing sessions, and most birth parents are able to find the support necessary to continue parenting their children. However, beyond these steps the RMI has yet to develop a full spectrum of family-based alternative care options. In Cambodia, a comprehensive set of alternative child welfare procedures were developed in 2009 with international assistance, closely adhering to the subsidiarity principle. These procedures were officially adopted as ministerial regulations in October 2011 after two years of being piloted, and initial indications are promising, especially at the very basic commune level where many of the traditional systems of caring for children seem to be reviving. The government needs to harness these resources and also bring additional assistance in order to protect the child's right under the subsidiarity principle. The greatest challenge to family preservation efforts will come when intercountry adoptions to the U.S. resume; if adequate protection is not in place, the enormous sums of money that enter the system could decimate any progress that has been made.

Protection from Commodification

In both countries children were used as commodities in the hands of local finders and adoption mediators, through financial inducements and other promises to birth parents. Much of the funds paid by adoptive parents enriched those involved in the schemes, from locals in the village who referred a mother to an orphanage to high ranking officials. In the RMI, the promise that the adoptive families would maintain on-going contact exploited the cultural tradition of open adoptions; with the birth families later realizing they had been lied to by those profiting from adoption.

As mentioned previously, financial inducements and solicitations for adoption are criminal offenses in the RMI, punishable by imprisonment or a substantial fine, or both. This has had a chilling effect on such activities; however, solicitations still occur via the Compact's visa-free provision which is available as long as travel is not for the express purpose of placing a child for adoption. Now brokers tend to bring women out early in their pregnancy and have them relinquish their rights in the USA after the child is born. Short of a pregnancy test at the time of obtaining the RMI passport or at the point of entry into the USA, such clandestine practices are difficult to detect, although U.S. courts are increasingly becoming wary and are refusing to grant such adoptions.

Best Interest Determination

The best interest of the child—the *paramount* consideration in intercountry adoption (CRC Art. 21)—was often ignored in both countries, as adoptions were largely conducted in order to supply the 'right' children to adoptive families rather than finding the 'right' families based on the needs of the children. Little thought was given to the child's relationships with their parents and siblings, within their extended family network and communities. The child's sense of identity within his or her culture and ethnicity was given little consideration in the frenzy to meet the demand of the adoption business or in ill-informed efforts to 'rescue' children from poverty. In Cambodia, some adoption agencies and orphanages worked together to find and place children, often smoothing the way with bribes, a situation far from the ideal of carefully matching each individual child with the appropriate family. In the RMI the desire for younger babies pushed the timeline ever forward, until mothers were being smuggled out so that the baby could be delivered into the waiting arms of adoptive parents.

The impact of the RMI law, the USA implementation of the Hague Convention in April 2008, and the process of accrediting USA agencies, combined with rumors of courts refusing 'smuggled-in' adoptions have largely stemmed the tide of illegal and unethical adoptions in and from the RMI. In addition, the RMI central authority was trained to carefully consider the child's right to familial, ethnic and cultural identity, and to undergo a child's best interest study in each case. Child-centered adoption procedures emphasize not only ethical procedures but the life-long wellbeing of the child. A part of this emphasis is to require cultural education for parents who adopt from the RMI with a minimum time to be spent on location.

The Cambodian law also emphasizes a careful consideration of each child's needs, consideration of in-country alternatives, and counseling and informed consent of birth parents. It seeks to regulate those involved in the adoption process, and to centralize government functions. Gaps remain, however, particularly in relation to controlling improper financial gain, removing conflicts of interest, and providing strong enforcement mechanisms. These gaps will have to be filled by regulations that build upon the law, the development of which is an ongoing effort. For Cambodia, the biggest challenge will be in ensuring that the on-the-ground process truly reflects the ideals enshrined in the law.

Conclusion

Human rights are intended to protect all people, but particularly those who are the least powerful in society. Children and birth families participating in intercountry adoption are often poor, have fewer economic and social resources, and are easy prey for exploitation. The rights enumerated in the CRC, the Optional Protocol on the Sale of Children, and the Hague Convention, when implemented appropriately in the social and cultural contexts of the countries of origin, can go a long way toward ensuring core human rights in intercountry adoption. The experiences of Cambodia and the RMI demonstrate that many factors influence the recognition of these rights, perhaps none more important than the political will to protect them.

Chapter 5
Fraud in Intercountry Adoption: Child Sales and Abduction in Vietnam, Cambodia, and Guatemala

Karen Smith Rotabi

The Hague Convention on the Protection of Children and Co-operation in Respect of Intercountry Adoption (HCIA; Hague Conference on Private Law, 2008a) has the goal of promoting the best interests of children and preventing child sales and abduction under the guise of intercountry adoption (ICA; Bergquist, 2009; Hollingsworth, 2003; McKinney, 2007; Rotabi, 2008; Smolin, 2010). Signatory nations must develop their own laws to govern ICA activities, including regulation of associated child welfare practices.

Standards of practice for child placement include ethical relinquishment and abandonment processes, a thorough investigation of child background and other critical ICA activities. In the USA and many other industrialized nations, private adoption agencies perform or interface with those services (Bailey, 2009). The pay-for-service nature of agencies poses challenges to Convention requirements for financial transparency and reasonable and professional compensation, especially in interactions with low resource nations and extreme poverty (Freundlich, 2000b; Rotabi, 2008; Rotabi and Gibbons, 2012).

Unfortunately there have been cases of inappropriate, unethical, and illegal practices that range from adoption irregularities and fraud to child sales and abduction, called child trafficking by some (Smolin, 2004, 2006). The idea that vulnerable children's cases are mismanaged or even trafficked by social service agencies as intercountry adoptees is repugnant, and those committed to ICA as a practice agree that the Convention is an important step forward (i.e., Joint Commission on International Children's Services [JCICS], n.d.a). However, there is some resistance among ICA professionals, advocates, and consumers to the idea that child sales and abduction occur frequently enough to be considered a significant problem (Freundlich, 2000b). Some ICA proponents assert that problems are isolated events (Bartholet, 2007). This position has been defendable because unethical and illegal practices are carried out 'backstage' or underground. As a result, only the most egregious examples of fraud and child trafficking are known, contributing to the appearance of 'isolated events' (Oreskovic and Maskew, 2009).

The Intercountry Adoption Act (IAA; PL. 106-279), passed in 2000 to implement the HCIA in the USA, provides a mechanism to prosecute those who engage in illegal activities while carrying out adoptions between the USA and other Convention nations. Though the IAA has not been used to prosecute anyone successfully to date, it does provide for such a legal process. In combination, implementation of the IAA and HCIA was a watershed moment. Acknowledgement that adoption fraud and child trafficking disguised as ICA must be prevented was a significant step forward. There has been a dramatic shift in policy and practices. Over 300 ICA agencies with main offices in the USA developed new administrative policies and procedures to meet new convention standards (Council on Accreditation, 2007; Rotabi and Gibbons, 2012; U.S. Government Accountability Office, 2005; JCICS, n.d.). In the context of this dramatic change, it is important to glean lessons from adoption fraud, including child sales and abduction. How has such activity been perpetuated? The answers inform planning for systems improvement or 'best practices' as explored in Chapter 19.

Three post-conflict countries with significant ICA problems are Vietnam, Cambodia, and Guatemala (Bunkers, Groza and Lauer, 2009; Joe, 1978; Rotabi, 2008, 2009; Rotabi and Bunkers, 2008; Smolin, 2004, 2006; United States Department of State [U.S. DOS], 2008). These three nations, all of which have experienced some form of moratorium, have unique histories of adoption fraud that intersect with USA child adoption history.

Because adoption fraud relies on unethical and illegal activities, it is very difficult, if not impossible, to conduct an exploratory research study using interviews or other documentation. Research in this area underscores human participant risks as well as research ethics dilemmas due to the nexus of some of those activities with organized crime. However, historical documents are available, including human rights reports and testimony, government investigatory documents, and legal proceedings. Additionally, media and popular press materials, including undercover investigations, also offer evidence and insight. For this chapter, multiple sources are used to create a narrative about how adoption fraud and human trafficking operated in the past.

Case Examples: Three Post-Conflict Child Sending Nations and Lessons Learned from Vietnam, Cambodia, and Guatemala

Vietnam

One cannot begin discourse about Vietnam without mentioning the Vietnam Babylift (Bergquist, 2009), a catalyst event (Altstein and Simon, 1991) which created ethical discourse amongst professionals and the general public about child rescue practice in the context of war (United States Agency for International Development [USAID], 1975). As Bergquist (2009) points out in Chapter 3, this evacuation resulted in 2500-3000 children being airlifted at the end of the

Vietnam War. This action, funded in part by the USA-government (i.e., use of military aircraft), was controversial in both Vietnam and the USA. In response to public criticism and a class action lawsuit by the families of some of the children (USAID, 1975), USA social workers involved in the airlift have provided some insight into the evacuation. In 1983, Ryan wrote that:

> … when the Vietnamese children were airlifted, there was a strong criticism of removing these children from their country of origin. Some critics of intercountry adoption equate the practice with the slave trade of earlier centuries, characterizing it as the ultimate expression of American Imperialism. (p. 51)

These ideas have been further explored by Altstein and Simon (1991) in their review of ICA history and the realities of a war and conflict are important to consider when one asks *why* a post-conflict nation is vulnerable to fraud. Human rights abuses, including human trafficking, are more likely to occur in an environment of limited civil society and rule of law.

Another social worker responding to the Babylift, Barbara Joe (1978) writes of this controversy in her manuscript *In Defense of Intercountry Adoption:*

> The Vietnam Babylift, due to errors common to emergency endeavors, crystallized official opposition to intercountry adoption with the Child Welfare League of America demanding a halt to the 'uprooting' of children, Caritas (World Catholic Relief) denouncing the airlift as 'deplorable,' and the International Union of Child Welfare condemning "the large-scale evacuation of these children. (p. 2).

Further, when discussing ICA more generally, Joe explores "financial considerations" (p. 13) and adoption agency irregularities versus professional fees. Specifically, she raises issues of birth mother payments for expenses versus incentive for child relinquishment.

> In [the US], it seems that the line between paying legitimate fees and buying a child is arbitrarily crossed when the natural mother herself accepts a direct cash payment, though not if she receives goods and services. When cash exchanges occur in the child's country of origin, even if not illegal there, we are quick to condemn them as 'irregular' or 'black market.' However, paying more for an adoption than some set 'usual and customary fee' even when part of the excess may find its way into the natural mother's pocket, does not invalidate adoption as the best plan for all concerned. (p. 13)

Joe's exceptionally transparent position, a largely unacceptable professional viewpoint in the post-Hague Convention environment, underscores the complexities of ICA and the inherent dilemmas related to financial incentives in the process—especially payments for parental relinquishment. Such payments to biological families, bribes to officials for birth certificates (sometimes altered to indicate 'orphan' status), and the vast financial sums involved in the multimillion dollar service of ICA (Riben, 2007) has been referred to as the "baby trade" (Kapstein, 2003).

Some sending countries impose moratoriums once problems of adoption fraud (i.e., coercive and/or paid relinquishments) become exacerbated to the point that the general public becomes aware and resistant to ICA (i.e., Romania, see Chapters 2 and 7). Altstein and Simon (1991) asserted that Operation Babylift had a backlash effect in Vietnam, noting that just six years later in 1980, ICA as a practice had all but ceased. It was not until 1995 that the practice resumed and in 2000, 728 children were adopted by USA citizens (Bartholet, 2010b). Several years later there was a another decline and closure of adoption services due to allegations of child sales with "14 individuals arrested in Hanoi for buying children from poor families, paying up to $70 a child, selling them to individuals in other countries for $1,000 to $1,500" (Freundlich, 2000b, p. 46).

It was not until 2005, upon reorganization of adoption services at the government level, including a new bilateral agreement that adoption services resumed to the USA. By 2008, the USA government refused to renew the agreement and allowed it to expire due to evidence of serious irregularities and renewed concerns about adoption fraud and child trafficking (U.S. Department of State, n.d.).

An investigatory report by U.S. Department of State (2008) indicated that financial incentives in the ICA process—specifically monetary donations to institutions from adoption agencies in the U.S. and other nations—were distorting adoption patterns and the availability of desirable children. This included evidence that institution directors were pressured to make child permanency decisions favoring ICA over biological family reunification or domestic adoptions in Vietnam. A disturbing and telling dynamic related to child desertion and abandonment, was explained by U.S. DOS as follows:

> Under US Immigration law, children can be adopted if they are orphans due to the whereabouts of their birth parents being unknown (desertion) or if one or both birth parents have permanently relinquished custody of their child to the orphanage, (termed "abandonment" by US Immigration law, but commonly referred to as relinquishment). Prior to the suspension of adoption in 2002, 80% of cases were relinquishments, and 20% were abandonments. Since the Memorandum of Agreement (MOA) [Bilateral Agreement] went into effect in 2005, those figures have flipped with over 85% of the cases involving desertions. Orphanages not involved in ICA, however, have reported to the Embassy that they have not seen any increase in the number of deserted children, and the vast majority of children in these facilities are children in care. Post [the embassy] has received multiple, credible reports from orphanage officials that facilitators are deliberately staging fraudulent desertions to conceal the identity of the birth parents. (U.S. Department of State, 2008)

This particular report describes an array of problems, including asserting that institution directors were interfacing with a financially incentivized system fueled by fees from prospective adoptive families. A market dynamic emerged and violations of child rights resulted. The report was a pre-cursor to closure of the Vietnam-USA adoption system and it is not likely to reopen until Vietnam joins and ratifies the Hague Convention (U.S. DOS, n.d.b). One final note that illustrates the complexities and even paradoxes of global ICA practices is the fact that as late as the spring of 2011 Spain and other Western European HCIA nations have continued adoptions from Vietnam, even in the face of significant problems.

Cambodia

Cambodian adoption fraud is well-documented and provides us with one of the most notorious examples of child trafficking under the guise of ICA (Smolin, 2005, 2006). This case summary is based on the USA government investigation entitled "Operation Broken Hearts," which resulted in the arrest and conviction of sisters Lauryn Galindo and Lynn Devin (Cross, 2005). Their adoption business paints a picture of unethical and illegal activities including bribery, immigration visa fraud, and money laundering. These organized crime activities of child sales were even more horrifying when the investigation uncovered use of unsanitary 'stash houses' for waiting children. Galindo lived in Cambodia, where she claimed she engaged in humanitarian work—a claim sometimes used by child traffickers as a disguise. She called herself an "adoption facilitator" but her work history did not indicate that she trained as a child welfare professional. Devin, on the other hand, was a trained counselor and she headed *Seattle International Adoptions*, an agency she operated from her personal residence, accepting applications and fees totaling hundreds of thousands of dollars. Together the sisters successfully developed an international 'adoption' agency which placed approximately 700 children with adoptive families in the USA, some of whom were clearly victims of a child trafficking scheme. When Galindo and Devin both pled guilty to a variety of charges including money laundering, they avoided a court hearing and the full extent of their illegal activities was not disclosed as formal testimony (United States District Court, 2004).

However, the investigating officer, a U.S. Federal Marshal, described their illegal activities with alarming details (Cross, 2005). Devin operated the USA-side of the 'adoption' business while the child-sending side of the process was organized by Galindo, who used her contacts with the Cambodian government, to whom she admitted paying bribes which she called "tips." In this process, a fraudulent paper trail was created and the children's identities were erased or "laundered" (Smolin, 2004, 2006). With new names and histories, the information was placed on falsified birth certificates to obtain travel documents. Fraud occurred when unsuspecting adoptive parents applied for immigration of these 'laundered' children as 'orphans,' as per USA orphan visa guidelines.

To commit this crime, Galindo collaborated with a number of Cambodians who recruited poor birth families for child sales. One tactic recruiters used was to entice birth families with stories of the wonderful life awaiting their children in the USA including photographs of happy, healthy Cambodian children living with their adoptive families. These photos were of children enjoying lives in relative wealth compared to birth families typically living in extreme poverty. Some defrauded birth families were led to believe that they could regularly visit their children or reclaim them in the future—believing that they would enjoy an ongoing relationship. Financial transactions included payments of $20 to $200 USD and a bag of rice, further inducing families and ultimately leading to sales and purchases of children.

Reportedly, Galindo reimbursed recruiters for costs associated with child medical exams, travel, and other expenses—including the actual payments for purchasing children. USA federal investigators found that recruiters also received a $50 USD commission per child. Their work was similar to independent contractors or freelance locators who are compensated by contingency fees for each child successfully secured for ICA. Contingency payments fuel the dishonesty and coercion inherent in adoption fraud and human trafficking.

Adoptive families were instructed to carry $3,500 USD in hundred dollar bills when they traveled to Cambodia to pick up their children; they were told that the money would be used as donations for humanitarian purposes. Groups of twenty parents would travel to pick up children, handing large sums of cash directly to Galindo. Investigatory evidence indicated that Galindo deposited this money into offshore personal accounts in Asia (in multiple deposits of $3,500), failing to use the money as promised.

Earning an estimated $9 million in just a few short years, Galindo was investigated for money laundering, which ultimately resulted in the USA government's seizure of her $1.5 million beachfront home and luxury automobile for tax fraud (Cross, 2005; Schuster Institute for Investigative Journalism, n.d.). Galindo was sentenced to 18 months in prison on visa fraud and money laundering (United States District Court, 2004). Devin received a lesser sentence (Cross, 2005); and Cambodia has failed to prosecute the case entirely. Short sentences translate into a failure of the justice system, in both the USA and Cambodia and ultimately illustrate the impotency of the IAA in these cases. It was not possible to prosecute the case as a violation of the IAA because Cambodia was not a party to the Hague Convention at that time (Bromfield and Rotabi, 2012; Rotabi and Gibbons, 2012).

It should be noted that the nation is now working towards implementing the Convention with a new 2009 adoption law (U.S. DOS, 2011b; see Chapter 4). In the spring of 2011, the USA government recognized Cambodia's improvements, however the nation remains in USA moratorium dating back to 2001. A recent statement by the USA Central Adoption Authority sheds light on the concerns as follows: "Issues related to transparency in fees, procedural safeguards, determination of a child's eligibility for intercountry adoption, criminal penalties and the creation of a strategy to formalize and strengthen the domestic adoption system will all need to be addressed effectively" (U.S. DOS, 2011b).

Guatemala

Guatemala instituted an adoption moratorium at the end of 2007 after a number of years of controversy (Bunkers et al., 2009; Gresham, Nackerud and Risler, 2004; Rotabi, Morris and Weil, 2008). A new system of ICA is currently emerging, informed by past problems related to adoption fraud (see Chapter 9). During the peak era of Guatemalan adoptions, called a 'baby market' by some, approximately 30,000 exceptionally young children (as much as 90 percent being infants or toddlers) left the nation bound for the USA (Casa Alianza, Myrna Mack Foundation, Survivors Foundation, the Social Movement for the Rights of Children and Adolescents Human Rights Office of the Archbishop of Guatemala and the Social Welfare Secretariat, 2007).

Similar to Vietnam and Cambodia, Guatemala experienced problems related to multiple underlying issues of a post-conflict and deeply impoverished nation with a track record of significant human rights abuses (United Nations Economic and Social Council Commission on Human Rights, 2000; Rotabi et al., 2008). Rotabi and Morris (2007) and Rotabi and Bunkers (2008) identified multiple problems in a systems analysis focusing on specific nexus points for fraud. Their conclusions pointed directly to the previous attorney or "notary" based system of ICA which allowed the adoption process to occur with little family court oversight. Working in concert with attorneys were well-paid birth mother recruiters acting as critical agents. The notary system, birth mother recruiters, and agency adoption facilitators were a problem of the *past* given the new phases of systems reform, which include the new Guatemalan adoption law passed in late 2007, which meets HCIA criteria (Bunkers et al., 2009; Rotabi et al., 2008). Under this code, notary processes, birth mother recruiters, and adoption facilitators are no longer viable as private or pay-for-service providers.

The focus of this discussion is on two activities that have been less frequently discussed than the notarial system: how children have actually been commodified via 'manufacturing' of children (Riviera, Bromfield and Rotabi, 2009) and child abduction in coordination with DNA test fraud (Rotabi, 2009; Cruz, Smolin, Rotabi, Dilworth and DeFilipo, 2011).

The manufacturing of children[1] is best illustrated by a personal account from a USA medical doctor working in a voluntary medical mission in Guatemala. White (2006) wrote:

1 The term 'manufacturing children', used by some Guatemalans, has been used here instead of 'baby farming.' The latter term has historical significance in regards to infant sales, see http://darkwing.uoregon.edu/~adoption/topics/babyfarming.html..

> Last week a thirteen-year-old pregnant girl named Marta [last name withheld] came into my office. Her father works on a coffee plantation not far away, and she grew up on the verge of starvation in a cardboard house, with eleven siblings, six of whom are still alive. A man came in a car a year ago, and offered her family three hundred dollars—a year's wages for her father—for each baby she can make and give to him. She now lives and works in his house, tends his garden, washes clothes, was impregnated by men unknown to her, and only wants from me a checkup, perhaps some prenatal vitamins, so the baby she will soon give away will be as healthy as possible. This visit to see me is to be a secret; such things are not allowed by the man and his wife. The babies are delivered by the owners in the house. No hospital. No doctors. There are six other girls, ages twelve to fifteen, in the same house, same situation. One recently died in child birth, but the baby was saved, to be sold for three thousand dollars in Guatemala City, she tells me … White was warned by Guatemalan friends against speaking out against Marta's captors and told that "these people not only deal in selling lives; they launder money, sell narcotics, and trade in arms and explosives." (p. 5)

White's reports to local police in Guatemala, as well as human rights organizations on a national and international scale, drew no response to Marta's plight. Nothing more is known about the outcome of the young mother or her infant (White, 2006).

Due to concerns about illegal adoptions, including abduction and sales, the U.S. Department of State and other governments such as Canada required DNA tests to verify relationships between birth mothers and children (Bunkers et al., 2009). In fact, many adopting families were comforted by this form of identification as a safeguard—an insurance policy of sorts. However, that assumption relied on the validity of such tests, and there is now evidence that one of the critical nexus points for fraud may well be the DNA tests themselves (Associated Press, 2008a, 2008b).

Ana Escobar's story brings these DNA tests into question (Estrada Zepeda, 2009). Ms. Escobar reported that her infant daughter was kidnapped while she worked in a Guatemala City shoe store where she was held at gunpoint and threatened with death (A. Escobar, personal communication, August 9, 2009; Associated Press, 2008a, 2008b). Immediately, Escobar claims to have gone to the police to make a criminal report of the kidnapping and asked for help in rescuing her child. Escobar recounts that she was met with suspicion by the authorities and faced accusations of selling her child into adoption—she was treated as a perpetrator of crime instead of a victim. This police allegation is not entirely surprising because, by this late point in the Guatemalan adoption system, it is asserted that birth mother payments for relinquishment signatures had become routine (Bunkers et al., 2009; Rotabi and Bunkers, 2008). Not to be deterred and without benefit of law enforcement assistance, Escobar searched for her daughter and in a chance sighting passing in the Guatemalan National Adoption Council office, she recognized her daughter and immediately identified the child due to a unique physical characteristic. In response, Escobar convinced government authorities to DNA test the child, confirming her allegation of kidnapping (Associated Press, 2008b). The child's adoption paperwork was fraudulent, including a previous DNA test matching her to a woman who *claimed* to be the biological mother. The 'adoption' which had been arranged for a USA-based family was cancelled and neither the USA-based agency nor anyone else involved in the case irregularities or the associated crimes have ever been held accountable for their roles. However, Escobar's case sheds light on DNA fraud and issues of biometric testing. There are theories as to how this crime was executed and Escobar's case is not the only example of known child abduction case or DNA-test fraud (Associated Press, 2008a; 2008b; Rotabi, 2009).

Unfortunately other cases of alleged child abduction have yet to be fully investigated and ultimately prosecuted despite concerted efforts from leading human rights defenders in Guatemala. Formal requests for DNA tests by the Government of Guatemala to the U.S. Department of Justice have not yielded results (Cruz, 2010; Cruz, Smolin, Rotabi, Dilworth and DeFilipo, 2011). Even with requests for intervention by U.S. Senator Landrieu, a leader within the U.S. Congressional Coalition on Adoption and outspoken proponent of prosecuting criminals who undermine ethical adoptions, there appears to be an impasse in USA collaboration with Guatemalan law enforcement (Cruz, 2011). However, at least three mothers periodically make starvation protests in Guatemala (Rotabi, 2009) and their cases garner international attention. These cases have become symbolic of women who have forcibly lost their children to intercountry adoption in a country that was riddled by corruption (Comisión Internacional Contra la Impunidad, 2010; Estrada Zapeda, 2009).

Conclusion

Freundlich (2000b) in her exploration of the market forces in intercountry adoption poses some critical questions, including the following:

> Is undue pressure being exerted to force women in developing countries to place their babies for adoption? Are women being induced to have babies specifically for the purpose of international adoption? Do facilitators and adoption professionals—who most directly benefit financially from international adoption—take advantage of the dire economic status of many women in developing countries? (p. 51)

The answers are complicated and these case examples frame the answers highlighting the unique dynamics in each post-conflict environment.

This historical case study is presented not only to consider the issues identified in Freundlich's questions, but to underscore the methods of fraud, child sales, and abduction. This is in part, to encourage greater awareness of the structures that conceal or even perpetuate adoption fraud. All three examples illuminate child laundering (Smolin, 2004, 2006), and some children were ultimately sold into highly lucrative and sophisticated networks. While each nation has unique dynamics, there are commonalities such as exploitation of vulnerable biological mothers and families and their very young and healthy children (Rotabi and Gibbons, 2012).

Adoption attorneys, agencies, and government bureaucrats hold a great deal of power in the process of adoption and practice ethics. The fact that 'recruiters' have been involved in ICA underscores a serious problem and anyone alarmed by what has been called the "Orphan Crisis" (JCICS, n.d.) should ask *why* such a role exists? Why the need to extract children when millions of orphaned and vulnerable children are available around the world? Why the need to pay extraordinary fees to adoption attorneys and agencies if everyone involved is concerned for the welfare of children rather than financial gain? The conditions of a post-genocidal era, specifically in Cambodia and Guatemala (January 2007) where "social cleansing" left a lasting scar, leaves one to wonder if ICA is an aftershock of genocide in some cases. And, 'humanitarian donations' in this context of societal disintegration and rebuilding efforts may actually distort or interfere with ethical child placement decisions (Doyle, 2010; Freundlich, 2000b; Rotabi and Gibbons, 2012). In an era of reform, we must ask if new Convention standards will control the problems identified in Vietnam, Cambodia, and Guatemala as well as other nations (see Chapter 19). In this chapter, I have outlined some of the ways fraud can be perpetuated to provide direction for eliminating fraud in the future. As Maskew (2010) said during an international Adoption Summit, "think like a bad guy, write like a lawyer."

Chapter 6
Perspectives on Child Welfare: Ways of Understanding Roles and Actions of Current USA Adoption Agencies Involved in Intercountry Adoptions

Mary Katherine O'Connor and Karen Smith Rotabi

Adoption agencies are critical nexus points in ethical intercountry adoption (ICA) practice and fraud prevention (Freundlich, 2000b). In industrialized or high-resource nations, they are organizations that recruit or market to potential families; carry out home study assessments; develop service plans based on certain family and child needs; organize immigration and other critical paperwork; and provide pre- and post-adoption support for families who adopt children internationally. Under the Hague Convention on Intercountry Adoption (HCIA), adoption agencies are recognized to be brokers of services that must be regulated to prevent child sales and abduction and ultimately child trafficking (Hague Conference on International Private Law, 1993). Inevitable tensions result. Some of the underlying issues have received considerable attention (see Chapters 2, 3, 4, 5, 6, 7, 11, 12, 18, 19, and 21).

Most adoption agencies in the United States are based on a social entrepreneurial model fundamentally, because of their structure and vision, ICA agencies are usually nonprofit organizations operating for-profit ventures to generate revenues. Many times, the revenues from ICAs are used to support other services provided by the adoption agencies. We are not unaware that some adoption agencies, while fitting into the nonprofit category, are really in the 'baby business' with the profit motive that that entails (Kapstein, 2003; Riben, 2007). We are also aware that some adoption agencies might object to the above characterizations, preferring a more progressive understanding of the designation "social entrepreneur," such as that of Bornstein (2004) who sees the social entrepreneurial position as a transformative force, an entity that provides new ideas to address major problems (in this case children in need of permanent homes world-wide). Bornstein sees social entrepreneurs as relentlessly pursuing their visions; not taking 'no' for an answer; constitutionally incapable of giving up until their ideas have spread to achieve systemic change that involves shifting patterns of behavior and perceptions. Entrepreneurial organizations, according to O'Connor and Netting (2009), identify with goals of individual liberation through individual empowerment. This determination to liberate and empower may, indeed, run counter to the capitalistic underpinnings needed for intercountry adoption efforts.

The tensions surrounding USA adoption agencies and the HCIA, regardless of the type of entrepreneurial organization engaged in ICAs, may be better understood by looking at the competing values of child care policy in the USA and elsewhere. This chapter's aim is to describe the tensions, underlying values and differing expectations, and needs in ICA using a framework devised by Lorraine Fox Harding (1991). Examples of various USA agency experiences and their interactions with different country and cultural contexts will serve to illustrate the challenges as the competing values are clarified. Finally, the chapter will close with both lessons learned from the field and recommendations for policy and practice changes in ICA.

A Framework for Understanding Child Welfare Policy and Adoption

In the USA, the child welfare policies are layered in complex ways that include Federal regulations, State laws, and human service agency policy and procedures; all of these have been shaped by differing professional and personal ideologies (Stone, 2002). Harding (1991) identifies four value-based perspectives in child welfare policy that influence how care is provided for children, based on preference. Stone (2002) suggests that what determines the perspective adopted and ultimately policies for childcare is not only values, culture, and tradition, but also power as enacted in politics. Much of the confusion regarding adoption agencies and their interface with low-resource nations and needed system reform may be more understandable and, therefore, more malleable if viewed in terms of four value-based perspectives; those perspectives are (1) *laissez-faire* and patriarchy; (2) state paternalism and child protection; (3) modern defense of the birth family and parent's rights; and (4) children's rights and child liberation (Harding, 1991).

Laissez-Faire *and Patriarchy*

Laissez-faire and patriarchy have been apparent in the USA during the 19th and 20th centuries through today. This perspective grants the family the position of power and decrees that the family should not be disturbed except in very extreme circumstances. The role of the State is minimal in order to family life undisturbed. Because intervention is not benign, when intervention does occur, fair warning is given to parents and clear restrictions of power are placed on State officials. Grounds for intervention are very precise, and, therefore, limited. This limit is preferred because of the belief that the State benefits from minimal societal intrusions; a weaker State has stronger families and freer individuals.

This perspective holds that society benefits by families living without interference, and that parents have the right to choose how to raise their children. It also recognizes the psychological parental bond, including children's need for their biological parents. Because damage can be done to children if the parental bond is disrupted, the connection between parent and child is only interrupted in extreme cases and only to avoid greater evil. When intervention occurs, there is a mandate to find a new permanent family as soon as possible so that the State can withdraw and the newly constructed family can create its own family life. Aspects of the USA public and private adoption systems fall within this perspective. Children's Home Society of Minnesota (n.d.), a long-standing adoption service provider, describes its services as guiding "children into loving, nurturing homes." This view of orphaned and vulnerable children suggests that they were 'unloved' prior to adoption, which is contradictory to findings of birth mother research (see Chapters 9 and 11; Roby and Matsumura, 2002). This statement also implies that an adoptive family is 'better' and more 'nurturing.' This conception of superior family life further justifies *laissez-faire* adoption practices of child placement into ICA as quickly as possible to 'nurture' the child by preserving healthy child growth and development (see Chapter 13).

The *laissez-faire* approach is demonstrated in the historically lax governmental regulation of intercountry adoption, that is, instead, managed by attorneys and private agencies operating under a 'business model' as social entrepreneurial organizations. Interactions between adoption agencies in the USA and India illustrate the *laissez-faire and patriarchy*values perspective in policy and its practice outcomes.

India is a nation with serious and persistent ICA problems. Smolin's (2005) analysis criticizes the nation's HCIA-system, pointing out multiple problems such as notoriously bad adoption facilitators; a known problem often connecting agencies to unethical adoptions (Freundlich, 2000b; Rotabi, 2008). Bhargava (2005), a founding member of the India Central Adoption Authority, provides a rather complex analysis of problems from the Indian perspective. Her critique includes how traditional culture in this largely impoverished society interfaces with relatively sophisticated adoption agencies with vast financial influence and a demand for healthy and young children. In an attempt to highlight the need to further restructure policies beyond initial changes under the Hague Convention, Bhargava outlines a number of problematic observations based on *laissez-faire* ICA practices present in Indian intercountry adoptions. Ultimately, the practices Bhargava identifies illustrate the fact that even with Hague Convention reform, inappropriate and even illegal activities continue to persist in India, ultimately violating requirements for transparent and ethical adoptions. With limited Indian regulatory influence and a high price tag on children, foreign (U.S. and others) and collaborating agencies in India (and their Indian partners) are using any means to acquire children for adoption. They may encourage relinquishment by distressed unwed mothers, who do not feel they have the option of keeping and parenting their children. Because the children are valuable commodities and agencies are committed to expediting adoptions, adoption agencies and their Indian intermediaries rarely give any financial assistance, support, or counseling to help mothers to keep their children. Often, agencies avoid involving the extended family in taking care of a relinquished child, because their perspective is to allow the newly constructed 'better' international adoptive family to create an undisturbed family life as quickly as possible (Bhargava, 2005). This is a clear violation of the HCIA, specifically the principle of subsidiarity that requires a search for biological family-child placement first (see Chapter 18).

A *laissez-faire* entrepreneurial business model seems operant in India as agencies are keen to place children in families abroad because of the sums of money involved. According to Bhargava (2005), foreign agencies are funding Indian agencies, which means that a regular business relationship between Indian agencies and foreign concerns has emerged, with money taken by in-country agencies and intermediaries in advance for a certain number of children placed through them. This unfettered capitalism and the commodification of infants to be adopted is possible due to the hands-off nature of the Indian State's value position that assures that the role of the State is minimal in order to create undisturbed family life.

State Paternalism and Child Protection

State paternalism and child protection, the second value-based perspective, appeared in the late 19th century and continues into the 20th and 21st centuries in the USA. This is exemplified by the child rescue approach of a child welfare system that assumes the legitimacy of extensive government intervention to protect a child. The intervention by the State is authoritarian and prescriptive, with norms of child rearing defined and imposed. The parental bond is undervalued by the belief that good quality substitute care is favorable when parents are inadequate. In fact, this perspective is punitive to parents; their rights are not valued, only their duties. Parents who do nothing to bring up their children cannot expect to keep them because children should be protected from poor parental care (e.g., the term "child protective services" emerges from this perspective).

Here children are seen as central in society and its future and given high priority. They are seen as separate individuals with the right to quality care as judged by experts. There is recognition of the psychological parent bond and a belief that this bond does not need to be biological in nature, because there is awareness that biological parental care is not always good care. When parents fail due to psychopathology or other problems, State power is readily and extensively used to provide something better. In these cases, agencies tend to have low levels of trust in parents; thus they may readily initiate actions that exclude parents, including removal of the child from the home. The USA adoption agency interface with Russia represents an example of practice within *state paternalism and child protection.*

The child in Russia is valued as an important member of society who must be protected, as indicated by the year 2007 being nationally recognized as the *Year of the Child* (Schmidt, 2009). This value perspective has resulted in controversy related to child care institutions in the nation. There have been recent efforts

Table 6.1 Values Perspectives

LAISSEZ-FAIRE PATRIARCHY	STATE PATERNALISM-CHILD PROTECTION
Minimalist State role. Intervene only in extreme circumstances. Sanctity of parent-child relationship. Family is private domain. Intervention is not benign.	Authoritarian State intervention to protect child from poor parental care. Recognizes parental duty over parental rights. The problem is poor parenthood due to individual psychopathology. "Child rescue." Child is separate entity from parents.
CHILREN'S RIGHTS & CHILD LIBERATION	**MODERN DEFENSE OF BIRTH FAMILY & PARENT'S RIGHTS**
Free children from adult oppression. Emphasizes strengths over vulnerability. Recognizes child rights over child duties.	Large role of State in intervention is supportive of families. The problem is that parents are oppressed by class, poverty and deprivation. Children's needs not distinct, but part of their family's needs.

Source: Adapted from Harding, L.F. (1991). *Perspectives in Child Care Policy.* London, UK: Longman.

and political promises to significantly reduce the use of institutions to care for orphaned and vulnerable children (Schmidt, 2009). However, the State continues to intervene as the 'child protector' in child removal or as a 'safe place' for abandonment with placements of children into various forms of alternative care, including overcrowded institutions and, sometimes, adoption.

Child protection, a central value in Russia's largely paternalistic system, is enacted when children are being inadequately parented or placed at threat of harm. As a result, large institutions, smaller group homes, and foster care are used commonly throughout the nation. The large numbers of children in State institutions has been called a "crisis" (Bowring, 1999, p. 125; Schmidt, 2009). The large numbers of institutionalized older children—a known dynamic in Russian ICA—is another characteristic of paternalism and child protection: life in an institution cared for by experts is assumed to be better than what happened to the child before being institutionalized. Under the perspective of State paternalism and child protection, the role of 'specialist' is highly valued. In Russian institutions there are usually more than four specialists providing service—experts in psychology, social pedagogy, social work, and speech therapy (Schmidt, 2009).

Recently, gaps in pre-placement social history and mental health assessment, home studies, post-placement care, and information sharing indicate that Russia's policies and practices may have been drifting from State paternalism towards a more *laissez-faire* model of child welfare services with the State taking less responsibility for child protection. This assertion is based on well-publicized ICA problems between the USA and Russia, including alarming adoption dissolutions and even child deaths. Outrage in Russia has resulted in controversy, even being debated within Russian Congress for legal changes if not a moratorium, have led to a new 2011 bilateral agreement developed to strengthen services and control the market forces in ICA (Rotabi, 2010a; Rotabi and Heine, 2010; U.S. Department of State, 2011d; see Chapter 19). The new requirements related pre-placement reports, home studies, and post-placement follow-up visits are an attempt to control *laissez-faire* practices.

Modern Defense of the Birth Family and Parents' Rights

The third perspective, modern defense of the birth family and parents' rights emerged as a perspective in the USA after World War II. Under this perspective, State intervention is legitimate, but must be supportive, defending and preserving birth families. This mandate is based on the assumption that poorer and socially deprived parents are victims of heavy-handed State action and require help and support to fulfill their parental responsibilities. Included are the recognition of parental rights and mandates to keep families intact whenever possible because the biological/psychological bond is the basis of the best provision of care. The role of the State is one of active support so a child will not require substitute care. The child is placed in out-of- home care only as a last resort; is allowed to keep in touch with parents; and is returned as quickly as possible.

In this perspective parental duties, rather than rights, are valued and state intervention is extensive, but not coercive. Birth parents are supported in their caring roles. Their emotional needs are responded to because the biological parent-child link is crucial, unlike what was seen in the first two values perspectives. When a child is placed in substitute care, family contact is continued, encouraged, and the child is returned as soon as possible. The role of traditional adoption is unclear when there is an assumption that problems in the care and protection of children are the result of the State giving insufficient attention to sustaining families. Insufficient care of children from this perspective is a social class issue, that requires overcoming poverty and deprivation to assure 'best interest' of the child, rather than placement out of the home to achieve a 'better' life.

In the USA and elsewhere, open adoptions and parental choice of the placement family have become common features of many private adoptions; these changes can be traced to this perspective (see Chapter 22). Support for open birth records in the USA also falls within this perspective (Babb, 1999) because open birth records allow the possibility of a relationship between a child and her biological family.

The *defense of the birth family and parental rights* is codified in Shari'ah law in Islamic societies. Islam places great importance on parentage, family relationships, and genetic lineage. As a result, one does not see ICA from Northern Africa and Middle Eastern countries or other largely Islamic nations in Asia. When there is a need to provide alternative care for a child *Kefala* is often practiced. The word itself means "to feed" (O'Halloran, 2009, p. 380) and relatives and kin of the orphaned or vulnerable children develop care plans solving the problem as a group. Often the child is raised by a relative or a member of the tribe who honors the birth family and the child is even viewed as a bridge across families—deepening relationships between members of the society. This is consistent with traditions in many non-industrialized societies with limited social welfare structure (Rotabi and Gibbons, 2012). There are also examples of strict legal protections for birth families in nations with histories of fraudulent adoptions, as is the case in Argentina which bans ICA altogether and in El Salvador which places significant restrictions on ICA (see Chapter 24).

The Marshall Islands is a nation that has codified birth family rights as a result of that nation's previous ICA problems (see Chapter 4). This was the result of birth mother mis-understanding of ICA as a clean and legal break of family relations, lack of informed consent for adoption, and coercive adoptions in some cases (Roby and Matsumura, 2002). Today, preventive and legal safe guards include Family Group Conferencing (FGC), as an intervention that allows a child's family and kin to come together to make a safety and/or alternative care plan for the child that usually does not include out-of-family adoption (Roby and Ife, 2009; Rotabi, Pennell, Roby and Bunkers, 2012).

Children's Rights and Child Liberation

The children's rights and child liberation perspective can be said to be both postmodern and quite extreme, at least from USA norms on the role of children in civil society. Under this perspective a child has independent rights similar to those of adults. The goal of this perspective is to free the child from adult oppression by granting children more adult status. Rather than decisions being made by the child welfare system or other adults, the child is recognized as an autonomous actor. Self-determination on the part of the child is preferred and the child should be allowed to do things that adults do legally, such as living independently, refusing to go to school, and working. This perspective assumes the fundamental competence and strength of children. Based on this, there should be no curtailment of children's liberties to the extent that what constitutes 'best interest' and child welfare is defined by the child.

This position emphasizes children's strengths over their vulnerabilities with neither parents nor the State having special rights vis-à-vis children. The State role is limited with children being expected to assume adult-like responsibilities regarding the law, policy, education health care and family life. This position recognizes child rights over child duties. However, adult level decision making is expected; when the child does wrong, adult consequences follow, such as death penalty sentencing for minors.

Examples of the perspective of *children's rights and child liberation* are evident in Romania and Brazil. Child rights were played out in Romania when two nine-year-old girls successfully blocked their intercountry adoptions to Italy through legal means (*Pini and Others v. Romania*,as cited in O'Halloran, 2009). While this was most certainly a legal precedent and not the norm in Romania, it should be noted that the HCIA demonstrates this values perspective with its requirements for children, based on their maturity, to be involved in decision-making in adoption plans (Hague Conference on International Private Law, 1993).

Child rights are also the focus of child welfare in Brazil, where under the national constitution children's rights supersede adult rights and where the Children's Statute or Children's Code is more progressive than the UN Convention on the Rights of the Child in that the code is connected to the Brazilian constitutional position that children's rights precede all other rights. However, this values perspective has not as yet achieved full operationalization in the national child welfare infrastructure as seen both in its challenges with street children (Garcia and Fernandez, 2009) and in Brazil's problematic ICA history including irregular and illegal adoptions with Israel (Jaffe, 1991) and other nations (Abreu, 2009; Fonseca, 2009; Herrman and Kasper, 1992). Currently the country engages in limited ICA sending practices under the 1990 Children's Code, which makes ICA a last resort after domestic adoptions. It should be noted that domestic adoptions were only recognized as a culturally acceptable and nationally regulated option in the 1990s (Abreu, 2009; Fonseca, 2009).

The Value-based Perspectives and Lessons for Intercountry Adoption and USA Agencies

From the above discussion it should be clear that policies and practices differ with respect to the values-based perspective that underlines them. Certainly, there are many more details and subtleties to the story of adoption in the USA and ICA and competing priorities which highlight Harding's framework (see Hermans' Adoption History Project, n.d. and the U.S. Department of Health and Human Services Child Welfare Information Gateway, n.d.). In this section, we show how competing value-based perspectives exacerbate the complexity of USA adoption in general and intercountry adoption in particular.

Though the four perspectives are very different, sometimes setting up paradoxical mandates for agencies and professionals in the child welfare field, there are some convergent values that might be bridges to implementing adoption reform globally. Regardless of the valued-based perspective, all focus on children. They also all recognize a role for the State in child protection. Finally, all perspectives demonstrate recognition of the parental bond, but not unfettered parental rights. The first three perspectives (minus the child rights perspective) also converge on two points: There is a societal role in supporting the biological family; and, the child is not autonomous.

The points of divergence are powerful and problematic, not only politically but culturally, when the focus is ICA. We see these elements of divergence in current Federal policy, State law, and the programs that derive from each in the USA. We also see them in the practices in the various nation States involved in the Hague

Convention. There is little understanding or agreement about what constitutes child welfare or what exactly is in the "best interest" of a child (Zermatten, 2010). There is little agreement regarding the role, definition, and functions of the family. The origins of family problems as being within the individual, the family or in the context of the environment are debated; as is the role of the State in responding to family and child welfare problems. Finally, the concept of rights is not agreed upon, especially as those rights relate to women and their children (see Chapter 18).

The divergences and the congruencies establish an unremitting conflict between the rights and needs of children, their biological parents, those seeking to adopt, and the agencies serving the adoption triad in the USA. The complexity regarding what is ethical and in the best interest of those involved is exacerbated by differences in prevailing cultural norms and political ideology. Within ICA there are not only conflicting perspectives on child welfare, but on another important factor—the entrepreneurial, economic motive in intercountry adoption.

What We Know about Agencies in the USA

Pertman (2011) aptly called the USA an "adoption nation." Although, there is no exact count of the number of ICA agencies in the USA, just over 300 USA-based ICA agencies applied to be evaluated to become approved service providers under HCIA (Rotabi, 2008). At the time of this writing, over 100 agencies are listed as approved providers of ICA adoption services by the USA Central Authority. In a small study of 300 USA-based adoption agencies in 2009, 100 randomly sampled websites were analyzed (Witwer and Rotabi, 2011). Findings indicated that 74 percent of the agencies reported being Hague Convention-accredited, while the other 26 percent made no reference to accreditation nor to the Hague Convention on the website.

Humanitarian activities were claimed by 63 percent of agencies, but many of the agencies did not demonstrate programs with specific goals, objectives that would adhere to Bornstein's (2004) definition of the social entrepreneur. The most common ICA programs were in China (62 agencies), Russia (46 agencies), Guatemala (41 agencies), Ukraine (40 agencies), Ethiopia (36 agencies), Kazakhstan (29 agencies), Nepal (23 agencies), South Korea (21 agencies), Taiwan (18 agencies), and Vietnam (17 agencies). It is important to note that Guatemala and Vietnam were on moratorium for USA adoptions at the time of the investigation, which indicates that some agencies continued to advertise presence in a nation (i.e., resolving pre-moratorium cases) without noting problems; some even suggested ongoing opportunities to adopt from closed nations (Witwer and Rotabi, 2011).

Implications: Old Issues and New Ideas for the Future

The large role of the State in supporting families is not really present when adoption, especially ICA is the option, because ultimately sending nations are deferring to private adoptions in receiving nations for alternative care rather than developing family support and domestic adoption services. Many nation States involved in ICAs do not seem to embrace the idea that parents of vulnerable children are oppressed by class, poverty, and deprivation while some ICA service providers justify child rescue from poverty in their *laissez-faire* approach. *Modern defense of the birth family and parents' rights* values seem largely absent. With the exception of the Marshall Islands, none of the sending nations considered here demonstrates pro-birth family policies for ICA, nor is there measurable recognition that children's needs are not distinct, but are often a part of a distressed family system with needs frequently related to poverty and gender inequality (see Chapter 25).

The impact of adoption agencies and ICA on vulnerable and impoverished families and child welfare has been discussed in the literature for well over twenty years (Dickens, 2009; Freundlich, 2000b; Hollingsworth, 2003; Joe, 1978; Rotabi and Gibbons, 2012) and the human rights dimensions have been explored (Bartholet, 2007; Roby and Ife, 2009; Roby, 2007; Smolin, 2007b). Serious concerns have been expressed about the inherent market dynamics and their effect on ethical practice and the best interests of the child (Freundlich, 1998, 2000b; Riben, 2007). Ngabonziza (1991) states that ICA "… in many instances functions like a market according to the laws of a market; and takes place between members of an advanced and well organized society with plenty of social [adoption agencies] and legal institutions on the one hand, and on the other, *ad hoc* institutions and or isolated individuals such as lawyers, magistrates, social workers, who act as intermediaries, often motivated only by the gain" (p. 100).

Historical/political and cultural changes within the USA have affected the adoption arena. The acceptance of single motherhood in the USA beginning in the 1970s altered the nature of adoption in that shame of illegitimacy is no longer the over-riding reason for placing an infant for adoption in the USA (Fessler, 2007; Gailey, 2010). However, shame and unaccepted single motherhood have persisted as dynamics in many ICA sending nations. As fewer babies were available to USA-based agencies, those agencies shifted to other nations to serve the market for infants. As USA adoption agencies began to look elsewhere for healthy and younger children, countries with endemic poverty, limited social welfare systems, and fragmented families due to war and disaster were targeted as part of entrepreneurial agencies' market plan. This is because those countries' social problems resulted in more 'available' children (Fronek and Cuthbert, 2012). As systems tightened, such as China's increasingly strict criteria for adoption (Dowling and Brown, 2009), new requirements in Russia (Rotabi and Heine, 2010), and closure of Guatemala (Bunkers, Groza and Lauer, 2009; see Chapter 7)—market shifts pushed elsewhere (e.g., Ethiopia; see Chapter 8). It would appear that USA agencies and their international collaborators have illustrated the unbridled capitalism of the *laissez-faire* and paternalistic approach to child welfare. So what does this mean for practice?

- The Hague Convention stands no chance of full implementation until sending nations have the capacity to counter the financial challenges in-country regarding adoption. Biological parents should have the resources to raise their children and should be supported in their efforts to do so. When children are sold into ICA for their long-long term survival, their "best interests" may be distorted to justify the adoption. Not only is sale of children illegal, but the best interests of a child is for family support across a child welfare continuum. Ultimately, poverty in sending countries must be addressed for the Convention to reach its stated goals.
- Clarity about the values of both sending and receiving nations must be reconciled. Best interest of the child without the consideration of the best interest of the birth family and kinship group must become truly unacceptable politically and otherwise. Implementation of the Convention must be expected to make this an absolute policy requirement in all nations involved in intercountry adoptions.
- The business aspects of intercountry adoptions must be recognized and managed such that the acceptable entrepreneurial perspective undergirding the economic side of the enterprise must more consistently resemble Bornstein's (2004) social entrepreneur definition that requires developmental reinvestment in the context where services are needed and provided. This means that intercountry adoption agencies and local agencies receiving international money must be required to reinvest in the quality of family life in the countries that have opened their borders to intercountry adoption. Such reinvestment must not be distorted by 'humanitarian giving' (i.e., building maternal health clinics) that is constructed to develop networks that entrap families into intercountry adoption (Rotabi and Gibbons, 2012).
- National policies and practices should be moved more decidedly to a defense of the birth family and parental rights perspective in order to assure a more even handed attention to children's contextual values (Roby, 2007). Enacting social interventions which include the entire family, such as Family Group Conferencing, when children and their families are at risk would solidly implant this values perspective world-wide.
- In the era of HCIA reform, new and emergent problems are becoming apparent. Older and waiting children are now beginning to receive more attention and they have inevitable developmental challenges for placement families. As these placements become more common, many agencies are largely unprepared to provide post-adoption and highly intensive clinical services for these 'special needs' children (or any other). This is partly because post-adoption services are expensive and families are commonly (a) unprepared to pay for such additional services when planning their adoption, and (b) agencies lack the professionally prepared personnel to carry out intensive clinical case management. Once the child is placed in the USA, a laissez-faire approach supporting an unfettered family life will not meet the needs of these families built through adoption. These newly

constructed families must receive support in keeping at least with State paternalism, if not the modern defense of birth family perspective. These policy and service deficits must be addressed; capacity must be built to respond to special needs children; and the entrepreneurial approach in USA ICAs must adapt to these challenges.

PART II
Sending Country Perspectives

Chapter 7
Child Welfare in Romania: Contexts and Processes

Cristina Nedelcu and Victor Groza

This chapter provides an overview of child welfare in Romania. The contexts for child welfare include history, the role of communism, the impact of intercountry adoption and current developments. The processes include the various reforms initiated and the impediments to developing a modern child welfare system.

Romanian Child Welfare Under Communism

For 45 years, from 1944 to 1989, Romania was subject to the "Communist Experiment," an effort to create a great economic power, and perhaps a strong military power (Jackson, 1981; Moskoff, 1980). According to Linden (1986), Ceauşescu's manipulation of the political system strengthened his power and control during the early years of his rule when there was rapid economic development, but undermined the country's capacity to react to economic changes. Subsequently, by the mid to late 1980s it was clear to many Romanians that the Communist experiment in Romania was failing (Pacepa, 1990).

The failures of the communist system and abuses of its people were secreted behind the Iron Curtain; for many years the West was unaware of the many human rights violations in Romania, particularly the violation of children's rights (Cojocaru, 2008a; Roth, 1999). The Ceauşescu government decreed that each woman must have at least five children or face stringent fines and penalties; this in a country where light bulbs were regulated by the government and food was rationed (see Behr, 1991). Pronatalist policies (Keil and Andreescu, 1999; Moskoff, 1980) resulted in couples having large numbers of children (some unable to support them), and then relying on the State to take them into state-run facilities that promised to care for the children. This included children with chronic illnesses, mild to severe disabilities, and those with low birth weights. Low birth weight babies were reportedly 100 times more likely than normal weight babies to be placed in an institution following hospitalization (Bascom and McKelvey, 1997). Low birth weights were a direct result of food rationing; pregnant or newborn parents had no access to fortified baby formula, vitamins or baby food (see Groza, Ileana and Irwin, 1999). The Ceauşescu Government perpetuated a propaganda campaign that favored child placement in institutions; parents were encouraged to believe the State could raise the children as well or better than they would be raised by their own parents. Unable to provide proper care for their children and convinced by the Communist Party that institutionalized care would be best, parents placed thousands of children into orphanages every year, a problem that continues (Morrison, 2004).

In essence, the Communist System promoted "social orphans"; these are children who had parents but the parents gave custody and care of children over to the state because they were unable or unwilling to care for them. Children would be moved without parental notification and a network of large institutions was created to house the growing number of children; many of these were located in rural areas away from public scrutiny. By 1989, there were over 150,000 children in institutions and over 16,000 were dying annually of easily treatable illnesses (see Groza, et al., 1999).

The system of large orphanages was common in Eastern Europe (Harrison, Rubeiz and Kochubey, 1996; Sloutsky, 1997). Neighboring countries such as Russia, Belarus, Ukraine and Bulgaria had similar systems. Romania gained worldwide notoriety in 1989 when the abhorrent circumstances of institutionalized children were revealed by the media. Images displayed around the world showed children tied to their beds, malnourished, neglected, with their heads shaved, emaciated and listless (Groza, et al., 1999; Johnson and Groze, 1993).

Traditional practices of child welfare, such as child care by the extended family or neighbors, were undermined by the Ceauşescu policy and security police who promoted fear and mistrust (Deletant, 1995). The collectivist model practiced in Romania under Ceauşescu focused on dismantling extended kinship and social networks in an effort to control the population. Strong social and familial networks were viewed as a threat to State control (Kideckel, 1993; Kozinski, 1991; Pacepa, 1990).

During this time family-based services were lacking and the only child welfare intervention considered and provided to children was institutional care (Morrison, 2004). Also, very few domestic adoptions occurred (Groza, 1999a; Tabacaru, 1999). Romanian adoptions were legally initiated at the level of Tutelary (County) Authority offices that were affiliated with the mayor's offices in different districts. The staff of the Tutelary Authority were usually high school graduates with no training in social work or any helping profession. It is important to note that under the Ceausescu regime, schools of social work and psychology were closed because of the view that Communism eliminated serious social problems and, thus, eliminated the need for professional helpers. As a result, largely-untrained public workers were assigned the responsibility of processing adoptions. Their assessments focused primarily on very practical issues such as housing and financial ability to provide for the child's basic needs. The adoptive family was mandated with obtaining a legal document from the birth parents certifying that they agreed to the adoption proceedings. This was a very difficult procedure and required having to locate the birth mother and/or father.

Most adoptions were due to infertility of the adoptive parents. The inability to conceive carried significant cultural stigma and many infertile couples were advised to adopt and keep their adoption secret from their family and community. There were no formal programs designed to assist adoptive families with the long life issues in adoption. The families who adopted children from institutions were unprepared for the many challenges posed by the neglect of institutionalization.

In summary, prior to 1989, changes in the child welfare system could not be pursued, even if there had been interested individuals or organizations, because every attempt at change was interpreted as an attack against the Ceauşescu government. The Revolution of December 1989 revealed for the first time the deplorable state of the child protection system, specifically the institutions for children.

The Opening of Gray and Black Markets in Romania for Adoption

In January 1990, within a few days after the execution of the Nicolae and Elena Ceauşescu, the press was publishing stories about thousands of children in Romania living in horrific institutions (Groze and Ileana, 1996). As a response to the television coverage, families started to arrive in Romania with the intention of adopting the babies they had seen on television. This, at a time of chaos within government services, resulted in legally and logistically ambiguous adoption processes. The legal framework for how to process adoptions of foreign nationals of Romanian children (i.e., intercountry adoption) did not exist.

Initially, kind individuals as well as entrepreneurs stepped forward to help searching adoptive families find children. These facilitators had at least one skill needed in order to facilitate connecting potential adoptive families with children; they were bi-lingual. Within a few months, more and more Western Europeans, North Americas, and Australians traveled to Romania to adopt children. It was commonly known that one major hotel lobby became the rendezvous of seeking parents and Romanian navigators. Although there were individuals with legitimate desire to help families find children, many were motivated by the quick money that was playing a critical role in the number of intercountry adoptions being facilitated. A quid pro quo arrangement was developed that included a specified amount of money for a middleman or facilitator to locate a child, arrange for the family to take temporary custody of the child, navigate the court system, and leave the country with a baby. To further expedite the process and bureaucracy involved in intercountry adoption under the post-communist government, in August 1990, the requirement for presidential approval for adoption was eliminated. As a result, independent (private) adoptions grew exponentially. Between August 1, 1990 and July 17, 1991, about 10,000 Romanian children were sent out of the country for adoption (United Nations Children's Fund [UNICEF], 2007a).

The media fueled the baby buying and selling market that developed in Romania. While initially children were adopted from the horrific institutions, within the first year, the navigators transformed into brokers and some families were selling their children to the highest bidder. Not only were children coming directly from families, but families who had previously placed their children were now taking their children from institutions, so that institutional staff did not get the money involved in providing a child for intercountry adoption; rather the birth family would receive the cash. In some instances, families went to Romania to adopt from an orphanage, only to have adoption from an orphanage closed to them (Greenwell, 2007; Groza, et al., 1999).

By the time Romania closed intercountry adoptions in 1991, as a reaction to the criticism as well as recommendations made by child advocacy groups such as the Defense for Children International, it was clear that a system of unethical adoption practice had developed, some of which could be considered child trafficking (Smolin, 2006). The moratorium on adoptions was meant to allow Parliament to draft appropriate legislation to deal with the problems generated by the adoption system. While the moratorium was expected to last only about six months, it was not until June, 1993 that Romania passed the Judicial Declaration of Child Abandonment (Groza, et al., 1999). The Romanian Committee on Adoption (RAC) was redefined by the Parliament and given a new and clear mandate. A new central registry of children available for adoption was designated, and a procedure for identifying children as abandoned and therefore eligible for adoption was developed. The new legislation strengthened government control over adoptions by making it illegal for parent(s) to select a child to adopt and requiring that all adoptions be processed through adoption agencies approved by RAC.

One positive aspect of the new system was the continued centralization of adoption decisions rather than depending upon individuals at the orphanage and local or district level who might require or demand bribes in order to move cases forward. A second positive aspect was the attempt to have agencies that facilitated adoptions contribute to the development of child welfare in Romania. Alas, this last provision, along with the underfunded and overworked RAC, caused other complications. The establishment of agencies providing services to develop Romania's child welfare system was never implemented; neither adoption agencies or the RAC knew exactly what agencies were supposed to do, so there were many interpretations, but none that led to systematic change. There were also complaints that the RAC was as corrupt as the previous intercountry adoption system.

There were also large gaps in child protection legislation. If birth mothers left the maternity hospital without providing their identity document, their children could be left without their own identity document or birth certificate, leaving them stuck within the system. Typically the abandoned babies would be housed in maternity hospitals; sometimes someone managed to get them the appropriate documentation enabling them to transfer to a different institution and sometimes they remained at the hospital, although not for a medical reason. To get the child processed, the birth mother had to be identified, located, and convinced to complete the necessary forms or to show up in court. In some locales the birth mother had to go to court numerous times to declare that she was, in fact, abandoning her child.

Locating the birth mothers with the scant records that were available brought its own myriad of challenges. It required a great deal of time, skill, resources, and expertise; unfortunately, the RAC had very little of these.

There was also an assumption that directors of maternity hospitals and directors of other child care institutions (e.g., pediatric wards or wards for dystrophic children) would identify and refer children to the RAC. However, institutional budgets were tied to the number of children they served. Therefore, there was limited motivation for institutions to release a child from the institution for placement in adoption if it resulted in decreased funds for the next month. If the referred child was not replaced by a new child, the facility would have a reduction in resources. Thus, there was an incentive not to refer children and to keep children within the walls of the institution.

Eventually, when it became apparent that the RAC would have difficulty fulfilling their mandate to make sure children were clearly abandoned according to the law, they began to rely on international adoption agencies to identify abandoned children, secure the necessary documentation, and obtain the consent to adopt by the birth parents. However, there was supposedly no guarantee that a child referred to the committee would subsequently be referred to the same adoption agency for placement with a foreign adoptive family. The RAC was, by now, very concerned about appearances of impropriety and possible unethical adoption practice. The process then got bogged down with the steady stream of children entering the child welfare system, the general inertia of government agencies, and the lack of training and technical assistance that the RAC members needed to function well. Eventually, a system somewhat akin to points was awarded to each agency that provided technical assistance, training, and funding to develop local child welfare services and programs in Romania (Gaetan, 2005), but it was not always clear how and why points were awarded. However, it was clear that the ability to place Romanian children and the number of children referred to a specific agency for placement in intercountry adoptions were awarded based on points. This new system led to corruption and conflict once again, resulting in international criticism, especially by the European Union (Dickens, 2002). In 2001 adoptions were closed a second and final time, causing great concern and outrage from receiving countries.

Gaetan (2005) asserts that the post-communist government left the previous strict State bureaucracy in place, making it difficult for child welfare reform. Moreover, the EU and the USA were diametrically opposed to each other with respect to the role of intercountry adoption in child welfare development; the EU viewed the moratorium as essential while the USA pushed for the continuation of intercountry adoption. As the decade of the 1990s closed, foreign NGOs were leaving Romania *en masse* (Groza, et al., 1999) and efforts to modernize the child welfare system were largely unsuccessful (Dickens and Groza, 2004).

The impact of child welfare reform that had begun in the mid-1990s began to show signs of success by the early to mid-2000s. Gaetan (2005) suggests there have been three phases in Romanian child welfare reform: the provision of humanitarian assistance (1990-1996), decentralization (1997-2000), and institutional reorganization (2001-2004). At the time of her dissertation, Gaetan (2005) concluded the following:

> There are at least three quantitative indicators of successful reform in Romania's child welfare regime: 1) Fewer children lived in residential childcare institutions in 2004 than in 1990. 2) More abandoned children were cared for in family-like settings in 2004 than in institutional settings. 3) The rate of child abandonment in 2004 was lower than in 1990. In 1990, approximately 150,000 children lived in state-run institutions. In December 2004, the number dropped to 32,679 children protected in state or private institutions (out of a national population of five million minors) and 50,239 children under the age of eighteen were cared for in substitute families, of which 34,405 were living with their extended families and 15,834 were in foster care—a form of child protection that did not exist in 1990. (p. 6-7)

Yet the results she presents are overly positive. While fewer children lived in institutions compared to earlier periods, disabled children still were institutionalized at a very high rate and Romania lagged behind other Eastern European countries in the high rate of institutionalization (UNICEF, 2007a). While more abandoned children entered foster care and the rate was lower than in 1990, maternal abandonment of newborns remained a problem; with almost 5,000 infants being abandoned a year. While there is an obvious connection between poverty and abandonment of children, other Eastern European countries with similar economic conditions as Romania had a lower child abandonment rate (UNICEF, 2007a).

Abandonment in Romania is a remnant of the particular type of communist legacy that encouraged mothers to abandon their children to State care; such ideology is difficult to change. Many families continued to expect the State to take responsibility for children when they themselves were unable and unwilling to do so. Changing a value system and social understanding around abandonment proved more difficult than expected.

A Snapshot of the Child Welfare Innovations in Romania

While child welfare system changes were uneven and developed over a period of time, including many steps backward before moving ahead, there were a number of child welfare innovations that did occur, did positively impact children's lives, and have been documented so that important lessons were learned in the process. These innovations were led by the NGO sector and by public agency-NGO partnerships. A few of those improvements are presented below.

Domestic Adoption

Both authors were involved in the first study of domestic adoptions in Romania (Groza, 1999a). Nongovernmental organizations, such as Holt International

Children's Services (a private, nonprofit agency recognized as a leader in the field of intercountry adoption and permanency planning for children aka Holt), had taken the lead in placing Romanian children in domestic adoptive families. Holt started working in Romania in 1991 with USAID funds to promote deinstitutionalization, promote the role of social work in child welfare, and demonstrate alternative care programs such as foster care and domestic adoption to prevent institutional care. From 1994-1999, about 500 children were placed with domestic Romanian families for adoption through Holt.

In the study, families consistently identified the bureaucracy of adoption as a barrier to their own satisfaction with the adoption (Groza, 1999a). The second biggest issue for families was related to how to discuss adoption with their child and the members of their informal network (family, friends, neighbors). There were no formal support systems in place for adoption and often families felt very alone in their unique situations. It did appear, however, that most of the families received informal support from their extended family. When families mentioned the need for more formal types of support, examples given included financial support, parent education, counseling, and social engagement with other domestic adoptive families.

Results from this first study on domestic adoption outcomes were very positive and adoptions were viewed favorably by the adoptive parents. Most Romanian adoptive families had cherished their children and were committed to the adoption. What the study could not tell was how families and children were doing, especially in cases where the family chose to keep the adoption a secret from the child and other family members. Another limitation of the study was that the data involved families with very young children, as at the time of the study the majority of domestic placements were of infants or toddlers. Results over time and when the children were older were not reported in this study.

Data from Romania's publicly available database on children (www.copii.ro) were used to obtain the number of adoptions from 2000-2008 (the latest data available) and the rate of adoption (number of adoptions/number of children in out of home care). As presented in Table 7.1, the rate of domestic adoption did not change over this time period.

Groza, Muntean and Ungureanu (2012) conducted a mixed methods study in 2009 of 62 adoptees living with two parent families (62 percent, n=18) and 38 percent (n=11) with single parent families. Overall, children and families are doing well in adoption, perhaps without great support from the community. Most of the children came from institutional care before adoption and appear to be doing as well as children who were adopted from foster care. The majority of children (58 percent) are securely attached. The adoptive families have strong parent-child ties and the children are developing well. The stigma against having a child without being married does not seem to carry over to the families who adopt and disclose the adoption.

Yet the domestic adoption program is not strong. More effort needs to be made to develop and improve the domestic adoption program.

Table 7.1 Rates of Domestic Adoption in Romania, 2000-2008

Year	Number of children in out of home care	Number of Domestic Adoptions	Rate of Domestic Adoptions
2000	56,804	1,291	.023
2001	53,792	1,271	.024
2002	54,169	1,346	.025
2003	51,495	1,383	.027
2004	48,807	1,422	.029
2005	45,999	1,136	.025
2006	45,676	1,421	.031
2007	45,308	1,294	.029
2008	45,609	1,300	.029

Note: Table was obtained from manuscript under review by Groza, Muntean, Tomita and Ungureanu.

Foster Care

Foster care has grown tremendously as an alternative to institutionalization. Foster family care, like domestic adoption, was first implemented by nongovernmental agencies. The growth of foster care had the direct effect of decreasing the number of children in institutions, as is presented in Table 7.2 (courtesy of Groza, Muntean and Ungureanu (2012). The data-bank does not have complete information but has the best information available about the status of children in Romania.

The children placed in foster care were triaged. First, infants and toddlers were placed in foster care. Then, older children were placed. Finally, children with disabilities and children with HIV were placed.

Foster parents were paid a salary and their time fostering counted toward their pension. Foster parents had to participate in monthly meetings and had many of the same obligations as foster parents in Western Europe and North America. The model that Romania chose for fostering was long term fostering as practiced in most of Western Europe.

Families were recruited to foster through the public agency. A public agency social worker completed a home study and then decided whether the family was appropriate to be licensed as a foster family. The license was issued for a three-year period and could be renewed. Social workers were obligated to visit foster families on a monthly basis. However, this had been quite challenging. Families were located in geographically dispersed areas and the time and resources needed to visit them was limited. Another challenge facing the foster care program initially was that there were more families licensed than there were children to be placed because of shortages in funding to pay the families.

The criteria for families to be licensed included the following: (a) a foster parent could not be older than 55 years of age, (b) a foster parent must have another

Table 7.2 Number of Romanian Children in Institutional and Foster Care, 1998-2008

Year	Number of Children in Institutional Care	Number of Children in Foster Care
1998		479
1999		3,058
2000	51,647	5,157
2001	45,422	8,370
2002	43,234	10,935
2003	37,870	13,625
2004	32,973	15,834
2005	28,786	17,213
2006	26,105	19,571
2007	25,114	20,194
2008	24,427	20,642

source of income, (c) a foster parent must have suitable living arrangements, and (d) a foster parent must be willing to participate in visitation and foster parent group meetings. Foster families earned salaries each month, similar to the wage of the lowest paid social workers. In addition, they are given two supplementary child allowances per child and received some food (rice, flour, sugar) each month.

Matching a specific child with a specific family was the responsibility of the public agency social worker. The foster parent's attitude was an important factor in child placement. Rejecting a child because of his or her skin color, ethnic or racial background, or religion was not allowed. After the presentation of the individual child and his or her situation to the foster parent by the social worker, a face-to-face meeting between foster parent and child was held. At that meeting the social worker provided more details about the child and his or her needs. The foster parent visited the child one or more times (depending on the distance of the foster family to the institution) at the institution (most institutions have a specific location where visitations take place). After the visits the child moved to the home of the foster parent and the protocol was for a social worker to visit within the first 30 days.

All foster families enjoyed talking about their children and could easily identify strengths in their children. Most of the children were reaching appropriate developmental milestones and had no serious health problems, sensory difficulties, or attachment issues. Most Romanian foster families have positive attitudes about their children and are committed to fostering their children until they reach majority age.

What was not known was how the experience in this county was similar to other regions. This county had strong public-private partnerships and a young professional work force that had completed university degrees in social work or psychology. Also, like the adoption study (Groza, 1999a), this was a cross-sectional study involving foster families early in the process of promoting foster care. Unlike the adoption study, the children in foster care ranged in age and included children with significant disabilities. These limits and strengths must be kept in mind.

One problem in foster care is that it is reaching a crisis; there are now too few foster parents for the children needing family placement. In spring 2011, Romanian Children's Relief reported a situation similar to that which occurred over 20 years ago. More infants and toddlers are being left in maternity and pediatric hospitals, even though they are medically ready for discharge. Romania has not increased the budget for foster care, essentially capping the program, at the same time that abandonment prevention programs, domestic adoption, and family reunification programs are underdeveloped.

Child Welfare in Romania in the New Millennium

Romanian child protection has progressed well towards European standards despite the initial negative predictions that Romania could not improve the situation of the most at-risk children (Jacoby, Lataianu and Lataianu, 2009). There were several phases of policy change that resulted in the creation of a new system of child welfare, similar to the phases proposed by Gaetan (2005) but with somewhat different elements.

In the first phase, 1989-1996, domestic professional work forces and institutional capacity were weak and many Romanians were hesitant to embrace change. The international pressures to change the child welfare system were met with resistance and the changes that did take place were minimal and disorganized. There were some exceptions; regional model projects were implemented by NGOs but were too limited to have the impact Romania needed. The second phrase, 1997-2001, was highlighted by increased pressures for integration in the European Union and a committed response from Romanian authorities, the donor community, and even practitioners to create legal changes to expand capacity to deal with abandoned children. The Romanian capacity for child welfare system development was improved but intercountry adoptions were extremely problematic with corruption and scandals. A third stage of policy change emerged after 2001; the domestic capacity increased in new areas like foster care and domestic adoption, at the same time that intercountry adoptions ceased. This third phase of reform marked the dismantling of the old institutional system and its replacement with a new modern child welfare system in accordance with EU standards, although specific populations of children such as disabled children have not benefited so much from the changes.

Those initiatives were accompanied by substantial aid aimed to decrease the number of institutionalized children, assist families at risk of abandoning their children, and the development of foster family care. The EU also supported Romanian public awareness campaigns about children in need. Domestic adoptions and alternative services to assist families in need were presented more in the media. The post 2001 reforms consolidated institutional capacity and active steps were taken to prevent abandonment, close or transform the old-style orphanages, develop family-like child care protection and increase domestic adoptions.

In pursuing child welfare reform, Romanian laws and policies set in motion an active policy of de-institutionalization by prohibiting the use of residential institutions for very young children. With the exception of a child with severe disabilities, no child under the age of two years could be placed in an institution. For older children, priority was given to reintegration of into the birth family or extended family over the use of institutional care. The new law focused on a continuum of care options with the extended family taking precedence over foster care and foster care taking precedence over institutional care.

The new legislation has provisions for the social inclusion of children with disabilities and underlines the right of the disabled child to education, rehabilitation, and integration. The local and central administrations are responsible for developing new programs and services aiming at the needs of disabled children and their families.

After years of criticism, the EU recognized the Romanian authorities' efforts to give vulnerable children, especially children without parental care, priority and even suggested that Romania could play a leadership role with other former communist countries in child protection (Jacoby et al., 2009). In the most recent period, the proportion of institutionalized children under the age of three years who remained in placement for more than three months showed that Belgium had almost double the rate of Romania and that Romania had only slightly more than either Finland or France (Jacoby et al., 2009).

On January 1st, 2007, Romania became a member of the European Union. Two years previously it had implemented new child protection and adoption legislation. According to Bainham (2003), USA reactions to the passage of these laws have focused largely on a single issue: the prohibition of intercountry adoptions from Romania. The USA media have reported extensively on the issue; the most common assertion was that the effect of the new laws would be to trap abandoned Romanian children in institutions.

Despite its numerous struggles in an environment were EU officials and academics were highly skeptical, a new system has emerged in Romania. There is more acceptance of foster care and domestic adoption, social work has been established at the universities, a new job classification for professional social workers has been established, and there has been a tremendous growth in the nonprofit/nongovernmental sector. This is remarkable, especially considering the major shifts in ideology that were required of the Romanian public.

Conclusion

Despite the initial grim predictions and its dire starting point, the Romanian Child Welfare system has developed and is now functioning at the level similar to other European child protection systems. A remarkable aspect of this success was the willingness of Romanian authorities to try new approaches and make mistakes, with the overall goal of creating a child welfare system that protected vulnerable children.

Romania struggled with having to dismantle an infrastructure of institutions. Throughout this process, there were stages of legal chaos that allowed human trafficking to take place, severe criticism from international child protection entities, and an internal struggle for cultural change. Romania has developed a vibrant network of young social work professionals, many with graduate degrees, who are competent and enthusiastic about program development and service delivery, consistent with European standards. Yet, this enthusiasm must be tempered with the continued problems: capitation of foster care, lack of growth in domestic adoption, and the failure to develop community based services such as family preservation and family reunification (Cojocaru, 2008b). Tremendous change has been achieved, but tremendous changes are still needed.

Chapter 8

Challenging the Discourse of Intercountry Adoption: Perspectives from Rural China

Kay Johnson

This chapter presents the challenge that my fieldwork on Chinese birth families and domestic Chinese adoptive families (Johnson, 2004)[1] poses to two closely related adoption discourses that have dominated North American thinking on these topics. One is the discourse of international China adoption—a discourse that attempts to explain the rise of China as the major sending country in the world today, focusing on traditional Chinese culture and its persistence in the context of government policies to control population growth. The basic outline of this discourse can be found in a wide range of venues—on adoption agency websites, popular news media and magazine articles, websites for adoptive parents dedicated to the discussion of China adoption, articles and books on China adoption, and scholarship on closely related topics. A second related discourse that my field studies challenge is the dominant critique of intercountry adoption (ICA) that has recently emerged out of five decades of ICA, a critique that alerts us to systemic problems of trafficking and corruption in the practices of ICA.

The perspectives and experiences of Chinese birth parents and Chinese adoptive parents who I have talked to over the last 15 years of research in rural Central South China resonate with some aspects of these two discourses, but fundamentally challenge some of the basic tenets of both narratives. The perspectives from the ground in China suggest a re-evaluation of our understanding of the rise of China as a sending country and of the ethics of intercountry adoption from China, past, present and future.

The Discourse of Intercountry China Adoption

China has been a dominant force in ICA as a sending country for over fifteen years. Shortly after the Chinese government began to allow foreign adoptions in

1 Thirteen years of research and fieldwork, including hundreds of interviews with Chinese families involved in child abandonment and domestic adoption is reported in Johnson (2004) especially Chapter 4, based on research done with Huang Banghan and Wang Liyao. In 2009/2010 I returned to the same areas to continue to interview and follow up on this research.

the early 1990s,[2] China rapidly became a major supplier of children to international adopters in wealthy countries. Since 1994 China has been among the top three 'sending countries' and from 2000 to 2011 it has been the world's number one source of intercountry adoptees in all but one year. In 2005, the peak year of ICA from China and near peak for all ICA, China contributed 14,000 of the 44,000 children adopted internationally, and 8,000 of the roughly 22,700 intercountry adoptions to the USA. Why and how did China become the major supplier of adoptable children for the world's receiving countries, primarily North America and Western Europe?

Traditional Chinese Culture and the Rise of China as a Sending Country

The standard discourse of intercountry adoption from China explains that healthy infant girls, the most desirable object in ICA, became available in large numbers in the 1990s because of the clash between an ancient patriarchal Chinese culture and the government's effort to control runaway population growth through a set of policies commonly referred to as the 'One Child Policy.' Less than 40 percent of the country's population falls under a strict 'one child policy,' primarily those who live in urban areas (Ebenstein, 2010). Most rural areas allow a second birth four or five years after the birth of a daughter, known as a '1.5 child policy'; a few rural and minority areas allow two, and sometimes more, widely-spaced births, regardless of the gender of the first child. Under these restrictive birth policies, according to the dominant narrative, peasants' strong desire for sons as heirs and family labor led traditional-minded rural Chinese families to jettison girls in droves.

Thus, all agreed that at the heart of female infant abandonment was profound gender discrimination, the result of thousands of years of tradition that simply could not be changed quickly. United States adopters even became familiar with traditional Chinese sayings such as "girls are the maggots in the rice" and "daughters are goods on which one loses." A deep cultural disdain for girls is a central theme in many books about China adoption aimed at the adoption community (Dorow, 2006b; Hopgood, 2009; Xinran, 2010). The message is clear: as a traditional culture and people, Chinese 'do not like girls.' They—at least the most backward, traditional segment of the rural population that has been the primary source of abandoned girls—do not value daughters.

The fact that many adoptive parents, as well as Chinese officials, see this policy as 'necessary' to save China from the catastrophic consequences of a dire population crisis reinforces the tendency to put it aside as a culprit in causing widespread female infant abandonment. The abandoned children are, unavoidably, collateral damage because of the difficulty of quickly changing embedded Chinese culture in the face of a population crisis. That international adopters can help deal

2 Small numbers of ICA occurred before the early 1990s but under guidelines that restricted adoption only to those of Chinese heritage or with a "special relationship" to China.

with this collateral damage, while also gaining the children they seek, seems like a moral good, a win-win solution for China, for the adopters, and for the children.

United States and Chinese scholars explain skewed sex ratios, abandonment of daughters, and female infanticide in terms of Chinese culture. With its disdain for daughters as the major culprit, Chinese culture will require persistent, long-term efforts to alter. Indeed most demographers explain the skewed sex ratios by simple reference to 'traditional son preference' and the widespread availability of prenatal sex selection technology. While few dismiss the government's 'one child policy' as a factor, most point to the skewed sex ratios in Korea and India, two other highly patriarchal Asian societies that have no such policy, as evidence that culture, not policy, is the key explanatory factor.

Yet, an emphasis on a nearly static, unchanging traditional culture as primary culprit removes from center stage the role and power of the state in producing the pool of adoptable female children available for intercountry adoption. The massive coercion that has characterized this policy over most of the last thirty years becomes less visible as state policy is effectively moved to the wings of this story.[3]

The Creation of an Intercountry Adoption Pool through Political Coercion

No one doing research on the topic of abandonment and adoption, including myself, would seek to deny that girls are disadvantaged in various ways compared to boys, suffer discrimination in a variety of venues, and are not so central to the strength and survival of the family in the minds of many if not most rural parents. Persistent patrilocal patterns of marriage and family formation require that daughters, but not sons, transfer their obligations, as well as residence, from parents to in-laws at marriage, making a son the basis of his parents' social security in old age. But neither attitudes toward daughters nor the need for a son are static features of rural Chinese culture; contemporary attitudes, perceived needs, and family behavior have been heavily influenced by government policies. Indeed, not merely a persistent cultural hangover from the past, the need for a son escalated in the 1980s and 1990s when economic policies dissolved the agricultural collectives that provided cooperative health care and minimal welfare protections for the sonless destitute (Ebenstein and Leung, 2010).

Ironically and cruelly, this collapse occurred just at the time that the 'One Child Policy' was sweeping in like a tornado, or as one local account put it, "hit the village like a bombshell" (Huang, 1989, p. 176). Our fieldwork suggests that in

3 In Chinese versions of this discourse—official, popular, and scholarly—it is virtually invisible (China's Sex ratio at birth). A recent example of the invisibility of birth planning policy in abandonment stories is an article on the reuniting of an internationally adopted teen and her birth family that appeared in *Beijing Review* in August 2010. Although the birth parents told the adoptive family that they abandoned the second born girl due to birth planning pressures so they could try again for a son, the story in *Beijing Review* said merely that "their living circumstances were difficult" at the time (Liu Y.).

the 1990s when rural families were without any source of security other than a son, their higher partiy daughters were put at risk of abandonment during birth planning campaigns. The highly coercive campaigns threatened to strip these families of their ability to survive unless they made a "choice" to jettison a child in order to have another. Ironically, much evidence suggests that the value of daughters was actually increasing in many areas of the countryside during this time, even as female abandonment escalated in response to birth planning campaigns (Greenhalgh and Li, 1995). In parent narratives about abandonment and adoption, we saw both sides of this painful, complicated confluence of changing attitudes, felt needs, and coerced choices (Johnson, 2004).

For over 15 years, the stories we have heard from birth parents who hide, surreptitiously adopt-out, or abandon their children invariably begin and end with the coercive pressures of birth planning, the need to hide births and children in order to avoid economically ruinous fines (two to five times annual income), loss of jobs, destruction of homes, forced abortion and, perhaps the worst fear, forced sterilization if the birth of an overquota child is discovered. A recent account from a villager in Jiangxi (Birth Planning Methods, 2009) described the behavior of local birth planners who launched an attack against his home, tearing out the windows and physically threatening his family because they had refused to be sterilized; he described the birth planning officials as "barbarians," morally equivalent to "9/11 terrorists." Another mother told us recently that her and her husband's family would have "ceased to exist in this village" if her hidden overquota daughter was discovered. Without the backdrop of coercion and fear, the difficult choices made to abandon or try to surreptitiously adopt-out a second or third born daughter would never have been made according to the narratives of the parents we have interviewed. Wanting a son would not require getting rid of a daughter were it not for the pressures of birth planning.

"Traditional Son Preference" vs. "A Son and a Daughter Make a Family Complete"

Furthermore, the choice to abandon or send a daughter out of the family was rarely taken unless the family was sonless and already had one or more daughters. Hence 'son preference' must be contextualized as arising primarily when a daughter is already present. In rural central and south China, where parents are allowed to have a second birth if the first child is a girl, parents do not clearly prefer a son unless they already have a daughter, at which point 'son preference' may escalate quickly to an urgent need. Sex ratios in these areas are near normal for first births (Hesketh and Zhu, 2006). Thus, out of over three hundred cases of families we found who abandoned or adopted-out healthy daughters, only a bare handful gave up a first-born daughter; and only one parent said "we don't like girls" to explain why an infant daughter was abandoned. Having at least one daughter was usually a precondition, indeed a necessary cause, for the pursuit of a son at the expense of giving up an additional daughter.

Furthermore, sonless couples' decision to send away a higher-parity daughter occurred only in the context of coercive birth planning. When campaigns waned, as they sometimes did in the 1990s, people who had abandoned a daughter at the height of the last campaign often kept the next overquota daughter because they could get away with doing so during a relaxed period, without being heavily fined and forcibly sterilized. Few people wanted to abandon or send away their daughters, no matter how many they had. On the other hand few sonless couples were willing to be caught and sterilized until they had a son.

We found again and again that families universally wanted a daughter, even if they felt strongly that they needed a son for social security in old age. So while the felt need for a son under coercive state-imposed birth planning could drive people to make choices they would not otherwise make, a desire for daughters also existed alongside the felt need for sons. The near universal hope in the area of our research was for both a son and a daughter, expressed in the common saying, "A son and a daughter make a family complete" (儿女双全). Indeed in some interviews people said a daughter was preferred as a first birth because it allowed for a second legal birth and put the ideal of one son and one daughter within reach without having to risk fines or penalties. Because of the importance of insuring that the second birth was a son, at least some people managed to use ultrasound for prenatal sex selection, skewing sex ratios for second and higher births among those whose first child is a girl (Chu 2001a; Hesketh and Zhu, 2006). But in families with a son and no daughters, one could predict a strong daughter preference' for any additional birth. Recent analysis demonstrates that this 'daughter preference' even shows up statistically among higher parity births to mothers who have one or more sons and no daughters, although it is not as clear as 'son preference' after the birth of daughters (Ebenstein, 2010). Parents we interviewed who succeeded in birthing a girl after having a son almost invariably said to us that the resulting fine, and sometimes forced sterilization, "was worth it." As one proud rural father spontaneously offered as we talked to his wife holding their four-year-old overquota daughter, "'A son and a daughter make a family complete' is part of Chinese culture! We are happy for this daughter no matter the penalty." This view of 'traditional Chinese culture' showed the popular shift toward valuing daughters while still wanting one son. The older saying "more sons, more prosperity" (多子多福) was never heard except to say such sentiment no longer existed.

In short, the static, monolithic, hegemonic view of Chinese culture found in the discourse of China adoption distorts and oversimplifies this much more complex picture of 'Chinese culture,' abandonment, and attitudes toward gender drawn from our fieldwork in central south rural China, the heartland of intercountry adoption from China throughout the 1990s and early 2000s.

Chinese Adopters: In Adoption Discourse and in Reality

The emphasis on Chinese culture and its alleged ancient disdain for girls also cannot readily explain a parallel phenomenon that we found widespread in the countryside in the 1990s and early 2000s, namely, the growing desire among those who already had sons to adopt daughters, as well as a willingness to adopt girls among those who were childless. Demographic analyses showed that domestic adoption, mostly *de facto* (i.e., unregistered, informal, customary), was common and began increasing in the 1980s and early 1990s, disproportionately involving girls (Johansson and Nygren, 1991); most adopted children in our sample of over 1,000 domestic adoptive families gathered in the late 1990s and early 2000s were girls, the majority abandoned girls of unknown parentage (Johnson, 2004). While the felt need for a son for social security and family survival was a factor shaping female infant abandonment of second, third or fourth daughters in sonless families, a dynamic popular culture of customary adoption along with a growing desire for daughters provided a ready-made counter-balance to female infant abandonment.

The very existence of hundreds of thousands of Chinese adopters in the 1990s flies in the face of the standard discourse of China adoption. The absence of Chinese adopters serves two functions in this discourse. Most importantly it justifies and confirms the need for ICA adoption to save China's abandoned girls. More subtly it bolsters familiar images of a Chinese cultural other that provides a contrasting backdrop against which intercountry adopters may see and define themselves as legitimate parents of Chinese girls. The power of these images of Chinese as son-seeking non-adopters derives from their congruence with longstanding images of China and Chinese in U.S. popular culture.

Thus alongside the jettisoning of girls from son-seeking birth families, the discourse of adoption from China asserts that blood ties, especially through male bloodlines, are crucial to Confucian traditions and to Chinese families. Hence adoption outside close male bloodlines is frowned on by Chinese culture, in sharp contrast to the progressive liberal attitudes toward adoption and gender held by North Americans and Europeans who readily welcome Chinese girls into their families as their own daughters. This construction highlights U.S. adopters as liberal and progressive, non-racist and committed to gender equality, while masking or muting the hierarchy of race and authority implicit in the White parent/Chinese child family. Such contrasting images of Chinese and Americans (traditional versus modern, backward versus progressive, authoritarian versus democratic, familistic versus individualistic, hierarchical/patriarchal versus egalitarian, etc.) can be found in American popular culture and sinology since the nineteenth century, so the belief that they 'are not like us' comes easily to U.S. adopters (Klein, 2003; Said, 1979; Zhang Longxi, 1999). Above all, the presumed unwillingness among Chinese to adopt, especially unrelated girls abandoned by strangers, made it clear that there was no other solution but intercountry adoption to provide homes for large numbers of Chinese girls discarded by their birth families.

The urgency of this situation was brought to public attention in the mid-1990s by a shocking British documentary called *The Dying Rooms: China's Darkest Secret* that portrayed the horrifying conditions of these discarded girls living in over-crowded, underfunded, poorly-staffed orphanages where care ranged from indifferent to cruel and intentionally fatal.[4] The message was that, due to a misogynist culture and indifferent rulers, China was a place where people "threw away baby girls like kittens in a bag." It was clear to Americans that there were large numbers of unwanted girls in China who urgently needed homes and parents who would love them. In this way, a whole generation of international adopters were primed to see China as a 'win-win' situation for intercountry adoption, through which unwanted baby girls, the most highly sought-after child in ICA, could find well-off parents who desperately wanted children to raise 'as their own.'

These features of the adoption discourse are well illustrated in a July 4, 2003 *Boston Globe* op-ed piece by Ellen Goodman (2003), grandmother to a baby girl adopted from China. In "Cloe's First Fourth," Goodman waxes eloquent about the new country and new family that has embraced this young child discarded by her Chinese parents and her country, a child who had no future but an orphanage in the land of her birth due simply to her gender:

> Cloe, this little girl with shiny black hair and a quiet, curious stare, has come to America and to us. We have embraced her with a loyalty that is all the more tenacious for having not been preordained by biology. We have the sort of attachment that the word "adoption" cannot begin to describe. (Goodman, 2003, p. A13).

Through adoption to the USA, the "entire arc of her short life had gone from being abandoned to being treasured," (Goodman, 2003, p. A13) as she joined the American birthday party as its latest newcomer.

Yet the notion that abandoned girls like Cloe had no future in China except an orphanage was very far from the truth that we saw on the ground. No doubt Cloe was "treasured" by her American family, but the arc from "being abandoned to being treasured" might have been traversed within the same village or county in China. Customary adoption took place in the shadows outside of government channels, but was nonetheless widespread throughout the countryside despite government efforts to suppress the practice. Cloe, in fact, was among a minority of abandoned baby girls who landed in orphanages. There is no doubt that the local, spontaneous adoption of girls increased in the 1990s, absorbing many of the increasing numbers of available healthy female babies resulting from birth planning pressures.

Our research (Johnson, 2004) as well as the research of Weiguo Zhang (2006) confirms the increased popularity of daughter adoption throughout this period. So why, then, were thousands of abandoned baby girls still flooding into the orphanages in the early 1990s if local Chinese were willing to adopt them?

---

4 In many parts of China there is a long history of customary adoption among friends, relatives and strangers, taking various forms and serving a variety of purposes at different times. (Lee and Wang 2001).

The Suppression of Domestic Adoption in the Rise of Intercountry Adoption

A crucial unseen piece of the picture of rising female abandonment in the 1990s, and the overcrowding of orphanages, was the active suppression of domestic adoption as part of the birth-planning regime. The failure of customary local adoption to absorb all of the abandoned babies, was, like abandonment itself, a result of government population policy, not Chinese culture or tradition. The purpose of the National Adoption Law of 1991 was to control and suppress domestic adoption to prevent it from interfering with birth planning efforts. The Law made it illegal to adopt any child other than a disabled child or true orphan (parents deceased), unless one was over 35 and childless. Few in our sample of over 1,000 families fit this profile; if childless they were too young, if over 35 they were not childless at the time of adoption. With these restrictions, the one-child adoption law aimed precisely at eliminating most local adoption practices, practices that had been quickly mobilized as a way to hide and circulate overquota, out-of-plan children when villages came under attack by birth planning campaigns.

Thus, a central component of enforcing the one child policy was the active suppression of domestic adoption, a policy likely to increase abandonment further, while discouraging local people from providing new families. This included especially tight restrictions on the adoption of abandoned children, or 'found children' (*jiande*), most of whom were presumed to have been born of out-of-plan and to have living parents. Birth planning penalties were often meted out to those who adopted these children in violation of the restrictions. Sometimes the adopted child was seized and put in an institution.

This active suppression failed to stop local *de facto* and customary adoptions, but it probably prevented adoption from growing as much as it otherwise would have. Local adoption also went underground, creating many tens of thousands of unregistered "hei haizi," or "black children" who lacked official existence, a legal family status, and basic citizenship. It also opened an unregulated space for various forms of adoption facilitation and organized child trafficking, a problem that became more serious in the 2000s as the ready supply of children available for adoption declined. Finally, adoption policy kept most domestic adopters from adopting from state institutions because of the strict legal requirements, even as these became overcrowded.

In effect, the government sought to channel abandoned children out of the hands of domestic adopters into the hands of the government. As a result tens of thousands of abandoned children (out of hundreds of thousands) ended up in state institutions as waves of vicious birth planning campaigns, armed with a law suppressing most popular adoption practices, descended on rural areas in the 1990s.

Intercountry adoption from China, far from being necessitated by traditional Chinese culture, a disdain for girls, and a presumed lack of Chinese adoption traditions, was promoted precisely at a time the government, in an effort to bolster birth planning restrictions, was seeking to suppress local domestic adoption. The government viewed local informal adoption as a means of hiding out-of-plan, healthy infant girls. Of course, legally qualified domestic adoption from orphanages was still allowed, but the domestic pool of legal adopters was unnecessarily small by design. Because of the stranglehold of birth planning on adoption policy, intercountry adoption in the 1990s would be one of the few routes out of a state institution for a child unlucky enough to have landed there. ICA, perhaps more importantly, also provided an additional source of funding for overburdened and underfunded institutions that were suddenly saddled with the task of caring for disabled and homeless children. This created a significant financial incentive for the institutions that participated in the program, an incentive that could potentially fuel efforts to find healthy babies, perhaps 'baby trafficking,' if and when the supply of adoptable children declined, as it finally did in the early 2000s. Thus, when the adoption law was revised in 1999 to enlarge the domestic pool of adopters by lowering the legal age of adoption to 30,[5] many orphanages shunned legally qualified domestic adopters in favor of intercountry adopters, adding yet another obstacle to domestic adoption (Johnson, 2002).

China and the Critique of Intercountry Adoption

Our fieldwork among birth parents and Chinese adopters also presents a challenge to the main critics of intercountry adoption today, not because of what they include but for what they miss in their critique.

After several decades of rising numbers of ICAs throughout the world, peaking at over 45,000 in 2004 (Selman, 2009d), the system and practices of intercountry adoption and the happy win-win characterization of the practice have come under attack primarily due to problems of corruption and child trafficking that easily emerge in the context of massive structural inequalities that allow the rich to exploit the poor. These are the concerns that frame the Hague Convention efforts to regulate ICA, ensuring that "international adoption serves the best interests of the child" and "prevent(s) the abduction, sale of or traffic in children." Until very recently China has been exempted from criticism within the terms of this discourse, set aside as one of the few international adoption programs that is ethical by the standards considered most important by critics and by those enshrined in the Hague Convention. Reports of baby-buying and trafficking by certain welfare institutions in 2006 finally raised some concerns, but these concerns have not been widespread, nor do they look beyond the issue of trafficking and profiteering.

The Dominant Critique of Intercountry Adoption: Trafficking and Corruption

A recent articulation of these concerns appeared in an article in *Foreign Policy* by E.J. Graff titled "The Lie We Love" (2008). Graff lays out a fundamental

5 Johannsen estimates there were 300,000 to 400,000 adoptions per year in the late 1980s.

critique of ICA as a far-flung business propelled by the high demand for children among couples in rich countries, backed by money and intense emotions. With prospective parents willing to spend large sums of money to adopt infants and young children, Graff states "adoption agencies work not to find homes for needy children but to find children for Western homes." This in turn creates a pool of adoptable children in poorer countries who can enter international adoption through various forms of corruption, solicitation, and child trafficking. In the words of David Smolin (2005, 2007a), another prominent critic, these children are "laundered" through the adoption system, passing through orphanages, NGOs and lawyers that certify them as 'orphans' legally eligible for adoption. Graff argues that although UNICEF says there are millions of 'orphans' in the world, 95 percent of these are over five and most live with relatives. Few are the healthy infants or younger children that are in high demand by intercountry adopters. The pool of such desirable children is built directly and indirectly by the huge sums of money that change hands in the process of intercountry adoption. As Graff asserts, "... remove cash from the adoption chain and, outside of China, the number of healthy babies needing Western homes all but disappears."

Graff explains that China is excluded from this problem because it has a large number of "truly abandoned" institutionalized children in need of families due to the one child policy and traditional son preference; thus the China program has been able to proceed free of trafficking and corruption. Smolin (2005; 2007a) similarly exempts China from charges of widespread "child laundering" to create legally adoptable children.

Thus, even critics of intercountry adoption have found China's international program to be an ethical one for both children and adopters exempting China from the major criticisms leveled at most other intercountry adoption programs. For both Graff and Smolin, a pool of children created by the 'One Child Policy,' interacting with traditional Chinese culture, is acceptable by international standards. Their blindness or indifference to the role of political coercion in separating children from birth families is perhaps due in part to the aforementioned widespread belief that drastic population control has been necessary to save China from famine and ecological collapse, as well as the fact that the policy is part of the legal regime of the state. The allegedly large role played by difficult-to-change Chinese cultural beliefs in the creation of adoptable children also takes the onus off policy makers for creating this problem, implicating instead a set of stubborn popular attitudes, especially prevalent in "traditional" rural areas, that the government itself has long opposed and tried to reform.

Concerns about Child Trafficking and Corruption in China's Adoption Program

In recent years, those following the money trail and looking at practices that lay behind the 'manufacturing' of adoptable children do not so quickly exempt China from charges of unethical adoption practices (Goodman, 2006; Stuy, 2006). The case that first caught attention occurred in late 2005, around the time China ratified the Hague Convention. Orphanage directors in Hunan Province were put on trial, along with a private ring of child traffickers, for the crime of buying and selling children to institutions that did intercountry adoptions, adoptions that drew in a mandatory $3000 donation from each international adopter. The children, presumably abandoned or surreptitiously given up by birth parents, had been trafficked from neighboring Guangdong. According to court records, between the early 2000s and 2005, the traffickers received ever-escalating 'finders' fees' from the institutions for securing the children. No evidence of kidnapping was brought forward, although lawyers for the prosecution claimed that at least a few children may have been abducted.[6] The accused insisted that they were getting the children into government hands where they would enter into legal adoption channels rather than into illegal *de facto* domestic adoptions.

Nonetheless, such highly organized, profit-driven practices were declared by the Hunan court to constitute illegal child trafficking. One institution director and nine traffickers were found guilty of "buying and selling children" and sent to prison for sentences ranging from one to 15 years. Over a dozen Hunan orphanages were implicated. Further, it appeared that many more Chinese institutions than those on trial were paying 'finders' fees, a practice that was widely considered acceptable when it involved small amounts to reimburse expenses or provide small compensation for the trouble. But as abandoned children grew scarcer, as happened in the early 2000s in Hunan, while ICA was increasing, the fees had grown larger to provide a monetary incentive to finders. The publicity that surrounded this case tainted the Chinese adoption program, a program once assumed to be clean, predictable, and free of corruption (Stuy, 2010).

Around the same time as the Hunan verdicts were announced, there was a report in a Chinese newspaper about village officials who seized 11 unregistered, hidden 'black children' from their parents, presumably all 'found children' adopted in violation of birth planning and adoption regulations (United in grief farmers lament loss of children 'stolen' by officials, 2006). It was reported that some of the seized children were over quota children being "hidden" by birth parents as "found" children in an effort to hide an overquota birth. The children were to be held until the parents paid huge fines, equivalent to birth planning fines, to get their children back; understandably the parents called this "ransom." At least a few of these children were sent to the nearby Shaoyang orphanage and adopted by others before their parents could pay the fines.

This story of direct government coercion in taking children from parents in the name of birth planning regulations drew little international attention or concern compared to the Hunan story of corruption and trafficking involving the sale of children for profit. Not until another case, published in 2009, linked local birth planning officials' seizures of over-quota children to a plan to "sell them into international adoption" through a state orphanage in Zhenyuan, Guizhou Province,

6 On the heels of *The Dying Rooms*, Human Rights Watch Asia (1996) published a similarly devastating and even more extreme critique of Chinese orphanages.

was the problem of political coercion in the name of birth planning added to concerns about child trafficking in the China adoption program. Several months later the Zhenyuan story was picked up by the *L.A. Times* and disseminated widely in the international China adoption community (Demick 2009, Groves 2009). Even so, this was a story not primarily about excessive government coercion on behalf of birth planning but about illegally trafficking children into intercountry adoption for profit, as if birth planning had become merely a ruse for trafficking children.

As Smolin and Graff stress, 'money is the root of all evil' in intercountry adoption and, with the power of a dominant discourse, all evils tend to be fit into this paradigm, this 'regime of truth.' The exercise of governmental biopower to regulate reproduction and control population growth, however coercively, is left invisible by this 'regime of truth' and thereby implicitly legitimized in the adoption process, as long as it remains in the realm of political power used to enforce a policy or discipline a population and is not aimed at trafficking for profit.

Abandonment vs. Trafficking: Contrasting Perspectives of Intercountry Adopters and Birth Parents

In the wake of the news stories on trafficking related to China adoption, international adoptive parents became alarmed that their child might have been trafficked into the institution and that the 'finding papers' may have been intentionally fabricated. The 1990s were, in contrast, seen as 'the good old days' of China adoption when large numbers of children were 'truly and legitimately abandoned' and infant girls really needed to be saved from overcrowded institutions. There was no 'supply problem' in those days and hence no trafficking. However in recent years, international adoptive parents have begun to worry that they might have inadvertently adopted a 'trafficked child', for whom money had been paid in order to get her into the adoption system (Groves, 2009).

If the parents secretly hand a child over to a 'finder' to be taken to an institution or to an adopter and money changes hands in the process (e.g., the "finder"receives payment from the orphanage or adopter), is that morally worse or more troubling than when a child enters the institution as the victim of a desperate and potentially life-threatening act of outright abandonment on the side of a road?

From the perspective of a birth parent, the answer is almost certainly "no." I venture that few parents with whom I have spoken would prefer to place a baby unprotected in a public place instead of handing her directly to a person who could safely pass her to an institution or an adopter. In my interviews, I have found that the pain of outright abandonment casts a long shadow, far longer than the act of secretly adopting-out a child or surreptitiously carrying out a successful 'adoption plan' by placing a child on the doorstep of a family that will adopt her. The pain of outright abandonment was illustrated well by a birth mother we interviewed many years ago whom I saw again in 2010. She had abandoned a second newborn daughter in 1993, the 'heyday' of female infant abandonment and beginning of intercountry adoption. When I first met her in 1996 she was still grieving heavily the loss of this daughter, still wracked with pain, guilt, and fear because she did not know what had happened to her child after she was left on the streets of Hefei. The leavers, her in-laws, were supposed to stay and see who took the baby and where they took her, but they panicked and left before the child was picked up. Seventeen years later, this birth mother still bore the emotional scars of that loss and still wept whenever she thought about it. The missing daughter left a permanent hole in the family, a family that now included a younger son, as they once hoped for, in addition to the 18-year-old first-born daughter. She said, "I just need to know if my daughter is alive somewhere in this world so my heart might finally rest."

This birth mother would have readily chosen to use a person who had the ability to transport the child secretly to an institution or an adoptive family, without caring if the person got paid for this or not. But at the time she had no way out of her terrible predicament except to let her in-laws leave her vulnerable newborn baby on the street near a police station in the wee hours, hoping that someone would take her quickly to a safe place and find her a new home.

In recent interviews we have found that new ways of arranging adoptions have emerged in lieu of the old methods of abandonment or targeting the doorstep of a likely adopter, as was common in the 1990s. Sometimes money passes hands to a go-between, such as hospital staff who may help hide the identity of the birth parent and arrange an adoption of an 'abandoned baby.' Or an informal broker may emerge who, using personal social networks, can find adopters for birth parents hiding a birth or vice versa. Such arrangements might be masked as 'abandonment' or registered as a birth to the adoptive parent, depending on circumstances and the ability to gain cooperation from local officials, invariably at a price. The reasons for arranging adoptions were similar to those for abandonment in the 1990s—out-of-plan children without official legal status who needed to be hidden from birth planners in order to avoid ruinous fines, loss of job, and forced sterilization.[7] Informal adopters, were childless though often underage or had son(s) and wanted a daughter. Most of these practices would be considered 'trafficking' or a violation of Hague rules prohibiting the unregulated use of money in exchange for a child.

The risk that an out-of-plan child will be separated from its parents is created in the first instance, not by traffickers, greed, and illegal behavior, but by a legal government policy that prohibits the birth of such children and severely punishes their parents for producing them. The government places a high price on the head of an out-of-plan child through the fines and punishments meted out to those who dare give birth to or illegally adopt these children into their families. In the state's struggle to strictly limit parents' reproductive behavior, the child often loses its citizenship and perhaps its parents, sometimes more than once.

7 A revision to the law lowered the legal age of adoption to 30 and allowed parents with one child to adopt a child living in an orphanage, although this latter clause was resisted by many local authorities.

Conclusion

The out-of-plan children are the ones who have filled the pool of children available for intercountry adoption from China. It is the dynamics of coercive and punitive government policy, not the presence of greedy finders and traffickers, nor the simple grip of ancient cultural norms, that make it difficult for parents to keep their own birth children, that forces them to make impossible choices about having and keeping children. Only later in the genesis of adoptable children do the dynamics of coercive reproductive policies morph into various forms of child trafficking,' 'child laundering,' and money-making via international (and domestic) adoption as well.

Secondly, the ready availability of domestic Chinese adopters eager to provide homes for abandoned or otherwise available adoptable healthy children also raises questions about the ethics of the intercountry adoption program. Many potential domestic adopters have been prevented from adopting by government policy and many have had adopted children seized from them and placed back into the adoption pool, including the international adoption pool. Sometimes even adopters legally qualified under the post-1999 adoption policy have lost out in the competition with richer foreigners to adopt children living in institutions. Every healthy child that is adopted internationally from China is a child that could be adopted by a qualified Chinese adopter now waiting in long lines at those Chinese institutions that still have a few healthy children. This behavior by local institutions, permitted by the national adoption authorities, is not illegal by any Chinese law but it is a violation of the subsidiarity principles stated in the Hague Convention (see Chapter 18).

If building an international adoption program with a pool of children who have been separated from birth families and domestic adoptive families by overtly coercive political policies is ethical by the terms of the current discourse, then those terms need to be challenged and changed. The Hague Convention on intercountry adoption (HCIA) focuses almost entirely on preventing the sale, abduction, and trafficking of children in intercountry adoption and is virtually silent on the issue of government power or political coercion in withholding citizenship, separating children from their parents, and preventing them from finding new adoptive homes in their community or country of birth. This is not surprising since the Hague Convention was negotiated and signed by sovereign states unlikely to implicate their own policies. China would not have signed such a document.

Moving forward, China's intercountry adoption program can be made ethical only to the extent that every child adopted internationally is one who cannot be placed in a good adoptive home in China. This will leave a small pool of children, most with special needs that cannot be readily accommodated in Chinese adoptive families today, for ICA. In fact these are not the children that most international adopters have sought in China over the years, although there is a minority of international adopters who have wanted to provide families for these children. These latter adopters might become the basis of an ethical intercountry adoption program from China, providing families for children who truly need homes and who would do better in a permanent family abroad than in a temporary foster care or institutional setting in China.

With both the fertility rates and the abandonment of healthy children declining in China in recent years, this may be the direction the program is heading even without any principled intervention on the part of government decision makers or international adoption organizations. In 2009 intercountry adoption from China had declined to 4,400 from the high of 14,000 in 2005; about 50 percent of these children had 'special needs.' In 2010, the figure fell further to below 4,000. How long the Chinese adoption authorities will continue to send children who could easily be placed with legally qualified Chinese parents into intercountry adoption is unclear. What is clear is that this violates the principle enshrined in the Hague Convention that intercountry adoption should occur only when appropriate domestic placement is not possible.

Chapter 9
Intercountry Adoption and Child Welfare in Guatemala: Lessons Learned Pre- and Post-Ratification of the 1993 Hague Convention on the Protection of Children and Cooperation in Respect of Intercountry Adoption

Kelley McCreery Bunkers and Victor Groza[1]

In this chapter we review the role of intercountry adoption in Guatemala and the limited domestic child welfare system, including structures, service delivery and trained workforce, prior to ratification of the 1993 Hague Convention on the Protection of Children and Cooperation in Respect of Intercountry Adoption (henceforth referred to the Hague Convention, Hague Conference on Private International Law, 1993). We explore the subsequent development of a domestic child welfare system that moved from reliance on intercountry adoption and institutional care as the primary solutions to at-risk and abandoned children to domestic family-based care for at-risk children. This process has seen successes and challenges and can provide cautionary lessons for other low- resource countries with a history of intercountry adoption.

Country Overview of Guatemala

Guatemala is a country in Central America and is approximately 108,890 square km and is divided administratively into 22 departments and 332 municipalities. The capital is Guatemala City with an official population of approximately 2.5 million but unofficially towering towards four million (Central Intelligence Agency [CIA], 2008).

1 This chapter is based, in part, on Bunkers, K.M., Groza, V., and Lauer, D. (2009). International adoption and child protection in Guatemala: A case of the tail wagging the dog. *International Social Work*, 52, 649-60. © Sage.

Guatemala has a great diversity of cultural and linguistic groups (Freedom House, 2010) with more than 23 languages officially recognized. Guatemala's population is approximately 13.3 million inhabitants with an annual population growth rate of 2.1 percent (CIA, 2008). Close to half of the population are children 0-17 years old (United Nations International Children's Fund [UNICEF] and United Nations Development Programme [UNDP], 2007). The cultural groups include *Ladino* (mixed Spanish heritage) estimated to be 55 percent of the population and indigenous Mayan, making up approximately 45 percent of the population (Freedom House, 2010). Guatemala rates 122 out of 182 on the Human Development Index; only Nicaragua (124) rated lower in Latin America (UNDP, 2009).

Guatemala maintains one of the highest birth rates in Latin America with an average of 3.6 children per mother. Rates within indigenous populations average 4.5 children per mother compared to 3.1 for Ladino women (Schieber, 2010). Half of Guatemalan children (49 percent) suffer chronic malnutrition, the second highest rate in the world (Marini and Gragnolati, 2003). The malnutrition rate for children under the age of five is 36 percent in urban areas and 55 percent in rural areas. Among Ladinos, 36 percent of children are malnourished, but 69 percent of Indigenous children are malnourished (Aldeas and Red Latino America de Acogimiento Familiar, 2010).

Guatemala is infamous for the 1956 overthrow of the democratically elected government with USA involvement via the United Fruit Company (Kinzer and Schlesinger, 1999) resulting in military rule. During the almost four-decade internal conflict (Hegre, Ellingsen, Gates and Gleditsch, 2001), over 200,000 Indigenous civilians were tortured and killed (Ball, Kobrak and Spirer 1999; Freedom House, 2010), and thousands displaced internally by a scorched earth policy that razed 400 indigenous villages (Archdiocese of Guatemala, 1999; Freedom House, 2010).

The internal conflict ended with the 1996 Peace Accords. Although the conflict is considered officially over, the last fifteen years can be characterized as an increasing culture of violence, with a current murder rate three times that of Mexico (Llorca, 2010). Violence against women occurs in such large numbers that it has been coined "*femicidio*" or femicide (Costantino, 2006; Rotabi, Morris, and Weil, 2008; Velzeboer, Ellsberg, Arcas, and Garcia-Moreno, 2003).

The combination of high birth rates, extreme poverty, migration, chronic malnutrition and a culture of violence are all prominent factors that contribute to or exacerbate intra-familiar violence, family disintegration, migration, child neglect, and abandonment (Bunkers, Groza and Lauer, 2009). To date, governmental and non-governmental services in Guatemala have been under-developed and under equipped to combat family violence, prevent family disintegration, increase school attendance, remediate child neglect, or respond to cases of abandonment. Until the end of 2007, the domestic child welfare system could be characterized as a combination of weak program implementation outside the capital city, failure to implement protection policies, minimal national budget assigned to child and family welfare, over-centralization of service-providers within the urban areas, and use of intercountry adoption as the major child welfare intervention for vulnerable children (Bunkers et al., 2009).

Intercountry Adoption Prior to Ratification of The Hague

Intercountry adoption in Guatemala expanded at an astounding rate after 2000. In 1999, 1,002 children were adopted from Guatemala, of whom 65 percent were placed with adoptive families from the USA (Selman, 2009d). By 2003, the number of intercountry adoptions had more than doubled to 2,677 children, and almost doubled again to 4,888 children in 2007 (Selman, 2009d, see Chapter 1). By 2007, virtually all the adopted children from Guatemala were going to the USA as European countries had stopped allowing adoptions due to concerns about system corruption.

In 2000, a UN-sponsored report on intercountry adoption in Guatemala raised serious alarms around unethical adoption practice (United Nations Economic and Social Council Commission on Human Rights, 2000). The report stated:

> What started out as genuine efforts to place quickly children in dire need of homes turned into lucrative business deals when it became apparent that there was a great demand in other countries for adoptable children. The situation within Guatemala, including the extreme poverty, a high birth rate, and lack of effective control and supervision of adoption proceedings, sustained this trade, and the demand was further increased in 1997 when neighboring Honduras began to take measures to stop illegal adoptions in that country (United Nations Economic and Social Council Commission on Human Rights, 2000, para 11).

This UN report became the impetus for another special investigative report commissioned by UNICEF and completed by the Latin American Institute for Education and Communication, commonly referred to as the ILPEC report. The ILPEC Report highlighted concerns around private adoptions occurring without government oversight, a demand-driven adoption system instead of a child-centered adoption system, and concerns around limited safeguards to protect the rights of children and birth parents. It also was the first to document concern about the number of children in long-term institutional care not being considered for adoption, given that they do not fit the profile of child that the "demand" side of the equation of children wanted for adoption (Hague Conference on Private International Law, 2007; ILPEC, 2000). This issue would later come to the forefront after the first national study on institutional child care was conducted and similar findings were documented (Perez, 2008).

By 2007, Guatemala had the highest sending ratio of children for intercountry adoption in the world; approximately one in every 100 children born was placed in intercountry adoption (Bunkers et al., 2009; Selman, 2009d). Guatemala became known as the adoption 'hot spot for babies' by adoption advocates and as an example of child trafficking by child rights advocates (Bunkers et al., 2009; Fieser, 2010; Rotabi, 2007; Rotabi et al., 2008). Guatemala became an attractive source of infants and toddlers because of proximity to the USA, the relative expediency of the process, the availability of young children, and the provision of foster care or group homes prior to placement (Bunkers, 2005; Bunkers et al., 2009).

Until 2008, intercountry adoption operated under a notary system. Private attorneys (notaries) facilitated all steps of the adoption, including identification of the child, matching with the foreign family, first meeting between parent and child, and placement of the child (Rotabi et al., 2008; Rotabi and Bunkers, 2008). In fact, the private notary, in most cases, represented the child and the adoptive family, an inherent conflict of interest (Casa Alianza et al., 2007). Judicial oversight was not robust; the main judicial involvement was an interview of the birth parents by a court social worker to ensure that the relinquishment was 'transparent' and 'in the best interests of the child.' The court social worker was not required to conduct a home visit to ensure the validity of the information provided in the child background study. Instead what typically occurred was an interview within the court itself, and possible payment to the social worker for issuance of a positive report (Rotabi et al., 2008).

There was also evidence of child theft. In 2008, in a case well-publicized in the Guatemalan and USA media, a birth mother recognized her daughter who had been stolen from her 18 months prior (Rotabi, 2009; see Chapter 5). The child was at the Solicitor General's Office (known by its Spanish acronym PGN) in the final stages of an intercountry adoption. After a DNA test was performed and confirmed the mother's claim, the birth mother and child were reunited (Associated Press, 2008a). There have been several alleged cases of children abducted for adoption purposes, only some of whom have been reunified with their families (Noel, 2008; Rotabi et al., 2008). Rumors of child abduction have, on multiple occasions, ended in public lynchings and mob violence within indigenous communities (Rotabi et al., 2008). Even the use of genetic testing to bring safeguards into the adoption process by verifying the birth mother was in fact a genetic match did not curtail inappropriate and unethical adoption practices. Greater detail about the aforementioned problems of child abduction and DNA fraud is found in Chapter 5.

Child Welfare Prior to 2008

Guatemala ratified the United Nations Convention on the Rights of the Child (hereafter referred to as the CRC) in 1990 (World Bank, 2002). Thirteen years later, Guatemala followed the trend of other Latin American countries and implemented core tenets of the UNCRC related to child protection and care in what is known as The Integrated Protection Law for Children and Adolescents (henceforth referred to by its Spanish Acronym the *PINA* Law). The *PINA* Law reflects very similar tenets as the CRC, including the best interest of the child, the right to survival and development, the right for the children's opinion to be heard in matters concerning them, and the right to alternative care and protection. The State, as the primary duty bearer, has the responsibility to ensure that these rights are fulfilled for all children. In spite of the *PINA* Law being an excellent legal framework for the protection of children in Guatemala, the part of the law related to the care and protection of children outside of parental care was not developed into meaningful programs or services until 2007 (Bunkers et al., 2009). In spite of the strong tenets in the *PINA* Law that promoted family-based alternative care, the Guatemalan child welfare system was institutionally-based; that is, if children were not in their birth or kin families, the state's response was to place them in one of many institutions (i.e., orphanages) throughout the country, both state run and privately run (Bunkers et al., 2009; Perez, 2008).

In 2008, the first national assessment on institutional care in Guatemala was completed (Perez, 2008). Over 6,000 children were found living in institutional care. The assessment located 133 residential facilities for children, 95 percent of which were privately owned and operated. Interestingly, this finding supported concerns raised in the 2000 UN report that stated that the private child care facilities (also referred to as orphanages or children's homes) were growing to support and provide children for intercountry adoption (United Nations Economic and Social Council Commission on Human Rights, 2000, para. 14) although a later report would have contradictory findings. Perez's 2008 report found that private child care institutions did not adhere to internationally-recognized care standards and 50 percent did not have qualified staff to meet the needs of children in their care (Perez, 2008). Perez also found that although some institutions were used as transit or recruitment grounds for intercountry adoption, the larger group were not necessarily involved in intercountry adoption and were caring for children, sometimes long-term, without parental care.

The two major reasons identified for institutionalization were abandonment (21 percent) and family violence (25 percent) including domestic violence and/or physical abuse of the child. Once placed in an institution, many children remained there indefinitely—there was no plan in place for any child to return to his or her family. Under the *PINA* Law, institutional care can only be considered as a temporary measure. For some children, institutional care was given as a permanent care option through the judiciary, in clear violation of the *PINA* Law that requires institutional care to be a temporary option (Bunkers et al., 2009).

Up until 2002 there were few dedicated social workers involved in child welfare. There was an established state-funded School of Social Work and there were hundreds of graduates of the program, but only undergraduate degrees were offered. The graduates had minimal training in child welfare; most of the training focused on community development. There were some social workers involved within the intercountry adoption process, but they were court-based and part of the problem (Hague Conference on Private International Law, 2007).

One aspect of a child welfare system was in place as a result of the elements of the private adoption system. The private adoption system developed an informal network of private caregivers and most children were placed in 'foster care' prior to placement in intercountry adoption (Bunkers, 2005; Gibbons, Wilson, and Schnell, 2009; Rotabi, 2010b; Wilson and Gibbons, 2005). What was concerning about this, besides that the fact that it was all done outside of government regulation and oversight, is that "foster care" was overseen by the private attorneys and the scant supervision of foster care programming was mostly done by secretaries or other professionals—not social workers (Bunkers, 2005; Bunkers et al., 2009). Foster parents were not trained nor were any systematic assessment of potential foster parents conducted. An additional issue that needed to be addressed was the total lack of birth mother counseling by any type of qualified professional (Wiley and Baden, 2005).

The Hague Convention, the major international policy framework designed to help States regulate intercountry adoption and associated ethical practice, has an interesting history in Guatemala. It was ratified in 2002 by Government Decree 50-2002 and entered into force in March 2003. In September 2003 the Constitutional Court declared it invalid (McKinney, 2007; Sohr, 2006) because the opposition claimed the President overstepped his powers to deciding to accede to a multilateral convention (Sohr, 2006). In the complex dynamics of Guatemala it was also concerning that members of the constitutional court had ties to intercountry adoption. After the Constitutional Court decision, several European countries participating in intercountry adoption stopped working with Guatemala, recognizing that corruption and bad practice were the norm (Bunkers et al., 2009).

In May 2007, a new ratification process took place for The Hague Convention and the Guatemalan Congress ratified it in Government Decree 31-2007 (Congreso de la República de Guatemala, 2007a). The 2007 Congress then passed an adoption law (Congreso de la República de Guatemala, 2007b) domesticating the contents of The 1993 Hague Convention, a significant event that would help shape child welfare reform in Guatemala.

Adoption Law 77-2007 provided for designation of an independent and autonomous Central Authority (known in Spanish as the *Consejo Nacional de Adopciónes* or *CNA*) charged with providing guidance on how to implement the best interests of the child principles in all matters and decisions related to adoption. The Adoption Law also ruled out the use of private attorneys and required a judge to determine a child's adoptability status (articles 10 and 36 of Law 77-2007). The law clearly defines the best interests of the child principle (Congreso de la República, 2007b) and the process is consistent with subsidiarity principles of the 1993 Hague Convention. Article 4 of the Law 77-2007 specifies that the best interest of the child is to ensure protection and development of the child within his or her biological family, and only if this is not possible, within another permanent family (Congreso de la República, 2007b). The law goes on to state in article 13 that the "best interests" principle should be the guiding criterion in selecting prospective parents (Congreso de la República, 2007b). Article 10 of the law also reflects the contents of the 1993 Hague Convention in stating that inducement in any form is a violation of the law (Rotabi et al., 2008).

The Nascent Child Welfare System in Guatemala after Hague Ratification

In the years after ratification of the HCIA and passage of Adoption Law 77-2007, several concurrent actions have been taken by the Government, non-governmental organizations, and UNICEF. Those actions have focused on regulating intercountry adoption and strengthening the national child welfare system, specifically family-based care.

The Government of Guatemala, under President Alvaro Colom, started a cash transfer program modeled after best practice examples from Mexico and Brazil (see Vadapalli, 2009). The program, entitled My Family Progresses (*Mi Familia Progresa*), targets vulnerable families such as female-headed households. It is a substantive program that provides conditional cash transfers of approximately \$40 per month if parents are willing to ensure that the children in their care are guaranteed health, nutrition, and education. Although a conditional cash program such as *My Family Making Progress* has had success in Brazil and Mexico (Fernald, Gertler, and Neufeld, 2008; Fiszbein and Schady, 2009), in the complicated context of Guatemala there have been challenges from the beginning. Critics complain that the Executive Branch (specifically the First Lady) was too closely involved and that lists of beneficiaries were not shared, leading to suspicions of favoritism and political interests (Freedom House, 2010). The conditional cash transfer program was also mentioned in the CRC Concluding Observations, specifically noting concern for lack of clarity in selection criteria and limited possibility for sustainability. The CRC Committee recommended a time-bound and comprehensive national plan of action for children be developed as part of the country's development strategy (United Nations Convention on the Rights of the Child, Committee on the Rights of the Child, 2010).

Domestic Adoption

In 2008, the first national survey on attitudes about adoption was conducted (UNICEF and Vox Latina, 2008). Results indicate that more than 55 percent of Guatemalans believed that Guatemalan children would be happier with a Guatemalan adoptive family, and 93 percent said they would not be concerned about adopting an indigenous child (Seijo, 2008; UNICEF and Vox Latina, 2008). This finding challenged the rhetoric of intercountry adoption supporters that inherent racism in the country would preclude Guatemalans from adopting indigenous children (Bunkers et al., 2009). Results of the study were published on the front page of the national newspaper *La Prensa Libre* in an effort to raise awareness around adoption issues and promote domestic adoption (Seijo, 2008). Although the numbers are not large, there has been an increase in the number of domestic adoptions since 2008. In 2009, 222 prospective Guatemalan adoptive families were assessed and 172 domestic adoptions were finalized (Justo Solorzano, UNICEF Guatemala, personal communication January 25, 2010).

Social Workers

As a response to the lack of child welfare government programs, UNICEF, in conjunction with the Government of Guatemala, hired a team of social workers to administer the birth mother support program, domestic adoption program, and the institutional care program. As part of this initiative, UNICEF funded training by a team of social workers from the USA and Europe to increase understanding of social work within child welfare, and specifically within the aforementioned program areas. Little by little, a core team of social workers was making progress in implementing contemporary child welfare services and perspectives. Using Colombia and Chile as models of strong child welfare programs, Guatemala made small steps to strengthen the continuum of care for vulnerable children. Colombia is one of the Hague countries that is frequently touted as a best practice example and social workers play a strong role within all areas of child welfare, including alternative care.

Some progress has been made in terms of improving the domestic child welfare system through strengthening the social worker workforce with skills and knowledge related to child welfare issues, increased family support, and expansion of foster care. Significant challenges remain. The UN Committee for the Rights of the Child, in their Concluding Observations for Guatemala in 2010, reported concerns over:

> the high number of children in institutions, as well as at the insufficient implementation of minimum care standards and monitoring systems for these institutions. The Committee notes the State party's intention to address the institutions' problems, including the lack of trained staff. However, the Committee remains concerned at the placement of more than 1000 children in a big institution (*Hogar Solidario*) in the capital (United Nations Committee on the Rights of the Child, 2010, para. 58, p. 11)

Specific recommendations included strengthening family reunification programs, ensuring the right of identity of the child; strengthening community programs such as foster care including prioritizing family-based care for young children (e.g., foster care); creating and implementing programs for children in institutional care that help promote community integration; and, utilizing the United Nations General Assembly Resolution A/RES/64/142 adopted on 20 November 2009 (United Nations Committee on the Rights of the Child, 2010, para. 59 (a), (b), (c), (d). The aforementioned resolution adopted the UN Guidelines for the Alternative Care of Children. The Guidelines are intended to enhance implementation of the CRC and relevant provisions of related international instruments. As such, they provide more detail and guidance as to how States should implement alternative care systems and programs for children outside parental care or in vulnerable families at risk of separation (SOS Children's Villages and International Social Service, personal communication, March 11, 2011).

Intercountry Adoption

With Hague ratification and the accompanying adoption law, there was a temporary moratorium on all new adoptions beginning January 1, 2008. The adoption cases that were already in process ('transition' or 'pipeline' cases) were allowed to continue but came under tight scrutiny. The National Adoption Committee has focused on two main activities related to intercountry adoption. The first is the review of approximately 3,000 transition cases initiated under the old law, but not yet processed through the court systems. The review involved a significant allotment of time and resources as cases were investigated at length. In the initial review, 10 percent of the first 150 cases had questionable records and 40 percent of birth mothers did not participate in the hearings to ascertain whether coercion or inducements influenced their decision to adopt (Bunkers et al., 2009).

The second focus of the CNA has been to develop a new intercountry adoption program based on the Law 77/2007. In November 2009 the CNA announced a two-year pilot program for intercountry adoption (CNA, 2011). The program was designed to approve a small number of special needs children—older children, children with physical disabilities, and sibling groups—to be adopted by a limited number of selected countries (CNA, 2011). Before the program was initiated it was already running into problems. In the spring of 2010, the pilot program was assessed by members of the International Social Service and the ensuing report mentioned several areas of concern related to appropriate safeguards and procedures (International Social Service, personal communication, March 11, 2011). In October 2010, the US State Department withdrew the interest of the USA from participating in the new pilot program over concerns regarding the proposed process (http://adoption.state.gov/news/guatemala.html). The UNCRC Committee, in the 2010 Concluding Observations for Guatemala, also made specific mention of intercountry adoption and recommended "continue suspension of international adoptions until child rights can be totally guaranteed in the adoption proceedings" (United Nations Committee on the Rights of the Child, Concluding Observations for Guatemala, 2010, p. 12)

Significant limitations remain in the development of domestic adoption in Guatemala as observed by the United Nations Committee on the Rights of the Child. The report states:

> the Committee remains concerned at the persistence of private adoptions, and at the fact that the National Adoption Council is only present in the capital city, which makes it difficult to provide an adequate response in the whole country (UNCRC, 2010, p. 12).

The CRC Committee recommends that the CNA make efforts to increase promotion, awareness and accessibility of domestic adoption in all parts of the country (UNCRC, 2010).

The International Commission against Impunity Report

The International Commission against Impunity in Guatemala, or CICIG as it is referred to by its Spanish acronym, was launched three years ago at Guatemala's request to dismantle illegal groups and end criminal impunity (Llorca, 2010). As part of its mandate, CICIG was asked to look into criminal networks that were or continue to be active in the area of adoption. Specifically, the CICIG investigation focused on illegal activities subsequent to the passage of Adoption Law 77/2007.

There were four main findings highlighted in the CICIG report (2010). The report found that intercountry adoption had converted into a lucrative economic activity involving criminal aspects. The report also specifically mentions the presence and involvement of trafficking networks of children and illegal adoption procedures with a criminal, transnational element. Also very concerning was the finding that these corrupt adoption processes and procedures have occurred with the participation or acquiescence of authorities and/or institutions that are supposed to ensure that transparent and ethical procedures in accordance with the law are in place. Finally, the report found that approximately 60 percent of the children considered adoptable have irregularities in their documentation and/or in the adoption process. The CICIG report recommended that the Ministry of Interior take the lead in prosecuting those who are involved in illegal adoption practices, specifically using the Law against Organized Crime as a mechanism for prosecution. Finally, the report suggested closer collaboration with financial intelligence agencies to track financial profits gained through criminal activity associated with illegal adoption. Given that the CICIG report was only publicly released in December 2010 it is difficult to say what the implications will be, although it is clear that the country has a long way to go before it is finally rid of corrupt practices that continuously violate the law and children's rights.

The UN Committee on the Rights of the Child made specific mention of the CICIG report in its Concluding Observations. The report states:

> The Committee recommends that the State party ensure strict transparency and follow-up controls and prosecute those involved in illegal adoptions and sale of children for adoption purposes. The Committee further recommends that the State party implement all the CICIG recommendations made in its recent report on Actors Involved in Irregular Adoptions in Guatemala, since the entry into force of Adoption Law (decree 77-2007), and take adequate measures to eliminate corruption and impunity, prosecute and sanction the perpetrators (UNCRC, 2010, p. 12).

Twisting the CRC to Promote Intercountry Adoption

In spite of documented reports of baby-buying and human rights violations the pre-2008 intercountry adoption system continues to have supporters. Bartholet has utilized child rights' based arguments to not only denounce moratoriums on intercountry adoption, but to promote systems such as the one in Guatemala before adoption reform.

In 2009, Bartholet argued in front of the Organization of American States that moratoriums on intercountry adoption violate a child's right to a family using the specific examples of Guatemala, Peru, and Honduras, (Bartholet, 2009). Bartholet (2009) has also decried the increased use of domestic foster care as a violation of this right. McKinley (2007) suggests that only placement of children in permanent families (typically middle-to-high-resource adoptive families outside of the child's country of origin) ensures a child's basic rights to shelter, food, health care and education, and fulfils a key principle of the CRC. This perspective tends to exclude or demean traditional family care systems such as kinship care, as well as foster care.

There is no right to a family in the CRC. The CRC discusses children's rights related to their family and discusses a family environment but does not claim that every child has a right to a family (Brooks, 1998; N. Cantwell, personal communication, May 20, 2010). What the CRC does include are several articles related to life within a family environment, the role of the State to support families, and the provision of family-based care for children outside of parental care. Brooks (1998) stated that although children have a right to *respect of* family life they do not have the right to a family, per se, under international law. In other words, suggesting that children have a right to a family under the CRC is a problematic argument as there is, in fact, no legal basis for this argument.

Summary

The proponents and opponents of intercountry adoption share a common concern for the welfare of children in low resource countries. They differ on the approaches they take to promote children's wellbeing. The history of Guatemalan child welfare services reinforces lessons learned from other low resource countries and provides new lessons with respect to the negative role intercountry adoption can play.

When low resource countries begin to address illicit or unethical adoption practices by better monitoring ICA typically slow down. The 'demand' or 'market' is pushed elsewhere, to countries with inadequate child protection mechanisms. This was the situation in Ethiopia, a non-Hague country and the second highest country for intercountry adoption in 2010, largely due to inadequate protections for children (see Chapter 10).

The challenges for developing child protection in Guatemala are profound. Intercountry adoption must not be a priority over the development of a strong domestic child welfare system. Guatemala provides an extreme example of what happens when the cart is put before the horse. Steps should first be taken to create a strong, viable, and family-based child welfare system domestically. If there is a weak social welfare system, it is easy for unethical intercountry adoption to flourish. Intercountry adoption must be part of the continuum of services and be at the end of the continuum rather than the beginning, in accordance with HCIA and the CRC. Guatemala also provides lessons in the challenges of implementing a Hague framework quickly without the appropriate structures, mechanisms, workforce, budget, and public awareness in place to support a continuum of care (i.e., subsidiarity). It is perhaps easier and more effective to take initial steps required for developing a Hague friendly system, including a committed budget to fund workforce, programming and service delivery before ratification so that once it is completed, the system is ready to function.

Leadership must come from the public agency responsible for child protection. In Guatemala, the status of child protection will only be raised if the Secretariat becomes a ministry (for example, a Ministry of Family) or a current ministry is expanded to encompass child protection (for example, Health and Social Welfare). There is no way to give the welfare and protection of children the status it needs without raising the prominence and accompanying resources of those whose mission it is to protect and help Guatemalan children and families.

In addition, child protection expertise cannot be built into a public system if all the middle managers are removed after every election. For consistency of expertise, not only the direct providers of service, but also the managers of service providers must be civil servants hired for their competency and retained over administrations. Only competent and strong leadership and a stable workforce will begin to provide the structure needed for child protection modernization.

Political will is mandatory. Legislators must be educated about the issues by child welfare professionals and not by those seeking to benefit from international adoption. Education is the first step and advocacy is the second step. Both education and advocacy will help shape political will to both pay attention to child protection issues and develop strategic planning for the improvement of child protection

A strong civil society includes both a government that functions by rule of law and a non-governmental sector collaborating with them. Government should develop policy frameworks, set standards of care, and provide oversight. Civil society actors can be direct service providers thus providing more coverage and enhancing what the State is able to do for vulnerable children. A strong civil society is important but it is the responsibility of the State, as primary duty bearer for children's rights, to ensure that that services and support are being delivered to and are accessible by children and families. Under this framework, civil society organizations can assist in developing intervention innovations, advocacy for change, and provide direct services.

Predictability and consistency are mainstays of contemporary public child protection. Laws and policies not only have to be developed, but be implemented and monitored by competent authorities. This could be especially challenging in Guatemala where the rule of law is almost absent. While regional variations are necessary, there should be one protocol for assessing family situations, evaluating child maltreatment, preparing a child for foster care or adoption, making placement decisions, etc. The ability to develop, implement, and monitor a predictable system will make Guatemala's child protection system effective and responsive to children's needs. Also this creates a framework for accountability.

Of course, there are many critiques of the policy and program changes proposed and implemented as Guatemala tries to curtail international adoption in order to develop a contemporary child protection system (Sohr, 2006). From an empowerment and developmental perspective (Dickens and Groza, 2004), what is most important is that Guatemala decide what child welfare should be and specifically what the role of intercountry adoption will be within that system. Inevitable in change are mistakes, but the critical element in developing a continuum of care is putting children's needs first.

Chapter 10
Ethiopia at a Critical Juncture in Intercountry Adoption and Traditional Care Practices

Kelley McCreery Bunkers, Karen Smith Rotabi, and Benyam Dawit Mezmur

Introduction

The Hague Convention on the Protection of Children and Co-operation in Respect of Intercountry Adoption (HCIA) provides a framework for ethical practice in intercountry adoption (ICA) and sets measures to safeguard the best interests of the child and prevent child sales and abduction under the guise of ICA, as outlined in Article 1 (Rotabi, 2008; Vite and Boechat, 2008). To date, over 80 States have ratified the Convention, including most receiving States, and several more are considering ratification at the time of this writing (Hague Conference on Private International Law, 2011b).

For countries of origin that are Contracting States to the HCIA, this means that the State has its own legal code and processes that domesticate and reflect the contents of the HCIA to insure ethical child placement (Rotabi, 2008), including verification of child relinquishment and/or abandonment and making a determination of a child's adoptability. Take China as an example. The Chinese Central Authority verifies the status and identity of the child by completing a background investigation and, if appropriate, places the child on an eligibility list for approved agencies in other nations, such as adoption service providers in the USA and Western Europe.

The subsidiarity principle of the HCIA requires a continuum of child welfare services prior to ICA (see Chapter 18). At a minimum, this includes verification that the biological family and kinship group is not able to care for the child, that there is no opportunity for a domestic adoption, and that the child meets the nation's criteria for ICA placement. This bureaucratic process is characterized by paperwork, child identity, and health documentation with a clear demonstration that family-based care options have been sufficiently explored within the country of origin.

This chapter explores how current ICA activities in countries that have not ratified the HCIA have resulted in worrisome and irregular practices. Ethiopia is examined as a case in point because it has become an active country of origin for as many as thirteen receiving States, and has neither acceded to nor incorporated many of the international standards under the HCIA. Thus, it is important to scrutinize current adoption processes in Ethiopia and offer recommendations for ways in which these practices might be improved. First, the authors begin with a review of what is known about the irregular adoption practices, utilizing a specific case example from the USA. Secondly, the authors give an analysis of this case example and identify the link between adoption agency accreditation procedures within the USA and larger problems within the system of child care and adoption in a country of origin. This provides an insightful look into the increasing risks for vulnerable children in Ethiopia should the practice continue *status quo,* while also examining how the USA can and should tighten its own requirements for adoption service providers. The authors conclude by presenting the current scenario as an opportunity for Ethiopia to be an example of how acknowledgement of irregular practices can be a catalyst for change.

Receiving Nations: The United States and Accredited Adoption Service Providers

Because the United States receives more children for ICA than any other nation in the world (Selman, 2009d), its ICA policies and procedures have a great impact on countries of origin. The US Department of State (U.S. DOS) is the designated Central Authority in the USA and the 2000 Intercountry Adoption Act, in addition to the HCIA, guides child sending and receiving practices. Critical steps towards reform were the new requirements for approved adoption service providers (ASPs) who are "accredited" to carry out adoptions between the USA and other HCIA nations. Over 300 adoption service providers applied to the U.S. DOS to be evaluated for agency accreditation (Rotabi, 2008) based on uniform standards of practice (Council on Accreditation, 2007; Rotabi and Gibbons, 2012 . Most agencies have now been evaluated and either approved, denied, or temporarily accredited and each agency's status is available on the U.S. DOS website.

Accredited ASPs in the USA meet financial transparency criteria, including documentation that demonstrates that only reasonable professional fees are paid for ICA. This is clearly outlined in Articles 8 and 32 (1, 2, and 3) of the HCIA. Also, bureaucratic processes must be followed; including and not limited to proof of ASP financial solvency, bonding and insurance, appropriate staff credentials, training for agency staff and prospective families in ICA-specific information, home study standards, and appropriate medical protocol and documentation (Council on Accreditation, 2007). Also, foreign service providers (e.g., adoption facilitators) in other Contracting States require criteria for oversight and supervision by the adoption agency. Agency personnel in the USA and their "foreign supervised providers" must refrain from child buying or any other process of incentivizing adoption (Council on Accreditation, 2007). While HCIA implementation and the agency accreditation system in the USA have been criticized (see Graff, 2010; Parents for Ethical Adoption Reform

[PEAR], 2010b; Rotabi and Gibbons, 2012, new safeguards are important due to previous irregular and corrupt practices (see Chapters 3, 4, 5, 6, 9 and 25).

USA Loophole: Leaving Ethiopia and Other Non-Signatory Countries at Risk

In the case of USA implementation of the HCIA, the Convention only applies to ICA cases/practices in which *both* countries have ratified the international agreement. This is despite the presence of a Special Commission Recommendation of the Hague Conference on Private International Law that calls on countries that are Contracting States to the HCIA to apply, "as far as practicable … the standards and safeguards of the Convention to the arrangements for inter-country adoption which they make in respect of non-Contracting States" (Hague Conference on Private International Law, 2001, para. 56). As such, there are several countries of origin, some of whom are the main providers of children for ICA placement in the USA, for which the HCIA does not apply. The result is that numerous *unaccredited* USA ASPs can continue to practice ICA with countries that are far less regulated. In essence, this loophole in the policy endorses unaccredited adoption service providers involvement with States that have been documented as having unethical and irregular adoption practices. One such case is Ethiopia.

Ethiopia is a country that has experienced an ICA boom in recent years (Heinlein, 2010a; Selman, 2009d; see Chapter 1). It falls within this loophole as it has not yet acceded to the HCIA and, yet there are currently 62 adoption service providers from 13 countries operating in Ethiopia. This is particularly worrisome because the country has a significant number of orphaned and highly vulnerable children. According to the 2007 Single Point Prevalence statistics from the Ministry of Health, there are an estimated 5,459,139 orphans in Ethiopia (Ethiopian Federal Ministry of Health, 2007). However, it should be noted that being an orphan cannot be equated with being deprived of a family environment (Abebe, 2009). Therefore, although there are a large number of orphans in Ethiopia, what is frequently absent from discussions about child welfare in Ethiopia is the tradition of strong and centuries-old caring mechanisms such as kinship care and the practice of informal adoption (referred to as *guddifachaa* or *gudifecha*) (Abebe and Aase, 2007; Beckstrom, 1972; Bunkers, 2010; Negeri, 2006).

The lack of a strong protective legal framework in Ethiopia, the high number of vulnerable children, and the increasing demand for young children by prospective adoptive parents has pushed the adoption market towards this East African country (Rotabi, 2010b). The number of children being placed in ICA has risen dramatically in the past four years, almost tripling the number of children sent to the USA (Rotabi, 2010b). Seven years ago, one in 200 children adopted by USA families was Ethiopian; in 2010 that number had increased to one in five (Heinlein, 2010b). See Figure 10.1

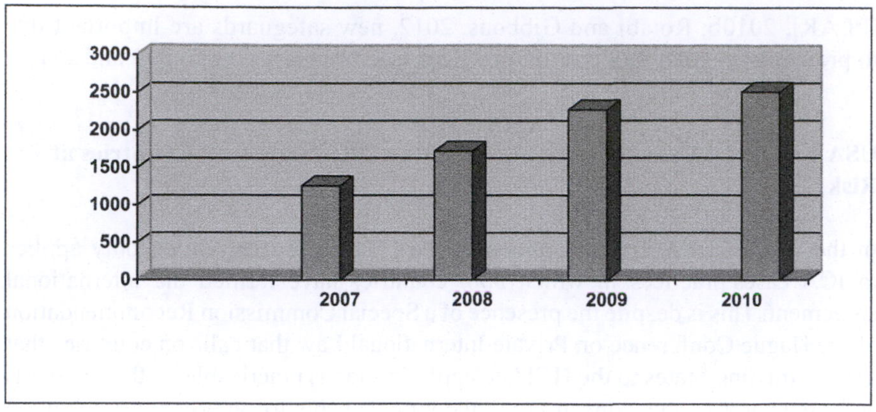

Figure 10.1 Adoption of Ethiopian Children to the USA
Source: U.S. DOS, 2011a.

It should be noted that the above data does not indicate adoptions to other nations. Notably, Ethiopia has also become one of the top countries of origin for Spain, Italy, and France. Together those countries as well as several other receiving States processed approximately 4,676 ICA cases in 2009 (see Chapter 1, Table 1.10). To the best of these authors' knowledge, there are no officially and publicly announced/available aggregated adoption statistics provided by the Government of Ethiopia.

Adoption statistics for the USA in 2010 showed a total of 2,511 Ethiopian children being adopted. The largest age group of children (approximately 1,100) was between one and four years of age (out of which 871 were under one year of age; U.S. DOS, 2011a). Adoption statistics from Ethiopia demonstrate changes in the profiles of adopted children. The number of children adopted under the age of one year remained the same from 2007 to 2010. Children between one and four years old accounted for 35 percent of the total adoptions from Ethiopia in 2007, but for almost 44 percent in 2010 (U.S. DOS, 2011a). Interestingly, this increase coincides with a decrease in the number of children between the ages of five and 12 years old being placed in ICA. In 2007, this group of children accounted for 25.5 percent of the total children adopted, while in 2010 it was 18.3 percent (U.S. DOS, 2011a). Although these numbers are not dramatically disparate, one could extrapolate from the changes that the growing demand from adoptive families is for younger children.

Case Example: A USA-based Agency Denied Accreditation But Working in Ethiopia

A good example of an adoption agency that was denied accreditation in the USA but chose to focus on adoptions from Ethiopia is *Celebrate Children International*

(CCI; U.S. DOS, n.d.a). At one point, the agency reported that the time between applying and receiving a child placement was three months or less, an exceptionally quick referral. The agency website neither addresses the fact that the organization was denied HCIA accreditation in 2009, nor the extensive complaints against the agency in the State of Florida.

The agency originally came under scrutiny given its involvement in Guatemala, a country that has had notorious ICA problems (*Comisión Internacional contra la Impunidad*, 2010; see Chapters 5 and 7). The agency's location in Florida is important to note because it is a USA State that has adoption laws and child placement agency licensing standards that do not fully address ICA practices (Siegal, 2011; Keller, 2010). Because CCI is a licensed child placement agency in Florida, complaints against the agency are a matter of public record. There are more than 1500 pages of complaints and related documents against CCI (Siegal, n.d.). An example of such a complaint was filed in a 2009 letter from a prospective adoptive parent in the Ethiopia program:

> The "relinquishment" videos we received have the mothers being interviewed by [the agency director], which according to other adoption service providers and sources is undeniably a conflict of interest and could easily be perceived as persuasive and unethical [The agency director] told us that CCI has nothing to do with the relinquishment process, and yet, she is interviewing the birth mothers … Parents with their children appear to be waiting in the background and lined up to be interviewed, leading us to believe that there is some type of child harvesting or recruitment going on at the time these videos were taken.
>
> We have asked multiple times about the events leading up to the relinquishment, and the reasons the mothers were unable to care for the children. We have been referred by [the agency director] back to the videos over and over again. We asked [the agency director] to remove the music and after much persuasion through an outside source, she finally complied. Then we found four local Ethiopian Americans to translate the videos. All four who saw the video have advised us to be very cautious, as at least one mother does not appear to understand about adoption. We have taken their advice. When the mother is shaking her head 'no' when asked if she understands about adoption, and after four Ethiopians told us to be very cautious, how could we in good conscience proceed without asking questions? Why is CCI even talking to birth mothers about adoption anyway? Are these mothers truly unable to care for their children, or are they being told by adoption service providers that their children will have a better life in America? Or are they being told their children will be educated and returned to them?
>
> When we could not get answers to the questions we went to another CCI adoptive mother to compare stories and ask questions. Without any explanation, we were removed from the [agency internet support group] and our client login was disabled.

> When we found out that all three children have living birth mothers with no documented reason for relinquishment we simply ask why … These children may be legally relinquished, but are they morally and ethically relinquished? (Siegal, n.d.)

This narrative of wrong-doing is made by one individual, and it cannot be verified as entirely factual. However, when reviewing *many* of the complaints made available by the State of Florida (using the Freedom of Information Act), this complaint is an example of countless negative reports of adoption practices which include dishonesty, threats, and other issues of violations of social work ethics (Siegal, n.d.).

The complaint itself underscores a troubling practice of video-cataloging of children. In the above case, CCI apparently has video-taped birth mothers and their children as a marketing technique. Apparently, these children are not, in fact, living in institutions; rather they have some intact family life as is indicated by the presence of a birth mother on film. Additionally, what is caught on film appears to be, in some cases, women who do not entirely understand the Western notion of adoption. The complainant rightly asks if these women have been made promises, such that their children will be educated abroad and later returned to them.

A recent Dutch documentary on Ethiopian adoptions (having no relation to the aforementioned USA agency) highlighted a case of fraud whereby a child was declared an orphan due to the death of both parents, when, in fact, both parents were living (KRO Brandpunt, 2011). Another case involving two Ethiopian children that were abducted, sold (allegedly for a $100 USD), and adopted by a family in Austria was also put under the spotlight in 2007 (Copies of correspondence between the authorities in Ethiopia and Austria on this matter on file with authors secured through a personal communication with a Government official, 15 September 2009). This latter case involved intermediaries, institution personnel, and relevant government administrators working at the *kebele* level (which is the lowest administrative level) who played a role in the adoption. In several other cases highlighted, birth parents declared that they did not understand adoption and its implications (Joyce, 2011; Heinlein, 2011a). This misunderstanding of the permanence of adoption especially pertinent in Ethiopia where simple adoption is the legal norm and birth parents never lose full parental rights[1] (*Federal National Gazetta of the Federal Democratic Republic of Ethiopia*, 2000). Collectively these cases call into question how many children are placed within ICA under falsified documents or through inadequate informed consent of their birth parents.

Part of the problem in relation to unethical and sometimes illegal adoptions from Ethiopia lies with the way consent is secured. In Ethiopia, Article 191 of

---

1 Under Ethiopia law, all adoptions are considered simple meaning there is no permanent severance of bonds between the child and the biological family. In what is considered full adoption, the ties between the child and the biological child are completely severed from a legal perspective.

the Revised Family Code (RFC) indicates that "[b]oth the father and the mother of the adopted child must give their consent to the adoption where they are alive and known" (*Federal National Gazetta of the Federal Democratic Republic of Ethiopia*, 2000, p. 57). In addition, "where one of the parents is not willing to give his consent and the child is ten and above years of age, the court may approve the adoption upon hearing the opinion of the other parent and of the child" (*Federal National Gazetta of the Federal Democratic Republic of Ethiopia*, 2000, p. 57). Those provisions are not further solidified under the RFC. For instance, the need to secure free and *informed* consent is not an explicit part of Ethiopian law. It appears that families give their consent without appreciating the nature of ICA (PEAR, 2010b). Further compounding the possibility for unethical practices, including improper financial gains, is the fact that there is no clear legislation nor practice in Ethiopia that emulates the "no initial contact" rule of Article 29 of the HCIA. It appears that the apparent gaps in the legal framework regarding consent and other elements of the ICA process have resulted in increasingly irregular practices leading the US Embassy in Addis Ababa to issue a warning, amongst others, in December, 2010: "The Department of State continues to be concerned about reports highlighting adoption related fraud, malfeasance, and abuse in Ethiopia, and acknowledges the concerns expressed by families over the integrity of the adoption process" (U.S. DOS, 2010d).

The RFC largely fails to address child laundering issues. The only provision that comes close to being related to child laundering is Article 194(3)(e). This Article requires the court, before approving an agreement of adoption, to consider the "availability of information which will enable the court to know that the adopter will handle the adopted child as his own child and will not abuse him" (*Federal National Gazetta of the Federal Democratic Republic of Ethiopia*, 2000, p.59). Furthermore, while the Revised Criminal Code (RCC) of 2004 has generally improved on the provisions of its predecessor in the context of child laundering, the relevant provisions are quite weak. In Article 597 of the RCC, there is reference to trafficking of women and children only for the purpose of labor (*Federal National Gazetta of the Federal Democratic Republic of Ethiopia*, 2004); thus cases of child laundering for adoption fall outside its scope. The current legal framework pertaining to child laundering is inadequate, thereby making prosecution very difficult. In fact, the authors could not find any court case where either individuals or organizations were found guilty of child laundering for adoption purposes.

Current ICA practices, including the aforementioned video cataloguing of children, lack of free and informed consent, limited understanding of the implications of relinquishment, and falsified documents fueled by adoption fees pose a threat to traditional responses to orphaned and vulnerable children. Many children being placed in ICA are relinquished from the extended family network and/or originate from regions known for the traditional practice of *guddifachaa.*

The Traditional Practice of Guddifachaa at Risk in the ICA Environment

Abebe and Aase (2007) state that "orphanhood, both biological and social, is a significant structural feature of Ethiopian society" (2007, p. 2059). They claim that orphans have been a part of Ethiopian culture and families for centuries, and that Ethiopians have dealt with children without parental care in constructive ways (Abebe and Aase, 2007). Care within the extended family has been the most frequent response to children outside of parental care reflecting similar practices across the African continent. Lombe and Ochumbo (2008) state that close to 90 percent of assistance to orphans in Sub-Saharan countries has been provided by traditional family networks.

In addition to kinship care, the indigenous practice of informal adoption, locally referred to as *guddifachaa,* has been a traditional family-based response most common in the Oromia and Amhara regions of the country. Its meaning is understood as the upbringing and full assimilation of an outsider (child) into a family (Beckstrom, 1972; Negeri, 2006). Legal *guddifachaa* is a formal process recognized by the judicial system and cultural *guddifachaa,* involves a ceremony and oath-taking in front of the community or tribal leaders (Beckstrom, 1972; Negeri, 2006). There is minimal formal literature regarding the practice of *guddifachaa* but the research that has been done on the topic demonstrates that children's right to identity, protection, and inheritance are respected within this type of care (Bunkers, 2010; Negeri, 2006). Duressa (2002) in his research on the practices finds:

> *Guddifachaa* practice provides (an) invaluable solution for foundling abandoned and orphaned children. If such children are adopted (in)to a society with such fertile ground of cultural and value system, they can easily be integrated into the community and get access to resources and status. Encouraging and expanding such local and traditional adoption [would] enable monitoring and evaluation. (p. 148)

The increase in the number of children being placed in ICA could put these traditions at risk through targeting vulnerable children that would, if ICA and associated practices did not exist, most likely be cared for within extended family and community. It is not uncommon for extended family members who are caring for orphans to be targeted for relinquishment. In a recent review of adoption statistics, the French Embassy in Ethiopia found that 245 out of 392 ICA cases processed in 2009 were relinquishment; 102 or 39 percent of those were relinquished by extended family members (M. Diallo, personal communication, June 28, 2011). For the USA Embassy, 81 percent of adoption cases are relinquishment; 18 percent of them by extended family members (U.S. DOS, 2011a). Furthermore, a large percentage of children being placed in ICA come from the Oromia and Amhara regions where the practice of *guddifachaa* is common. Statistics provided by the French Embassy show that 59 percent of the 392 ICA cases processed in 2009 came from the two regions; Amhara accounted for 43 percent of all cases and Oromia 16 percent (M. Diallo, personal communication, June 28, 2011).

The increasing number of children being relinquished from extended family members, encouraging relinquishment for improved educational opportunities (PEAR, 2010b), and targeting children from specific regions should raise concern about how ICA has and will continue to erode the practice of indigenous care responses.

Ethiopian Government Controls

In light of the aforementioned concerns, Ethiopian government structures have started to respond. In March 2011, the Ministry of Women's, Children's and Youth Affairs (MoWCYA) issued a directive saying it will process a maximum of five inter-country adoptions a day, effective March 10, 2011 (Heinlein, 2011b); a 90 percent decrease in the number of cases that were being reviewed. The Ministry acknowledged concerns about irregular practices and the spokesperson for MoWCYA acknowledged concerns, specifically mentioning issues of abuse and illegalities in some adoption cases. The spokesperson went on to explain that new directives will help pave the way for the development of new safeguards (Heinlein, 2011b). Investigations mentioned in Heinlein (2011b) also show that birth parents have been tricked into relinquishing children, documentation has been falsified and significant sums of money have been passed at certain stages of the intercountry adoption process. In addition to the slow down in case review, several key ministries have also been involved in an assessment of institutional child care settings (Family Health International, Children's Investment Fund Foundation, and UNICEF, 2010). The assessment has resulted in the planned closing of approximately 46 institutions; primarily those involved in identifying children for ICA ("46 Foster Homes," 2011). The formal acknowledgement by government institutions of the connections among an increasing number of children being placed in ICA, institutional care settings as recruiting grounds for ICA, and other irregular practices such as falsified documentation is an important first step in developing more appropriate and formal safeguards for children. Although initial steps have been made to address concerns regarding the ICA process, significant work remains to be completed to strengthen the legal framework, build capacity to appropriate oversight by mandated institutions, increase public awareness about the implications of ICA, and promote better understanding and implementation of the subsidiarity principle.

Conclusion

In an article published in an Ethiopian online newspaper in 2009, "People in *Merkato* jokingly say that if you go to '*Bomb Tera*' [a name of a place in *Merkato*] there is nothing you cannot buy, including a child" (Maru, 2009). This commentary underscores the availability of everything at Africa's largest outdoor market, but it also illustrates the "market" approach to finding children for ICA and the weakness of systems to protect vulnerable children. This commodification of children has occurred in other countries before Ethiopia.

Ethiopia appears to be at an important crossroads whereby irregular practices have been identified and publicly acknowledged by the government, foreign embassies and other organizations such as the United Nations Children's Fund (UNICEF; Heinlein, 2010a; Heinlein, 2011b). Ethiopia has a choice between continuing down the current path or addressing the irregular and illegal practices that have been identified with a thoughtful response for reform. For reform to occur Ethiopia's accession to the HCIA is fundamental and there are signs that this may occur by the end of 2011 or in 2012. The authors argue that this is a unique opportunity. Ethiopia has the chance to construct a stronger legal framework that protects birth families, adoptive families and most importantly, children. Acknowledging traditions of indigenous care practices and their inherent value is also needed if kinship care and *guddifachaa* are to be continued. The recent boom of ICA in Ethiopia and its accompanying array of concerning practices do not necessarily have to end in the same way that other countries have experienced. Rather this could be an opportunity to demonstrate how documented problems can be acknowledged, addressed, and turned into a beneficial change for children. If this opportunity is not embraced then Ethiopia will most likely become another statistic in the on-going intercountry adoption saga, with children having the most to lose.

Chapter 11

Maternal Thinking in the Context of Stratified Reproduction: Perspectives of Birth Mothers from South Africa

Riitta Högbacka

Over the past decade the annual numbers of intercountry adoptions to the affluent parts of the world have varied between the peak of 45,000 in 2004 to roughly 30,000 in 2009 (Selman, 2010c). What is less often emphasized is the other side of those figures: the birth mothers left behind in low resource countries. It is precisely those women we know little about. At the same time, there is a growing body of research on the circumstances and rights of women making a plan for domestic adoption in Western Europe and in North America (Fravel, Mcroy, and Grotevant, 2007; Grotevant, 2009; Modell, 1994; 2002; Neil, 2006; Smith, 2007; Solinger, 2002).

This chapter focuses on South African birth mothers' understanding of the circumstances leading to the adoption of their child. How do birth mothers view their alternatives; and how do they talk about their lives without the child afterwards? From my larger project conducted from 2006 through 2009 with birth and adoptive parents in intercountry adoption, I describe thematic interviews with 32 Black (or 'Coloured')[1] South African (and some Zimbabwean) women who had relinquished a child (24) or who were pregnant and had made an adoption plan (8). Slightly fewer than half had relinquished two to 12 years previously, whereas for the other half the experience was more recent. The ages of the women varied between 14 and 43, the majority being between 19 and 25. Birth mothers were recruited through homes for pregnant women (15), an aftercare skills development program (6), and through social workers who worked for three large organizations arranging adoptions (11). At four different locations in South Africa, I conducted the interviews, including 29 in English and three with the help of an interpreter/social worker in Afrikaans. I also draw on interviews I conducted with ten South African adoption social workers. All names in the text are pseudonyms.

I refer to the birth mothers' beliefs, sentiments, and practices concerning their children as maternal thinking, following the anthropologist Scheper-Hughes (1992) who argued that maternal commitment is contingent on the particular

1 South Africans themselves still distinguish between 'blacks', 'whites', 'coloureds' and 'Indians' (see Alexander 2006, 24-5 for further clarification). I will therefore be using these categories in this chapter.

social and economic circumstances. Her study showed that in the context of high infant mortality and the unavailability of birth control or other help, impoverished Brazilian women withheld maternal care and emotions from newborns they thought were 'doomed.' Those findings are compatible with newer approaches based on evolutionary theory that emphasize maternal ambiguity rather than a single universal and fixed maternal script or 'maternal instinct' (Hrdy, 1999, 2008). In environments with extremely scarce resources and no social support, human mothers have had to weigh the chances of successfully raising this particular infant against investing in the survival of themselves and their existing or future children. Such circumstances make mothering more difficult and can lead to reduced maternal commitment and to the abandonment of infants (Hrdy, 1999, 2008; Johns and Belsky, 2008; Keller and Chasiotis, 2008).

Using the framework of maternal thinking under difficult circumstances, I look at the tradeoffs and dilemmas that birth mothers face. It will, however, be shown that maternal commitment is generally not withdrawn in the case of birth mothers of internationally adopted children in South Africa. Birth mothers' perceptions and options are framed by their place in the new global division of reproduction, where children are seen as the new 'gold' and are transported from the less developed world to countries with the resources to absorb them (Ehrenreich and Hochschild, 2003). This system of "stratified reproduction" (Colen, 1995) simultaneously creates the adoptive family and the birth family. In the South African context, the high value placed on children along with the importance of the extended family and traditional child fosterage, all influence the meanings of child relinquishment. As a large number of children do not live with their birth mothers all the time or are raised by kin or non-kin at some point, adoption tends to be viewed not as a permanent erasing of ties. Most of the birth mothers I interviewed saw intercountry adoption as a way to provide their children with better opportunities. It will be shown that for many, motherhood does not end with the relinquishment of the child.

Although intercountry adoptions from Africa have until now been rare compared to other continents, this appears to be changing mainly due to a decline in numbers of small children available in other countries and the growing 'demand' for children in the West (See Chapter 1, Table 1.10). Intercountry adoptions from South Africa started relatively late, in the 21st century, with a sudden increase in the number of Black children entering children's homes. The Hague Convention (1993) was entered into force in 2003. A Children's Act, passed in April, 2010, regulates adoptions and domesticates the Convention (Government of South Africa [GOVSA], 2005). Although based on the Western model of exclusive adoption, in which legal ties between the child and his/her birth parents are terminated, the new legislation also introduces the concept of a post-adoption agreement (in domestic adoptions), regulating the possible maintaining of connections. Before turning to the South African case, other studies of birth mothers in intercountry adoption will briefly be reviewed.

Birth Mothers' Vulnerable Positions

Birth mothers in countries of origin live under oppressive economic, social, and political conditions. Economic reasons were at the top of the list in the Marshall Islands: most birth mothers were simply too poor to raise another child (Roby and Matsumura, 2002), especially as they had three or four other children to support. Similarly, most Latin American children in state institutional care are not the first children of teenage mothers, but the third or fourth children of very poor mothers (Fonseca, 2003).

Birth mothers lack other alternatives. In the Marshall Islands there were no governmental or other programs for temporary care of the children (Roby and Matsumura, 2002). Poor mothers in Ecuador (Leifsen, 2009) and Brazil (Fonseca, 2003) have no in-between solutions. If they do not have the means to support their child, the only option available is adoption. The desperation of birth mothers is particularly striking where intercountry adoptions have occurred directly from birth families, such as Romania in the early 1990s (Kligman, 1995) and Guatemala in the early 21st century (Cantwell, 2003). In Eastern European countries poverty, deprivation, and lack of support for families in difficult situations lie at the heart of why children enter children's homes (United Nations Children's Fund [UNICEF], 2001).

In most cases birth mothers have no social support. Records of Argentinean birth mothers show that the women were poor, young, largely uneducated, and had migrated to towns in search of work; they were alone without the support of a family or birth father (Giberti, 2000). In the Marshall Islands, the grandmothers, who traditionally help in looking after their daughter's children, put pressure on their daughters to relinquish the child (Roby and Matsumura, 2002). Social support is also lacking in cultures that attach a heavy stigma on unwed motherhood. In India the shame and discrimination brought on by having a child out of wedlock, combined with extreme poverty, are reported as important factors behind adoptions (Bos, 2007). The majority of the children leaving South Korea for adoptions abroad are born to single mothers, who are discriminated against by society and who have little or no support (Dorow, 1999; Sang-Hun, 2009).

Little is known about the consequences of adoption for birth mothers; however, the evidence points to emotional distress, longing, and a wish to know how the child is faring. In China, where state policies and the need to have a son drive the abandonment of girls, some birth mothers reported that they still felt the loss of the child, while others said it was less painful over time (Johnson, 2004). See Chapter 8. Chinese birth parents interviewed in a recent documentary by Changfu Chang said they had never been able to forget their child. A tearful birth father said to the cameras about the baby girl given up over ten years ago: "All these years, every night, your mother and I have been talking about you, thinking about what you look like" (Chang, 2008).

Recent media reports (Geoghegan, 2009; Jolley, 2009) paint a grim picture of intercountry adoptions from Ethiopia (see also Chapter 10). Some birth mothers interviewed in a documentary stated that they were homeless and without the means to feed children (Geoghegan, 2009). In addition, birth mothers were despondent and did not understand they were permanently giving up their children. One birthmother said: "I do not regret. But when the lady took him away she said she would let me know his address. She said she'd assist me and my other kids when she took him away. At that time I was homeless (crying). Until now, I've heard nothing. It's almost 3 years."

Many poor families in Brazil whose child had been adopted did not know that their child had been declared abandoned, nor did they know the meaning of signing (Cardarello, 2009; Fonseca, 2003). Some thought the child could visit or would return. In the Marshall Islands Roby and Matsumura (2002) found that local child care through informal foster arrangements clashed with practices of permanent adoption. Most birth mothers believed they would receive photographs and letters about their child, and that the child would return when of age. Informal child fosterage that does not cut all ties with the natal family is indeed common in many countries of origin, including Oceanic societies (Modell, 2002), various Latin American countries (Fonseca, 2003; Hoelgaard, 1998; Leifsen, 2009; Leinaweaver, 2008), and Africa (Goody, 1982; Therborn, 2006).

The Context of Raising Children in South Africa

Children and fertility are highly valued in Africa (Therborn, 2006), although the total fertility rate has declined in several African countries. It is currently 2.5 in South Africa (UNICEF, 2008b). Motherhood is still almost universal in South Africa, and women carry the sole responsibility for the children (Swartz, 2003). Marriage prevalence for South African women is low, and there is a high rate of marriage breakup (Therborn, 2006). The legacy of the destruction of the Black family that started during Apartheid can still be seen in the patterns of disruption. Strict pass laws allowed only men to enter cities, as workers in the mines, while families (women and children) remained in the countryside. This strained family life (Thomas and Mabusela, 1991). Fathers were often absent. Births registered in 2008 revealed that 67 percent of birth certificates lacked information on fathers (UNICEF, 2008b). In some South African areas, the father is totally missing in over 50 percent of Black families (Lund, 2006). At the end of 2004, 37 percent of all households were women-headed (South African Institute of Race Relations [SAIRR], 2006).

Another distinctive feature of child rearing in Africa is the widespread and common informal fostering of children, and the importance of the extended family (Goody, 1982; Therborn, 2006). In 2001, almost 45 percent of Black households and well over 30 percent of 'Coloured' households in South Africa consisted of extended families (Amoateng, Heaton and Kalule-Sabiti, 2007). The expectation has been that pregnant women and girls bring the child home to the extended family and the *gogo*, the grandmother, most often the woman's own mother, will look after the child. Over 60 percent of South African children who have lost one or both parents live with their grandparents (UNICEF, 2003). Informal fosterage has typically been high among the Black population in South Africa. Urban couples or single women might leave young children in rural areas with grandmothers, and rural families might leave their school-age children with relatives in urban areas, in order that they might attend better schools (Makiwane, 2003). In fact, 27 percent of children with both parents and 35 percent of paternal orphans in South Africa do not live with their birth mother (UNICEF, 2003).

South Africa's HIV/AIDS epidemic is the largest in the world: in 2009 there were an estimated 5.6 million people living with HIV (UNAIDS, 2010). Life expectancy has been reduced from 61 years in 1990 to 52 in 2008 (UNICEF, 2008b). The HIV/AIDS epidemic, along with high unemployment, has put stress on the extended-family system. For example, all members of the extended family might be unemployed; grandmothers and other female relatives might have too many children to care for.

In 1994 South Africa carried out a remarkable political reform, as the Apartheid government stepped down. However, social and economic reforms are still lacking (Bond, 2006). There is increasing division between those with good permanent jobs and education and those with no skills and no employment (Seekings and Nattrass, 2006). There are no governmental support systems for poor mothers or families. The child support grant, introduced in 1998, is insufficient (For example, in 2005 it was 180 ZAR or about 26 USD a month; Lund, 2006). Patterns of unemployment and poverty are gendered and racialized. The expanded unemployment rate[2] for Black women in 2005 was 56 percent, compared to 39 percent for Black men and 10 percent for White women (SAIRR, 2006).

The Current Study: South African Birth Mothers' Perspectives

I now turn to my research on birth mothers. First, I will describe the circumstances of the women and thereafter their emotions and beliefs regarding adoption.

Birth Mothers' Tradeoffs: Survival or Reproduction

When the adoption plan was made, the situation of the birth mothers was desperate: most were struggling financially and many did not have a roof over their heads. Their everyday life was a matter of survival, of having enough food. A social worker acting as an interpreter said about Louisa, 25, and her household, consisting of her older child, her mother and sister: "They are all living below the poverty line. … They can't look after anybody else. They just have to look after

2 The expanded unemployment rate includes those people that had given up looking for work.

themselves." Elsie, 27, was unemployed, HIV-positive and already had one young child: "I can't keep the child, because I must look after myself."

Given the high unemployment rates and lack of benefits, finding employment is crucial. Those with no jobs would have taken any kind of work. Many dreamed of a cleaning job. Lily, from a poor rural area, had come to the city looking for work. When I met her, the baby was two months old and had been placed in a nursery of the adoption agency. Lily visited the baby every day and very much wanted to keep her. Her two older children were living in the rural area with Lily's aunt who was also unemployed. Lily faced an impossible equation.

> … I can't go to [her home in the rural area] because I'm not working. … and if I'm staying in the [her home in the rural area], it is too far, I haven't money for transportation. It's too far. There's no jobs. And here I don't have a place to stay. (Lily, 37, gave birth two months ago)

Others with some kind of employment but with very little pay were struggling hard to find a so-called good job so that they could support themselves. Most of the women (22 of 32) had children and were working hard to provide a better situation for them.

> Biggest problem at the moment is a job … Stable job. I need a stable job to support my children. Any little money that I get, I don't worry about myself. I always see that my children have it first. A stable job, I'm struggling so hard to get a stable job. … (Meg, 22, relinquished child three years ago)

Some women were working and pursuing studies at the same time. Natie, together with 850,000 other Black South African women (SAIRR, 2006), found employment as a domestic worker. Domestics cannot have their children with them, so Natie's two older children were living with her mother, and she saw them on the weekends.

> … Then during the school holiday I got this job as a domestic worker. I can't leave that job, so I'm doing management assistant part-time, so that I can go to work. Then, afternoon I will attend classes for management assistant. … you have to work hard to create something for yourself and the other children. I have to work hard. (Natie, 27, relinquished child a year ago)

Birth mothers strongly believed or knew that the way out of poverty would be through education. Many of the women were hoping to study, but often had to choose between the last-born infant and school. As Bontle, 18, explained: "I cannot afford to support both the babies and then me and at the same time attend school." Miriam contrasted education and "going nowhere," and many others said even more dramatically that without education death awaited you.

> Now I'm looking for a job. At least, if they can pay me 1.500 [about 218 USD] per month, so then I can take myself to a school. … Because if you don't have education you are not going nowhere. (Miriam, 25, relinquished child over a year ago)

Many of these mothers stated that they wanted to be "proper" parents to their children. This included being able to pay school fees and also not having always to say "no" to their children's needs. Mary had joined an aftercare skills development group for birth mothers and was able to earn some money from temporary employment in a weekly sewing and baking project. She came from a poor rural area, where her other three children were being taken care of by her aunt, who was also unemployed. Mary sent what little money she made to her aunt to care for the children.

> … Because for now I'm homeless. I'm not working. … My other children at home don't even have shoes to go to school. … The thing that I was thinking about was … the right job, working for my children, to give them … things they need. … start from the beginning to support the child like a parent. … So I want, the time that say, he said to me mom, we have the trip at school so I just give that money, give him to go to that trip. (Mary, 34, relinquished child a month ago)

In addition to taking their own needs and those of their other children into consideration, mothers may have to put supporting other close kin ahead of investing in a new infant (Keller and Chasiotis, 2008). Many of the birth mothers were helping relatives or taking care of younger siblings. The two Zimbabwean women also had a hard time in South Africa. They were without work, support or protection, and, as immigrants, faced discrimination and hostility (Landau and Freemantle, 2010). Flora and Hope both sent what little money they managed to earn home to Zimbabwe to their parents, siblings, and other children. Flora, 23, had just given birth. She pointed out that even a hundred rand (about 14 USD) could make a difference to her older child and parents in Zimbabwe. She said: "And my child, it can survive with that hundred rand." Hope was in South Africa illegally, looking for work and supporting her own mother, her other child, her older brother's little child, her younger brother, her 18-year-old sister and the sister's boyfriend and their baby, all living together at Hope's mother's place. Hope, just like a number of other birth mothers, had discovered her pregnancy too late for abortion. Legal abortion has been available in South Africa since 1997, and at the moment there are over 45,000 abortions annually (SAIRR, 2006).

> … if I have a baby where I'm going to stay with this baby because I don't have place, I don't have money, I'm not working. … I discovered I'm pregnant when I was five months. And then I don't have money to support this child 'cause I have one child. … I support my mom, I support my child. There's child of my brother. She is at school, and then my brother. He's at school. So I must send them books

> and food to eat, to go to school. … if I send something to my mother at home I'm feeling happy all the time. (Hope, 20, relinquished child a week ago)

The mother's health and overall condition are also important. The energy allocated to somatic effort reduces the energy available to reproductive effort (Johns and Belsky, 2008). The four HIV-positive women in my sample were healthy, with the prospect of receiving the new anti-retroviral drugs later. Their HIV-positive status was, however, an important factor in the adoption decision. Most had been shocked to learn about being HIV-positive at the maternity clinic when they were pregnant with the child they later relinquished. They worried because they did not know how long they would live, and had other children to consider:

> … I had to give up the baby. I thought I'll never give it up because it was so difficult for me thinking that I went and tested the other one, so I found out she was also HIV- positive so it was just rough for me. So I couldn't bear thinking that I'm bringing this baby to life and then she's going to be miserable and I wasn't going to give her nothing but misery. But I could give her life and then give it to somebody who'll give her such a wonderful life, education, everything so that I can struggle with this other one. … (Simphiwe, 29, relinquished child two years ago)

Lack of Social Support

What is apparent in the women's narratives is the lack of supportive networks. The Zimbabwean women stated that they have "no family here." Immigrants and migrants to cities from rural areas have in common the absence of family and kin. The feeling of being on one's own was evident in the majority of the interviews.

> I can't raise a child on myself, on my own. I'm unemployed, I don't have clothes, I don't have anything. What can I give the child? (Elsie, 27, relinquished child a year ago).

> … at this point I cannot raise my child, though I've grown fond of my baby, but I can only really think of myself right now, here alone, I can't. (Lebohang, 19, pregnant).

According to Hrdy humans have evolved as "cooperative breeders": mothers have always needed and received help in rearing their young (Hrdy, 1999, 2008). The role played by maternal grandmothers in particular and other female kin is of great importance: it diminishes child mortality and can make a real difference even in conditions of poverty (Hrdy, 1999, 2008; Johns and Belsky 2008; Keller and Chasiotis, 2008). In South Africa the *gogo*, the maternal grandmother, is a central character in helping out with the children of her daughters (Duflo, 2003;

UNICEF, 2003). Many birth mothers talked at length about the importance of their own mother. Those who had mothers helping them talked about them in highly appreciative terms. Sometimes, even the presence of a mother, would not be enough for the women to cope. One of these was Simphiwe, 29, who was struggling with poverty, HIV and desertion by her husband. To the question of who helps you she, like many others, replied: "It's my mom. Yes, my mom is always there for me." Edith, 19, replied: "Family? It's my mother. She has always been there for us, in the hardest times of my life." Edith, in fact, later changed her mind as her mother will help and "would never allow adoption."

Other women whose mother had died, or who did not have a close relationship with their mother, mentioned that as an important reason behind their adoption decision. "If only I could have told my mother" or "I just so wished my mother was still alive, maybe I wouldn't have done it" were frequent comments.

> To keep that baby? If I had a good relationship with my mother I think. Because she didn't know me when I was a baby, so I think if we had a closer relationship with each other, even if his father ran away, maybe my mother would advice me and support me. … (Cindy, 22, relinquished child a year ago)

While it is mostly maternal kin who help, support from the child's father is also important. Men's commitment to their offspring, however, is dependent on the quality of their relationship with the child's mother (Geary, 2008). According to Hrdy (1999) men prioritize quality over quantity in children under conditions of high paternity certainty and high infant survival rates. If a man cannot expect to live far into middle-age and the relationship patterns are disrupted, he would instead tend to try to sire as many children as he can hoping that some of them would survive. In South Africa those latter conditions prevail, and fathers are absent in almost half the families (Lund, 2006; UNICEF, 2008b). Four women I interviewed were pregnant as a result of rape by unknown men. Three of the four HIV-positive women and numerous others were deserted by men after learning they were pregnant.

> … he [birth father] said to me he doesn't want a positive child, and then positive mother. … I find him disappear, take his clothes, everything. So when I tried to contact him I didn't find him anywhere. And then I was afraid to tell my parents that I'm pregnant because they didn't know that I'm pregnant a second child. And if my stepfather will chase me away because with my firstborn he chased me away…. (Elsie, 27, relinquished child a year ago)

According to birth mothers, the men often used arguments such as "it's not my child" before they disappeared. Some men would have several girlfriends at the same time. Many women I interviewed made it clear that they did not even think about relying on a man; instead, they dreamed about having all their children and young siblings and their own mothers in a home of their own.

> … If things go exactly the way I want them to go I see myself with my kids. No men. … a house, maybe with my family, in my own house. (Sibongele, 20, pregnant).

> … no man, I want to be independent. The man is on the site but I'm not putting him in the picture, I'll put him in the picture when I have everything. So I know when he leaves me, I still have my things, so he can go with whatever he gave us. … (Meg, 22, relinquished child three years ago)

However, some birth fathers are present and can be relied upon. One such example is Margaret, 33, who had recently given birth. Margaret and her husband have a long-term relationship and have four other children together. They are experiencing severe financial difficulties in trying to make ends meet and to provide for their children. Margaret and her husband decided together about the adoption.

No Viable Alternatives

Birth mothers had very few other options. It was generally: either keep your child (which because of your economic and other immediate circumstances you cannot do) or give it up forever. There was no viable third way. Foster care was not really an option for these women as it was only granted in cases of severe negligence or abuse of the child. There was also no other temporary help available for the women; nor were there programs at the governmental level to help single or poor mothers keep their children. Social workers commented: "There is a real sense of desperation in the moms that we work with because we can't offer them what's needed most." Another experienced social worker said: "They're giving up because they can't do anything else."

Other social workers said that they saw changes in some women's circumstances six to twelve months or two years after relinquishing. This implies that if there was a way to support birth mothers or to provide temporary child care, many might improve their situations, and be able to take back their children. I also know of birth mothers who came back after two or more years saying that their situation had improved, and they wanted to have their children back.

Some social workers tried to find funding for housing and child care for the mothers, to help them to look for jobs and get back on their feet, but to no avail. Other social workers told me they stretched the rules and let children's homes keep the children for three to six months or longer while the mother tried to improve her situation. The situation of students, in particular, made social workers wonder because these women might in the very near future be in a far better financial situation but "based on their immediate need they make the decision for adoption." The same social worker continued: "I often wonder about them."

Among the birth mothers I interviewed Lily, Simphiwe, Rose, and Edith did not or had not wanted adoption. They would have preferred temporary care. Edith, 19, was seven months pregnant, and was in a home for pregnant women. She told me that she did not want to put her child up for adoption, but that it was difficult in the home because the atmosphere was so pro-adoption. She had made an appointment with a social worker to discuss her other options. She remarked: "Here in this place, I think it's only the girls that are here they are all for adoption. ... I haven't heard anyone [talk] about foster care. Everybody here is for adoption." Social workers of the organization confirmed that they did not allow women who wanted to keep their babies to live in the home, because "it had a bad effect on the other girls." Later this organization, however, founded another home for 'parenting-minded' pregnant women.

Rose was HIV-positive and had another young child. She had relinquished her last born child three years previously. Rose lived in an informal settlement, in very bad conditions, while her child stayed with the paternal grandmother during the week. Her own parents were no longer alive. Rose would have preferred temporary care to adoption.

> ... I wanted the local one, but they said there aren't local one.... Because I think maybe I can contact ... . I was only told about the overseas ones. ... So now I can't do anything now until she's reached the age. (Rose, 43, relinquished child three years ago)

Maternal Emotions: Thinking about the Child

Adverse circumstances, with limited social support, can make mothering extremely difficult, and can result in the withdrawal of maternal commitment (Hrdy, 1999; Scheper-Hughes, 1992). The birth mothers I interviewed did not, however, generally show signs of withdrawn maternal commitment. Research on birth mothers in domestic adoptions in Western Europe and North America have found that the child, mostly born to young White single mothers, remains 'psychologically present' to the mother; thus, even after decades, the child is 'in the heart of or on the mind of' the birth mother (Fravel et al., 2000). Many of the mothers I interviewed were dealing with sadness, grief, and longing, and some even regretted the adoption.

One of the saddest stories was that of Lily, 37, who had given birth a month previously. She wanted to keep her baby, but did not have any means to do it. She was crying almost all the time. One factor making the situation more difficult for Lily was her age. She commented on it saying she was old and that this was her last child. Studies show that mothers near the end of their reproductive cycle cannot be so selective with the allocation of investment as younger women (Keller and Chasiotis 2008).

> You see, I'm very worried. Every day I'm worried and they are coming to see me every day if they are ready to take the baby. ... Because it is not easy. (Cries) ... I want to take baby but I can't. Because I have got nothing. I have got nothing. ...

> And you know I tried to forget this baby but I can't forget. Now I'm not sleeping, I'm not okay. (Lily, 37, gave birth a month ago)

Simphiwe had relinquished her child two years previously, but could not get over it. She also cried through the interview.

> ... I don't know what time I'll ever forget it. I just wondered will my baby one day ask, mom where were you when I started to walk, mom where were you when I started teething. That's quite bad. (Cries) (Simphiwe, 29, relinquished child two years ago)

Other mothers also felt grief and loss after adoption. One mother who had relinquished her child more than ten years previously said: "After giving her up there was a time when I wanted to commit suicide so many times." The child Rosina had relinquished about a year previously was born as a result of rape. Yet, she remained sad about the loss of her child.

> ... The worst thing is me, I'm lonely, alone. ... I feel like no one. ... (Cries) I end up starting to drink every day.... It doesn't help and I had to stop myself before I was addicted. But now when I'm lonely, I just cry before I go to sleep. ... I cry myself to sleep. But at times, it doesn't happen every day, I can pass a week, and I feel like I forgot him, not thinking about him, not crying for him, I feel like I forgot him and I'll cry, then I stop myself. It's better to think about him, not cry about him. And I try every day when I get up to pray for him where ever he is. It gives me a good start for the day. (Rosina, 22, relinquished child a year ago)

Birth mothers were thinking about their children, wondering how they were. Both those who had relinquished several years previously and those with more recent experiences recalled thinking about their child. With time, many felt the pain lessen.

> ... I thought about him every day. But I told myself I just have to like pull myself together, you know, and go on, because I have other kids to look after. (Cathy, 30, relinquished child seven years ago).

According to the birth mothers, the birthday of the child is always very difficult. The feeling they shared was one of powerlessness of not being able to do anything for the child on the birthday. "It's his birthday and I can't do anything." Another mother said that sometimes she did not get out of her bed the whole day on her child's birthday. The other difficult encounter was seeing children of the same age, which brought back memories.

> When you see just a child. ... You start asking yourself some questions. How is he? His mind, his hands, or he's grow, how much he's now, he's bigger, smaller,

> fatter, how, the colour? We always ask ourselves that. (Elsie, 27, relinquished child a year ago)

Even though those mothers did not withdraw maternal commitment, other mothers may differ. Among my interviewees, one woman reduced investment. Sibongele, 20, was about seven months pregnant. She explained to me that she already had two toddlers cared by her parents in a rural area. She herself was in the city in order to complete a course on body guarding, after which she would have a good chance of finding employment. Her father was paying the expensive school fees. She could not and did not want to care for a new infant. The baby would be put up for adoption. Sibongele also emphasized that relinquishment would not be difficult, and that she would never come back. It is also reported that abandonment of babies at hospitals or other areas has, from 2008 onwards, increased in South Africa (Van Schalkwyk, 2008). These desperate women may have had no other option but to withdraw commitment.

Maternal Commitment and Global Hierarchies

"I know that they love them throughout of my experience of coming across them, they love their kids," a Black social worker wanted to add at the end of the interview. In the birth mothers' narratives the four most frequently found idioms often appeared together: "I love my child," "better life for child," "I don't want the child to suffer" and "I had no choice." It was evident that motherhood means looking after the child and its needs. In the context of scarce resources and opportunities and the weakening of the extended family system, the highest proof of a mother's love begins to mean parting with the child instead of staying together (Beck-Gernsheim, 2011).

> … if you are a mother you must think about your baby. … I'm not giving them 'cause I don't love him. I love this baby. But I don't have choice in the situation. (Hope, 20, relinquished child a week ago).

> Sometimes, when I'm alone, I just think about her. How is she doing? Is she crying wherever she is? Is somebody picking her up? You know, all those kinds of things. And most people think that I just did that because I'm selfish, you know, and I do not think about her, I do not love her. The reason why I did this is because I really, really, really love her. (Molly, 20, relinquished child a year ago)

The context of stratified reproduction and hierarchical global structures present a new situation for the mothers' decision making. The birth mothers were well aware of the unequal power relations behind the giving and receiving of children in adoption. Some people have all the wealth in the world but cannot have children, while others have children but no means to raise them (Yngvesson, 2010). Birth mothers knew or had been told by social workers that there was "a long list of prominent families" who did not have children, but very much wanted to have them. The birth mothers also understood the value of a very young child.

> ... she told me that you know there are very, very well off people who doesn't have kids, who are able to take care of kids, so I just wanted to leave her in good hands, I don't want that the child is going to grow up and suffer. So they told me there is a long list of prominent families who want to adopt kids and this is a newborn and usually a newborn has a better chance of adoption because they don't know nothing. (Lucille, 38, relinquished child 12 years ago)

The birth mothers clearly wanted the child to have more opportunities than they themselves had. It was perceived that the child would have "a chance to get a better schooling, a better life from better parents." Another mother said: "You must just tell yourself that maybe I'm not going to give her life, maybe those other people will be able to give everything, see (cries)." Those other people are affluent adoptive parents from high resource countries. Natie, 27, had relinquished her child a year previously. She was also supporting her younger siblings and her mother, who looked after her two other children. She hoped that adoption would give her child "education, love, education, a better future," and importantly that the child would land in a higher social position.

> ... I couldn't kept my child because I'm not working. Actually I can't support the child, even though right now I'm the breadwinner at home. I have sisters and brothers, but I'm the breadwinner at home. ... so my mother and the other two at home, and my two children. So I think my mom understood that, you know, if she doesn't do this, then the child will suffer more. And I didn't have the support of the father, I didn't have myself financially, I didn't have anything to give the child. So I thought this is the best thing that this child can get better than myself. (Natie, 27, relinquished child a year ago)

The child becomes almost an extension of the mother. Those other people in higher positions whose families are formed out of the unequal global structures are perceived as being able to give the child such things as an education that the birth mother herself never had. Others talked about toys or other utensils and opportunities they never had.

> They even told me that in [their country] the education is fine. That's why I was so happy because me, I couldn't go to school (starts crying), even now, I still want to study ... (Miriam, 25, relinquished child a year ago)

Many birth mothers emphasized the well-being and happiness of their child somewhere else. They seemed to have a very idealistic picture of "overseas" as this "wonderful," "safe," "clean" place. One birth mother said: "I wanted a better future for it. Cause there's a lot of crime [here]." Another mother remarked: "The good thing is happiness and safety of the child, and environment, clean and safe environment. … It's a big thing for a child." Adoptive parents were described as "better parents," "good people" or "wonderful people." Several birth mothers expressed a wish to go away themselves if they could.

> … I made overseas adoption because I knew there's a life in there, she will get the best education, she will get the best job. Here kids are getting raped, terrible things are happening to kids in South Africa, you always have to be scared when you are at work. … It's so bad for the kids in here so if I could choose I would go there even myself. … that's why I did this because she will have so much opportunities. (Simphiwe, 29, relinquished child two years ago)

Maintaining Connections

The majority of birth mothers expressed a wish not to lose touch with their child. They explained to me that "I did not want to throw away of my child altogether." Similar wishes were made by the women I met randomly at the various homes. Pam was just 14 and was eight months pregnant. She chose adoption together with her mother because of her young age and due to the fact that their family was already struggling to make ends meet. She also said she did not want to "lose connections" with the child. Wanting to receive information about how their children were faring after adoption was very common. Only three of the 15 birth mothers I contacted at random through the homes thought they would not want any information. The rest of my interview sample (15) was more concentrated among those who were receiving or hoped to receive information through social workers. Two women had recently come back, wanting to know something about their children. They said it had bothered them all these years, not knowing.

The policies of the agencies allowed information to be sent for a period of two years. The actual practices varied, however. Sometimes the sending of letters and photographs stopped, and in other cases, it continued if both the adoptive parents and the birth mother wished. Some adoptive parents thought that communication had to stop after two years; and some birth mothers did not know communication would end. Other birth mothers did not receive anything despite promises. It still is up to the adoptive parents whether they want to send any information back to the social workers or the birth mother.

> … they told me that I'm gonna get letters and pictures every after four months for period of two years. … And then I mean two year period that's nothing. … the year's already gone. And then I'm only left some few months. And then they haven't done any. So sometimes when I think about that, I just get angry. That why are they doing this to me? Why aren't they sending me pictures anymore? Have they forgotten about me? … (Molly, 20, relinquished child a year ago)

Margaret, 33, who had just signed the adoption papers, told me: "Sometimes it's like you're throwing her or what. And maybe to know something, it will help. Just to see how she's doing, is she smiling or …" (cries). Other birth mothers who were receiving information confirmed that information did help. Photographs and letters could ease the birth mothers' sorrow and longing for the child. Information alleviated pain and lessened anxiety. Letters and photographs are also tangible objects. They can be put away and then taken out when one feels the longing.

> At first it was not so easy. I was always thinking about him, but now I'm not thinking about him. I know that where he is he is happy because I see the pictures. When the child is not happy we can see on his eyes that he's not happy. So I don't worry about my child. … But when the times goes on or I get the pictures my heart is having joy, enjoying. … Because I'm not trying to forget him. I just want to accept. If you see something you'll accept rather than not to see. (Elsie, 27, relinquished child a year ago)

> … when I'm pretty lonely I read the letters and look at the pictures. It does help. … It keeps me going. It's tough, but just seeing him in the pictures, I know he is still there. He is out there and he is fine and I feel much better. (Rosina, 22, relinquished child a year ago)

Birth mothers hoped and believed that one day they would meet up with their child, or that the child would come back. The idea of the future return of the child was expressed by both those birth mothers I met randomly through the homes and those who were still in some contact with the adoptive parents through the social workers. Usually it was thought that the child would return when of age. Mary: "I love the child, I want, when he was eighteen, God knows, maybe I will be alive. So when he meet me." Hope: "That baby, she will come maybe after eighteen years. She want to see me." Even in cases where the child was a result of rape, mothers expressed the wish to one day meet their child. Lebohang had been raped by unknown men.

> … I don't want to lose contact, I still want to know what's going to happen throughout the years, and hopefully one day he or she will understand and I will want to meet him. (Lebohang, 19, pregnant)

Many birth mothers still thought of the child as 'their' child and as part of the birth family and kin. I heard expressions such as "It's still my child," "At the end of the day, it's my child" or "He is my blood" even though "he's not with me." The clean break of Western adoption clearly does not happen in the minds of the birth mothers. The perceptions of birth mothers echoed more the norms of traditional child circulation, where ties are not erased (Fonseca, 2003; Leinaweaver, 2008).

Conclusion

It is clear that the South African birth mothers I interviewed were in difficult, some even desperate, situations. The inability to afford the economic necessities, lack of social support, and the need to support older children dictated their decisions. At the same time many birth mothers I met just seemed down on their luck temporarily. Others would have wanted some kind of assistance instead of permanent adoption. This raises critical questions related to the practices of intercountry adoption. Is intercountry adoption currently the last resort it is meant to be after all attempts at family preservation or finding temporary solutions have been exhausted (Smolin, 2007b). This question is all the more important as South Africa has been an early proponent of the Hague Convention and its inter-country adoption program is carefully monitored and transparent. Every effort is made to ensure ethical practices. If the rights of the birth family cannot be protected even under such conditions, one wonders what the situation looks like elsewhere.

Intercountry adoption also legally erases the birth mother through its exclusivist 'clean break' approach that vests all rights to the child in the adoptive family, while terminating those of the family of origin (Högbacka, 2011; Yngvesson, 2010). The birth mother no longer has any role in the child's life; nor is there any obligation for the adoptive family to send news about the child. By contrast, most birth mothers I interviewed were extending or hoping to extend the boundaries of their nonexistent legal motherhood. They still thought about their children and wanted to stay in touch. The opening of intercountry adoption with the right for birth parents to receive information about their child's well-being, already advocated by Triseliotis, Shireman and Hundleby (1997), needs urgent attention.

The birth mothers I interviewed wanted to send their children to a safe environment with better opportunities. Thus, their children were not only not orphans, but also not unwanted nor abandoned. In such cases, adoption seen from the birth mothers' viewpoint has a closer resemblance to that of fostering than permanent termination of parenthood. How could this perspective be incorporated in the practices of intercountry adoption?

Acknowledgements

This research has been funded by the Academy of Finland, the Jenny and Antti Wihuri Foundation and the Kone Foundation. It has also been supported in part by the Beatrice Bain Research Group, at the University of California, Berkeley.

Chapter 12
Exiting or Going Forth? An Overview of USA Outgoing Adoptions

Dana Naughton

The United States (USA) has long led the world in the adoption of children from other countries, with over 300,000 adopted in the last 30 years (see Chapter 1). Given this magnitude of foreign-born adopted children living in the United States, it is not surprising that academic works have focused on the adjustment, development, and well-being of these children and their adoptive families. Missing from this academic canon, however, are the experiences of adoptive parents, birthparents, and adoptees that comprise a smaller subset of USA adoptions known as *outgoing cases* (U.S. DOS, Bureau of Consular Affairs, 2009a, 2011). This official Department of State (U.S. DOS) descriptor covers those intercountry adoptions, in which USA children, mostly Black and Bi-racial infants are adopted by citizens of Canada, the United Kingdom, Germany, France, Italy, the Netherlands, Switzerland, and other countries. The USA, with respect to intercountry adoption, is both a receiving and a sending nation. Indeed, from 2003 to 2009, nearly 1,500 USA-born children were adopted by foreign nationals in 14 countries (see Chapter 1)

This chapter outlines some of the issues surrounding outgoing adoptions, provides an overview of the process and ends with a brief discussion of an exploratory qualitative research study conducted by the author with USA and Canadian adoption professionals involved with these adoption cases over time. The discussion is framed within the context of the Hague Convention on Intercountry Adoption (HCIA) and the Intercountry Adoption Act of 2000 (IAA; Intercountry Adoption Act of 2000, 2000), and is focused on USA infant adoptions to convention countries.

Exploring Outgoing Cases

Although numerous socio-legal constructs of intercountry adoption practice are inverted by outgoing USA adoption practice, this phenomenon is remarkably absent in scholarly literature (Avitan, 2007). Adoption of USA children by foreign nationals falls into several categories of adoption lexicon. It is an *international* or *intercountry adoption* (ICA; terms used synonymously), which involves the legal adoption of a child from his or her country of origin into the country of the adoptive parent. All parental rights are transferred to the adoptive parent, and the child immigrates to the adoptive parents' country through a permanent, legal relationship (U.S. DOS Office of Consular Affairs, 2009). Because most of these emigrating children are Black or Bi-racial going to White families (Davenport, 2004), they are also *transracial adoptees*. These adoptions are also considered *outgoing cases*, a term used, to mean:

> (a) The child being adopted is resident in the United States; (b) the prospective adoptive parent(s) is (are) resident in a foreign Convention country, where they will move the child after adoption in the U.S. or plan to move the child for the purpose of adoption; and (c), the prospective adoptive parents initiated the adoption process by applying to the Central Authority in their country of residence on or after April 1, 2008. (U.S. Department of State, Bureau of Consular Affairs, 2009, Part II (b))

Mapped against traditional paradigms of intercountry adoption, these outgoing cases are exceptional for numerous reasons. First, ICA is almost universally seen as the transfer of children from low resource countries characterized by poverty and conflict to high resource Western nations (Dorow, 2006b; Dubinsky, 2008; Grice, 2005; Kapstein, 2003; Olsen, 2003; Solinger, 2002). The USA is one such nation, presumed to have abundant resources and families to support and adopt its own children as well as the children of other countries. Sending children to other countries contradicts this assumption.

Second, the desire for an infant adoption is a major criterion in domestic and intercountry adoptive parent decision-making (O'Neill, 2005; Stein, 2001). Although placement initiatives support outgoing adoptions of older children in USA public care (Court Appointed Special Advocates for children [CASA], 2010) most outgoing cases involves the adoption of infants (Child Welfare Information Gateway, 2004). These adoptions must be considered, then, against a complex racialized landscape. That is, are USA prospective adoptive families, as Dorow (2006a) or Rothman (2005) suggest, bypassing USA Black and Biracial infants in favor of 'less Black children' (from China, Eastern Europe, or Russia) or foreign-born Black children (from Ethiopia or Haiti) whose adoptions may be tethered to humanitarian notions of rescue? Are USA birthparents placing infants with foreign families because of experiences of racial discrimination in the United States? And are foreign adoptive parents who adopt USA children doing so, as Balcom and Dubinsky (2005) suggest, not just because of the child's young age, but because they are also motivated by beliefs that their country is less racially divisive than the United States?

Third, transracial and transnational adoption in the United States has a long, contentious history (Alexander and Curtis, 1996; Bartholet, 1991; Curtis, 1996; Goddard, 1996; Hansen and Pollack, 2010; Hollingsworth, 1998, 1999; Lee, 2003; Perry, 1993; Simon and Altstein, 1996). Most (though not all) of the emigrating children are Black or Bi-racial, and in the majority of these cases, they are being placed with White families (Davenport, 2004). Adoption researchers (Simon and Roorda, 2000) argue the need for transracially adopted children to have access to same-race communities and role models, an outcome that may be seriously challenged by placement in some foreign countries and communities. For example, in the last 20 years nearly 300 Black children have been placed in British Columbia, where Blacks account for less than 0.7 percent of the population (Armstrong, 2005).

Fourth, the decision to place an infant with a foreign parent must be made by the birthparent and determined by the state court in which the child resides as being in the best interest of the child. Adoption agencies and providers cannot facilitate contact between prospective adoptive parents and the birthparents prior to adoption. The infant's subsequent emigration, initiated through birthparent choice of adoptive parents, stands counter to international and USA child welfare instruments, which privilege the principle of subsidiarity (see Chapter 18). Subsidiarity holds that domestic or in-country options must be explored before an intercountry adoption can be considered. Only after birth, relative or kinship groups, or domestic non-relative adoption possibilities have been considered and proved unsuccessful in identifying a placement, is ICA to be considered.

In USA outgoing cases, birth mothers identify and choose a foreign family—and often a foreign White family, over a USA Black, White, or Bi-racial family. The birthmothers' decision-making process, which may involve review of adoptive parent 'Dear Birthparent' profiles in print or via Internet, lies well outside of all intercountry adoption protocols. In effect, the right of the birthmother to plan for her child takes precedence over the principle of subsidiarity. Although there is a limited but growing body of knowledge that considers the birthmother's voice in intercountry adoption (Bos, 2007; Dorow, 1999; Gibbons, Wilson, and Schnell, 2009; Jones, 2007; Roby and Matsumura, 2002), the agency of U.S. birthmothers—and in particular, Black birthmothers (Fessler, 2007)—is absent from those accounts. Birthmother choice in these adoptions is a dominant focus in legal studies (Avitan, 2007; Hollinger, 2008), the only discipline to date to offer scholarly investigation of the issues that regulate, promote, and impede the intercountry adoption of USA children. Hollinger (2008) notes the USA's contradictory relationship to subsidiarity in the matter of USA intercountry adoptions. That is, while the USA has favored limiting subsidiarity for incoming adoptees (i.e., "not requiring specific, prolonged or diligent efforts to find an in-country placement" [p. 113]), it takes a stronger viewpoint toward "due consideration" when sending out its own adoptees (p. 113). Nonetheless it allows several exceptions "to reasonable efforts requirement in states that permit a birth parent to select a related or unrelated identified PAP in another Convention country" (114).

In April, 2008, the USA fully enforced the Hague Convention on the Protection of Children and Co-operation in Respect of Inter-Country Adoption (HCIA). This instrument, implemented in the United States through the Intercountry Adoption Act of 2000 (Pub. L. 106-279, 42 U.S.C. 14901-14954), identifies U.S. DOS as its enforcement entity, working in concert with state adoption courts to determine that intercountry adoption is in a child's best interests.

It appears that currently, the USA is the only high resource country to regularly allow non-relative adoptions of its children by foreign nationals. As Pertman, observed "… people in other countries are adopting American children. That is occurring to this day, and no one to my knowledge has done a serious examination of the practice or its implications" (quoted in Wegar, 2006, p. 64). Pertman's observation is particularly disturbing because it suggests that for years, these best interest determinations have been conducted without any systemic, empirical investigation. And, for years it has been determined that for some of our nation's children, their best interests means growing up outside of the USA.

An Overview of the Outgoing USA Adoption Process

The IAA paved the way for implementation of the HCIA in the United States, and Section 104(b)(2) and 303, "Adoptions of children emigrating from the United States," and Title 22 Parts 96 and 97 of the federal regulations implementing the IAA are specific to outgoing adoptions. The IAA, which affects only adoptive placements of USA children to other Convention nations, states as one of its three purposes, "to improve the ability of the Federal Government to assist United States citizens seeking to adopt children from abroad and residents of other countries party to the Convention seeking to adopt children from the United States" (Intercountry Adoption Act of 2000, p. 2). The HCIA requires designation of a state entity—a Central Authority—to carry out enforcement and monitoring of convention responsibilities, and, as noted, U.S. DOS was identified as the Central Authority. U.S. DOS in turn chose the Council on Accreditation (COA) as the only national organization empowered to monitor accreditation standards and approvals of adoption services providers (agencies or persons). The Intercountry Adoption Act of 2000 P.L. 106-279 201; and the 22 CFR §§ 96.12—96.15 outline in detail the criteria to be met by an accredited agency, a temporarily accredited agency, an approved person, a supervised provider, an exempted provider, or a public domestic authority. Agencies and persons must also meet the criteria determined by their state under licensing criteria specific to state laws. Accreditation requirements do not apply to public domestic authorities in a Convention adoption case: For example, Oregon's Department of Human Service, which engages in relative adoptions across borders, (Englander, 2010) does not have to seek accreditation through the COA to do so. When the Hague Convention entered into force in the United States on April 1, 2008, it outlined a structure of outgoing adoptions in terms of how they are defined, processed, and for the first time, tracked. Documentation of ICA cases through a case registry mechanism is now required whether the adoption is an incoming or outgoing case, and regardless of its Convention status. On its website, U.S. DOS offers both web page summaries as well as longer documents to guide state authorities, approved providers and prospective adoptive families.

The following is a summary of the outgoing adoption process as described in U.S. DOS (2011), *The Hague Convention on Intercountry Adoption: A Guide to Outgoing Cases from the United States*.

The outgoing process appears relatively direct and very similar to any ICA process. It includes identification of a child in need of placement, a background study on the child prepared by an appropriate provider, prospective adoptive parents who have been approved in their home country and have filed with the Central Authority in their country, demonstration by USA adoption providers that reasonable efforts to locate a domestic family have been made, application approval by central authorities in both countries, agreement that placement with the family is in the best interests of the child, and submission of a formal placement proposal. After acceptance of the placement match, approval for the child to enter the foreign country must be secured by the authorizing entities along with documentation that the child will be allowed entry and permanent residency in the foreign country. Prospective adoptive parents petition the state court with jurisdiction over the adoption, and the court may either undertake a preliminary review which would grant guardianship to the prospective adoptive parents and allow the parents to return to the receiving country pending finalization of the adoption abroad, or, to (if needed) return to the USA for finalization. In either case, before the order for adoption or custody can be issued, the IAA stipulates that the USA court must provide evidence that the best interests of the child are met with the proposed placement, that standards for the child home study were upheld, that a home study has been conducted on the proposed parents, that the child will be allowed to enter the receiving country, and that the respective Central Authorities approve the adoption.

Two Convention documents verify recognition of a Convention adoption—the Hague Custody Declaration (HCD) and the Hague Adoption Certificate (HAC). They ensure that the adoption (or child custody) will be recognized in the receiving country. The former verifies that custody has been officially granted to the prospective parents for the purpose of adoption abroad (or to allow travel abroad pending finalization in the USA) and the latter document indicates that the USA adoption court has followed the standards of the IAA and the adoption should be recognized by Convention countries. Both require documents from the USA state court which indicate the adoptability of the child and recognition that the best interests of the child are being upheld with the granting of custody or adoption. Furthermore, documentation must be submitted that meets the full spectrum of concerns found in the IAA. With issuance of the HCD or HAC, the child may emigrate to the receiving country (Bistransky, 2010).

Klarberg (2010) identifies areas where this process becomes decidedly less 'straightforward.' He draws attention to sections of the law 22 CFR 96. 54 (a) and (b) which require the Adoption Service Providers (ASP) to demonstrate its reasonable efforts to find a domestic placement for a child, while at the same time, it outlines exceptions to this rule, which may include adoption by relatives, or, in cases when birthparent(s) have identified specific adoptive parents. To comply with these laws, the ASP presents evidence of reasonable effort in the recruitment of domestic parents, and dissemination of information related to the available child. This is to be accomplished through various media outlets including the listing of the available child on national or state adoption exchange for sixty days post-birth. More specifically, the CFR standards read in part:

> § 96.54 Placement standards in outgoing cases.
>
> (a) Except in the case of adoption by relatives or in the case in which the birth parent(s) have identified specific prospective adoptive parent(s) or in other special circumstances accepted by the State court with jurisdiction over the case, the agency or person makes reasonable efforts to find a timely adoptive placement for the child in the United States by:
>
> (1) Disseminating information on the child and his or her availability for adoption through print, media, and internet resources designed to communicate with potential prospective adoptive parent(s) [PAP] in the United States;
>
> (2) Listing information about the child on a national or State adoption exchange or registry for at least sixty calendar days after the birth of the child;...

It also states,

> (b) The agency or person demonstrates to the satisfaction of the State court with jurisdiction over the adoption that sufficient reasonable efforts (including no efforts, when in the best interests of the child) to find a timely and qualified adoptive placement for the child in the United States were made.
>
> (c) In placing the child for adoption, the agency or person:
>
> (1) To the extent consistent with State law, gives significant weight to the placement preferences expressed by the birth parent(s) in all voluntary placements. (Accreditation of Agencies and Approval of Persons under the Intercountry Adoption Act of 2000[IAA])

Additionally, ASPs cannot facilitate contact between birth and adoptive families. Indeed, birthparent agency to choose a foreign family is contingent on their having done so "without the assistance of the ASP or its agents" (Klarberg, 2010). However it is the state law in which the birthparent resides that determines if pre-birth contact can be conducted, or if birthparents can review prospective parent profiles. As the U.S. DOS explains (U.S. Citizenship and Immigration Services [U.S. CIS], 2006):

> If the State where the birthparent(s) reside permits them to review prospective adoptive parent(s) profiles before the referral or adoption or consider non-relative referrals, then the practice is not per se prohibited, but must comply with any specific State requirements, such as those on who may present the information on (attorney for prospective adoptive parent(s) or birthparent(s) or adoption service provider). If State requirements are completely silent, then direct contact practices are not allowed. … pre-birth contacts are permitted in Convention cases if they are allowed by the relevant State law or public domestic authority and the contacts occurred in accordance with required conditions. (USCIS, 2006, section II)

Outgoing adoption cases are almost always infants whose birthparent(s) relinquish at birth (Avitan, 2007). Detractors of outgoing adoption see these prohibitions on contact and emphasis on domestic recruitment as necessary protections for the USA child, and birth parents. That is, to allow the child to remain in its birth land and culture and to protect birth parents from coercion or abuse. Some supporters see these prohibitions as discrimination. Avitan (2007) argues that Black families may not seek adoption of non-relatives because of a culture of kinship in which families care for other family or community members' children. A culture of kinship care may mean that fewer Black families pursue non-relative adoption. In withholding a population of foreign parents who may be interested in an infant regardless of its race, Avitan argues that protections can also serve to discriminate against the child and birthmother and cause unnecessary delays in placement.

In the first year of HCIA enforcement most outgoing cases were in fact 'transition cases,' already in process before the start date of April 1, 2008. Initially, the "sixty day rule" (#2 above) in particular, was seen as likely to end outgoing adoption practice. The first year was rife with ambiguity as sending and receiving agents struggled to determine how birthmothers in voluntary adoption situations could even consider a foreign adoptive family if they were not allowed to go through accredited agencies to locate a family or if their child had to be publically abandoned and advertised. However, in March, 2009, just as Hague Convention implementation was nearing its first anniversary in the United States, U.S. DOS issued, *Outgoing Cases: Guidance on 22 CFR 96.54(a)* (U.S. DOS, 2009b) the outcome of which was to reveal how these adoptions could proceed. The Guidance clarification notes:

> Specifically, if the birthparent(s) have identified specific prospective adoptive parent(s) consistent with applicable State law, the prospective adoptive parent recruiting procedures set forth in 96.54(a)(1)-(4) do not apply. (para. 3)

And,

> An accredited adoption service provider may provide adoption and other services to a birthparent(s), including providing access to information on prospective adoptive parents, without jeopardizing its accreditation status. However, only the birthparent(s) can identify the specific prospective adoptive parent(s) in order for the exception to the adoptive parent recruiting procedures set forth in 96.54(a) (1)-(4) to apply. (para. 5)

The Guidance, in effect, precludes sole reliance on Federal guidelines, by deferring to state law. States vary in their adherence to the subsidiarity principle. Birthparents can choose foreign adoptive families, if they have also considered domestic families, have received counseling regarding the implication of the adoption, and state law permits. Moreover, ASPs can assist with the placement with the international family if state law permits and the court determines that the choice of the birthmother is in the best interest of her child. More specifically, the Guidance concludes:

> Some birth parents may prefer that their child be placed with a relative in another country who has the capacity to provide suitable care for the child. Other birth parents may prefer a non-relative placement abroad. Nothing in the Convention or the IAA warrants taking a course different from applicable State law on the question of birthparent preferences (Guidance on 22 CFR 96.54(a) (final paragraph).

Additionally, reasonable efforts to recruit domestic adoptive families may be exempted in states that "permit a birth parent to select and related or unrelated indentified prospective adoptive parent in another Convention country" (Hollinger, 2008, p. 119). State laws can also regulate the provision of living expenses for birth mothers and can eliminate the Federal 60-day waiting period. This variance in adoption court practices and state regulations is of concern to some adoption experts. Balcom (2011), for example, warns that some states may be seen as 'easier locales,' from which to adopt USA children.

Views from Canadian and USA Adoption Professionals

A qualitative study was conducted with ten adoption professionals in the United States and Canada focusing on their perspectives and experiences with outgoing adoptions. Professionals were agency directors, attorneys, and social workers and their experience ranged from one year to over twenty-five years in practice. Several participants commented on the countries' past history of cross-border adoptions with the contiguous border seemingly facilitating a practice of adoptions by networking. Participants noted the changing demographics with available infants in the USA now being mostly Black and biracial children; a shift from early years when White infants were also placed across the border. Participants also remarked that not all [Canadian] prospective adoptive parents are White with one adoption worker clarifying that strong kinship ties in Canadian Caribbean and African communities made it easier for prospective parents from these ethnic groups to adopt from the United States than from Canada. With regard to influences on USA birthparents' (and most professionals framed this as birthmothers') decision to place a child with a Canadian family, they noted two related but somewhat different factors:

> (1) Idealized perceptions of Canada as racially integrated, diverse with less racial divisiveness, and better social care—offering better opportunities for a Black or mixed race child.
>
> There is this very strongly held myth that Canada is somehow gentler, less racist and has a more open society than America. Real or not, it is what is believed. Birthmothers chose Canada because they believe it's diverse and there will be less discrimination for their child. This is the dominant myth or belief.
>
> Is this a matter of choice? The prevailing belief and sentiment is that kids should stay in their own country, in the country of their birth... . On the other hand, mothers should have a say. Some mothers in relinquishing their child do so because of their belief that [her] kid will have a better upbringing in Canada. Canada can be seen as a sort of friendly, not too far, accommodating place—less crowded, more sedate than the U.S.
>
> (2) Experience of the United States as a racially conservative society where Black and Biracial families face significant discrimination and a belief that a child's best interests exist outside of the country.
>
> ... My anecdotal experiences with birth moms show ... a woman of color may be very rational about her decision to launch her child in an environment that she may consider to be more open, receptive, and tolerant than her conservative state historically, on racial issues.

These views align with reports from media accounts (Corley and Ludden, 2005; Davenport, 2004; Glaser, 2004: Stahl, 2005) of outgoing adoptions in which adoption professionals from Georgia, Illinois, and Florida among other states also noted the interplay between experiences of discrimination and racism as one factor influencing birth parents' choice.

A third factor is USA birthmothers' increasing desire for more openness in adoption and more post adoption contact which they perceive as more likely in Canada:

> ...the other part of this is that at least in [this part] of the United States, adoptive parents are typically less receptive to openness in their adoptions, and the

> Canadian families typically are more receptive to openness. So that's one reason why birth moms pick Canadian families.

> … The Canadian families are typically more receptive to openness … It really comes down to philosophies of adoption. And the birth moms, I think are … sensing their own empowerment by having a lot more control of the adoptive situation that they want, and the openness issue is not a problem.

Adoption professionals in this study, and professionals and birth mothers interviewed in media accounts (Stahl, 2005), observed that sometimes it is sense of connection to a family, provided through the parent profiles, that determines a placement and not the nationality of the parents.

> I do think that yes there is a comfort level with [Canadian] society. It's not so strange that they feel that they're sending their kid out, or away, … I really think it comes down to, they consider Canadians along with Floridians.

Why do Canadian families look to the United States to adopt? Participants identified several factors including, (1) the desire for an infant, (2) proximity and good medical or psychosocial histories, and (3) interest in open adoptions and ongoing contact with the birth family.

> There is no other place in the world where you could adopt a new born baby out of the hospital than in the United States, period! So if as an adopting parent this is your driving motivation, and certainly this is not the case for all adopting parents, but if it is to be a parent from day one, then the U.S. is one of the best possibilities.

> We know on this end if we send a family … to the U.S., they are going to get a healthy child with a relatively lot of information, a good medical and it's a relatively successful program for the adoptive parents.

Transnational and transracial adoption literature often speaks to the rescue fantasies of adoptive families, or the altruistic motivations held by parents when choosing adoption as a means of building a family (Dubinsky, 2008; Volkman, 2003). While this factor was not identified in this study, it has been noted by scholars as contributing to Canadian parent decision-making in looking to the United States (Balcom and Dubinsky, 2005). Additionally, while adopting from the United States might be less expensive than adopting from China or Russia (O'Neil, 2005), this factor was not noted by professionals on either side of the border.

None of these factors can be viewed in isolation; they are intricately and dynamically related to one another, creating a Gordian knot of sending and receiving forces, the effects of which are largely unknown. For example, Canada may be idealized as a civil, diverse, multi-cultural and progressive country by USA birthparents but researchers also note discrimination against Blacks and, media interviews with Canadian families and their USA children present a more complicated picture (Balcom, 2011; Glaser 2004; Milan and Tran as cited in Lalonde, Giguere, Fontaine, and Smith, 2007). Moreover, Canada's heterogeneous Black population is an ethnic mix primarily from the Caribbean and it is unknown as to how U.S. Black children are adapting to this culture or to the White dominant culture.

Research indicates that exposure to activities that promote racial and cultural diversity and includes mentors or representatives from birth country communities can help children integrate the dualities in their adoptions (Paulsen and Merighi, 2009). Study participants and popular media reports noted the existence of support groups for parents and children, social activities that bring Canadian transracial families and specifically USA–Canadian adoptees together as well as websites and newsletters on transracial parenting issues. Moreover, USA adoption workers were unequivocally impressed with the pre-adoption training offered to Canadian parents in preparation for transracial adoption.

Conclusion

Outgoing USA adoptions should be located in the crosshairs of debate that question why these adoptions occur and who benefits. Balcom, (2011), Baden (2002), Dubinsky (2010), Eng, (2003) Gailey (2010), Hollinger (2008), Hübinette (2007c), Quiroz (2007) and others offer exceptional adoption-related studies and critiques that can provide powerful legal, historical, sociological, psychological, feminist and political frameworks and arguments from which to address issues inherent in these adoptions.

However, is it fair to argue the practice as being either exploitative or benign when, quite simply, so little is known about it? Whether USA outgoing adoptions are a forced exit, a loving plan, or something else is unknown. The voices of those who can best tell us—birthparents, adoptive parents, and children are missing and we need to hear them.

PART III
Outcomes for Intercountry Adoptees

Chapter 13
Review of Meta-Analytical Studies on the Physical, Emotional, and Cognitive Outcomes of Intercountry Adoptees

Femmie Juffer and Marinus H. van IJzendoorn

Since intercountry adoption started in the second half of the twentieth century, a large number of studies have examined the developmental outcomes of internationally adopted children and adolescents. How does one make sense of the findings, particularly when results are heterogeneous or contradictory? Adoption policy and practice badly need evidence-based information about the developmental outcomes of intercountry adoptees to both adequately support adoptive families and adoptees and to inform counselors and policy makers.

A meta-analytic approach provides a method to summarize and analyze adoption research, by computing a combined effect size of all studies examining the same aspect of development (Rosenthal, 1991), e.g., adopted children's attachment security. A meta-analytical approach also results in the evidence-based knowledge needed for adoption policy and practice. Following the same example, the outcome that children adopted after their first birthday are at elevated risk for insecure attachment, implies that children should be adopted as early as possible, preferably before their first birthday, and that families adopting older children should be supported with interventions. In this chapter we draw on our meta-analytical database in which we included more than 270 empirical studies with more than 230,000 participants to examine adopted children's adjustment (see also Juffer and Van IJzendoorn, 2009; Van IJzendoorn and Juffer, 2006).

In an authoritative review, Palacios and Brodzinsky (2010) provided an historical analysis of adoption research, distinguishing three historical trends: the first focusing on risk in adoption and identifying differences between adopted and non-adopted children's developmental outcomes; the second examining adopted children's recovery from early adversity; and the third focusing on factors and processes underlying variability in adopted children's adjustment.

In this chapter we examine adopted children's developmental outcomes from a meta-analytical perspective while using the framework provided by Palacios and Brodzinsky (2010) as a connecting thread. For each developmental domain we first focus on the comparison between adopted and non-adopted children, then examine possible recovery, and finally elaborate on potential moderators explaining why some adopted children show better outcomes than do other adopted children. For the first focus, we compare adopted children with their non-adopted classmates or friends ('current peers'). For recovery we compare adopted children's development with their own baseline, i.e., their adjustment when they were adopted, or with the development of children living in comparable circumstances but who were not adopted, e.g., children in institutional care ('past peers'). And for the third focus we report whether the meta-analytical outcomes were different for subgroups of adopted children, for example domestic versus international adoptees.

Along these lines, we start with the developmental domain of physical growth, continue with attachment security, cognition, behavior problems, and end with self-esteem. The meta-analytical outcomes are presented in Cohen's d (Cohen, 1988), with $d = 1.00$ converging with a difference of one standard deviation (SD) of the pertinent measure between the adopted and non-adopted group.

Physical Development

In many cases adopted children were living in group care in an institution before adoption. Institutional care is often qualified by a lack of sensitive care and a risk of malnutrition, neglect and abuse (Gunnar, Bruce, and Grotevant, 2000; Miller, 2005a). These experiences may have negative consequences for children's social-emotional development and for their physical growth (Dobrova-Krol, Van IJzendoorn, Bakermans-Kranenburg, Cyr, and Juffer, 2008; see Chapter 14). Indeed, based on findings from eight empirical studies (including 919 participants) we found that the longer children are in institutional care, the more delayed their height, with a strong negative correlation between height for age and the number of years in institutional care, $r = -0.62$ (Van IJzendoorn, Bakermans-Kranenburg, and Juffer, 2007).

Adopted Versus Non-Adopted Children

Physical growth of adopted children has been studied in 33 empirical studies, including more than 3,500 international adoptees. A series of meta-analyses revealed that adopted children showed serious delays in height, weight, and head circumference compared to their non-adopted, current peers when they arrived in their adoptive families. (For details, see Van IJzendoorn et al., 2007). The children's mean chronological age at adoptive placement in the pertinent studies was 30 months in the case of height assessments, and 23 months for weight assessments. The combined effect sizes for the delays in height, weight, and head circumference at adoptive placement were very large, $d = -2.39$ to $d = -2.60$ (15 to 27 studies with 1,331 to 3,753 adoptees).

Recovery

After an average of eight years in their adoptive families, the internationally adopted children showed a remarkable catch-up in height and weight compared to the baseline at adoptive placement (Van IJzendoorn et al., 2007). The lags in height and weight had decreased to $d = -0.57$ and $d = -0.72$, respectively (23 and 18 studies; 3,437 and 3,259 adoptees, respectively). However, some years after adoption the combined effect size for the delay in head circumference compared with non-adopted, current peers remained large, $d = -1.56$ (6 studies; 527 adoptees). Thus, the catch-up in height and weight was far more impressive than the catch-up in head circumference.

To further investigate this issue, four studies with longitudinal data were identified and included in a separate meta-analysis. The set of studies, including 448 adopted children, again showed that the catch-up of head circumference across a similar average period of 19 months (mean chronological age at adoptive placement) to 49 months (mean chronological age at follow-up assessment) was significantly smaller than the catch-up of height and weight. We therefore concluded that catch-up of head circumference was slower and remained incomplete, even several years after adoption (Van IJzendoorn et al., 2007).

With respect to long-term recovery processes, our series of meta-analyses showed some evidence that height of adoptees seemed to lag more behind the non-adopted current peers from nine years of age onwards. Precocious puberty may be one of the reasons for this lower final height than may be expected on the basis of the rapid catch-up before puberty (Van IJzendoorn et al., 2007).

Variability in Outcomes

The meta-analyses of physical growth included internationally adopted children only and therefore contrasts between domestic and intercountry adoptees could not be analyzed. Regarding the delays in height, weight, and head circumference, no differences were found between children adopted before or after their first birthday. However, after an average of eight years in the adoptive family, early adopted children (before their first birthday) showed a complete catch-up in height ($d = -0.03$), meaning that their height did not differ anymore from their non-adopted peers.

Attachment

In infancy, formation of a secure attachment relationship is a major developmental milestone (Bowlby, 1982). The frightening nature of severe insensitivity and enduring unresponsiveness in institutional settings may trigger insecure disorganized attachment in children, a category of insecure attachment with major psychopathological consequences (Van IJzendoorn, Schuengel, and Bakermans-Kranenburg, 1999). Children adopted from institutional care may develop insecure and disorganized attachment relationships with their new adoptive parents, based on their previous adverse experiences.

Adopted Versus Non-Adopted Children

In a meta-analysis of 17 empirical observational studies we examined attachment security in more than 750 adopted children. Overall, adopted children did not differ from their non-adopted current peers with respect to attachment security (Van den Dries, Juffer, Van IJzendoorn, and Bakermans-Kranenburg, 2009). In another meta-analysis of 11 observational studies including more than 450 adoptees, we examined the risk of insecure disorganized attachment and found that adopted children showed more disorganized attachment compared to their non-adopted, current peers. We computed that 31 percent of adopted children showed disorganized attachment, significantly more than the 15 percent found in normative samples (Van den Dries et al., 2009).

Recovery

It should be emphasized that there seems to be an impressive catch-up in attachment organization and security of adopted children, because children in institutions do show much higher rates of insecure, and in particular, disorganized attachment (e.g., Vorria et al., 2003; Zeanah et al., 2005). Across six studies of institutionalized children, Van IJzendoorn et al. (2011) found that 72.8 percent of attachments to the favorite caregiver were disorganized.

Variability in Outcomes

Children who were adopted before their first birthday showed secure attachments as often as non-adopted children. However, children adopted after 12 months of age showed significantly less attachment security than non-adopted children compared to children adopted before 12 months (d = 0.80 vs. d = 0.08; Van den Dries et al., 2009). For disorganized attachment, no differences were found for age at placement (before or after 12 months). With respect to domestic and international adoptees no differences were found for attachment security or attachment disorganization.

Cognitive Development and Learning Problems

Institutional care is often characterized by insufficient sensitive care and a lack of stimulation. These conditions may have negative consequences for children's cognitive development, either while living in the institution or after transition to the adoptive family following a history of institutionalization.

In a meta-analysis of intelligence (IQ) of children in institutions (Van IJzendoorn, Luijk, and Juffer, 2008) we included 75 studies (with 3,888 participants) on IQ of children in institutions (children's homes, orphanages, and other group homes). Children in institutional care were compared with non-institutionalized children or with norms. For these 75 studies we found a large, significant effect (d = -1.10). This outcome means that on average children in institutions develop an IQ of about 84, which can be considered as a delayed cognitive development (the mean IQ of normative children is 100 with a standard deviation of 15).

Adopted Versus Non-Adopted Children

In a large set of 42 studies with 6,411 participants, we found that adopted children's IQ was not different from that of their non-adopted current peers (d = -0.13; Van IJzendoorn, Juffer, and Klein Poelhuis, 2005). However, compared with non-adopted children, we found small but significant delays in adopted children's school achievement (d = -0.19; 52 studies including 78,662 children) and in language abilities (d = -0.09; 14 studies with 15,418 participants).

Relatively many adopted children appeared to show learning problems (d = -0.55; eight studies including 3,018 adopted children; Van IJzendoorn et al., 2005). We found that adopted children were referred to special education twice as often as non-adopted children. However, it should be noted that the percentage of children with learning problems that need treatment or referral to special education is generally rather small—both in the adopted group (12.8 percent) and in the general population (5.5 percent)—and that this finding is based on a small number of studies (Van IJzendoorn and Juffer, 2005). Adoptive families seek more help and support to cope with the learning problems of their child. This higher rate for learning problems may also be related to a lower threshold for adoptive parents to seek assistance for the problems of their adopted child (Warren, 1992).

Recovery

We found massive catch-up of the adopted children compared with the children left behind in the institutions (past peers), both for IQ (d = 1.17; six studies including 253 children) and school achievement (d = 0.55; three studies with 523 children; Van IJzendoorn et al., 2005).

Variability in Outcomes

The outcome that IQ of adopted children was not different from non-adopted peers was equally true for domestic and international adoptees and for children adopted before or after their first birthday.

Later adoption (after the first birthday) and experiences of serious pre-adoption adversity such as severe neglect in Romanian institutions were associated with delays in school achievement (Van IJzendoorn et al., 2005). Children adopted before their first birthday and children without experiences of extreme pre-adoption trauma did not lag behind in school achievement. There were no differences in school achievement between domestic and international adoptees.

Behavior Problems and Mental Health Referrals

How do adopted children adjust several years after their adoption? Behavioral adjustment may be considered as one of the indices of the long-term consequences of being adopted (e.g., Verhulst, Althaus, and Versluis-den Bieman, 1990). Based on their histories of early deprivation before adoption and possible feelings of being different after adoption (Brodzinsky, Schechter, and Henig, 1992; Juffer and Tieman, 2009), adopted children may be at elevated risk for behavioral difficulties.

Adopted Versus Non-Adopted Children

In a comprehensive meta-analysis including 25,281 adoptees and 80,260 non-adopted comparisons, adoptees presented more externalizing (e.g., aggression), internalizing (e.g., depression), and total behavior problems, but effect sizes were small (d: -0.16 to -0.24; Juffer and Van IJzendoorn, 2005). Adoptees (N = 5,092) were overrepresented in mental health services, and this combined effect size was large (d = -0.72).

Recovery

When our meta-analysis of behavior problems was conducted, there were no studies available comparing the behavior problems of adopted children with their own baseline (at adoptive placement) or with children in institutional care (past peers). Since that time, some new evidence has emerged, pointing to the negative effects of institutionalization and the positive effects of family placement on behavioral adjustment. In Spain, Palacios and Sánchez-Sandoval (2005) found that institutionalized children (especially boys) showed more behavior problems than a matched group of adoptees. Another study found that internationally adopted children from South Korea living in the USA showed fewer behavior problems than institutionalized children in Korea (Lee, Seol, Sung, and Miller, 2010). Converging with this evidence, in the Bucharest Early Intervention Project it was found that children with histories of institutionalization showed more psychiatric problems than children without such histories, while children randomly assigned to family foster care had significantly fewer problems than children who remained in institutional care (Zeanah et al., 2009).

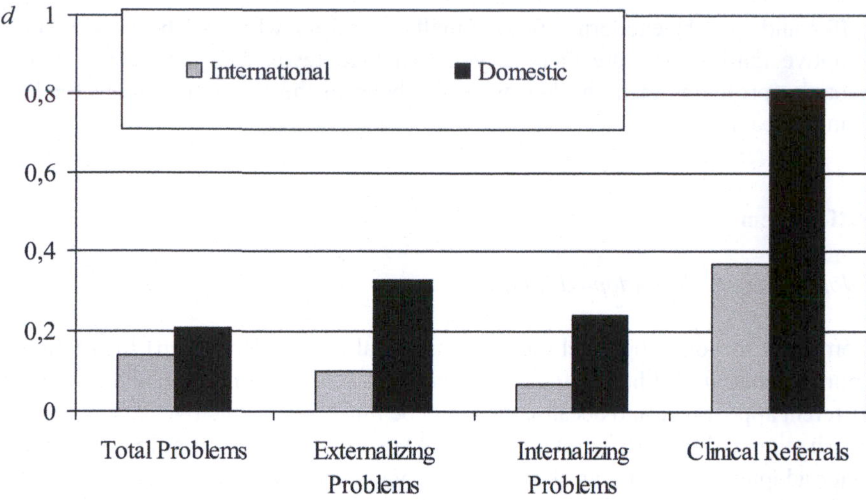

Figure 13.1 Meta-analytic Comparisons (all significant) of International and Domestic Adoptees on Behavior Problems and Clinical Referrals

Source: Based on Juffer and Van IJzendoorn, 2009, p. 182.

In addition, comparing the very small combined effect sizes in the meta-analyses of adopted children's behavior problems with studies examining behavior problems in institutionalized children (e.g., Simsek, Erol, Oztop, and Munir, 2007), we assume that catch-up and recovery of adopted children's behavioral adjustment is a realistic possibility.

Variability in Outcomes

Remarkably, international adoptees showed fewer total, externalizing and internalizing behavior problems than domestic adoptees (see Figure 13.1). Also, international adoptees were less often referred to mental health services, $d = -0.37$, than domestic adoptees, $d = -0.81$ (Figure 13.1; Juffer and Van IJzendoorn, 2005, 2009). We computed that international adoptees are referred to mental health services twice as often as non-adopted children, whereas domestic adoptees are referred four times as often as their non-adopted counterparts.

International adoptees with severe pre-adoption adversity, for example children adopted from Romanian or Russian orphanages, showed more total problems and externalizing problems than international adoptees without evidence of extreme deprivation. For children adopted as infants (0 to 12 months) compared with children adopted after their first birthday, there were no differences for total behavior problems, externalizing problems, or internalizing problems.

We also found that international adoptees presented more total behavior problems in childhood than in adolescence ($d = 0.23$ vs. $d = 0.09$, respectively;

Juffer and Van IJzendoorn, 2005). Finally, children who had been with their adoptive family for more than 12 years showed fewer total and externalizing behavior problems than children who had been in their adoptive home for less than 12 years.

Self-Esteem

Adopted versus Non-Adopted Children

Compared to non-adopted children, trans-racial and (older-placed) international adoptees may find it harder to develop positive self-esteem, because they have a different appearance and because they may be hindered by negative experiences of deprivation in their early childhood years. Also, problems may arise in adolescence when adoptees start thinking about how they value themselves. To address this issue we conducted a meta-analysis of adoptees' self-esteem. Surprisingly, we found no difference in self-esteem between adoptees ($N = 10{,}977$) and non-adopted, current peers ($N = 33{,}862$) across 88 studies ($d = 0.01$; Juffer and Van IJzendoorn, 2007).

Recovery

In a small set of three studies with 300 participants we found that adoptees showed more optimal levels of self-esteem than their past peers, i.e., non-adopted, institutionalized children ($d = 0.58$; Juffer and Van IJzendoorn, 2007).

Variability in Outcomes

The outcome that adoptees and non-adopted, current peers did not differ on self-esteem was equally true for international, domestic, and transracial adoptees. We found no differences in self-esteem between children adopted before or after their first birthday, nor did self-esteem assessments of adoptees in childhood, adolescence, or adulthood differ. Moreover, studies that used the view of the adoptees themselves (self-report measures) showed the same outcomes as studies that relied on the perception of teachers or parents (other-report measures).

Conclusion and Discussion

Meta-Analytic Conclusions

With a meta-analytic approach the available empirical adoption studies on adopted children's developmental outcomes were systematically reviewed, analyzed, and synthesized. Because adopted children often have histories of pre-adoption adversity, delays and difficulties were expected in every developmental domain.

At the same time, catch-up growth and recovery after adoptive placement were expected as well, while heterogeneous outcomes for various groups of children were also hypothesized.

Following Palacios and Brodzinsky's (2010) historical analysis of adoption research, we *first* examined risks in adoption and focused on adopted versus non-adopted children's developmental outcomes. According to this first approach, adopted children are indeed at risk compared to their non-adopted, current peers. But the risks are not present in every developmental domain as we found no differences between adopted and non-adopted children regarding intelligence and self-esteem. Also, the risks were not equally large for each developmental domain: substantial delays and difficulties were found for physical growth, disorganized attachment, learning problems and mental health referrals, but much weaker effects were found for language abilities and behavior problems.

According to the *second* focus in adoption research, recovery of adopted children also is an important theme in adopted children's developmental outcomes. Our meta-analyses indeed show impressive and massive catch-up after adoptive placement in all developmental domains, including physical growth, attachment, cognitive development, behavior problems, and self-esteem. Based on these outcomes we conclude that adoption is a highly preferable option compared to institutional care.

Converging with our meta-analytical evidence, comparable positive effects of placement in a family setting were found in the Bucharest Early Intervention Project (BEIP), for example on institutionalized children's IQ (Nelson et al., 2007). A strong feature of the BEIP study is that children were randomly assigned to either foster family care or prolonged institutional care, thus preventing a possible bias of positive selection of specific children for family placement. It should be noted that the BEIP data were analyzed with an 'intent-to-treat' principle, meaning that children who had been randomized to prolonged institutional care but were placed in families during the project, were still considered as institutionalized children. Therefore, the BEIP findings probably underestimate the positive catch-up of the children randomly assigned to family care. Concluding, based on our meta-analytical outcomes and the experimental findings from the BEIP study we can be quite certain that placement in family care (adoptive or foster family) provides unique and powerful chances for recovery in institutionalized children.

At the same time, our meta-analyses show that adopted children are not able to catch up completely with their current peers, particularly with respect to attachment disorganization, school achievement, learning problems and mental health referrals. We therefore also conclude that adoptive families and adopted children need support to help them cope with delays and difficulties.

The *third* focus in adoption research considers variability in adopted children's developmental outcomes. The meta-analyses discussed in this chapter provide some first indications that some adopted children develop in a more optimal way than do other adopted children. Later adoption (after the first birthday) is associated with incomplete catch-up in height, more insecure attachment and less optimal school achievement compared to children adopted in their first year of life. Internationally adopted children are not at higher risk of maladjusted development compared to domestic adoptees, and for behavior problems they are even at lower risk. Children with histories of serious pre-adoption adversity, including severe neglect, abuse, and malnutrition, are at higher risk of delays in school achievement and more problem behavior.

Implications for Policy and Practice

The following key points for adoption policy and practice can be inferred from the meta-analytical evidence in this chapter:

Physical Growth

- Health care professionals should be aware that at the time of adoptive placement moderate to severe delays can be present in adopted children's height, weight, and head circumference.
- Impressive and substantial catch-up growth can be expected for height and weight, but less so for head circumference.
- Children adopted before their first birthday may catch up completely in height.
- Adopted children may not reach the same final height as non-adopted children, while a small minority (but a larger minority than in non-adopted children) will show precocious puberty.

Attachment

- Children adopted after their first birthday are at risk of insecure attachment, in contrast to children adopted earlier. Therefore children should be adopted as early as possible, preferably in their first year of life.
- Although adopted children do show relatively high rates of disorganized attachment, these rates are substantially lower than in institutionalized children, suggesting that there is recovery after adoption.
- The risks of disorganized attachment and insecure attachment (for children adopted after their first birthday) point to the need of intervention. Attachment-based interventions may support the adoptive family and provide the child with corrective attachment experiences.

Cognition

- In and shortly after institutional care, children's IQ may be delayed, but after adoption children are likely to catch up and ultimately reach IQ's in the average range.

- School achievement may be delayed. For children adopted before their first birthday catch-up of school achievement may be complete, but children adopted at older ages may need extra assistance at school.
- Children with histories of severe pre-adoption adversity may show a larger lag in school achievement and may also need extra help.
- Learning problems may often occur in adopted children and therefore adoptive families should receive support from well-informed professionals, including social workers, counselors, and school psychologists.

Behavior Problems

- In a minority of adopted children (but a larger minority than in non-adopted children) relatively more internalizing and externalizing behavior problems may be present.
- Professional social workers, counselors, and therapists should be aware that relatively many adopted families seek mental health services for their child. These professionals should have information about the specific needs of adopted children, and about evidence-based interventions for treating those difficulties.
- In contrast to public opinion, intercountry adoptees are not likely to show more behavior problems than domestic adoptees, and the opposite may be the case.
- Children with histories of severe pre-adoption adversity may show more behavior problems and need more help for their difficulties.
- Adopted children's behavior problems can be expected in middle childhood even more than in adolescence.

To-Do List for the Future

In the meta-analytical evidence presented in this chapter our current knowledge of adopted children's developmental outcomes is presented and summarized. Although numerous adoption studies have been conducted, there are still gaps in what we know about adopted children's lifelong adjustment, and we agree with Palacios and Brodzinsky (2010) that we have just started to explore the variability of adopted children's development, let alone the explanation of heterogeneous outcomes.

In a 'to-do list' for the future, a few topics should be mentioned as highly prioritized. First, the search for factors and processes underlying adopted children's development should be continued, including neurobiological (e.g., genetic and epigenetic factors; Van IJzendoorn, Caspers, Bakermans-Kranenburg, Beach, and Philibert, 2010), psychological, and contextual influences. For example, recent studies have indicated that varying pre-adoption rearing arrangements may result in different developmental outcomes for adopted children. Children who lived in a foster family before intercountry adoption showed better health, mental and motor development than children who stayed in institutional care before adoption (Miller,

Chan, Comfort, and Tirella, 2005; Van den Dries, Juffer, Van IJzendoorn, and Bakermans-Kranenburg, 2010). In the same vein, improved quality of institutional care may result in better health outcomes (Van Schaik, Wolfs, and Geelen, 2009) or in a boost in cognitive development (Bakermans-Kranenburg, Van IJzendoorn, and Juffer, 2008; St. Petersburg USA Orphanage Research Team, 2008).

Second, not only do rearing arrangements before adoption matter, but more optimal parenting behavior and preventive interventions in the adoptive family may offer the adopted child opportunities for (even more complete) catch-up. For example, attachment-based interventions may improve adoptive parents' sensitivity and promote attachment security in their adopted children (Juffer, Bakermans-Kranenburg, and Van IJzendoorn, 2005, 2008). In the near future, research attention should also be paid to the adjustment of special-needs adopted children and the support their families need, given the increasing number of children with special needs in intercountry adoption.

Third, longitudinal studies are needed to unravel adoptees' development from infancy to adulthood and beyond (Juffer et al., 2011). Longitudinal adoption studies are valuable because they can reveal long-term processes, mechanisms and predictors. For example, in a longitudinal adoption study we found that attachment relationships and parental sensitivity in early childhood predicted adopted children's social development in middle childhood and (indirectly) in adolescence (Stams, Juffer, and Van IJzendoorn, 2002; Jaffari-Bimmel, Juffer, Van IJzendoorn, Bakermans-Kranenburg, and Mooijaart, 2006).

Fourth and finally, most intercountry adoption studies have focused on the developmental outcomes of adopted children and adolescents, while studies on adopted adults are still relatively scarce (e.g., Storsbergen, Juffer, Van Son, and 't Hart, 2010; Tieman, Van der Ende, and Verhulst, 2005). It is important to examine the specific challenges for adoptees in adulthood, such as becoming a parent, searching for roots—or not—(Tieman, Van der Ende, and Verhulst, 2008), and how to give meaning to their cultural-racial identity (Baden, 2010).

During the past few decades research on adoption has been burgeoning and various applications to the practice of supporting families with adopted children have become available. It seems now time for global implementation of some of these applications.

Acknowledgments

The Adoption Meta-Analysis Project (ADOPTION MAP) is supported by grants from Stichting VSBfonds, Stichting Fonds 1818, Fonds Psychische Gezondheid, and Stichting Kinderpostzegels Nederland to F.J. and M.H.vIJ in cooperation with the Adoption Triad Research Centre (www.adoptionresearch.nl). Femmie Juffer holds the Chair for Adoption Studies supported by Wereldkinderen, The Hague. Marinus H. van IJzendoorn is supported by the NWO/SPINOZA Prize of the Netherlands Organization for Scientific Research.

Chapter 14
Medical Status of Internationally Adopted Children

Laurie C. Miller

More than 40,000 children per year cross borders to enter new families, usually traveling from lower to higher income countries (U.S. Department of State, 2011c). These children arrive in their new adoptive countries with a variety of medical, growth, and developmental issues. Many of these issues relate to the conditions in which the children reside prior to adoptive placement. Although some children receive the emotional and physical benefits of loving foster care prior to adoption, most reside in orphanages where nurturing care and material resources are usually limited. In this chapter, the general health status—including growth, infectious diseases, and other medical issues—of internationally adopted children at arrival will be reviewed. Developmental and emotional issues are described in Chapters 13, 15, and 16.

Pre-adoptive Factors Affecting the Health of Children at Arrival

Institutional care presents many potential hazards to growing children (Frank, Klass, Earls, and Eisenberg, 1996; Miller, 2005a) including poor nutrition/growth, lack of medical care, increased exposure to infections, physical and emotional neglect, and lack of stimulation for cognitive development. Children may also experience health risks prior to entry into an institution. These include possible adverse prenatal exposures (drugs, alcohol, tobacco), perinatal complications (especially prematurity and low birth weight), toxic environmental exposures, and emotional difficulties prior to institutional placement (for example, living in an abusive or neglectful family). Some of those topics are addressed below.

Growth

One of the most striking findings in newly arrived children is poor growth. Many pre-adoptive factors, especially institutionalization, contribute to delayed growth. Sadly, in many circumstances, adequate types and quantities of food are unavailable due to financial constraints. Appropriate foods, for example infant formulas or weaning foods, may be in short supply. In many institutions, specific nutrients—especially those needed by growing children—may be limited. These include protein, fat, and micronutrients (iron, zinc, calcium, and vitamin D). Local customs or financial constraints may result in inappropriate food offerings (for example, tea instead of milk). Institutional feeding practices (such as bottle propping) also conspire to impair the growth of children. One of the most important factors contributing to poor child growth in institutions is inadequate staff: child ratios. This situation reduces the opportunity for infants to receive nurturing physical contact during feedings. Such contact is a necessary component of growth (Frank et al., 1996; Kim, Shin and White, 2003; Kuhn and Schanberg, 1998). In addition, children in orphanages may be understandably depressed, with resulting anorexia. Other reasons for anorexia include dental caries, medications, or even 'attention-getting.' For an emotionally deprived child, individualized attention from a caregiver encouraging him to eat may be more highly valued than food itself.

Growth delays are therefore a notable finding in newly arrived internationally adoptees (Miller, 2005a; Van IJzendoorn, Bakermans-Kranenburg and Juffer, 2007). Typically, growth delay is defined as one or more measurements <-2 z score or < 3rd percentile. However, this does not account for children with 'normal' measurements at placement whose growth then rapidly crosses percentiles within the normal range (e.g., from the 10th to the 50th percentile). It is likely that such children should be categorized as growth delayed at arrival, although this information is difficult to capture.

Other factors may also contribute to underestimation of the true prevalence of growth delays. Most adoptees have been in the care of their adoptive parents for several weeks or longer by the time they undergo medical evaluations and anthropometric measurements in their new country. Catch-up growth may be rapid in these circumstances, again leading to under-recognition of growth delays at the time of adoptive placement. Moreover, children may have been the beneficiaries of what may be termed 'the adoption bonus.' Although this has not been formally demonstrated, some research supports the notion that children receive better care after assignment to adoptive families. Staff attitudes towards the child may subtly shift after adoptive assignment (Andersen, 1999); the child is now viewed as highly valued and prized, rather than 'unwanted.' Although the effects of the 'adoption bonus' on growth have not been formally studied, pre-adoption growth spurts are commonly seen during the interval between adoption assignment and completion of legalities and transfer to care of the adoptive parents (usually over several months).

Among post-institutionalized children evaluated after adoptive placement, height, weight, and head circumference are <5th percentile (using international standards) in nearly 50 percent, 40 percent, and 40 percent respectively (Miller et al., 1995). Some differences are found between countries of origin (reviewed in Miller, 2005a). For example weights <3rd percentile were found in 30-86 percent of children adopted from India, Korea, and Africa, while weights <3rd percentile have been reported in 15-36 percent of children adopted from Romania.

Overall, mean weight z scores at arrival range from -0.75 to -2.30 in children from a variety of countries. Weight (as well as other measurements) tends to be considerably better in newly arrived children from Ethiopia—likely reflecting the usual assignment of such children to pre-adoptive centers prior to placement with their new families (a form of 'adoption bonus') (Miller, Tseng, Tirella, Chan and Feig, 2008).

Height at arrival also varies with country of origin, with mean z scores ranging between -1.04 to -2.20. However, duration of institutional care is likely a more important factor determining height delays than country of origin. In children adopted from China, Russia, or Romania, a direct correlation was observed between duration of institutional care and linear growth delays. For every ~3 months of institutionalization, children 'lost' ~1 month of height age (Albers, Johnson, Hostetter, Iverson and Miller, 1997; Johnson et al., 1992; Miller, 2005a). Similarly, the percentage of Romanian adoptees with height measurements <3rd percentile increased with age at adoption (Benoit, Jocelyn, Moddemann and Embree, 1996).

Head growth (which reflects brain growth) may also be delayed in intercountry adoptees. At arrival, head circumference mean z scores ranged from -2.10 to -1.03 in children from Romania, other Eastern European countries, China, India, and Guatemala. However, the range of z scores reported was quite broad—more so than for height and weight. Some children arrive with extreme microcephaly (z scores of ≤-4), while others arrive with scores in the solid normal range (+1 to +2). Thus, average scores may not be particularly meaningful. The broad range of head circumference z scores emphasizes the complex factors impacting brain growth, including both malnutrition and emotional neglect.

The growth status of newly arrived international adoptees was comprehensively reviewed in a recent meta-analysis (Van IJzendoorn and Juffer, 2006) (See also Chapter 13). This analysis of 33 papers with 122 study outcomes (as many as 2640 children for some variables) clearly demonstrated the association of duration of institutionalization with height delay (r= 0.62). Height delay increased with age at adoption; overall linear growth lag was estimated at ~8 cm at 30 months of age. Weight also was decreased (by ~3kg at 23 months), as was head circumference but neither of these parameters were related to age at adoption.

Few direct comparisons exist of children adopted from institutions vs. foster care. In a small group of pair-matched children adopted from Guatemala, those who had resided in foster care had significantly better growth measurements at arrival in the USA than those adopted from institutions (height -0.7/-1.3, p =.03, weight -1.0/-1.4 p=.05, and head circumference -0.9/-1.4 p=.04) (Miller, Chan, Comfort and Tirella, 2005). In the Bucharest Early Intervention Project, institutionalized children were randomized to foster care or usual institutional care. In the first 12 months after randomization, the foster care group had rapid increases in height and weight while those in the institutional care group showed no improvement (Johnson et al., 2010).

Growth Recovery After Adoption

What happens to these growth-delayed children after they arrive in their adoptive homes? The catch-up and recovery of growth in children after adoption has rightly been described as "massive" (Van IJzendoorn and Juffer, 2006). Catch-up growth analyzed by meta-analysis an average of eight years after adoption revealed dramatic but incomplete recovery for height (effect size from d=-2.43 to d=-.57). Children adopted before 12 months of age had more complete height recovery than children adopted at older ages. Weight also recovered, but this did not relate strongly to age at adoption. In contrast, recovery of head circumference was less complete; many children still had lower head sizes even eight years after adoption.

In one specific example, Indian children adopted in Sweden improved their height and weight measurements from about -2.2 SD to -0.7 SD within about two years (Proos, Hofvander, Wennqvist and Tuvemo, 1992). Completeness of catch-up was related to birth weight: children with less linear catch-up growth had lower birth weights. Those with lower height-for-age at adoption had the most marked catch-up but ultimately remained smaller. Similarly, malnourished Korean children adopted by USA families eventually surpassed typical height and weight measurements for Korean children, but remained shorter and lighter than American controls (Lien, Meyer, and Winick, 1977, Winick, Meyer, and Harris, 1975). Greek adoptees placed after two years of institutionalization had no differences in weight and height from family-reared children by age four (Vorria et al., 2006). Moreover, even severely growth delayed children adopted from Romania showed impressive catch-up after adoption in the UK, for height, weight, as well as head circumference (Sonuga-Barke et al., 2008). In general, the final height of intercountry adoptees is greater than that of reference populations in their countries of origin. However, adoptees remain shorter than non-adopted peers in their new country of residence.

Infectious Diseases

In addition to growth issues, infectious diseases are another common health problem in newly arrived international adoptees. Infectious diseases may present risks to the infected individual, family, and community (Table 14.1). Many of these infections are 'silent'; thus screening of new arrivals is essential to identify infected individuals and to minimize public health risks. Although children may be screened in their countries of origin prior to adoptive placement, such testing is considered inadequate due to possible laboratory errors or the chance that the child became infected at some time after testing was completed. Screening done as part of medical visa examinations (these requirements change frequently and vary among countries of origin) should also be repeated after arrival in the child's new country. Testing during the incubation periods of some infectious diseases may result in 'false negative' results. In this section, some of the common infectious diseases identified in newly arrived adoptees will be reviewed, along with current

Table 14.1 Occurrence of Serious Infectious Diseases in New Arrivals

	Approximate % of new arrivals with this infection unexpectedly
Intestinal parasites	25%
Tuberculosis	15% (latent)
Hepatitis B	3-5%
Hepatitis A	<1%
Hepatitis C	<1%
HIV	<1%
Syphilis	<1%

Note: All of these infections (except syphilis) may spread via 'ordinary household contact' and thus represent risk to the immediate family as well as potentially to the community.

recommendations for screening (Table 14.2). Some of these recommendations are country-specific. Further details of these infectious diseases may be found in standard references (Pickering, Baker, Kimberlin, and Long, 2009). Due to concerns about vaccines administered in most countries of origin, current recommendations include (re)immunization, or for older children, testing blood samples to verify appropriate immunity. Specific up-to-date recommendations are available at the Advisory Council for Immunization practices website (http://www.cdc.gov/vaccines/pubs/acip-list.htm (Atkinson et al., 2002).

Intestinal Parasites

About 25 percent of intercountry adoptees newly arrived to the USA have intestinal parasites. The prevalence varies depending on country of origin: infections are common in children from Eastern Europe, South Asia, and Africa but rare in children from South Korea (Aronson, 2000; Hostetter et al., 1991; Johnson et al., 1992; Miller and Hendrie; 2000; Miller, Kiernan, Mathers, and Klein-Gitelman, 1995, Saiman et al., 2001; Smith-Garcia and Brown, 1989; Staat, 2002). *Giardia intestinalis* is most frequently identified. Other parasites are often found, including *Entamoeba histolytica*, *Dientamoeba fragilis*, *Ascaris lumbricoides*, *Trichuris trichiuria*, Hookworms, *Hymenolepsis nana*, *Strongyloides stercoralis*. Some children (particularly those from Africa) have multiple parasites. *Blastocystis hominis*, various *Amoeba* species, *Cryptosporidium, Microsporidium*, *Cyclospora*, *Isospora*, and *Endolimax nana* are usually considered non-pathogens and do not require treatment.

Symptoms of infestation include diarrhea, flatulence, odoriferous stools, abdominal pain, failure to thrive, and anemia, although many children are asymptomatic. Interestingly, impaired neuropsychiatric function (unrelated to anemia) has been attributed to parasitic infection, with improved cognition after treatment (Boivin and Giordani, 1993; Guerrant et al., 1999; Nokes et al., 1999).

Table 14.2 Suggested Evaluation for Newly Adopted Post-institutionalized Children

Examination
Review of medical records from country of origin
Comprehensive physical examination
Hearing screen
Vision testing and referral for pediatric ophthalmology examination
Developmental assessment
Laboratory Testing
General health
CBC
Lead level*
Urinalysis
Liver function tests
Thyroid function tests
Calcium, phosphorus
Ferritin
Infectious diseases
Hepatitis B surface antigen, surface antibody, core antibody*
Hepatitis C antibody*
HIV Elisa (consider also PCR testing for infants < 6 months)*
Stool for ova and parasites
RPR (syphilis)
Tuberculin skin test (PPD)*
Consider also: Newborn Screen to State Board of Health (especially for young infants), Stool for H. pylori antigen (especially if gastrointestinal symptoms),
Dental evaluation
*repeat recommended ≥6 months after arrival

Note: Adapted from Miller, 2005a.

All newly arrived children should be screened for intestinal parasites. Three samples are recommended to improve detection rate (Staat, 2002); immunoassay of giardia antigen alone is inadequate. Follow-up samples should be obtained after treatment to verify eradication and to screen for additional parasites. Parasites are sometimes missed in initial stool screening; re-testing is advisable if later symptoms appear.

Other enteric infections also occur among intercountry adoptees, including *Salmonella*, *Shigella*, *Campylobacter*, and *Helicobacter pylori.* Careful testing for these pathogens is necessary in symptomatic children.

Tuberculosis

Intercountry adoptees have multiple risk factors for infection with *Mycobacterium tuberculosis*, including birth and residence in countries with high prevalence of this disease, poor access to health care, living in institutions where caregivers may not be screened for tuberculosis infection, young age (infants are particularly susceptible to infection), and malnutrition. Fortunately, few children arrive with active disease. Latent tuberculosis, however, is relatively common (Mandalakas and Starke, 2004). Most researchers report latent tuberculosis infection (e.g., positive tuberculin skin test [TST], no clinical disease) in ~5-20 percent of new arrivals (Miller, 2005b). Children from Russia and Ukraine appear to be at higher risk for this infection (Saiman et al., 2001). In a recent report of internationally adopted children in Italy, 30 percent of non-BCG (Bacille Calmette-Guérin) vaccinated children had latent tuberculosis infection (Vivano et al., 2006). It is vital to recognize that latent disease may activate; the risk is especially high in young children. This is dangerous for the child and also may create a public health hazard. For example, an outbreak of tuberculosis affecting 56 people in a small town in North Dakota was traced to a child adopted from the Marshall Islands (Curtis et al., 1999).

All children should be tested for tuberculosis after arrival and again six months later. The most commonly used test is the tuberculin skin test. In some circumstances, the newer interferon-γ release assays may be useful diagnostic aids (though not yet approved for use in all ages of children). Testing for tuberculosis should be done even in children who received the BCG vaccine in their country of origin.

Hepatitis B

Intercountry adoption and other types of immigration are now the most common history of children in the U.S. with Hepatitis B infection (Elisofon and Jonas, 2006). In a recent survey by the Centers for Disease Control, adoptees from China, Bulgaria, Russia, Phillipines, Ukraine, and Vietnam accounted for 32 percent of young children reported with Hepatitis B infection (Shepard, Finelli, Bell, and Miller, 2004). Overall, about three to five percent of intercountry adoptees arrive with this infection (Albers et al., 1997; Bureau, Maurage, Bremond, Despert and Rolland, 1999; Hostetter et al., 1991; Johnson et al., 1992; Miller, 2005b; Saiman et al., 2001). Hepatitis B is spread by blood or sexual contact. Many adoptees acquire this disease via vertical transmission (e.g., from infected mothers at birth). Other routes of transmission include exposure to contaminated needles or medical equipment. Unfortunately, reuse or improper disposal of needles remains a widespread practice in many parts of the world (Murakami et al., 2003) with nearly one-third of injections in developing countries administered using unsterile equipment (Keystone, 2005). Worldwide, about one-third of the world's population have present or past evidence of infection with Hepatitis B; nearly 75 percent reside in Asia (World Health Organization, 2008).

Hepatitis B screening is nearly universal for children prior to placement in intercountry adoptions. However, Hepatitis B is diagnosed in some children at arrival, even after negative tests in the country of origin. This seeming paradox likely reflects laboratory errors or infection which occurred after the testing was completed. All children should be tested on arrival, and again ~six months later (to identify children whose initial tests may have been in the 'seronegative window'). Immediate family members should be vaccinated prior to the adoptive placement, as Hepatitis B is highly contagious within the family via ordinary household contact, with transmission rates as high as 64 percent (Cobelens et al., 2004; Sokal, Van Collie, and Buts, 1995). Infected individuals are usually asymptomatic for many years, but over time, Hepatitis B may cause cirrhosis, liver failure, or hepatocellular carcinoma. Treatment is offered to selected children with this infection; for most, close monitoring only is required in childhood.

Hepatitis A

Hepatitis A is transmitted by fecal-oral contact (contaminated food or water). Although usually not a serious infection, Hepatitis A can be dangerous in elderly or immunocompromised individuals. Hepatitis A occurred in extended family members of some children adopted from Ethiopia (Fischer et al., 2008). Investigation of this outbreak revealed that adoptees could serve as vectors for this infection beyond their immediate households. Thus, recommendations for screening new arrivals have changed, and all children should be tested for Hepatitis A. Household and some family members should be vaccinated in advance of the adoption.

Hepatitis C

Hepatitis C infection is rare among international adoptees (~one percent) (Miller, 2005a), although some adopted children (primarily from Russia) are known to be born to mothers with this infection. Like Hepatitis B, this virus is spread by blood or sexual contact. Vertical transmission, however, is unusual as this virus is considerably less contagious than Hepatitis B. However, as with Hepatitis B, long-term carriage of Hepatitis C increases the risk of hepatocellular carcinoma (~1.9-6.7 percent of patients after 20 years of disease (El-Serag and Mason, 1999)), cirrhosis, and liver failure. Asians, Hispanics, Native Americans, and Pacific Islanders have the highest incidence of disease (El-Serag and Mason, 1999). All newly-adopted children should be screened for Hepatitis C at arrival and again ≥6 months after arrival (Maggiore, Caprai, Cerino, Silini, and Mondelli, 1998). Infected children should be referred to a specialist in liver diseases for consideration of drug treatment and ongoing management.

Human Immunodeficiency Virus Infection (HIV)

Many internationally adopted children come from countries with high rates of HIV infection. To date, however, very few adoptees have arrived in the USA with unexpected disease (Miller, 2005b; Miller, 2005a). In seven studies describing a total of 1,089 children adopted to the USA, Australia, and France, no child had unexpected HIV infection (Albers et al., 1997, Bureau et al., 1999, Hostetter et al., 1991, Johnson et al., 1992, Miller and Hendrie, 2000, Miller et al., 1995, Saiman et al., 2001). An informal multicenter survey of 7,299 adopted children evaluated in 17 international adoption clinics between 1990-2002 found only 12 infected children (0.16 percent, from Panama, Russia, Cambodia, Romania, and Vietnam) (Aronson, 2002). The actual proportion of HIV-infected children is likely somewhat less, as this survey included only children who were evaluated in specialized clinics. The reason for the low rate of infection may reflect accurate pre-adoptive testing in the birth countries and low (but not zero) risk of acquisition in institutions or foster care. However, with the change in distribution of countries of origin, the number of infected children may increase. Children with known HIV infection are also now considered 'eligible' for adoption, and many such children have been placed with American families.

Syphilis

The medical records of about 15 percent of children adopted from former Soviet Union countries indicate that their birth mothers were infected with syphilis. Untreated maternal syphilis may be transmitted to the fetus, causing serious birth defects. Mothers with active infection may also transmit the disease to their newborns at the time of delivery. Fortunately, most children exposed to syphilis are identified and properly treated as neonates; fewer than one percent have unexpected infection with syphilis after arrival. Occasionally, dental abnormalities are found in children who were exposed during fetal life (at the time of tooth formation). Syphilis may also be spread via sexual abuse. All children should be tested for syphilis exposure at the time of arrival.

Other infections

Less serious but important infections are also frequent in new arrivals. In many, lack of treatment in the country of origin may result in progress of these conditions to more severe forms than usually encountered by receiving country practitioners. Common examples include dental caries, scabies, lice, ringworm, impetigo, and tinea capitis. Other rare infections also occur (e.g., malaria, toxocara); management requires consultation with a pediatric infectious disease specialist.

Other Medical Problems

Anemia

Anemia is a common medical problem for new arrivals, affecting about 70 percent of children. In most children, the cause is iron-deficiency. Institutional diets tend to be low in iron content, iron-fortification of food is uncommon, and supplements are seldom provided. Other factors may contribute to iron deficiency, including intestinal blood loss due to parasitic infection. Iron is an essential element for normal brain development in the infant and young child; thus, iron replacement should be given to newly arrived children with iron deficiency.

Although iron-deficiency is widespread, other forms of anemia also occur in intercountry adoptees. Several hemoglobinopathies (hereditary anemias) are common in Asia, Africa, and the Mediterranean. The most common is thalassemia, a disorder of hemoglobin synthesis. These conditions can easily be diagnosed by appropriate testing. Anemia (especially in the presence of splenomegaly) in children from Africa should raise consideration of possible malaria.

Lead Poisoning

Lead poisoning is found in ~five percent of new arrivals, although the number of affected children has decreased in the past five years. Children may be exposed in their birth countries to contaminated paint, dust, fumes, food, or medicines. The prevalence of lead poisoning has been highest among children adopted from China: in a 2000 study of 492 Chinese adoptees, 14 percent had elevated lead levels on arrival in the USA (Miller and Hendrie, 2000). Elevated lead levels may be associated with later neurocognitive and behavioral problems, even after treatment (Bellinger, Stiles, and Needleman, 1992). Lead levels should be tested in all children on arrival and again >6 months later; this second test detects exposure in the receiving country.

Fetal Alcohol Syndrome and Other Prenatal Exposures

Prenatal exposures to alcohol, drugs, and other substances may affect many internationally adopted children. However, reliable information about these exposures is rarely available. Lack of information should not be construed to mean that exposure did not occur. Prenatal exposure to alcohol may impair growth and brain development. It may also cause birth defects (including characteristic facial dysmorphology) (Astley and Clarren, 1996), developmental delays, reduced global intelligence, behavioral problems, poor coordination, and challenges related to memory, learning, and regulation of attention and arousal. Many of these problems may be permanent. Children with characteristic phenotypic and neurobehavioral abnormalities are considered to have Fetal Alcohol Syndrome (FAS); incomplete forms such as Fetal Alcohol Effect (various terminologies are used to describe these problesm) are even more common. Alcohol use during pregnancy is particularly common in the former Soviet Union, although it occurs in nearly every country of origin. Characteristic facial features suggestive of FAS were found in 13 percent of young children surveyed in a group of Russian institutions (Miller et al., 2006). In another survey, 41 percent of birth mothers of children in Russian baby homes drank alcohol during the pregnancy (Miller et al., 2007).

Prenatal exposure to illicit drugs also may have longlasting effects on neurobehavioral function. In general, prenatal exposure to illicit drugs increases the risk of ADHD, learning disabilities, and behavior problems (Miller, 2005). Similar outcomes, although less severe, have also been observed in children exposed prenatally to tobacco. Accurate information about such exposures is exceedingly unusual.

Rickets

Rickets is a disorder of bone mineralization of the growing skeleton, caused by deficiency of calcium, vitamin D, and/or sunlight (necessary to activate Vitamin D). These conditions are common in many institutions. Although severe 'bowed legs' are uncommon, young children often have subtle physical features of rickets, including frontal bossing (prominent, thickened forehead), flared lower ribs, and thickened wrists. Usually, provision of adequate dietary calcium, vitamin D, and sun exposure is adequate to heal rickets and promote bone remodeling.

Uncertain Age

Some internationally adopted children arrive with uncertain ages. Some are children who entered care without documentation of their ages. This is usually not a problem for young infants, but is more difficult for children who are older at entry into care. In other situations, document discrepancies may result in confusion. Malnutrition, prematurity, neglect, and ill health often alter the apparent age of the child. Age reassignments are occasionally necessary for children after arrival. It is usually advisable to observe children for four to six months prior to determining age, obtaining serial assessment of growth, bone, and dental ages, cognitive, motor, social, and language development. Older children should be consulted before age is reassigned.

Precocious puberty

Precocious puberty, the premature onset of physical changes of pubertal development, is an uncommon pediatric condition. However, it has been observed with increased frequency among internationally adopted children. Girls, especially those from South Asia, seem to be affected more frequently than boys. Although the timing of puberty differs among various ethnic groups, early puberty has been seen in a small but important group of international adoptees. Various theories have been suggested, including alteration of hypothalamic hormones by early malnutrition followed by rapid catch-up growth, dietary changes, exposure to endocrine disruptors, and residence with unrelated males (reviewed in (Miller, 2006)).

Conclusion

Internationally adopted children may arrive with medical issues relating to their countries of origin, as well as the specific conditions they experienced before placement. These children deserve a specialized medical evaluation at arrival, as well as regular health follow-up to identify and treat these problems. Infectious disease problems, in particular, may affect not only the individual child, but also the family and the community. Thus, along with the joys and challenges that any new child brings to his or her family, intercountry adoptees also have specific health issues.

Chapter 15
Cognitive Competence, Academic Achievement, and Educational Attainment Among Intercountry Adoptees: Research Outcomes from the Nordic Countries

Monica Dalen

This chapter focuses on cognitive ability, academic achievement, and educational attainment among internationally adopted children. The knowledge presented here is based mainly on research outcomes from studies carried out in the Nordic countries during the last ten years. One has to keep in mind that intercountry adoptees represent a very heterogeneous group, although they have all been adopted from a non-Western country in the early years of their lives. Background information is sparse, and often limited to country of origin, gender, and age at adoption.

Cognitive Competence

Cognitive ability is one important indicator of adoptees' development, both as an outcome measure itself and as a potential mediator between early adversities and academic achievement and attainment. Many of the intercountry adoptees reaching young adulthood have to cope with the high educational demands of the labor market in post-industrial societies. An important determinant of educational attainment is cognitive competence.

Here we define cognitive competence as intelligence test scores (IQ) and language skills in a broad sense. How do intercountry adoptees perform in these two important areas?

Intelligence Test Performance

Few studies have actually focused on intelligence test performance (IQ scores) among intercountry adoptees, although this has been a common theme in national (domestic) adoption research (Duyme, 1990; Duyme, Dumaret, and Tomekiewicz, 1999; Scarr, 1992). One exception is a study of 159 internationally adopted children at age seven carried out in the Netherlands by Stams, Juffer, Rispens, and Hoksbergen (2000). This study documented that adopted children's intelligence was in the normal range or above average, although there were large differences related to the children's country of origin (See Chapter 13). Other studies on children adopted from Romania to the UK have revealed that children adopted before the age of six months have IQ scores at the same level as non-adopted children at the same age (Rutter et al., 2009). Children adopted at an older age had lower IQ scores compared to non-adopted children. The results from these two important studies indicate that there are at least two very important variables influencing adopted children's IQ (age at adoption and country of origin).

In the last 10 years there have been important contributions to knowledge with respect to intercountry adoptees' cognitive development. Based on a meta-analysis, van IJzendoorn, Juffer, and Klein Poelhuis (2005) conclude that it is less clear whether adopted children's cognitive development is at risk in the same way as is their socio-emotional development. They found that adoptees did not lag behind in IQ compared to their environmental siblings or peers. Odenstad et al. (2007) found quite different results. In their study from Sweden, IQ test scores at conscription among male adoptees were compared with a non-adopted group. The adoptees were divided into two groups: intercountry and national adoptees. Many studies have documented a disparity among intercountry adoptees' performance in different areas showing adoptees from Korea to have superior performance (Dalen, 2001; Frydman and Lynn, 1989; Hjern, Lindblad, and Vinnerljung, 2002; Kvifte-Andresen, 1992; Lindblad, Hjern, and Vinnerljung, 2003; Verhulst, Althaus, and Verluis-den Bierman, 1990; 1992). The intercountry adoptees were therefore divided into two groups; one consisting of adoptees from Korea and one of non-Korean adoptees. The study also included siblings of adoptees for comparison. The results from this study showed that siblings of intercountry adoptees had the highest global test scores followed by adoptees from Korea and siblings of national adoptees. Adoptees from non-Korean countries and national adoptees had the lowest test scores with the non-adopted majority in a middle position.

With respect to age of adoption, there were only small differences. In the non-Korean group there were lower scores in the adoptees arriving after 4 years of age, but this was not the case in the Korean group. There was no effect of parental educational level on global test scores in the adoptee groups, whereas in the general population, such influence was prominent.

Language Development

Early research outcomes indicated that some internationally adopted children developed language problems (Dalen, 1995, 2001; Hene, 1988; Rygvold, 1999). Scandinavian researchers were among the first to point to intercountry adoptees' language development as a potential risk factor for delays in their further development. Rygvold (2009) points to the fact that the language acquisition of intercountry adoptees is neither bilingual nor monolingual. Adopted children have an interrupted language development; they develop a second first language. However, most of the internationally adopted children learn their new language very rapidly, and the development seems to follow the same pattern as in monolingual language development (Glennen, 2007; Glennen and Master, 2002; Pollock, 2005; Roberts et al., 2005; Rygvold, 1999). Although most of the adopted children show normal language acquisition, one third develop some form of language problem (Dalen, 2001, 2005; Glennen and Masters, 2002; Roberts et al., 2005). There seems to be a discrepancy between the children's mastery of day-to-day language and academic language. The day-to-day language represents the contextualized language in which meaning and understanding are anchored in the here-and-now situation, while the academic language represents a more abstract and de-contextualized language. The internationally adopted children's language problems are more related to delayed academic language than to day-to-day language (Dalen, 1995, 2001; Rygvold, 1999, 2009).

The Romanian study explored the association between early language ability and later cognitive performance (Rutter et al., 2009). Although the majority of the children had no language when they arrived in their adoptive homes, a minority was able to reproduce one or two words. The children who were able to say one or two words had significantly higher cognitive scores and enhanced language ability at ages 4, 6, 11 and 15. The children who had not developed any language before they left the institution in Romania were at much greater risk of cognitive delay and autistic tendencies. One has to keep in mind that the global deprivation experienced by the children adopted from Romania may be more marked than that experienced by other groups of internationally adopted children.

Academic Achievement

Here academic achievement refers to both school performance and educational attainment.

School Performance

The earliest studies to focus on intercountry adoptees' school performance, carried out in USA, Canada, and Europe, showed that these children managed very well at school compared to non-adopted children (Bagley and Young, 1980; Feigelman and Silverman, 1983; Pruzan, 1977; Simon and Altstein, 1981). This was somewhat astonishing because often those children had been raised in institutions or had come from other deprived conditions.

At the end of the 1990s a somewhat different picture emerged. In the Netherlands Hoksbergen, Juffer, and Waardenburg (1987) found that intercountry adoptees had lower school performance than non-adopted peers. In a large epidemiological study Verhulst, Althaus, and Verluis-den Bierman (1990) studied

2148 internationally adopted children aged from 10 to 14 years. The adopted children showed a lower level of academic achievement in school compared to Dutch-born children. Research carried out in Scandinavia also documented lower school performance among intercountry adoptees compared to environmental peers (Dalen, 1995, 2001; Kvifte-Andresen, 1992).

In the beginning of this century the knowledge on intercountry adoptees' school performance expanded (Becket et al., 2006; Dalen and Rygvold, 2006; Lindblad et al., 2003; van IJzendoorn et al., 2005). Research outcomes from those studies clearly documented that cognitive competence, language skills, and school performance are intertwined.

Studies on school performance display considerable methodological variations concerning the delimitation of the study group, age at follow up, and choice of outcome measure. This has resulted in partly contradictory messages from research on school performance of intercountry adoptees. Many studies are based on samples from a single adoption organization (Dalen, 1995, 2001; Dalen and Rygvold, 2006; Stams et al., 2000) or from only one or two sending countries (Bagley and Young, 1980; Dalen 2001; Dalen and Rygvold, 2006; Mylien, Meyer and Winick, 1977; Wickes and Slate, 1996).

Furthermore, there are large variations in age at follow up. Most studies contain a wide age range (Dalen, 1995, 2001 Dalen and Rygvold, 2006; Levy-Schiff, Zoran, and Shulman, 1997).

Moreover, school grades have seldom been used as outcome measures in research on school performance among intercountry adoptees. This stands in contrast to studies on national adoptions (Burrow, Tubman, and Finely, 2004; Miller, Fan, Cristensen, Grotevant, and van Dulmen, 2000). Instead, teacher ratings have been the most common indicators of school performance (Dalen, 1995, 2001; Dalen and Rygvold, 2006; Kvifte-Andresen, 1992; Stams et al., 2000). Some studies have also used parental reports (Bagley and Young, 1980; Dalen, 2001; Dalen and Rygvold, 2006; Verhulst et al., 1990).

School grades were used in a Swedish study measuring academic achievement at age 16 in a national cohort sample, including all intercountry adoptees (N=6,448) born 1973-1977 (Vinnerljung, Lindblad, Rasmussen, and Dalen, 2010). The adoptees' grades were compared to grades among environmental siblings of the adoptees and a Swedish-born group. Girls performed better than boys in all the groups. Siblings of intercountry adoptees had the highest grades of all groups, followed by adoptees from Korea and then the Swedish-born group. Adoptees from non-Korean countries had the lowest grades. Thus, the results documented a great disparity within the adopted group.

Non-Korean adoptees tended to have a more uneven grade profile (greater variability) compared to Korean adoptees and Swedish majority peers, with particularly low grades in physics, and in other theoretical subjects, but more or less comparable grades in music and sports. This suggests that Non-Korean adoptees tend to have problems in subjects where cognitive competence is needed the most.

School Performance Better than Expected from Cognitive Test Scores

In the Swedish studies there was a genuine chance to study the relationship between cognitive function and school performance in *male* adolescent adoptees. As mentioned before, those studies showed that the non-Korean adoptees had lower grade points than the *male* majority population. The results indicate that, when adjusted for cognitive test scores, the outcome was significantly better in the non-Korean group than in the majority population. Those adoptees performed better—reached higher grade points—than could be expected from the cognitive test scores compared to the majority group. In linear regression models, adjusted for gender and year of birth, lower maternal education was strongly associated with lower grades for the majority population group. However, in the two adopted groups, this gradient was quite weak.

Learning Disabilities

Quite a few studies have documented that a higher percentage of internationally adopted children have learning disabilities (Dalen, 1995, 2001; Verhulst et al., 1990). In their meta-analysis van IJzendoorn, Juffer, and Klein Poelhuis (2005) also found that adopted children showed significantly more learning problems. The learning disabilities were often related to some kind of hyperactive behavior and language difficulties (see section on language development).

Hyperactive behavior The prevalence of hyperactive behavior has been found in several studies of intercountry adoptees (Dalen, 1995, 2001; Kvifte-Andresen, 1991; Lindblad, Dalen, Rasmussen, Vinnerljung, and Hjern, 2009; McGuiness and Pallansch, 2000; Rutter et al., 2009). This hyperactive behavior has been discussed in different ways, most often as Minimal Brain Dysfunction (MBD) and Attention Deficit Hyperactive Disorder (ADHD).

ADHD is often described as a neurobehavioral developmental disorder characterized by inattention, impulsiveness and hyperactivity. Although there is considerable evidence that genetic factors are important in the etiology of ADHD (Wallis, Russell, and Muenke, 2008). Rutter et al. (2009) found that inattention/over activity was much more frequent among Romanian adoptees at age six than in a comparison group. Those findings indicate that environmental conditions such as duration of institutional deprivation must also be taken into account (Taylor and Sonuga-Barke, 2008).

In a study of children adopted from the former Soviet Union, McGuinness and Pallansch (2000) found that 13.3 percent of the children were reported by parents to have ADHD compared to between three to 6 percent in the USA population. Many of these children are born to women who had used alcohol during pregnancy, a practice that can result in Fetal Alcohol Syndrome, a birth defect that increases the risk for developing ADHD (McGuinness and Pallansch, 2000; Streissguth, Barr, Sampson, and Bookstein, 1994). Problems related to hyperactive behavior seem to interfere with learning processes by impairing working memory, attention regulation, and executive functions in many internationally adopted children who have experienced severe adversity (Gindis, 2005; Rutter et al., 2009).

One of the Swedish register studies focused on ADHD in intercountry adoptees (Lindblad, Ringbäck, Weitoft, and Hjern, 2010), as compared to the general population. The results showed that the rates of ADHD medication were higher in intercountry adoptees than in the comparison population for both boys (5.3 vs. 1.5 percent for 10 to 15-year-olds) and girls (2.1 vs. 0.3 percent for 10 to 15-year-olds). The prevalence of medication was particularly high for adoptees from Eastern Europe. The risk increased also with higher age at adoption.

Special needs education Several studies have documented that a higher percentage of intercountry adoptees are referred to special education services (12.8 percent in the adopted group compared to 5.5 percent in the non-adopted group; Bohman, 1970; Dalen, 1995; Dalen, 2001; Dalen and Rygvold, 2006; Verhulst et al., 1990). In their meta-analysis, van IJzendoorn, Juffer, and Klein Poelhuis (2005) documented a twofold increase in special education referrals for adopted children, compared to non-adopted comparisons.

However, this tendency can be explained in different ways. It could be that the internationally adopted groups do have a higher percentage of learning difficulties and therefore also more often need special educational treatment. Another explanation would be that adoptive parents are more concerned about their children's school performance and follow their achievement more closely. These families often have a higher level of education than the majority population and also higher financial resources (Dalen et al. 2008, Odenstad et al. 2009). This should mean better propensity for the identification of learning problems and at the same time convey a potential for seeking and utilizing psychological and educational support.

Educational Attainment

In a Swedish study from 2003, Lindblad, Hjern and Vinnerljung (2003) documented that intercountry adoptees had reached the same educational level as the majority group. However, the adoptees had not reached the level expected from their socioeconomic background. The same tendency was found in another Swedish study (Dalen et al., 2008). This study showed that a higher percentage having only completed basic education was found among non-Korean and national adoptees and the lowest percentage among siblings of intercountry adoptees and Korean adoptees. The highest percentage having completed a post-secondary education was found among siblings of intercountry adoptees and Korean adoptees.

The most striking findings of this study were the positive impact of adoption on educational attainment among intercountry adoptees. Given their cognitive competence, they had a better chance than the general population to reach university level. These results seem to demonstrate that families adopting internationally create an ecological setting that promotes education and fosters educational attainment. This is further underlined by the higher than average educational attainment of the biological children of these same parents. In contrast, national adoption did not have a positive effect on educational attainment and this was not explained by lower socio-economic level in these families compared with the adoptive families of intercountry adoptees.

Discussion

In this final section we will look at cognitive competence and academic achievement in relation to pre - and post adoption factors. As mentioned earlier the information on the children's pre-adoption history is very limited. When it comes to post adoption factors the information is limited to the adoptive families' socioeconomic status and level of education; we know very little about the psychological and educational climate within the adoptive family.

Gender

When intercountry adoptions started to be common in the Nordic countries mostly girls were adopted from abroad. Later on the percentage of boys increased and today the gender differences are not that large. However, some countries, such as China, still have an overrepresentation of girls for adoption. Most studies have focused on behavior problems and they document a higher percentage of externalized and hyperactive behavior among internationally adopted boys, both compared to adopted girls and also to non -adoptees (Dalen, 2001; Kvifte-Andresen, 1992; Stams et al., 2000; Verhulst et al., 1990). Most studies on school performance show that internationally adopted girls generally perform better than boys (Dalen, 1995, 2001; Kvifte-Andresen, 1992; Vinnerljung et al., 2010).

Although few studies have focused on intelligence among internationally adopted children, a study by Stams, Juffer, Rispens, and Hoksbergen from The Netherlands in 2000 revealed higher intelligence scores among adopted boys, and an interaction between gender and country of origin. The superior performance among boys could be explained by a higher percentage of those boys coming from Korea. The Swedish register studies on cognitive competence are limited to male adoptees so it is not possible to compare performance in this area between males and females.

Age at Adoption

The age at adoption is a classical variable in adoption research, but it is difficult to determine the effect of age at adoption on cognitive and academic outcomes. Some studies show that age of adoption has no effect on overall cognitive competence (Dalen, 2001; Kvifte-Andresen, 1992), while others give a quite different picture

(Beckett et al., 2006; Rutter et al., 2009; Verhulst, et al., 1990). Studies also differ in their cut-off points for an early or late adoption. In their latest longitudinal study Rutter et al. (2009) used the cut-off point of six months of age. Children adopted before the age of six months were not delayed in their cognitive development. Children adopted after that age experienced delays in their development, and did not catch up with non-adopted children at older ages. In their meta-analysis Van IJzendoorn, Juffer, and Klein Poelhuis (2005) did not find evidence for any general effects of age at adoption on adoptees' IQ. However, age at adoption did matter for school performance, revealing that children adopted before the age of one year had superior academic achievement. Thus, there is some evidence that age of adoption has a greater effect on school performance than on cognitive development in general.

Interestingly, age of adoption might not be the crucial factor. The environmental conditions the adopted children experience during their first months of life may be far more important. The Romanian adoptees are an example of children who have experienced severe pre-adoption adversity. Children adopted from other sending countries may have been exposed to much better quality of care during their first months of life. Swedish register studies reported that age at adoption had different effects related to country of origin. Adoptees from non-Korean countries with higher adoption age had lower cognitive test scores (IQ), while this was not the case among Korean adoptees. For this group age at adoption had only marginal effects on the mean scores. This result could be explained by different pre-adoption conditions in Korea compared to other sending countries.

Country of Origin

Children adopted internationally represent countries with a great variety in terms of quality of pre-adoption conditions, adoption procedures, and selection of children for adoption. Intercountry adoption is often seen as a humanitarian response to crises of war, famine, disease, and disaster that make it impossible to provide for all children within a certain country (Selman, 2000; See Chapter 3). The history of adoption in the sending countries has been very different, and even today there exists a large heterogeneity when it comes to adoption specific conditions.

Pre-adoptive environmental factors—in combination with different adoption practices—are likely to influence the cognitive development of children available for adoption in a given country. However, developmental outcomes related to country of origin have been less extensively studied than impact of age at adoption (e.g., van IJzendoorn et al., 2005).

Quite a few studies have documented that adoptees from Korea have better cognitive and academic achievement than adoptees from other sending countries (Dalen, 2001; Dalen et al., 2008; Kim and Staat, 2004; Kvifte-Andresen, 1992; Lindblad et al., 2003; Lindblad et al., 2009; Odenstad et al., 2008; Vinnerljung et al., 2010; Verhulstet al., 1990, 1991). However, those results reflect the conditions around intercountry adoptions in South Korea more than ethnic differences.

Selman (2000) points to the fact that South Korea has a special position among countries delivering children for intercountry adoption. When intercountry adoption started, South Korea was devastated by war and had a very low GNP per capita combined with a high birth rate (Fronek and Tilse, 2010). Today it is a prosperous country with a high level of education and sub-replacement fertility. However, there is continuing stigmatization of single mothers, related to cultural factors. The stigma, along with the absence of a comprehensive welfare system makes it, even today, almost impossible for a single mother to keep her child.

The effects of pre- and postnatal deprivation are far more severe in countries with low resources, making children born in these countries more vulnerable to cognitive developmental delays.

Adoption as a Positive Intervention

Adoption means a positive change for most children. They move from deprived or unfavorable settings to more positive environmental conditions in the adoptive family. The effect of adoption on children's overall development has been discussed in several studies (Bohman and Sigvarsson, 1980; Dennis, 1973; Hodges and Tizard, 1989; Rutter, Kreppner, O'Connor, and the ERA Study Team, 2001; van IJzendoorn et al., 2005; See also Chapters 13 and 14). Especially strong effects on cognitive development have been found when the adoption has brought about radical changes of environment (Duyme, 1990; Duyme et al., 1999; Rutter et al., 2009).

Adoptive parents seem to offer better than average environmental conditions in some respects, like parental education and socioeconomic level. This has been documented in the Swedish register studies. Although those studies do not find any effect of adoptive parental education on adoptees' cognitive test scores (IQ), the studies clearly showed positive effects on intercountry adoptees' school performance and educational attainment (Dalen et al. 2008, Lindblad et al. 2003, Lindblad et al. 2009, Odenstad et al. 2008, Vinnerljung et al. 2010). In those studies intercountry adoptees perform better at school and reach higher educational levels than could be expected from their cognitive test scores, compared to the majority group.

The low correlation between adoptive parents' educational levels and their adopted child's cognitive performance can to a large degree be explained by the genetic component of intelligence (Neiss and Rowe, 2000). The positive effect of parental educational level on adoptees' school performance and educational attainment can be explained by these families' ability to stimulate their children educationally. In their longitudinal study on school achievement among adoptees, Maugham, Collishaw, and Pickles (1998) came to the same conclusion.

McGuinness and Pallansch (2000) also found in their study on adoptees from the former Soviet Union that adoptive family environments were generally positive and accepting. They suggest that it is the family environment that is a more important protective factor than socioeconomic measures. They believe that it is the quality of the adoptive family social climate and circumstances that helps adopted children overcome, in part, some of the damage caused by early risk factors. Adoptive families in this study did not have excessive expectations for the adopted child's development. They put somewhat less than average emphasis on competitiveness and achievement in school activities, indicating that the parents are sensitive to the challenges that the children have faced.

Other studies have documented that adoptive parents are far more supportive of the child's school situation than parents of biological children (Dalen, 1995; 2001; 2005; Dalen and Rygvold, 2006). They more often help their children with homework and are more involved in the day-to-day life at school. This can easily lead to a positive effect on a child's academic performance. However, one should also be aware that adoptive parents sometimes set unreasonably high standards for their children's school performance. The study of Verhulst, Althaus, and Verluis-den Bierman (1990) did show that children adopted in families with low SES had better academic performance and were less often referred to special classes and special education than children adopted in families with higher SES. This may indicate that adoptive parents representing high SES families might have excessive expectations and demands concerning their children's academic functioning. Bohman's study from 1970 found the same result, and he discussed how chronic feelings of not being able to satisfy parental standards may be an important stress factor influencing the adopted child's self-esteem and learning process. Other studies have actually shown that there is a higher risk for social maladjustment in adoptive white-collar families than in blue-collar families. Furthermore, the rate of adoption disruption is higher in families from higher socio economic classes (Berry and Barth, 1990; Rosenthal, 1995; See Chapter 21). Although adoptive parents may encourage cognitive development, the adoptees' capacity for intellectual performance may be limited because of genetic and pre-adoption factors.

Van IJzendoorn, Juffer, and Klein Poelhuis (2005) introduced the term *Adoption Decalage,* that describes a gap between cognitive competence and actual school performance of adoptees. The *decalage* was largest for those children who came from extremely deprived preadoption backgrounds.

The Swedish register studies do not give support to the existence of an adoption decalage (Dalen, 2005; Dalen et al., 2008; Lindblad et al., 2009). Those studies documented that the adoptees with the lowest school grades (non-Korean group) performed better and reached higher grade points than could be expected from their cognitive test scores compared to the majority group. Furthermore, their pattern of grades differed from other groups, showing lowest grades in physics and highest in sports and music. This pattern supports the hypothesis that poorer school performance is related to a lower than average cognitive competence. We should be aware of this fact when offering special needs education to adoptees with learning difficulties. An assessment of cognitive competence is an important step for successful educational intervention for many intercountry adoptees for preventing secondary psychological symptom formation due to unrealistic expectations.

To summarize, there is a need for a developmental model in studying academic achievement among intercountry adoptees. This model should be longitudinal, following the children from the time they are adopted, through early infancy and into kindergarten and school years (Palacios and Brodzinsky, 2005). The model should include variables like gender, age at adoption and country of origin, but also variables referring to social development and cognitive competence. The model should also include variables related to the adoptive family with a special focus on standardized measures of the psychological and educational climate within the family.

Ethical Considerations

Research focusing on intercountry adoptees runs the risk of stigmatizing this very visible group in Western societies (see Chapter 17). Research outcomes have documented a great disparity within intercountry adoptees' performance. The outcomes that have been presented in this chapter clearly show that some of the adoptees perform very well, both on cognitive and academic achievement, even better than the majority population. At the same time, a fairly large group performs far below the normal range. When asked how intercountry adoptees are doing, what is the right answer? The best answer would be to point to the mixed picture and acknowledge that quite a few adoptees have problems with their cognitive and academic performance, and will need help and support during their formative years. On the other hand, adoption seems to be a very good intervention for children not able to remain in their biological families.

Chapter 16
Families with Intercountry Adopted Children: Talking About Adoption and Birth Culture[1]

Femmie Juffer and Wendy Tieman

Although most intercountry adoptees develop as favorably as do non-adopted children, it is well recognized that a minority of intercountry adoptees show difficulties at home or at school. At the same time, adoption can be seen as a powerful positive intervention in the lives of children who suffered severe deprivation in early childhood, offering them opportunities for catch-up and recovery in their cognitive and social-emotional development (see Chapter 13). A meta-analysis on behavior problems and mental health referrals showed that, compared with non-adopted children, intercountry adoptees appear to have somewhat more behavior problems, and they are referred to mental health services about twice as often as non-adopted children (Juffer and Van IJzendoorn, 2005).

It is important to examine the correlates of intercountry adoptees' behavior problems and to study the life stages in which they may particularly struggle with adoption issues. The above-mentioned meta-analysis showed that age at adoptive placement was not a significant moderator: intercountry adoptees placed in infancy presented the same levels of behavior problems as intercountry adoptees placed after their first or second birthday (Juffer and Van IJzendoorn, 2005). What did matter was the developmental phase of the international adoptees: in middle childhood they showed more behavior problems than in adolescence. We may speculate that intercountry adoptees start struggling with adoption and identity issues relatively early because racial and cultural differences between adoptive parents and adoptees are often obvious and visible (Juffer and Van IJzendoorn, 2005). It could also be assumed that some behavior problems are related to processes in the family, including understanding and interest in adoption, and communication about adoption and the birth culture. In this chapter we discuss outcomes from our studies on children's interest in

1 This chapter is based, in part, on Juffer, F. and Tieman, W. (2009). Being adopted: Internationally adopted children's interest and feelings. *International Social Work*, 52, 635-47. © Sage.

adoption and in their birth culture in families with transracially adopted children from several countries of origin.

Children's Understanding of Adoption

According to Brodzinsky and colleagues (Brodzinsky, Schechter, and Henig, 1992; Brodzinsky, Singer, and Braff, 1984) there are clear developmental trends regarding children's understanding of the concept of adoption and its implications for the involved persons. Most preschoolers—even adopted preschoolers—understand little of adoption. At about six or seven years, however, most children can distinguish between birth and adoption as alternative ways of forming a family. Also, in middle childhood adopted children start to recognize that being adopted means having two sets of parents, birth parents and adoptive parents. And they also begin to realize that being adopted not only means being wanted or 'chosen' (by the adoptive parents) but also being relinquished or 'given away' (by the birth parent). In this developmental stage, adopted children start to reflect on the separation between their birthparents and themselves, and they may experience a profound sense of loss for the first time. Brodzinsky et al. (1992) noted that in middle childhood adopted children's understanding and appreciation of the implications of the adoption grow at a profound rate, whereas at the same time a decline in positive attitudes about being adopted is shown. According to Brodzinsky et al. (1992) a rise in behavioral problems that are more common in adoptees can also be seen at this age (as has been confirmed in the meta-analysis by Juffer and Van IJzendoorn, 2005).

Although Brodzinsky's (1990) stress and coping model has been developed for domestic adoptees, it could be hypothesized that the same loss-related processes apply to intercountry adoption. However, intercountry, transracial adoptees not only have to deal with being different because of their adoptive status but also because of their different appearance and skin color (for a review of transracial adoption see Lee, 2003). Depending on the racial context of being reared in a North-American or European country, being different and looking different may interfere with children's feelings of attachment (Bowlby, 1982) and positive identification with their parents.

Children's Interest in Adoption and in the Birth Culture

Relatively few empirical studies have examined adopted children's understanding of and interest in adoption (Brodzinsky, Schechter, and Henig, 1992; Brodzinsky, Singer, and Braff, 1984), or their feelings associated with being adopted and looking different (Juffer, 2006). Importantly, these studies suggested that communication processes in adoptive families influence adopted children's psychological adjustment (Brodzinsky, 2006; Juffer, 2006).

Studying these issues in intercountry adoption is important, because the fact of being adopted—or adoptive status—is in many cases more visible than in domestic adoptions (but not always, e.g., Scherman and Harré, 2008). In most families the intercountry, transracially adopted children have a different skin color and physical appearance compared with their parents and peers, combined with another cultural heritage (Heimsoth and Laser, 2008; Lee, Grotevant, Hellerstedt, Gunnar, and the Minnesota International Adoption Project Team, 2006; Thomas and Tessler, 2007). Therefore, intercountry adoptees may not only feel different because of their adoptive status, but also because of their different looks.

Adoptive parents often face the dilemma that they are outsiders to their adopted child's birth culture (Tan and Nakkula, 2004). At the same time they realize that they should support their child's ethnic identity and adoption background. To cope with these issues, adoptive parents utilize a series of strategies, including communication about adoption, post-adoption support groups (Tan and Nakkula, 2004; Vonk and Massati, 2008), and involvement in cultural activities corresponding to the child's birth culture (Paulsen and Merighi, 2009; Thomas and Tessler, 2007). Many adoptive parents also initiate or encourage heritage trips, language classes or 'culture camps' to keep the connection with the birth culture alive.

Studies on heritage or return trips to the child's birth country are scarce (for an explorative study on five families see Ponte, Wang, and Fan, 2010), and the same is true for studies examining the role of 'culture camps.' In an explorative study Randolph and Holtzman (2010) suggested that adoptive parents utilize culture camps to pay attention to cultural and racial differences, whereas the adopted children reported that although the camps were fun, they did not do enough to address the racial challenges they faced.

How Does It Feel To Be Adopted?

In the studies discussed in this chapter we asked parents to report on their intercountry adopted children's understanding of adoption, their children's feelings about being adopted and looking different, and their children's interest in adoption. We also addressed the issue of talking about adoption in the family.

There are large numbers of intercountry adoptees in North America and Europe nowadays. Worldwide each year approximately 30,000 children are adopted among more than 100 sending and receiving countries, although a recent decline in intercountry adoptions has been observed (Selman, 2009a). The children in our studies were adopted from Sri Lanka, South-Korea, Colombia, China and India and transracially placed with White parents in the Netherlands. In this multicultural society, many ethnically mixed groups live together, although the big cities, such as Amsterdam, show more cultural diversity than do rural areas. About 17 percent of the Dutch population are first- or second-generation immigrants (Vedder, Boekaerts, and Seegers, 2005).

In the Netherlands, adoption predominantly consists of intercountry adoptions. Each year approximately 600 children are adopted internationally via six accredited adoption agencies versus about 20 domestic adoptions. The Netherlands has a medium intercountry adoption rate (intercountry adoptions per 100,000 population), 5.0 compared with 10.2 in Spain, 9.6 in Norway, 6.8 in the USA, and 0.6 in the UK (Selman, 2008).

Being Adopted: Feeling Different?

In a first study including 176 families with 7-year-old children adopted from Sri Lanka, Korea and Colombia to the Netherlands, we examined children's understanding of and interest in adoption, and their feelings about being adopted and looking different (Juffer, 2006). Virtually all children did understand the meaning of being adopted. Most children were interested in their adoption but almost one quarter of the children showed little or no interest in adoption. The children who did show interest in their adoption were particularly interested in their individual photo album of adoption.

Quite a few children (27 percent) had expressed the wish that they were born in the family rather than adopted. For these children the adoptive status seemed less desirable than being born in a family. Moreover, almost half of the children (46 percent) had expressed the wish to be White like their parents and peers. For these children, the most obvious aspect of the intercountry adoption experience—the physical differences between parents and children—may be particularly stressful during some time period.

These findings could be understood as an extension of Brodzinsky's stress and coping model (Brodzinsky, 1990) to intercountry adoption: the stress is related to being different, being adopted as well as having a different appearance than one's parents or friends. According to Juffer (2006), an additional or alternative explanation is offered by attachment theory. A common theme in both wishes, the wish of being born in the family and the wish to be White, might be that adopted children feel frustrated in their tendency to fully identify with their adoptive parents, which is a normative tendency in childhood and a logical consequence of early parent-child attachment relationships (Bowlby, 1982). For adopted children the wish of being born in the family and the wish to be White may represent their answer to the distance they experience between their adoptive parents and themselves in terms of family relatedness and appearance, despite their strong feelings of closeness and attachment to their parents. Importantly, these wishes predicted children's behavior problems, as reported by the parent and independently rated by the teacher (Juffer, 2006).

Interest in Adoption and Talking about Adoption

In our next studies we replicated and extended our findings to two samples of adoptive families with school-aged children adopted from China and India (Juffer and Tieman, 2009). We expected that most adoptees understood the difference between adoption and being born in the family. Based on our previous study we also expected that the adopted children had expressed wishes not to be different (by adoptive status or by physical appearance), and that they were interested in specific aspects of adoption (such as the story of their own adoption). Finally, we expected that most adoptive families did talk about adoption, since the visibility of intercountry adoption seems to exclude secrecy. To further extend our knowledge, gender and country of origin differences were explored.

Parents were requested to participate in a survey on intercountry adopted children from China or from India. Adoption agencies in the Netherlands were willing to approach all eligible families with children aged four to 16 years, and this resulted in a sample of 1,233 children adopted from China and a sample of 412 children adopted from India. As expected, based on China's one-child per family policy, resulting in relatively high rates of abandonment of female infants (Johnson, 2004; Tan and Marfo, 2006), a large number of girls were involved in the China study: 1130 girls (92 percent) versus 103 boys (eight percent). The children from China had been adopted at an average age of 19 months and their mean age at the time of the study was 7.1 years. The sample of children adopted from India consisted of 319 girls (77 percent) and 93 boys (23 percent). As in China, based on son preference, more girls than boys are being made available for adoption (Diamond-Smith, Luke, and McGarvey, 2008; Groza, 2006). Children from India were placed for adoption at a mean age of 14 months and they were on average 10.2 years old at the time of the study.

The two groups did not differ significantly from each other with respect to parental education. However, the sample of adopted children from India consisted of relatively more boys than the sample of adopted children from China ($p< 0.01$). Also, the adopted children from China were younger at the time of the study but older at adoptive placement than the children from India.

We asked the adoptive parents whether their children understood the concept of adoption, were interested in adoption, and talked about their adoption. Parents replied to the following questions:

- Does your child understand the difference between being adopted and being born in a family?
- How would you rate your child's feelings about being adopted?
- Did your child ever express the wish to be White (for the China survey: not to look Chinese)?
- Did your child ever express the wish that (s)he had been born in your family?
- Is your child interested in adoption?

- How would you rate your child's interest in the following aspects of adoption:
  - The story of her/his adoption
  - The book of photos of her/his adoption
  - The video of the trip to the country of origin
  - Children's books on adoption
  - Books/films with adopted characters.
  - Some families start talking about adoption with their child early while other families start later. How about your family?
- Who usually starts talking about adoption in your family?

Being Adopted and Looking Different

Almost all adopted children from China and India were reported to understand the difference between being adopted and being born in a family (90 percent and 89 percent, respectively). Children from both countries were reported to have rather positive feelings about being adopted. On a rating scale from 0 (negative) to 10 (positive), parents rated their children's feelings about being adopted as, on average, 7.2 (*SD*= 1.6) in the China group, and a similar average rating of 7.3 (*SD* = 1.8) in the India group (Juffer and Tieman, 2009).

According to the parents of the adopted children from China a substantial part of their children had expressed the wish to be White (not to look Chinese), at an average age of 5.2 years. Girls did express this wish significantly more often than boys, 34 percent versus 14.6 percent, respectively (see Figure 16.1). In the same vein, many parents of adopted children from India reported that their children had expressed the wish to be White, at an average age of 5.1 years. In this group a gender difference was also present: girls expressed this wish more often than boys, 52.2 percent versus 38.9 percent (Figure 16.1) (Juffer and Tieman, 2009).

Many children adopted from China had expressed the wish that she or he had been born in the adoptive family, at an average age of 4.3 years. Girls did express this wish more often than boys, 50.9 percent versus 35.3 percent, respectively (see Figure 16.1). Comparably, parents of children adopted from India reported that a substantial part of their children had expressed the wish to be born in the adoptive family, at an average age of 4.8 years. No gender difference was found in this group (Juffer and Tieman, 2009).

Interest in Adoption

The adoptive parents reported that a minority of the children were not interested in adoption: five percent for the China group and 13 percent in the India group. A sizeable number of adopted children showed some interest or were interested sometimes, 47 percent and 49 percent, for China and India, respectively. The remaining children were interested or very much interested (China: 47 percent and India: 38 percent) (Juffer and Tieman, 2009).

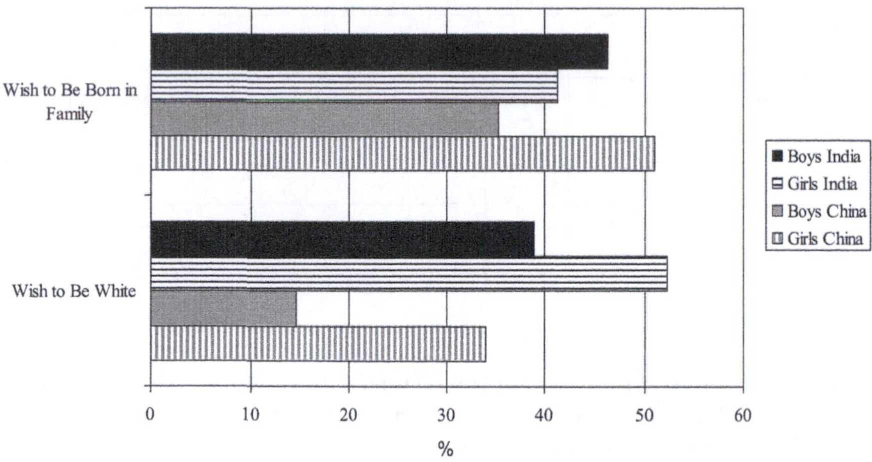

Figure 16.1 Children's Wish to be Born in the Family and the Wish to be White in Girls and Boys from China and India (%)

Parents also rated their children's interest in several specific aspects of adoption. The highest ratings were reported for children's interest in the book of photos of their adoption, children's interest in the story of their adoption, and the video of the journey to the country of origin (when the parents traveled for the adoption). Lower ratings were given to interest in children's books on adoption and book or films with adopted characters.

The child's interest in aspects of adoption was summarized by computing a standardized total adoption interest score and we found that the two groups of children from China and India did not differ from each other regarding their total interest in adoption. However, within each country, we found significant gender differences (Figure 16.2). Girls showed significantly more total interest in adoption than boys, and this was equally true for children from China and India.

Talking about Adoption

Only a few parents had not talked about adoption with their child yet. In both groups of adopted children from China and India, most parents started to talk about adoption immediately after their child's arrival in the adoptive family (80 percent and 71 percent, respectively). Parents also reported who usually started the conversation about adoption. Parents and children started talking about adoption equally often (China sample: 61 percent and India sample: 53 percent). Parents usually initiated the conversation about adoption according to some parents (21 percent and 29 percent for China and India, respectively). And in some other cases (China: 15 percent and India: 10 percent) the child was reported to start talking about adoption (Juffer and Tieman, 2009).

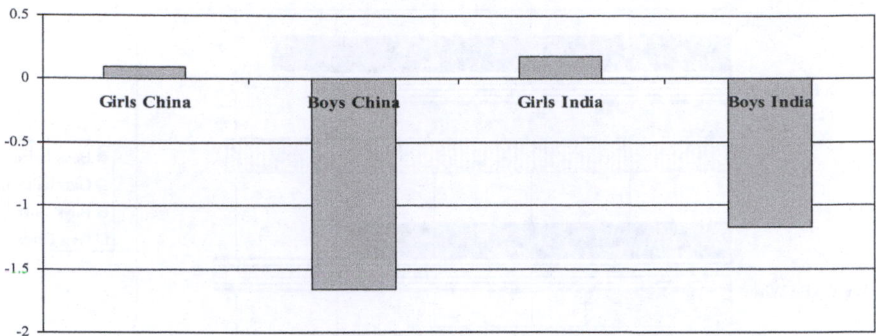

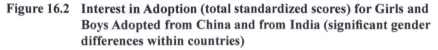

Figure 16.2 Interest in Adoption (total standardized scores) for Girls and Boys Adopted from China and from India (significant gender differences within countries)

Cultural–Racial Issues

In our adoption research we found that substantial numbers of children adopted from Sri Lanka, Korea, Colombia, China and India wished that they had been born in the family rather than been adopted while many adopted children had also expressed the wish to be White around the age of five years (Juffer, 2006; Juffer and Tieman, 2009). We found comparable patterns for five different countries of origin, implying that these wishes may exist in many intercountry adoptees.

In our studies on adoptees from China and India girls expressed the wish to be White more often than boys (Juffer and Tieman, 2009). Maybe girls are more aware of their physical appearance, or people outside the family address their different looks more openly than in the case of adopted boys. According to their parents, the wish to be White was expressed at the age of about five. At this age, children usually meet more peers and families outside their home and they may notice the differences between biologically related families and adoptive families. Moreover, like children from ethnic minorities, adopted children may receive negative comments on their (racial) appearance from people outside the family, and feel worried about it. They may be confronted with differences between their parents and themselves, whereas at the same time they feel close to their parents and like to identify with them (Juffer, 2006). It is important to be aware of these issues in the development of adopted children and respond with adequate cultural-racial socialization (Thomas and Tessler, 2007). Social workers may address these issues when counseling adoptive families, and additionally they may recommend relevant literature on adoption communication (for books for parents and/or children, see Harris, 2008; Watkins and Fisher, 1993; Wolfs, 2008).

Communication about Adoption

Our study confirmed that by middle childhood most children involved in intercountry adoption understand the concept of adoption. Also, most children from China and India were interested in their adoption (Juffer and Tieman, 2009). On a more detailed level, the highest ratings were reported for children's interest in their book of photos of the adoption, and in the story of their own adoption. It seems that especially the personal aspects are more interesting for children compared to the less personal examples of adoption in children's books and films. We found that the children from China and India did not differ from each other regarding their total interest in adoption. However, within each country, we found significant gender differences. Girls were reported to show more interest in adoption than boys, and this was equally true for children adopted from both countries. Interestingly, this finding seems to converge with clinical observations that female adoptees are more eager to search for their birth relatives than male adoptees (Brodzinsky et al., 1992), and with study outcomes that female adopted adults show more interest in their roots (Tieman, Van der Ende, and Verhulst, 2008) and think about their birth family more often (Irhammar and Cederblad, 2000) than male adopted adults. Parents and social workers should be aware of these gender differences and explore and discuss possible reasons and consequences.

Most adoptive parents started talking about adoption immediately after their child's arrival in the family. We think that this reflects the reality of intercountry, transracial adoption. Because this type of adoption is so visible, the adoption cannot be concealed. This should be evaluated in a positive way, because open communication about adoption may enhance children's coping and acceptance of their adoptive status (Brodzinsky, 2006; Brodzinsky et al., 1992).

Future Studies

Although in our studies most questions addressed current issues (such as the child's current interest in adoption), some questions asked the adoptive parents to reflect on issues in a retrospective way (for example the child's wish to be White). Future research should extend our findings by prospectively studying young, intercountry adopted children in the preschool years and examine these children's feelings of being different and their wishes to identify with the adoptive parents.

Another limitation is that in our studies we had to rely on parent report. Future studies should also examine self report of intercountry adoptees, for example with interviews (Reinoso, Juffer, and Tieman, 2012. In addition, future studies should examine the development of adoptees' interest in adoption and in the birth culture from early childhood to adolescence and adulthood (Meier, 1999). Also, the role of cultural experiences for ethnic identity formation should be investigated (e.g., Song and Lee, 2009).

Conclusion

We conclude that social workers and adoptive parents should be aware of the specific developmental needs and concerns of intercountry adopted children. Intercountry adoptees may feel different because of their adoptive status and because of their different physical appearance. Adopted children may need our support when they are confronted with these possibly stressful differences, challenging their normative feelings to identify with parents and peers. Because these concerns seem to start at an early age—three to six years—we should accommodate counseling and parent education about adoption communication and cultural-racial socialization to this fairly early time schedule. Also, adoptive parents should be informed about their child's possible worries and supported to offer their child comfort and reassurance.

Acknowledgments

We thank Wereldkinderen, Meiling, Stichting Kind en Toekomst, De Rode Draad, Renske Gast, and the participating adoptive families for their contributions to the studies described in this chapter. Femmie Juffer holds the Chair on Adoption Studies supported by Wereldkinderen, The Hague.

Chapter 17
Post-Racial Utopianism, White Color-Blindness and "the Elephant in the Room": Racial Issues for Transnational Adoptees of Color

Tobias Hübinette

Ever since the institutionalization of transnational (intercountry) adoption as a child welfare practice, as a reproductive technique, and as an international migration phenomenon (see Chapter 1), the subject of transnational adoptees of color and race has with few exceptions been glossed over or even ignored by researchers studying adoption, while adoptees have not merited any particular interest from ethnic and migration studies scholars. This omission becomes even more puzzling in light of the fact that domestic transracial adoption has been highly contested in decades-long debates in countries like the USA and the UK, with race as a central issue. The aim of this chapter is to try to understand why issues of race and the non-white bodies of transnational adoptees have received so little attention in adoption research. Race within adoption research can almost be compared to "the elephant in the room"—an obvious and uncomfortable topic that everyone avoids. The chapter begins with an attempt at understanding the relative invisibility of race within adoption research as a reflection of a hegemonic color-blindness which in its turn can be explained by the ideology of post-racial utopianism that surrounds transnational adoption as a field, continues with a summary of the existing research on transnational adoptees of color and race, and ends with a concluding discussion. Finally I criticize the tendency to pathologize and medicalize adoptees and argue for a stronger bridging of quantitative and qualitative adoption research.

Transnational Adoption and the Birth of the Hegemony of Color-Blindness

During the colonial period, mixed-race children in the global European empires were cared for in special homes where they were brought up to become something of an intermediary class between the White settlers and the indigenous people (Stoler, 2002; White, 1999). In the European settler colonies mixed-race children were classified as non-White, and generally deemed unfit to be adopted or fostered by Whites or taken to Europe, unless they were able to pass as White. In other words, it is fair to say that the post-Holocaust atmosphere and the beginning of decolonization in the 1950s created the type of transnational and transracial adoption that we know of today.

Transnational adoption in its modern sense grew out of the heightened number of orphaned and mixed-race children in Europe and Asia which followed World War II, although it had several predecessors (Hübinette, 2009). The first children were mainly dispatched to the USA, many from the newly occupied countries of Germany, Italy and Japan; this marked the beginning of permanent transnational adoption placements. Although the majority of the estimated 5,000 American transnational adoptions that were processed between 1946-1953 concerned White children, the mixed-race adopted children fathered by Black or White American soldiers in continental Europe or in Japan heralded the beginning of a revolution in transracial placements, and was soon followed by a new wave of transnational adoptees following the Korean War (Weil, 1984).

One of the pioneers of transnational and transracial adoption, who is nowadays largely forgotten as an adoptive parent, but who really epitomized the spirit of post-racial utopianism in the 1950s, was the African American expatriate singer, dancer, and artist Josephine Baker. Together with her White French husband, she adopted 12 children from every continent of the world, including a Korean child and even coined the expression "rainbow family" (Pratt and Guterl, 2009). Baker wanted to prove that after the Holocaust and at the time of anti-colonial uprisings and rebellions, race should no longer matter. As a celebrity she was able to convey this message widely through the media and through her children's book *The Rainbow Children*. She wrote:

> My ideal is so simple, yet so many people view it as a crazy dream. Surely the day will come when color means nothing more than skin tone, when religion is seen uniquely as a way to speak to one's soul, when birth places have the weight of a throw of a dice and all men are born free; when understanding breeds love and brotherhood. (Baker and Bouillon, 1995, p. 262-3)

Ahead of her time, Baker's utopian vision of a color-blind world where race, ethnicity, religion, and biological roots would become obsolete and completely irrelevant, was to become the ideological underpinning for transnational and transracial adoption when it was institutionalized after the Korean War. This form of adoption became increasingly socially acceptable, as well as seen as a politically radical act, in the 1960s and 1970s.

Simultaneously domestic transracial adoption in the USA, in the UK, another new child welfare practice, created a heated discussion. To date, the discussion is still not settled (Briggs, 2009). In this debate many minorities claimed that White families cannot provide children of color with strategies to combat racism in a White-dominated Western society and that the adoption of non-White children by Whites is a continuation of the colonial practice of forced removal of native children, who were placed at boarding schools and special institutions in order to assimilate and integrate them. The debate, however, has not spilled over to transnational adoption. This may be due to the fact that Asian children always have dominated transnational adoption, and Asian migrant communities have generally not been very vocal, nor visible, in the public sphere.

Western Research on Transnational Adoptees

If post-racial utopianism and color-blindness were the driving forces behind the birth of transnational adoption, it is not surprising that adoption research has also reproduced this unwillingness to speak about race. Research on transnational adoptees has been conducted ever since the first foreign-born children arrived in their Western host countries in the 1950s. The vast majority of studies have been based on small samples of children or adolescents, frequently with adoptive parents as the principal informants, who rate and assess their adoptive children's self-esteem and/or social abilities (Bagley, 1993; Feigelman and Silverman, 1983; Hoksbergen, 1986; Koh, 1981; Simon and Altstein, 1987; Valk, 1957). Most research on transnational adoption uses normative developmental models to focus on the adoptees' psychosocial adjustment, attachment to the adoptive family, and socio-cultural assimilation.

The outcomes are generally interpreted as positive, because without doubt, most adoptees rapidly change culture and language, attach to their adoptive families, and identify primarily with White society. Adoptees thus develop 'positive' self-esteem and identification consistent with normative models (Maury, 1999; Rørbech, 1989). The sensitive issue of race and racism is simultaneously minimized. Reported incidences of discrimination and racism are downplayed or denied, as the color-blind ideology is hegemonic in research on transnational adoptees of color. Many studies also advocate color-blindness and conclude that there are no differences at all between White children and adopted non-White children when it comes to psychological well-being and self-esteem. The few 'deviant' problems that have been identified in the form of psychological and social difficulties (for example feelings of bodily discomfort and self-loathing) are either glossed over or pathologized and medicalized, with the 'deviance' attributed to a combination of pre-adoption and genetic factors (Cederblad, Irhammar, Mercke and Norlander, 1994). In sum, mainstream Western adoption research tends to privilege childhood over adulthood, family over society, and the adoption factor over the race factor.

Further, this dominant Western adoption research rarely addresses the adult lives of adoptees, and there are still few studies with adoptive parents as research objects. Many researchers themselves have, until recently, been adoptive parents, adoption professionals, and/or affiliated with adoption agencies and authorities. At the same time, ethnic and migration studies in most Western countries rarely include adoptees as research participants, as adoption is not really conceptualized as a migration. Adoptees are therefore generally not seen as migrants or minorities neither in American ethnic studies nor in European migration studies.

However, during the past decade new quantitative adoption research has emerged in Sweden that specifically examines the situation of foreign-born adult adoptees of color. This research takes advantage of the country's unique population registers that make it possible to statistically examine every inhabitant, citizen and non-citizen alike. This new research has concluded that many adult adoptees have a lower psychological health, compared to both the Swedish majority population and migrants coming from the same countries as the adoptees. They exhibit, for example, increased levels of psychiatric illnesses, alcohol and drug abuse, criminality, and suicide behavior (von Borczyskowski, Hjern, Lindblad and Vinnerljung, 2006; Hjern and Allebeck, 2002; Hjern, Lindblad and Vinnerljung, 2002). In fact, no other demographic subgroup in Sweden has a higher suicide rate than adult intercountry adoptees, as completed suicide is four to five times higher among the group than among the Swedish majority population. In an international perspective, this is comparable to the staggering suicide rates registered among indigenous peoples in North America and Australia.

This new quantitative research has also revealed that many adult adoptees have substantial problems in achieving their adoptive parents' high socioeconomic status. For example, they may have difficulties establishing themselves on the labor market (Rooth, 2002). In spite of the fact that the adoptees have grown up in the most privileged strata of Swedish society (it is estimated that 90 percent of the adoptive families belong to Sweden's upper and middle classes), the adult adoptees rarely achieve economic success as compared to their non-adopted White siblings, their adoptive parents, and equivalent cohorts (Carlberg and Nordin Jareno, 2007; Lindblad, Hjern, and Vinnerljung, 2003). Both migrants of color and adoptees of color tend to end up in the lower strata of Swedish society as adults. Finally, adult adoptees of color more often remain childless and unmarried compared to both the majority and minority populations of Sweden.

The dominant explanation for those statistical results has been a combination of pre-adoption trauma and separation, genetic defects, and cognitive delays. This implies that pre-adoption factors such as maternal deprivation and separation, genetic influences, and low IQ cause the overrepresentations of psychological problems, high suicide rates, and high unemployment (Odenstad, Hjern, Lindblad, Rasmussen, Vinnerljung, and Dalen, 2008). An alternative explanation is that psychological and demographic indicators of lesser well-being are caused by systemic isolation and exclusion in everyday life, resulting from the presence of the adoptees' non-White bodies in heavily segregated affluent, and mostly White, communities. That is the hypothesis of my studies using autobiographical texts written by transnational adoptees and deep interviews with adult adoptees of color in Sweden.

Studies on Transnational Adoptees of Color and Racial Discrimination

Recently, a multidisciplinary field of critical adoption studies has emerged, inspired, in part, by critical race and whiteness studies and gender and queer studies. Those studies differ from mainstream adoption research in their non-linear and multi-dimensional approach to transnational adoptees of color. The studies focus on adult adoptees, recognizing that being a transnational adoptee is as a lifelong and fluid process. Identifications are viewed not as dichotomous, but as multiple and always under negotiation. In addition, the studies focus on issues of race instead of just behavioral adjustment and acculturation (Baden and Stewart, 2000; Brottveit, 1999; Eng and Han, 2006; Hübinette, 2004b; 2007a; Hübinette and Tigervall, 2008; Kim, 2000; 2004; Kim, Suyemoto, and Turner, 2010; Lee, 2003; McGinnis, Livingston Smith, Ryan, and Howard, 2009; Palmer, 2001; Park Nelson, 2007; Rastas, 2004; Schwekendiek, Kwon, and Jung, 2008; Shiao and Tuan, 2007; Shiao, Tuan, and Rienzi, 2004; Wekker, Åsberg, van der Tuin, and Fredriks, 2007).

What is striking in the empirical results of these studies is the always-present feeling and experience of profound bodily alienation and racial isolation, ranging from overt and systematic bullying, to irregular but intermittent teasing. This fundamental loneliness and 'exposedness' comes from almost always being the only non-White person in the close environment, such as among family and kin, in neighborhood and school, and at the workplace. Adoptees also report feeling distanced and isolated from both minorities from the same country of origin, as well as from other adoptees of color. Another observation of these studies is the tendency among significant others of the adoptees such as parents, siblings, friends, and partners to downplay, minimize or even silence these racializing experiences. Those close others may sometimes even question the adoptees' perceptual accuracy. However, some scholars argue that being an adoptive parent to a non-White child could potentially increase the parent's ability to understand racism in society at large (Lal, 2001; Marinara, 2003; Watkins, 2005).

> Johanna: My parents said—"Honey, we don't even think about that you look different, we are so used to you!" I tried to be one in the group, but it was impossible as I looked different, and it was uncomfortable. So I went home to my mother and tried to get some kind of confirmation, like—"Yes, you look different, but don't let others tease you," but she didn't understand! And it was the same in school, instead of saying—"Yes, you look different and we understand that it isn't easy," some kind of confirmation, but no, nothing at all!

In the following passages, I provide extracts from interviews with Swedish adoptees. A colleague and I have interviewed 20 adult transnational adoptees and eight adoptive parents with transnationally adopted children in Sweden (Hübinette and Tigervall, 2008; Tigervall and Hübinette, 2010). We investigated the experiences of racialization among adoptees as a way of studying how exclusion due to a non-White appearance is put into practice in contemporary Sweden. Like other Western societies, Sweden is characterized by marked solid racial segregation in the labor market, in everyday life, and in the formation of families.

In this context, adoptees are the ideal group to study to examine discrimination based on a non-White appearance. They are ethno-culturally Western, and unlike all other foreign-born 'first generation migrants' from non-Western countries, they share the privileged socioeconomic conditions of the wealthy native-born White majority. In other words, foreign-born adult adoptees of color are completely Western, and even White according to a performative understanding of Whiteness. Therefore, race is the only category at work when they are treated differently.

The adoptees we interviewed reported being noticed and singled out for their race:

> Linnea: I have always been singled out at home. As soon as there is something about Korea on television, they have said—"Look it's about Korea!" And if something about Korea comes up, they have always emphasized it towards me, as if I didn't get it in the first time. And my mother has her favorite stories, such as when I arrived in Sweden and sits on the floor. Her favorite story, I think she has told it hundreds of times, is that my cousin says, "Oh, it looks as if she is sleeping," because I have narrow eyes. This story has amused her so many times! Isabella: Me and my friend who is adopted from Colombia were in a shop, and we were followed by the shop owner, and it was quite unpleasant. Also, when me and the same friend and another friend who is wholly Swedish had been in Copenhagen, my Colombian friend was stopped at the customs, while me and my other friend could pass through without any problems.

What we found was that all adoptee informants could relate to being treated differently during childhood, adolescence, and adulthood due to their non-normative appearance. Their experiences occurred in both public spaces dominated by middle and upper- class White Swedes, where a non-White body is hypervisible, and in the intimate sphere of the home. Painful and destructive experiences of racial discrimination came even from parents and spouses.

> Andreas: I have experienced a lot, but I don't know if it's racism. Like on the bus, and I have only lived in areas with Swedes, not in immigrant-dominated neighborhoods. And when I am on the bus, no one wants to sit beside me, and they even prefer to stand. And then one wonders, well, I don't smell, and I don't look particularly ugly. And when I walk home during evening time, people seem to be afraid of me.

> Fredrik: Once I was with my former girlfriend and her friends, and I was withdrawing money from a cash dispensing machine. Behind us, there were some older Swedish guys, and immediately they started to say "damn negro" and so on, and they didn't say it in a subtle way but in a rather high voice. At

> that moment, you are very vulnerable, because I was with my former girlfriend and her friends.

Another observation in the study is that the adoptees are relatively protected from racializing experiences when they are in the company and physical proximity of their adoptive parents, which is of course the usual case during childhood; but from adolescence and on into adulthood, this secure situation naturally disappears.

The most common form of racialization reported by the informants is the constant bombardment of questions regarding the national, regional, continental, ethnic, religious, and racial origin of the adoptees; this sometimes reaches the level of harassment for both the adoptees and their parents. Some informants view these questions as 'natural' expressions of human politeness, while others attribute them to common and subtle forms of social exclusion, as though a Swede cannot possibly be non-White.

So in spite of being completely Swedish, including holding Swedish citizenship, speaking Swedish, having a Swedish, Western, and Christian name, and above all, being fully integrated within a White family network, adoptees are constantly racialized in their everyday life. Their non-white bodies are localized to a different geographical origin, connected to a different ethnicity, nationality, language, and religion, and sometimes linked to different cultural practices. This is, of course, similar to the migrant experience in most Western countries, but the main difference is that contrary to the majority of migrants who at least have their own families, friends, neighborhoods and communities, adoptees are almost always more or less completely isolated. They have no safe space where they can be left alone, and no significant others whom they can fully trust to defend or at least to understand and empathize with them.

> Emma: Many adoptees look upon themselves as whites, and they become shocked when they meet people who speak to them in English and who discriminate against them when they are adults. And if you haven't understood that you look different, and if you haven't got any strategies from your adoptive parents, how to deal with it when you become an adult? Then you have to invent these strategies yourself, and that cannot be easy!

However, the acquiring of a White identification has been made mandatory in mainstream adoption research, where it is termed adjustment and assimilation. Proponents of transnational adoption even argue that the acquiring of a White identity is exactly what so-called 'non-integrated' and underprivileged non-White migrants and minorities also need to develop in order to cope with a society dominated by Whites (Bartholet, 1993a). In a textual study of adoptees' self-narratives, I have instead argued that this identification with and performance of Whiteness is at the same time always interrupted, questioned, and disturbed by others (Hübinette, 2007a). It is, according to my analysis, precisely this transracial identification and instability which results in severe physical alienation, and I argue that this is also what explains the high frequency of suicide, mental illness, and social marginalization among transnational adoptees. This explanation opposes a dominant explanation based on attachment problems, separation trauma, or cognitive disabilities. On an intimate and psychic level, this transrace experience of having an inverted bodily self-image oftentimes leads to self-hate, self-loathing, and a permanent dissatisfaction with one's own appearance, leaving transnational adoptees perpetual strangers to their own bodies.

So the achieving of the kind of adjustment advocated by mainstream adoption research is not so simple and unproblematic as identifying fully with White society. Having a non-White body marked and inscribed with a long history of otherness in a Western culture imbued with colonialism and racism actually does matter. Despite being given a Western name and growing up in a White family, and in spite of speaking only a Western language and behaving like a White person, having a non-White body creates limitations to the adoptees' ability to sustain a White identity. In the end transnational adoptees of color are left completely alone to deal with this transracial experience.

Discussion

So why has the race factor been so largely ignored when it comes to research on transnational adoptees? Why are adoptees of color so absent in ethnic and migration studies? In the Western compartmentalization of research, transnational adoption has fallen into the domain of research directed towards adoptive parents, adoption agencies, adoption professionals and government bodies. The research aims to defend, legitimize, and uphold transnational adoption as a successful, and also profitable, reproductive technique that will benefit the adopters, the agencies, and the receiving countries. Therefore, adult adoptees are not in the focus for research. Ethnic and migration studies, on the other hand, address individuals and groups that differ culturally from the White majority; this means that transnational adoptees fall outside of their scope.

However, as has been mentioned, recent quantitative adoption research has revealed a high preponderance of psychological problems and socioeconomic deprivation among adult transnational adoptees of Sweden (Carlberg and Nordin Jareno, 2007). Although those outcome studies are represented as being caused by genetic or pre-adoption factors, I argue that the race factor has to be taken into consideration in adoption research. Only in this way can we fully grasp the specific and vulnerable situation of adult adoptees, including the staggering suicide rates. In order to provide a link between quantitative and qualitative research, I have referred in this chapter to, and cited from, my own qualitative studies with adult adoptees. The findings clearly show that the non-White bodies of the adoptees are always made significant in their everyday lives in interactions with the White majority population. The adoptees' experiences reflect historically embedded and scientifically produced ideas about and images of different races. Those images are still very much alive in everyday life in contemporary Western societies, and they refute the official declarations and celebrations of having achieved a post-racial and post-colonial world.

In order to foster the well-being of transnational adoptees, future research must therefore include the race factor. Fully grasping and understanding the specific and vulnerable situation of adult adoptees of color should also be a goal of the adoption community, including adoption agencies, adoption professionals, and adoptive parents. The focus on the cultural aspects of adoptees' birth cultures too easily becomes a way to avoid uncomfortable issues of racism. Adoptive parents could potentially play an important and crucial role when it comes to combating racism, discrimination, and segregation in Western society, given their privileged and influential status. The mere presence of their non-White adopted children in heavily segregated and highly affluent White neighborhoods and communities could potentially change the whole idea of Whiteness. But to accomplish that, color blindness and post-racial utopianism must be discarded.

PART IV
The Debate

Chapter 18
The Debate

Elizabeth Bartholet and David Smolin

Part I: Bartholet's Position

I welcome this opportunity to address issues central to the debate over international adoption. Given space limitations, I rely on my prior publications for documentation of claims made here (see http://www.law.harvard.edu/faculty/bartholet/), citing more specifically as necessary. I will respond to the three prescribed questions and then finally respond directly to Professor Smolin's position.

1. From a worldwide perspective, identify basic human rights, core human needs, and best interests of unparented children, those living without family care including those in institutionalized care.

There are many millions of unparented children worldwide living in dire circumstances—some 143 million orphans, 8-10 million children in orphanages, and hundreds of millions on the streets. A more limited number are in foster care or group homes.

Children's most basic needs include the need to be nurtured from infancy on by permanent, loving parents. Children have related needs to be protected against the conditions that characterize life in orphanages, on the streets, and in most foster care. Decades of social science and developmental psychology demonstrate that children need parents to develop normally in emotional, intellectual, and physical terms, and demonstrate as well the devastating damage children suffer when denied nurturing parental care, particularly in their early years (see Chapters 13 and 14). Studies show that even the best institutions fail to provide what children need, and most unparented children are living in terrible institutions that provide almost no human interaction, and often fail even to keep them alive.

Long-term solutions to the problem require preventing the poverty, disease, wars, and other disasters that produce so many unparented children. Ideally, parents should be able to raise the children they produce. But today we have hundreds of millions of unparented children, as we will have for decades, if not millennia, to come.

We should do what we can to get as many of these children as possible into nurturing homes. This means we should make efforts to support birth families so that some of these children can return home. But we know that limited numbers will or should return home. Resources to support family reunification will be limited. Many children were removed from their homes because of maltreatment, and family reunification under such circumstances puts children at significant risk of ongoing maltreatment, even when family support services are provided.

Adoption serves children's needs essentially as well as biologically-linked parenting, and far better than foster or institutional care. And adoptive homes will be found in significant numbers only through international adoption. The conditions that produce so many unparented children in poor countries also limit the number of prospective adoptive parents. Bias against adoption or against the racial minority groups from which many unparented children come often makes it hard to find in-country adoptive homes. Accordingly, international adoption should be embraced as one of the best available options for unparented children.

International adoption demands no resources from resource-starved countries. Indeed it more than pays for itself, since adoptive parents pay the costs of placing and supporting children. Adoption also brings new resources into poor countries through adoption fees and adoption-related humanitarian work and charitable contributions.

However, policy makers have failed to date to embrace international adoption. Instead they have surrounded it with restrictions, often citing "subsidiarity" principles and adoption "abuses."

2. How should we understand the subsidiarity principle of the Hague Convention and how do the expressions of that principle in the CRC and the Convention aid or hinder the best interests of the child?

The subsidiarity principle is generally understood to mean, in the context of international adoption, a preference for keeping children in their country of origin over placing them abroad. Many argue that this principle means children should be placed in international adoption only as a last resort, after exploring all in-country options.

These ideas are a corruption of the original understanding of subsidiarity, according to human rights scholar, and former Chair of the Inter-American Commission on Human Rights, Paolo Carozza. He says subsidiarity was designed to serve individual human rights, not state sovereignty, and the core idea was that children be brought up in a family—ideally their family of origin, but if not then a substitute family that can provide the same sense of intimate community (Carrozza, 2003).

The Convention on the Rights of the Child (CRC) and the Hague Convention on Intercountry Adoption (Hague Convention or HCIA) both defer to state sovereignty, leaving nation states free to ban international adoption altogether regardless of whether they can provide children with nurturing homes in the absence of such adoption. Both provide that if countries choose to allow international adoption, they should exercise a preference for placing children in-country. The CRC requires a more powerful in-country preference, mandating that in-country foster care and other "suitable" care be chosen over out-of-country adoption, and that "due regard … be paid to the desirability of continuity in a child's upbringing and to the child's ethnic, religious, cultural and linguistic background" (Bartholet, 2011). The HCIA requires "due consideration" of in-country placement before out-of-country, but prioritizes international adoption over any in-country placement except adoption and other "family" care (Bartholet, 2011).

Many powerful organizations like the U.N. Committee on the Rights of the Child (UNCRC), United Nations Children's Fund (UNICEF), and Save the Children have used subsidiarity claims in their efforts to restrict international adoption. They focus on the CRC rather than the Hague Convention, even though the HCIA was clearly designed to take a step beyond the CRC in the direction of validating international adoption and limiting the in-country preference. Since the Hague Convention is more recent and far more specific to international adoption, it should govern under accepted international law principles, but these organizations tend either to ignore its subsidiarity provisions, or to claim that they are no different than those in the CRC. They regularly promote in-country foster care over out-of-country adoption.

Although these organizations often say that they accept international adoption at least as a last resort, they often treat it as a non-option. They publish reports on solutions for unparented children that make no mention of international adoption, but recommend consideration of virtually all in-country options including group homes, sibling-headed households, and new improved institutional care. They recommend the creation of foster care and other in-country solutions that do not now exist, effectively condemning to ongoing institutionalization children who might have found international adoptive homes.

These treaties and these organizations have a powerful influence on nation states. All countries except the United States and Somalia have ratified the CRC, and almost all countries that engage in international adoption, including the United States, have ratified the Hague Convention.

Countries with many unparented children in need of adoptive homes may oppose international adoption for additional reasons. National pride often makes them reluctant to admit they cannot care for "their" children. Resentment against past colonialist domination and current disparities in wealth and power often makes them eager to attack international adoption as an exploitative move.

Accordingly, many countries ban international adoption altogether, or simply fail ever to make it an option. Many institute holding periods, requiring that institutionalized children not be placed abroad for periods ranging from six months to two or three years, while supposedly in-country options are pursued. Since there will be no good in-country options for the overwhelming majority of children, these holding periods generally mean simply delaying the possibility of adoptive placement abroad, or denying it altogether because as children age their possibilities for placement diminish. Holding periods also condemn even those children lucky enough to eventually be placed in adoption, to the harm caused by additional time in institutional care.

Many countries cut back on the number of children sent abroad for adoption, claiming they can take care of their children in-country. China made such an announcement a few years ago, although there was no evidence it had enough permanent nurturing homes in-country to serve all those baby girls stacked up in orphanages.

The form of subsidiarity written into the CRC, promoted by organizations like the UNCRC, UNICEF, and Save the Children, and adopted by many countries is contrary to children's best interests. Some important court decisions have recognized the conflict between extreme versions of subsidiarity and the principle that children's best interests should govern. They have ruled that when there is such a conflict, children's best interests trump according to fundamental human rights principles and, indeed, according to the CRC itself. They have found that children have a right to international adoption if the alternative is institutionalization.[1]

I believe there should be no preference whatsoever for placing children in-country, whether in institutions, foster care, or even adoption, if children's best interests are the driving consideration, as the CRC, the Hague Convention, and most participants in the international adoption debate say they should be. Instead the goal should be to place unparented children as early in life as possible, so as to maximize their opportunities to overcome damage suffered during the prenatal period, in the original biological home, or in institutional care, and provide them the best chance for healthy development.

For most unparented children the real alternative to international adoption is life, or death, in institutions or on the streets. Obviously children's interests are better served by placement in adoptive homes, as the above-noted courts recognized, and even organizations like UNICEF generally admit when pressed.

Preferences for foster care are also inconsistent with children's best interests. Typically there is no foster care available, and such preferences simply relegate children to continued institutionalization. Moreover, strong social science evidence indicates that even where foster care exists and is supported by significant resources (as in the United States), it serves children's needs much less well than adoption. There is no reason to think foster care will work better in desperately poor countries. Indeed there is evidence that in many countries the phrase "foster care" is used to describe something that bears no resemblance to the family care it is supposed to emulate. Often it is simply a euphemism for child slavery, as has been documented in Haiti.

Although many criticize preferences for in-country foster and institutional care over out-of-country adoption, most believe that there should be a preference for in-country adoption. However I see no evidence and no common sense reason to support such a preference, looking at the issue from a child's rights perspective. Any preference means, almost inevitably, delay in adoptive placement, which often leads to denial of placement. This was the experience in the United States

1 See discussion of decisions by courts in India, South Africa, and Malawi in Bartholet (2010a).

during the 1970s through the early 1990s, when preferences for placing children within the same racial group resulted in delaying and denying adoptive placement for significant numbers of black children. Moreover, the extensive body of social science accumulated on transracial and international adoption reveals no evidence that children suffer any harm from placement across racial, national, or other lines of difference. These studies demonstrate instead that the key factor in determining children's well being is how early in life they are placed in adoptive homes.

Arguments can be made that countries and groups that have suffered oppression in the past should have some right to hold onto children as a form of reparations or means of empowerment. But we don't think of countries as having the right to hold onto adult members of their populations, although various totalitarian regimes have often tried to wall in their populations. If we truly respect children's human rights we shouldn't treat children as reparations or affirmative action chits.

Nor is there reason to believe that holding onto unparented children is a winning strategy for national empowerment. Children growing up in institutions or on the streets represent significant costs, although they are often called "precious resources" by those engaging in debate over international adoption. Even grossly inadequate institutions are costly to support. Significant resources would be required to improve these institutions, or build foster care. And children graduating from even improved institutions or foster care will end up costing their countries dearly as the graduates move on in disproportionate numbers to unemployment, substance abuse, homelessness, crime, and incarceration.

Some argue that current law may limit policy makers' options. The CRC should be no problem, since the Hague Convention should govern. But the HCIA mandates a preference for in-country adoption over out-of-country adoption.

The Hague Convention should, however, be read in light of the overriding mandate in both the CRC and the HCIA that children's best interests trump other considerations. Any preference for in-country adoption over out-of-country should be implemented through a concurrent planning strategy, mandating development of pools of domestic and international adoptive parents simultaneously, and placement of children in international adoption if there is no domestic adoptive home immediately available.[2]

3. How should the law (and the governments of sending and receiving nations) respond to concerns with child trafficking, corruption, and adoption fraud in the intercountry adoption system?

Abuses exist in international adoption in the form of violations of the laws against paying parents to surrender parental rights, fraud against birth parents in connection with surrender, and kidnapping. But there is no persuasive evidence that such abuses are widespread; instead, they seem a very small part of the total

---

2 See the International Adoption Policy Statement (Child Advocacy Program, 2008), endorsed by numerous human rights and child rights organizations and experts.

international adoption picture, with the overwhelming majority of adoptions taking place in compliance with the law. Moreover, the evidence shows that international adoption serves children extremely well, with the children placed early in life doing essentially as well as children raised in untroubled biological homes, and those placed later helped enormously in overcoming damage suffered prior to adoption (see Chapter 13).

The serious, systemic abuses to children occur when unparented children are denied the nurturing homes that international adoption provides. Institutional care subjects the millions of children kept in institutions to horrible forms of neglect and often to active abuse as well. Institutional care often kills children, and it systematically destroys the life potential of those who live. Children who graduate from institutions or grow up on the streets are the ones who are at serious risk of abuses in the form of child trafficking for sex and other slavery, and exploitation as child soldiers. There is no evidence that international adoption serves as a front for any of these forms of serious exploitation.

The common response to law violations in the international adoption area is to shut down such adoption through temporary or permanent moratoria, and to impose increasingly severe restrictions that effectively if not officially shut down such adoption. For example, alleged baby selling was used to shut down Guatemala's international adoption program entirely for two years, and to help justify the strict new law that Guatemala boasts will limit such adoption to some two hundred children annually, as compared to the several thousand previously placed annually. Alleged abuses have helped justify bans on private intermediaries throughout Central and South America. Since these intermediaries served as the lifeblood of such adoption, these bans have effectively shut it down.

This response makes no sense as a way of addressing adoption law violations. It punishes unparented children by locking them into institutions and denying them the nurturing adoptive homes they need. It puts children at far greater risk of true trafficking and exploitation.

The response to adoption abuses should be the same as in other areas of law violation—enforce existing law, strengthen that law as appropriate, and punish those violating the law. Biological parents often violate the laws against abuse and neglect of children. Society does not respond by telling parents they can no longer take their newborns home from the hospital because henceforth all children are to be raised in institutions to protect against parental misconduct. Instead society enforces and sometimes strengthens the laws against parental misconduct.

Some say that it is hard for poor countries with limited infrastructure to enforce laws prohibiting baby selling and other adoption abuses. This may be. But it is also hard, indeed impossible, for these countries to guarantee nurturing parental homes for all their children. Even if adoption law violations occur, the harm such violations cause children and birth parents is minimal compared to the harm caused by shutting down or severely restricting international adoption.

Part I: Smolin's Position

I appreciate the opportunity to participate in this exchange of views with Professor Elizabeth Bartholet, and hope that this dialogue will help illuminate some of the conflicting perspectives concerning intercountry adoption. Given space limitations, these essays do not include footnotes. Extensive citations of sources can be found in my adoption-related writings, many of which are available at my website (http://works.bepress.com/david_smolin/). I too will respond to the three prescribed questions and then finally respond directly to Professor Bartholet's position.

1. From a worldwide perspective, identify basic human rights, core human needs, and best interests of unparented children, those living without family care including those in institutionalized care.

Human rights documents throughout the modern era make clear that the family is the fundamental group unit of society, and the child is a part of his/her family as a matter of both basic human need and fundamental human right. These fundamental human rights include the right of a child to remain with the family to which she was born, and the corollary right of parents to the care and custody of each child born to them. Thus, the family that the child belongs with, as a matter of the rights of the child and of her parents, is clearly the family into which the child is born. Further, the child is born not only to a father and mother, but also into a broader set of relationships, including siblings, grandparents, aunts and uncles, cousins, and so on. Thus, as a matter of widespread cultural practice, human need, and fundamental rights, the family into which the child is born extends beyond the parents, and beyond the nuclear family, to include an inter-generational and extensive family group.

The phrase "unparented children, those living without family care including institutionalized care," contains multiple ambiguities. Do "unparented children" include children residing separately from their living parents? Do "unparented children" include those living with extended family members (grandparents, uncles and aunts, etc.), but whose parents are dead? Is a child living in a long term foster care situation "unparented?" Does the phrase "those living without family care including those in institutionalized care" include all children living in "orphanages," boarding schools, group homes, and hostels? What counts as an institution? These ambiguities are similar to those which have developed over the more common term, "orphan." In the context of adoption, both domestic and intercountry, the question of when a child needs a new (adoptive) family is deeply controversial.

Beginning a discourse on adoption with the image of a child alone, without family ties, is inherently misleading. Children do not fall from the sky; they come into this world amidst a web of relationships. When a child is found alone, the first question that must be asked, therefore, is how the separation of child from parents and family occurred. The first relevant image is not of the child already alone, but of the child with her original family; the next relevant image is that of the event which tragically separated the child from her parents.

Put another way, there is, in one sense, no such thing as an "unparented" child. No one comes into this world without having parents. The phrase "unparented child" suggests a child who really, in fact, has no parent. Such a person has never existed.

A better term, then, might be a "separated child." A child separated from her parents and family is, as the CRC makes clear, highly vulnerable. The first right and need of such a child is a determined effort to reunify her with her family: first her parents, and if not her parents, then other family members. This effort should normally include an effort to determine the circumstances under which the separation occurred, and whether some kind of assistance might make a successful reunion possible.

Sometimes the most determined efforts to reunify a child with her family are unsuccessful. It may be impossible to identify the family of an abandoned child. The parents and extended family may be unwilling to raise their child. The parents may pose a severe threat to the safety of the child, and no relatives may be available to raise the child. Depending on the circumstances and age of the child, it may be necessary to provide such a separated child with another family who can love and provide for the child. This new family may be an adoptive family, although there are a variety of family settings that could accomplish the same end of providing a family environment for a child.

Some forms of institutional care are so profoundly destructive of children that they constitute an emergency situation, which should be remedied as quickly as possible. The profound developmental, emotional, and physical damage caused by poor quality institutional care, particularly of infants and young children, and sometimes of older children, has been well documented. Other forms of care which might be called institutional, such as some SOS Children's Village, or hostels/orphanages which provide an education, room, and board to impoverished children, are positive interventions which can provide better opportunities for some children than would remaining full-time in the family home. Thus, some forms of "institutional care" provide a family-like environment, and some are, in effect, boarding schools for the poor, providing children with opportunities for education and adequate nutrition not available at home. Sometimes the decision to place a child in what could be called "institutional care" reflects parental decision-making and responsible care, rather than parental abandonment. Thus, it would be wrong to assume that all children living without their parents in what could be considered an "institutional setting" are in need of adoption, or are "unparented."

Sometimes, the adjustments and adaptations that a particular adoptive placement would require are so extreme as to negate the benefits of placing an older child in an adoptive family. For example, transferring an emotionally-troubled American teenage "orphan" with behavioral, cognitive, and/or educational issues from a group or foster home, to an adoptive home in China with Chinese adoptive parents who speak no English, would be inappropriate. Assuming such teenager had no cultural or language affinities with China, the resulting demands for cultural and language adjustment would overwhelm the child. Although not always recognized, the reverse situation—moving a Chinese speaking teenager from a Chinese orphanage into an English-speaking American family—can be just as disastrous. Much-older children should not be placed into societies for which they lack the language, educational and cultural skills necessary for success, and are too old to attain these necessary skills prior to adulthood. The gain of a family, for a much older child, cannot make up for the wrong of transferring them into a world which requires adjustments of which they may be incapable.

2. How should we understand the subsidiarity principle of the Hague Convention and how do the expressions of that principle in the CRC and the Convention aid or hinder the best interests of the child?

The subsidiarity principle of the Hague Convention and CRC prioritizes interventions on behalf of a child separated from her parents and/or family, or facing a possible future separation. First, efforts should be made to reunify the child with her family, or to avoid a future separation of the child from her parents. The first priority is thus family preservation. If family preservation efforts are unsuccessful, then interventions on behalf of the child within the child's own nation have priority over international adoption. Thus, both the CRC and the Hague Convention clearly favor domestic adoption over intercountry adoption. The status of placements other than adoption, from foster care to various kinds of institutional care, is more controversial. Some would stress the temporary, insecure, and potentially damaging nature of such non-adoptive placements, and argue that intercountry adoption should have priority over all domestic placements short of full adoption. Others argue that even institutional care should have priority over intercountry adoption, and that nations are required to develop child welfare systems that provide adequate options for their children within the nation of origin. One middle position would divide between domestic foster care and institutional care, so that domestic foster care would be viewed as a family-like environment having priority over intercountry adoption, while intercountry adoption would have priority over institutional care. I would prefer a middle position that evaluates domestic options short of adoption individually, taking account of the quality and nature of the placement, as well as the age and capacities of the child. As indicated under question one, a placement that moves a much older child to a new country, language, and culture may be more destructive to the child than high quality foster or institutional care within her own nation, despite the advantages of receiving a permanent adoptive family. In addition, in some instances high quality foster or institutional care may serve as a relatively secure and positive care setting, particularly for older children; from this perspective, the negative label of "institutional care," while sometimes quite accurate, is too conclusory and imprecise a term to form the basis of a legal rule. The wide variety of placements short of full adoption, and the significant differences among children in regard to their needs, history, capacity, age, and situation, counsel against an absolute rule.

The subsidiarity principle implements the best interests of the child by safeguarding the child's relationships to her original parents and family. This conclusion follows from the fundamental principle, described in question one, that children and their families have corollary rights to preserve their familial relationships. These family ties represent a multi-generational heritage and set of connections which ground the child, as a human person, in a specific set of identities. Stripping a child of her identity and familial, community, and cultural heritage is a severe deprivation of rights, as the child generally has no choice in the matter and has her fundamental orientation to herself and the world altered without her consent.

The subsidiarity principle also preserves the child's right to maintain continuity with her culture, language, community, and nation, even when she cannot remain with her original family. Some dismiss the connection of children to the nation, community, or culture of their original family as merely nationalist or group ownership of children in derogation of children's rights. Such a dismissal of subsidiarity ignores the connection of human beings not only to their families, but also to the broader cultural, language, and societal groups to which they and their families belong. The well-recognized fact that many adoptees find it meaningful to return to their nation of origin even when they do not locate their original family, indicates the strength of the larger ties protected by subsidiarity. Adoption involves not only the loss of the original family, but also the loss of the original culture, community, and nation into which the child was born. The subsidiarity principle safeguards the best interests of the child by recognizing the losses inherent to adoption, and those specific to intercountry adoption; the subsidiarity principle favors interventions and placements that will avoid or minimize these losses to the degree compatible with the child's needs for permanency and day-to-day love and care.

The subsidiarity principle further safeguards the best interests of the child by protecting the child against powerful market forces that would commodify the child as an international asset to be sold to the highest bidder. While children are not and should not be viewed as commodities, market pressures have distorted the practice of intercountry adoption. There is a great unmet desire for children in developed nations: particularly children with qualities such as youth (i.e., infants), good health, a preferred gender, or a particular race. This unmet desire has created a huge demand-side pressure, which causes intercountry adoption to be practiced as a means of locating children for prospective adoptive parents in rich countries. The supply of legally available children in developing nations meeting these desired characteristics of youth and health is much smaller than the demand. The subsidiarity principle, properly implemented, prevents adoption agencies and facilitators from exploiting the poverty and powerlessness of poor families in developing nations to extract the kinds of children in greatest demand. Under the subsidiarity principle, the first obligation is to provide assistance that will allow families to keep their children, rather than exploiting imbalances of wealth and power to extract children for intercountry adoption.

Most children truly in need of adoption, in both the United States and other nations, are older children and children with special needs (including children with serious physical, cognitive, emotional, and educational disabilities or difficulties.) Absent the subsidiarity principle, those children are often ignored or passed over by a demand-driven adoption system seeking to extract children with the more desirable characteristics of youth and health. The subsidiarity principle is a necessary corrective that requires interventions to be chosen according to the rights and needs of the child and original family, rather than according to the desire of adults for healthy infants and adoption agencies and facilitators for monetary compensation.

3. How should the law (and the governments of sending and receiving nations) respond to concerns with child trafficking, corruption, and adoption fraud in the intercountry adoption system?

Significant segments of the adoption community are in deep denial about the prevalence and seriousness of abusive practices in intercountry adoption. This denial, and the subsequent failure to adequately respond to these abuses, constitutes the greatest threat to the future of intercountry adoption.

The historical and legal record indicates that "the abduction, the sale of, or traffic in children," as the CRC and Hague Convention describe it, is the most significant category of abusive practices. My work has termed these practices child laundering (although I did not invent the term). Typically, child laundering consists of obtaining children illicitly through force, funds, or fraud, providing false paperwork that indicates that the children are abandoned or relinquished "orphans," and then processing these "orphans" through the official intercountry adoption system. The preparatory materials of the Hague Convention, created between 1988 and 1993, name this kind of "trafficking" as the most significant abusive practice of the time, and indicate it was particularly prevalent in Latin American nations. The 1993 Hague Convention states that the creation of safeguards to prevent "the abduction, the sale of, or traffic in children" is one of the purposes of the Convention.

Unfortunately, in the years since the Convention was finalized, significant child laundering practices have arisen in many nations, including Cambodia, Chad, China, Guatemala, Ethiopia, Haiti, India, Liberia, Nepal, Samoa, and Vietnam. While the Hague Convention has some flaws, the principal reasons for these continued abuses have been the failure to ratify and properly implement the Convention. The United States, statistically the most significant receiving nation, did not effectively ratify the Convention until 2008. Even to the present day, the United States implementation of the Convention has fundamental flaws. These include a failure to limit the amounts of money that are sent to intermediaries (facilitators, attorneys, orphanages, and others) in countries of origin; a failure to make United States adoption agencies legally responsible for the illicit actions of foreign intermediaries or partners; a failure to require Hague accreditation or apply Hague standards to agencies placing children from non-Hague Convention nations; and a failure to provide for adequate investigation and prosecution of child laundering and other abusive practices.

The most fundamental problem is money. Guatemala is the most obvious example (see Chapter 7). Between 2002 and 2008, 24,778 Guatemalan children came to the United States for intercountry adoption, with the typical fee paid to Guatemalan attorneys in the range of 15,000 to 20,000 USD per child: a total of 371 to 495 million dollars over seven years. In a country with poor governmental capacity, chronic corruption, endemic violence against women, the scars of a 36 year civil war, and a significant percentage of the population living in extreme poverty, these unaccounted-for funds incentivized systematic child laundering. The United States government instituted single DNA, and then double DNA, testing, but it was eventually proven that even the system of double DNA testing had been violated (see Chapter 5). Fundamentally, no amount of regulation can overcome the incentives for abuse when such large amounts of money are introduced into vulnerable developing nations.

Despite a constant stream of substantial evidence of severe abusive practices, as documented by the Hague Conference on Private International Law, International Social Service, Terre des Hommes, the United States government, journalists such as E. J. Graff of the Schuster Institute for Investigative Journalism, my own work, and that of many others (see Chapters 2, 3, 4, 5, 7, 10), some adoption proponents have minimized the extent and significance of these practices. Reports of abusive practices have been interpreted as a conspiratorial attack motivated by ideological opposition to intercountry adoption. The result is tragic. Significant components of the adoption community react to serious wrongdoing by defending status quo practices that incentivize child laundering. Instead of demanding positive reforms that could safeguard intercountry adoption against such wrongdoing, much of the adoption community resists the necessary reforms in the areas of money and agency accountability. Some adoption "advocates" vainly hope that prosecutions of a few "bad" actors will be enough to safeguard the intercountry adoption system, in a developing nation context where those actors have been provided more than enough cash to buy their way out of trouble, and where the primary cause of the abuse is financial incentives for child laundering provided by over-generous fees and unregulated donations.

Some individuals are ideologically opposed to intercountry adoption, but I, and many others seeking to document abuses and safeguard the system from them, are not among them. In the end, the truest enemies of intercountry adoption are those who refuse to acknowledge the very real abuses, and resist the only reforms capable of safeguarding the system from those abuses.

Bartholet and Smolin Respond

Each author responds to the assertions made by the other in questions 1-3 in this section below.

Bartholet Responds to Smolin

On the first question, Smolin argues that the phrase "unparented children" is ambiguous, and its definition overly broad in including "those living without family care including those in institutionalized care." He says institutional care is really not so bad, and often better than what biological parents can provide. But experts in child welfare are united in their belief, based on brain science, social science, and developmental psychology, that institutions, even the better ones, are almost always terrible for children, brutally unloving in the short term, and seriously harmful to their life prospects in the long term. The USA Congressional Coalition on Adoption Institute (CCAI) recently initiated the Way Forward project based on this widespread consensus, with the goal of helping African leaders move children out of institutional care into families.[3]

On the second question, Smolin argues that the subsidiarity principle, as generally interpreted, serves children's best interests. He supports the classic positions argued by opponents of international adoption, promoting in-country solutions like foster and even institutional care over out-of-country adoption. He separates himself from such opponents by his claim that he would evaluate such in-country options individually rather than by a general preference rule. But his reasoning indicates that he too believes that in-country options are *generally* preferable because they serve children's interests in cultural continuity. He indulges in the classic false romanticism about the value of "cultural heritage" to children growing up deprived of the basic human right to the heritage of parental love. He ignores the horrible realities characterizing most unparented children's lives.

In my view subsidiarity, as generally interpreted to favor almost all in-country options over out-of-country adoption, has operated *contrary* to children's best interests. It has been used to justify locking children into institutions rather than placing them in available international adoptive homes. It is now being used to justify placing children in paid foster care in-country in preference to international adoption, although foster care has never worked as well for children as adoption. Paid foster care presents particular risks to children in poor countries, where desperation will motivate many to offer to "parent" for the stipend alone.

Some justify subsidiarity as serving the interests of in-country parents, both the original biological parents, and those interested in becoming foster or adoptive parents. Others justify it as serving the interests of sovereign nations. Neither are

3 I am one of the group of U.S. and African child welfare experts named as members of this Way Forward project.

worthy goals, if children's rights to grow up in nurturing homes are at issue. Parents and sovereign nations should be guided by the best interests of children, not their own interests in holding onto children they cannot care for, or in getting paid to foster. Nor will keeping children in-country enrich or strengthen impoverished nations. Subsidiarity does serve, of course, to enrich and empower organizations like UNICEF that work in-country.

On the third question, having to do with adoption abuses, Smolin says supporters of international adoption are in "denial." "Denial" is a favored claim by those who do not like the facts others put forth. Smolin has no evidence that serious abuses are extensive—abuses such as kidnapping, fraud on birth mothers inducing non-consensual relinquishments, and payments to birth mothers inducing relinquishment decisions they would not have made otherwise. A recent law review article by Richard Carlson gives the lie to Smolin's claims, addressing his arguments in detail. I summarize that article in my introduction to the issue, as follows:

> Richard Carlson's article … systematically tak[es] on all the important arguments made by critics of international adoption, analyzing them carefully and rationally in light of the actual facts.….[He] find[s] no reason to believe that corruption, trafficking, fraud, or other serious abuses are prevalent. He argues… that there is no persuasive proof that significant adoption abuse is widespread, and that while some illegalities exist in this area, as in all areas of human endeavor, they are far outweighed by the positive impact of international adoption on children as well as their families and countries of origin (Bartholet, 2010-2011, pp. 690, 695-6).[4]

Critics like Smolin never weigh the costs of adoption abuses against the costs of human rights violations to children when they are denied adoption. The truth is that institutionalization is responsible for the systematic violation of the fundamental rights of millions of children on a daily basis. The closing down of international adoption that Smolin and other critics encourage denies many thousands of children per year the opportunity to escape.

I want to address such serious adoption abuse as actually exists. But I want to do so by penalizing those perpetrating such abuse, and not penalizing innocent children as we now do by shutting down international adoption or restricting it in ways that deny institutionalized children the opportunity to find adoptive homes.

Smolin's claim that adoption abuses are common relies on use of the vague "laundering" term, merged with complaints that international adoption fees and donations are so large that they create the risk of corruption. But there is no reason to equate all funds connected to international adoption with corruption, while assuming that all other funds flowing to poor countries represent an unmitigated good.

4 See also Carlson (2011).

International adoption results in very significant funding for services for poor children and families in-country, and related humanitarian work. One measure of only a small part of this funding is the study conducted by the Joint Council on International Children's Services, an umbrella organization for agencies involved in international adoption. Its January 2011 newsletter reports that in just one country, Ethiopia, Joint Council partner-organizations contributed in just one year, 2010, $14 million in services, primarily in community development, including medical care, family empowerment and preservation, education, and foster and kinship care, serving over 1.6 million children and families, with less than 0.1 percent of them served through international adoption. Smolin characterizes this kind of funding as corruption, arguing that it encourages international adoption. But why not recognize that *both* this kind of funding for in-country services *and* international adoption help children?

UNICEF is involved in different kinds of funding deals. Together with the USA Government it pressured Ethiopia to reduce by 90 percent its international adoption program, based on alleged adoption illegalities. When the CCAI's Way Forward project met in Ethiopia a few months later, officials announced a USA grant of $100 million, with 10 percent channeled through UNICEF, for in-country services work. Those I consulted with, who had decades of experience on the ground there and reason to know what was going on, thought the quid pro quo clear—shut down international adoption and we'll give you $100 million USD. Why isn't this kind of apparent deal characterized as corruption? Why isn't it condemned as harmful to children, shutting off the international adoptive homes that represent for many their best option? Why is Smolin not interested in investigating any corruption or other misuse of funds given to organizations like UNICEF for in-country work?

Smolin's characterization of international adoption as "exploiting imbalances of wealth and power to extract children" reflects a classic claim that such adoption is simply a modern manifestation of the evils of colonialism. Colonialist exploitation was an evil. But the modern phenomenon of international adoption involves individual parents taking into their homes and hearts children in need for whom there is no other good option. A significant percentage of these parents are devoting their lives to trying to help children horribly damaged by pre-adoptive lives in institutional care recover and thrive. Sensible and caring policy makers should be able to recognize that this is not colonialism, and to regulate in a way that protects children's rights to nurturing homes

Smolin Responds to Bartholet

Professor Bartholet eloquently describes a prevalent adoption fantasy, in which the creation of a large-scale adoption system employing highly-paid private intermediaries can be operated ethically and with little collateral damage in nations where corruption, document fraud, bribery, poverty, deep inequality, and human trafficking are prevalent. According to this fantasy, all the law need do is prosecute the few wrongdoers and otherwise keep regulation to a minimum, allowing the system to match an endless number of vulnerable orphans with eager adoptive parents in the West. Unfortunately, without adequate monetary controls and regulation such adoption systems soon reflect the societies in which they operate, becoming themselves rife with corruption, fraud, bribery, exploitation of the poor and powerless, and human trafficking. Indeed, the infusion of millions of dollars from the United States into poor and transition economies creates new incentives for corruption, fraud, and human trafficking, effectively creating a market in children. Invoking the desperate situations of many children in developing nations and the human desire to protect and nurture, Professor Bartholet fails to account for how systems created to alleviate human ills can sometimes cause more harm than good.

Within Professor Bartholet's adoption fantasy, adoption is an inherent, rather than relative, good; she therefore dismisses or minimizes harms related to adoption that are generally considered serious issues in the broader adoption community.

For example, Professor Bartholet says there is "no evidence that children suffer any harm from placement across racial, national, or other lines of difference." This "no harm" assessment is consistent with her position that there should be no preference for domestic over intercountry adoption.

Similarly, Professor Bartholet appears to perceive very little loss or harm to children in regard to adoption generally, saying that "[a]doption serves children's needs essentially as well as biologically-linked parenting…"

There is little in Professor Bartholet's answers, and in her articles, that acknowledges one of the central themes of modern adoption literature: loss. It is one thing to say (as I would) that the gains of an adoption, domestic or intercountry, can be enough to outweigh the losses involved, making it the best option for a child under certain (generally tragic) circumstances. It is another thing to approach adoption (as Professor Bartholet appears to do) from a perspective that minimizes and dismisses the substantial losses involved in adoption.

Adoption involves the loss of relationship and connection to one's original parents, sibling, and extended family. Any perspective on adoption that does not, at the outset, understand this is as a significant loss and harm to both child and original family is, I believe, dangerous and deficient. This danger is particularly great in a culture like that of the United States, which practices a system of closed-record, secret adoption in which the law pretends that the child was born to the adoptive parents. It is not healthy to feed the legal and cultural pretense that adoptive children have no connection to the multi-generational family group that conceived and birthed them. In a world in which we (outside the context of adoption) acknowledge that both nature (genetics) and nurture matter, pretending that genetic inheritance and nine months of nurture in the womb mean nothing makes no sense. Such a pretense makes even less sense given the large numbers of older child adoptions in which children have spent a significant part of their childhood with their original family.

It also makes no sense to ignore the additional losses of culture, language, and nationality involved in intercountry adoption. Professor Bartholet ignores studies and adoptee accounts which amply illustrate the psychological difficulties and complexities created by these losses. For example, one recent survey of Korean adoptees by the Evan B. Donaldson Institute found that 78 percent of Korean adoptees during childhood considered themselves to be, or wanted to be, White. Surely it is a harm to feel psychologically driven to deny a significant aspect of one's body, identity, and genetic inheritance. Acknowledging that these very real losses and harms can be outweighed, in a given case, with the gains involved in an intercountry adoption, is very different from minimizing or denying the losses and harms involved in the first place.

Professor Bartholet's response to the harms caused by illicitly obtaining children through kidnapping, fraud, and child-buying is equally dismissive, saying there is "no persuasive evidence that such abuses are widespread." She further states that "the overwhelming majority of adoptions [are] taking place in compliance with the law." In doing so, Professor Bartholet brushes aside widespread evidence from a broad variety of sources documenting serious, systemic misconduct in many nations, including Cambodia, Ethiopia, Guatemala, India, Nepal, and Vietnam. While it is possible to bury one's head and issue "see no evil" pronouncements, such is hardly a sound basis for public policy.

Professor Bartholet similarly dismisses other difficulties by silence and inattention, saying little in these essays, as well as her articles, about the central problem of money in the intercountry adoption system. Instead of calling for limitations on the amounts of money that can be sent to intermediaries in developing nations, she specifically defends the role of "private intermediaries," calling them the "lifeblood" of adoptions from Central and South America. Lifeblood indeed!! A system that pays "private intermediaries" thousands of dollars to obtain children from vulnerable families living in extreme poverty in developing nations is inviting child laundering. How can the rights of children and poor and vulnerable families be protected in a system that so obviously incentivizes the illicit sourcing of children?

Professor Bartholet may be unconcerned about illicit sourcing of children because she assumes that with so many children in obvious need of intercountry adoption, it is not much of an issue. This picture of virtually endless numbers of children in need of intercountry adoption is misleading. For example, Professor Bartholet uses the estimate of 143 million orphans (presumably from UNICEF), while ignoring the clarification from UNICEF that their various estimates of "orphans" include those who have lost only one parent. Hence, about 90 percent of such "orphans" are still living with a parent, and thus are not relevant to discussions of the need for intercountry adoption. Similarly misleading is Professor Bartholet's presumption that Chinese orphanages still are overwhelmed with large numbers of baby girls, despite strong evidence that the numbers of healthy infants in Chinese orphanages has been sharply reduced, in part through (illegal but prevalent) sex selective abortion. Similarly, Professor Bartholet ignores extensive evidence that there are increasing numbers of domestic adoptions—and waiting lists for domestic adoption of healthy babies of both genders—in nations such as China and India. There are, I would argue, relatively few healthy babies or toddlers truly in need of intercountry adoption.

Lumping all "orphans," street children, institutionalized children, etc., together to demonstrate a need for intercountry adoption ignores important differences between such children, as well as the highly differential number of available, qualified adoptive parents. There are millions of Americans, many with fertility issues, yearning to adopt a healthy infant or toddler. There are, however, relatively few who can or should attempt a high-risk adoption of a much older, highly traumatized child—indeed, we don't even have enough adoptive parents for such children within the United States, given the many much older children waiting for adoption from our foster care system. In addition, many much older street and institutionalized children may be incapable of adapting to conventional family life, let alone making the huge adaptations of language and culture expected of intercountry adoptees. Thus, despite the existence of many older, special needs and disabled children both in the United States and globally who are separated from their families, there are very few of the kinds of children the vast majority of prospective adoptive parents seek: healthy young infants or toddlers. Hence, the existence of millions of institutionalized and street children does not prevent the illicit sourcing of the kinds of children most sought by prospective adoptive parents.

Professor Bartholet unfortunately ignores the capacity of monetary incentives for intercountry adoption to draw children unnecessarily into institutional care, creating the very kind of harm (the institutionalization of children) which she most decries. As the very "private intermediaries" she praises seek out the kind of children for which they will be paid, children are pulled, through various illicit means, out of families and into orphanages; while some of those children are eventually adopted (despite not being true orphans), others die or live out their childhood in these damaging institutions.

Professor Bartholet also over-states the influence of the Hague Convention, whether for good or ill, when she states that "almost all countries that engage in international adoption … have ratified" the Convention. In fact, a number of significant sending nations, such as Ethiopia, Russia, South Korea, Ukraine, and Vietnam, have not ratified the Convention, leading to a situation where a significant proportion of adoptions to the United States are non-Hague Convention adoptions. (The United States does not apply Hague Convention rules to adoption from non-Hague Countries.) Since the United States ratification of the Hague Convention was not effective until April 2008, and adoptions to the United States constitute approximately half of all intercountry adoptions, much of the development of the contemporary system has, until very recently, occurred outside the rubric of the Convention. Overall, the tendency of Professor Bartholet to scapegoat the Hague Convention, the CRC, and various human rights organizations for the ills of the system is unfortunate. While these documents and organizations certainly have their flaws, those pale in comparison to the poor practice standards endemic among the private adoption agencies that dominate intercountry adoption practice in the United States. It is those agencies that have created virtual bidding wars for adoptable children in nation after nation, while linking to intermediaries and partners who practice in a context of widespread falsification of documents, bribery, corruption, and child laundering. In this kind of context, it is very difficult to sort out ethical from unethical adoptions, and to engage in the kind of accuracy in documents and social work practice which would provide the best chance of success for high-risk adoptions of older and special needs children.

The intercountry adoption system is in trouble. Advocates for the system, such as Professor Bartholet, seek to blame an ever-widening circle of supposed "enemies" of adoption; instead, they would do better to change course and make common cause with those, like myself, who see serious reform as the only possible solution.

Editors' Note

The editors, Judith L. Gibbons and Karen Smith Rotabi, would like to thank Professors Bartholet and Smolin for bringing the differences in opinion about intercountry into sharp focus and for elucidating the complexity of the issues involved.

PART V
Pragmatists: Improving the Process

Chapter 19
Best Practices in Implementing the Hague Convention

Judith L. Gibbons and Karen Smith Rotabi

The Hague Convention on the Protection of Children and Co-operation in Respect of Intercountry Adoption (henceforth referred to as the HCIA or the Convention) was designed for the protection of children in intercountry adoption. The Convention states that "Recognizing that the child, for the full and harmonious development of his or her personality, should grow up in a family environment"… [the purpose is] "to establish safeguards to ensure that intercountry adoptions take place in the best interests of the child and with respect for his or her fundamental rights as recognized in international law" (Hague Conference on Private International Law, 1993, preamble). Because the Convention lacks specificity in how to implement its requirements, a second document, *The Implementation and Operation of The 1993 Hague Intercountry Adoption Convention: Guide To Good Practice* (Hague Conference on Private International Law, 2008b) outlines specific ways, or guidance, for how the Convention should be implemented in order to protect children and their families of origin. In this chapter we elaborate on the limitations of those documents and variations in the implementation practices that continue to put children at risk and fail to serve their best interests. We describe from both macro and micro perspectives ways of addressing the best interests of children.

Intercountry adoption is the product of global inequality and vulnerability resulting from poverty, disaster, war, corruption, and market forces (see Chapters 3, 5, 9, 10, and 11). It is also a child welfare strategy that has been described as "a successful natural intervention" (Van IJzendoorn and Juffer, 2005) for improving children's well-being. There is substantial evidence that children adopted internationally show better cognitive, emotional, and physical development than do their peers left behind (see Chapter 13). Moreover, recent evolutionary evidence suggests that humans may be predisposed to cooperative child rearing (Hrdy, 2009), so that child circulation and adoption are built-in human adaptations to our environmental conditions (Fonseca, 2003; Leinaweaver, 2007).

Many authors have made the link between social and economic inequities and intercountry adoption. But to reiterate the evidence for that relationship, in Chapter 1 Selman listed the five major receiving countries for intercountry adoption—the United States, Spain, France, Italy, and Canada. All five are categorized by the World Bank as high-income countries (World Bank, n.d.). Of the ten major countries of origin for intercountry adoption (see Selman, Chapter 1), two (Ethiopia and Haiti) are classified as low income economies, five (China, Guatemala, India, Ukraine, Vietnam) are classified as lower middle income economies, two (Colombia and Russia) upper middle income, and only one anomaly (Korea) is in the category of high income countries (World Bank, n.d.). In examining the per capita gross domestic product (GDP), the wealthiest sending country (Korea) has a per capita GDP that is slightly less ($29,326) than the poorest of the top five receiving countries (Italy at $30,080; United Nations Development Programme [UNDP], 2010). So, as many scholars have pointed out, intercountry adoption involves the transfer of children from low resource countries to high resource countries. Put another way, the correlation between the number of children sent (-) or received (+) among these 15 sending and receiving countries in the most recent year of data (Selman, Chapter 1) with the GDP per capita (UNDP, 2010) is .80 ($N = 15, p < .001$). What that statistic implies is that the number of children sent or received for intercountry adoption is very closely related to the income of that country. However, if we look just at the ten top countries of origin, the per capita GDP does not significantly correlate with the number of children sent ($r =$ .04, n.s.), nor to the ratio of children sent to children born ($r= 0.25$, n.s.). These results suggest that factors other than economic within sending countries (laws, traditional practices, accession to the Hague Convention) influence the numbers and proportions of children relinquished. Nonetheless, because of the economic disparity between sending and receiving countries, market forces often come into play in intercountry adoption (Smolin, 2004).

Within countries of origin, individual parents who make an adoption plan often cite poverty as the overwhelming factor in their decision (Bos, 2007; Roby and Matsumura, 2002; see Chapter 11). When poverty itself is not the overriding factor, coercive state policies may create an environment in which parents feel that abandoning or relinquishing their children is the only option (see Chapters 6 and 8). Although the stigma of unmarried motherhood may still be a factor in relinquishment in countries such as Korea (Dorow, 1999; Fronek, 2006) it pales in comparison to the economic and political pressures that most relinquishing families face.

Thus, at the broadest level, efforts to eliminate poverty and reduce economic disparities would not only foster economic justice, but also abate the conditions that promote intercountry adoption. This requires intervention at multiple levels of society, targeting structural inequality broadly, including gender inequality and poverty as the underlying causes of ICA.

Reducing or preventing the need for intercountry adoption requires the development of a range of child welfare strategies within potential countries of origin (e.g., Dickens, 2002). Article 4b of the Hague Convention states "An adoption within the scope of the Convention shall take place only if the competent authorities of the State of origin have determined, after possibilities for placement of the child within the State of origin have been given due consideration, that an intercountry adoption is in the child's best interests." This clause, known as the subsidiarity clause, was further elaborated in the *Guide to Good Practice* (Hague

Conference on Private International Law, 2008b). Countries are encouraged to develop comprehensive child and family welfare policies and procedures. These include measures to support families in order to prevent family segregation and to reintegrate separated families, known as family preservation. Care options for unparented children might include kinship care such as guardianship, national (domestic) adoption, and temporary measures such as foster care and institutionalization. The interpretation and implementation of the subsidiarity clause has been very controversial among intercountry adoption scholars and practioners (e.g., see Chapter 18).

Recent efforts to promote the well-being of unparented children in their countries of origin include strategies such as promoting national (domestic) adoption, as in Guatemala. The new Guatemalan law regulating adoption requires the presentation of an adoptable child's dossier to two Guatemalan families (and their rejection) before the child is eligible for intercountry adoption (Ministerio de Gobernación Guatemala, 2010). The Central Authority in Guatemala regularly hosts sessions about adoption for potential adoptive families, as one strategy to promote national adoptions (Consejo Nacional de Adopciones, n.d.). Also, a foster care strategy has been developed and a number of families have been recruited and trained to provide this service to children as an intermediary care option.

Other strategies have included Family Group Conferencing (Harper, Pennell, and Weil, 2002; Roby and Ife, 2009; Rotabi, Pennell, Roby and Bunkers, 2012) and the Family Care Model (Pardasani, Chazin, and Fortinsky, 2010) to assist families in collaboratively finding solutions within the extended family for children whose parents cannot care for them. These practices have been promoted, in part, because they are often based on cultural traditions of kin fostering or child circulation. As Pardasani and colleagues have written, "In traditional African culture, there are no orphans, as parentless children are cared for within kin systems" (Pardasani et al., 2010, p. 308). Because resources are scarce, the Family Care Model provides that kin who take in orphaned children receive supplemental food, regular visits from NGO staff members, caregiver support, and comprehensive health services; moreover, the orphaned children can attend nursery school or after-school programs. While these efforts show a great deal of promise in supporting families and caretakers of unparented children, the programs need further examination. Cheney (2010, 2011) has pointed out that providing incentives for orphan care may make children even more vulnerable to exploitation by adults, and that within a caretaking family, orphaned children may enjoy privileges that biological children do not. Moreover, some orphans who are cared for by extended kin suffer from heavy workloads and/or neglect (Oleke, Blystad, Moland, Rekdal, and Heggenhougen, 2006).

Care within institutions (orphanages) has generally been considered to be deleterious to children's physical, emotional, and cognitive development (Groza, 1999b). There is substantial evidence from the adoption literature that early institutionalization can lead to emotional and behavioral problems and developmental delays (Groza, 1999b; Hawk and McCall, 2011). Although children adopted out of institutional care at later ages generally exhibit more problems, the critical age for the transition is not well-established (Groza, 1999b; Hawk and McCall, 2011; Rutter, Kreppner, O'Connor, and the ERA Study Team, 2001). Because of the research findings concerning pre-adoption institutionalization, institutionalization (within the country of origin) is often considered to be the 'last resort' for children outside of parental care (see Chapter 18). Like other options, however, the complete picture may be more complicated. In many parts of the world, parents have used institutions to care for their children temporarily until the family situation changes. For example, a family living in poverty may need to feed a child 'today' while family members search for work. This was the case after the 2010 earthquake in Haiti, where the vast majority of institutionalized children were not classifiable as 'orphans' when assessments were made of their circumstances (Balsari, Lemery, Williams and Nelson, 2010).

And under extraordinary circumstances children raised in orphanages may have better outcomes than peers growing up in horrific conditions. For example, during the Guatemalan civil war, where the alternative to institutional care was being subject to extreme violence within communities, children raised in orphanages may have fared better than their non-institutionalized peers (Heying, 2010). At least one author has argued that the long term outcomes for children raised in orphanages can be positive (McKenzie, 1999). In addition, the adoption literature shows great heterogeneity among children with respect to the consequences of early institutionalization (Groza, Ryan, and Thomas, 2008; McCall 1999; Rutter et al., 2001). The varying outcomes may depend, in part, on the particular institutional conditions such as size of the facility, density of children, and child-caregiver ratio. Interventions to improve the quality of institutional care, especially increased and improved caregiver attention, have led to improvement in children's communicative abilities, and socio-emotional, cognitive, personal-social, and physical development (St. Petersburg USA Orphanage Research Team, 2008). The *Guide to Good Practice* states that, "it is, as a general rule, not preferable to keep children waiting in institutions when the possibility exists of a suitable permanent family placement abroad" (Hague Conference on Private International Law, 2008b, p. 30). And also that "institutionalisation as an option for permanent care, while appropriate in special circumstances, is not as a general rule in the best interests of the child" (Hague Conference on Private International Law, 2008b, p. 30). In sum, institutional care is not generally a preferred option for children living outside of parental care, but under certain conditions may be the best option available.

Cuthbert and Fronek (2012) propose a new paradigm for successive steps to address child welfare within a public health prevention framework, shifting from children being viewed as 'available' for ICA to children 'at risk' for ICA. This alternative lens requires State intervention oriented towards family preservation. Fronek and Cuthbert's approach to ICA may be operationalized as follows. Primary prevention includes providing State welfare supports such as economic opportunity and basic services such as health, education, and childcare for all families. Then, if a family appeared to be struggling with maintaining custody of their child, secondary prevention efforts would be implemented. These would include additional targeted family support services such as childcare, sometimes crafted for special needs children such as respite care, and other services such as visits by social workers and/or nurses. Secondary prevention would allow for flexible interventions that are culturally appropriate and are also aimed towards family preservation. Then, if secondary courses had been exhausted and it was clear that a child was not able to be maintained within the family, tertiary prevention would be implemented. At the tertiary level, options for alternative care would be explored, beginning with possible family and community placements. Tertiary prevention options would include guardianship of the child within the kinship system or domestic child adoption. If and when those options were exhausted, a State might determine that is a child was appropriate for ICA and release the child with documentation of identity and social history. The three phases of preventive response represent a continuum of family support and childcare and when executed correctly, the vast majority of children would *not* be routed to ICA as the social intervention of choice. Those children who were identified as eligible for ICA would be truly appropriate, rather than fast-tracked to ICA for the convenience of others, expediency, and financial gain (Ngabonziza, 1991). To our knowledge, the proposal of Cuthbert and Fronek (2012) has not been fully implemented in any country.

Roby (2007) applies a human rights perspective to child adoption, defining the child's rights before, during, and after adoption placement. Prior to adoption, children's rights include the rights to survival and health care, to grow up in a family and in her own culture. During the adoption, a child has rights to be determined to be adoptable, to be placed with a properly prepared family, to be matched with family who can provide for his needs, to be protected from commodification, to receive competent professional care, and to give consent or express an opinion about the adoption (depending on age and maturity). After adoption, a child has the right to full family membership, to social acceptance, and to access to birth and identity records, Like Fronek and Cuthbert, Roby argues that families should be preserved by eliminating conditions of poverty, but adds that nations should allow children the right to be adopted. Roby and Ife (2009) further explore the conceptions of a rights-based framework for adoption, applying those ideas to the Marshall Islands and Romania. Their approach is inclusive of biological families, when possible, in decisions about a child's future.

Based in part on the heterogeneity of possible placements, variability of contextual factors, time and resources required for implementing child welfare programs in countries of origin, and differential outcomes for children in similar circumstances, the implementation of the subsidiarity clause of the Hague Convention has been extremely controversial. Should intercountry adoption be the 'last resort' or should institutional care fall into that category? Should children languish in institutions while domestic placements are being sought? What exactly is a 'family setting' and is foster care an acceptable alternative? Those questions are at the core of effective implementation of the Hague Convention.

Along with sweeping structural changes such as the elimination of poverty and economic inequality and the development of effective child welfare systems, there are more specific ways that the Hague Convention might be implemented in order to further the best interests of children. Several critiques of the Hague Convention have identified loopholes, and possible ways that countries might enact laws, policies, and procedures to close those loopholes.

The *Guide to Good Practice* is the primary document that provides guidelines for implementing the Hague Convention, including how to establish a central authority, carry out four phases of national child care solutions, develop processes for intercountry adoption, and regulate the costs (Hague Conference on Private International Law, 2008b). In June 2010 the Hague convened a Special Commission, the Special Commission on the practical operation of the Hague Convention of 29 May 1993 on Protection of Children and Co-operation in Respect of Intercountry Adoption, to evaluate the current state of the Hague Convention and its implementation (Degeling, 2010b). At that meeting, members drafted a second set of guidelines for implementing the Hague Convention (Hague Conference on Private International Law, 2010). The document, commonly referred to as the *Guide to Good Practice No. 2* is not as of this writing in final form, but the draft focuses on the issues of accreditation and also on transparency and accountability in the costs of intercountry adoption. A chapter is devoted to the challenges for states of origin, and another to the challenges for receiving states. Also included are the perspectives of three states of origin (Colombia, Lithuania, and the Philippines) and those of three receiving states (Belgium, the Netherlands, and Sweden). The *Guide to Good Practice No. 2* promises to advance the implementation of the Hague Convention more effectively.

Among the various critiques of the Hague Convention (e.g., Graff, 2010; Hollingsworth, 2008; Parents for Ethical Adoption Reform [PEAR], 2010a; Rotabi and Gibbons, 2012) the most frequent criticism is that intercountry adoption involves transfer of large sums of money, is subject to market forces, and puts at risk persons and countries with fewer or lower resources. Among the suggestions for enhanced implementation is that cash transfers be prohibited, so that the exchange of money can be tracked (Graff, 2010; PEAR, 2010a). Rotabi and Gibbons (2012) also suggest that financial transparency be implemented with respect to humanitarian giving to countries of origin by agencies and adoptive parents. Another issue related to the potential monetary gain in intercountry adoption is that intermediaries may seek out or recruit potential relinquishing birth parents, and their potential for financial gain may promote illegal practices such as coercion of parents (Smolin, 2006).

Another way to combat illegal practices in countries of origin is to hold the agencies in receiving countries responsible for their foreign partners' actions (Graff, 2010; PEAR, 2010a, Rotabi and Gibbons, 2012). Among the illegal actions in some intercountry adoptions are the fabrication of paper work and the creation of 'paper orphans' (Smolin, 2006). Those practices need to be addressed by both sending and receiving nations. This is a very difficult prospect in countries of origin as millions of children globally are without birth certificates and subsequent documents are often difficult to substantiate. Combine this issue with graft and corruption and a chain of problems develop related to appropriate and legal paperwork for ICA, sometimes resulting in "child laundering" in which a child's complete identity is changed (Smolin, 2006).

While agency accreditation is required under the HCIA and the paperwork process is regulated to prevent child laundering (Rotabi and Gibbons, 2012), it is often difficult for agencies to ascertain if documentation is bona fide or forged. In some cases, agencies have looked the other way while a foreign facilitator 'arranges' a child's paperwork. Then, if the agency stands accused of lack of due diligence or incompetent practice, their willful blindness is often passed off as a 'we didn't know' response to the problem. Under USA HCIA criteria, an agency could just terminate a supervised contract with such a dishonest facilitator, after the fact or embarrassment of forged documents, and claim to have engaged ethically under HCIA accreditation standards. The only vulnerability would be *if* the agency were proven to be working in concert with document fraud in a systematic manner. However, the agency evaluation process, as it currently stands, has some inadequacies including lack of detailed and in-person field investigations of agencies that receive complaints in-between accreditation cycles (Rotabi and Gibbons, 2012).

A very important ethical issue in intercountry adoption is whether consent is fully informed and freely given by relinquishing parents (Babb, 1999; Freundlich, 2000b). Although the Hague Convention is designed primarily to protect children, there are also protections for birth parents. As Smolin (2004) points out, we must respect the rights and dignity of all members of the adoption triad—child, birth family, and adoptive family and by extension child, country of origin, and receiving country. Guaranteeing informed consent is complex and difficult, even when the full intention is to provide accurate information and encourage free choice. Studies from the Marshall Islands (Roby and Matsumura, 2002), from South Africa, (see Chapter 11), and from India (Bos, 2007) reveal that birth mothers may misunderstand the nature of intercountry adoption. For example, over 80 percent of birth mothers in the Marshall Islands believed that their children would return to them (Roby and Matsumura, 2002). In some instances (e.g., India, Korea, Brazil) it is clear that birth mothers felt pressured to relinquish by agencies, recruiters, their own families, or birth fathers, and did not truly feel free to make an autonomous decision (Abreu, 2009; Bhargava, 2005; Fonseca, 2009; Fronek, 2006). Some of the misunderstandings may stem from cultural understandings of traditional practices of child circulation in which parenting is shared by other than birth parents (Leinaweaver, 2007; Rotabi and Gibbons, 2012). In most traditional child sharing practices, adoption or fostering is open (all parties know and agree), parenting is additive rather than substitutive, and may be temporary rather than permanent. Birth parents often do not lose their rights nor their responsibilities to the child (see Chapter 6).

Poverty and marginalization contribute to the difficulties in making free decisions with respect to relinquishment. Green (2010) has pointed out the challenges to self-determination for marginalized persons. "Marginalized individuals often do not have choices … mechanisms such as empowerment, diplomacy, political pressure, sanction enforcement, external policing, and war are some of the measures employed to protect [their] self-determination (Green, 2010, Conclusion section). Self-determination is particularly challenging for women in low resource nations who often must 'choose' among a number of untenable options when making decisions for the well-being of their family. Ultimately it may be argued that it is impossible for the most impoverished women to make an informed consent decision in an autonomous manner, as their living conditions are coercive in and of themselves.

Cultural factors may enter into the relinquishment process in other ways as well. One of the strengths of the Hague Convention is that it allows contracting states flexibility "in deciding how its provisions are to be implemented" (Hague Conference on Private International Law, 2010, p. 10). Therefore, states might implement specific policies and procedures that take into account culture. For example, a prominent cultural distinction is that between individualistic cultures and collectivist cultures (Hofstede, 2001; Oyserman, Coon, and Kemmelmeir, 2002). The core characteristics of individualism are valuing independence and uniqueness and those of collectivism, enacting duty to the in-group and maintaining group harmony. The notion of informed consent is based in an individualistic perspective, that it is individuals who have the agency, personal freedom, and independence to make informed decisions. Those ideas do not transfer directly to more collectivistic cultures. In collectivistic cultures, children are considered to belong to extended families or to communities (e.g., Bos, 2007). While there is no research on cultural differences in decision-making about relinquishment, analogous studies about informed consent for participation in research provide ample evidence that in-groups assume or could be allotted some authority for consent in collectivist cultures (see Rotabi and Gibbons, 2012). An extension of the responsibility for children to nations is also a critical and contentious issue in ICA (Roby, 2007).

Further, ensuring informed consent in relinquishment for adoption is one of the most difficult practice areas of social work and often results in significant ethical dilemmas (Kaplan and Bryan, 2009; Wiley and Baden, 2005). This is especially true in low resource nations with limited social services, gender inequality, and poverty, where birth mothers may be faced with financial pressures or even coercion to relinquish (Freundlich, 2000b).

Because both countries of origin and receiving countries have leeway in implementing the Hague Convention within their own borders, they need to develop policies and procedures that both follow the letter of the spirit of the HCIA and are consistent with their local cultural traditions. This means a domestication of the HCIA in adoption laws such as the USA Intercountry Adoption Act (2000) or Guatemala's aforementioned law (Ministerio de Gobernación Guatemala, 2010). Some nations have better laws than others and variability of HCIA-implementation quality. Administrative policies at the Central Authority level as well as at the adoption agency level are derived from these laws—again some administrative policies and procedures better than others. By the time a law truly interfaces with a vulnerable family or birth mother considering relinquishment, the actual enactment of policy may look very different from the original intent, which began broadly with the HCIA.

In order to increase the well-being and promote the best interests of the adoption triad globally, nations might consider policies that include:

1. Additional rights for birth parents, including the right to know where their child is and to maintain contact if so desired.
2. Additional rights for adopted children, including the right to know the family of origin, including siblings whether they remained in the birth country or were adopted into other nations.
3. Ascertaining that agencies are properly accredited, and that they follow transparent financial procedures.
4. Providing services for adoptive parents, that include matching for their ability to meet the needs of adopted children, training and education prior to adoption, and support services following adoption.
5. Instituting regulations that clearly separate humanitarian giving by agencies from their involvement in ICA. See the draft version of Guide to Good Practice 2 for examples of good practice (Hague Conference on Private International Law, 2010).
6. Cooperation and collaboration between sending and receiving states to ensure that processes of ICA are legal and ethical.
7. Closing the loophole that allows for non-Hague nation adoptions to be exempt from best practice standards (see Chapter 10).
8. The development of a universal code of adoption ethics as a framework of practice above and beyond the HCIA and the guidance in the Guide to Good Practices.

Along with these global and local interventions to protect the rights and foster the well-being of all stakeholders in ICA (children, birth families, adoptive parents, communities and countries of origin, and receiving communities and nations), ethical considerations might be extended to encompass long-term outcomes in light of globalization. As the world becomes more intertwined, integrated, and interconnected, the well-being of children worldwide may become a more prominent part of humanitarian concern. Instead of imagining communities based on nation states, people may turn to imagining global communities (Singer, 2002). In terms of enhancing children's well-being globally, is it ethical to spend $30,000 on an intercountry adoption, when a mere $200 may save a child's life (Singer,

2002)? On the other hand, some of the controversies about intercountry adoption stem from nations protecting 'their' children. In a truly global world, would national boundaries be seen as barriers to promoting children's best interests and well-being? These are just a few of the issues that need to be addressed in order to create a more just and caring world.

Chapter 20
Intercountry Adoptions and Home Study Assessments: The Need for Uniform Practices[1]

Thomas M. Crea

Tragedies in adoptive families seem to occur with regularity in the media, and often shed light on the failures of the current system to protect children adequately and to support adoptive families in crisis. As in other placements with tragic outcomes, the recent case of Artyem Savelyev, a seven year-old adopted boy sent back to his home country of Russia by his adoptive mother with a note stating, "I no longer wish to parent this child" (Williams, 2010), seemed to expose a string of problems within intercountry adoption practice (Rotabi and Heine, 2010). While many of the facts of this case are sealed under agency confidentiality regulations, the adoptive mother's public abandonment of the child in another country raises many questions (Rotabi, 2010a): How well did the agency prepare this mother to adopt a special needs child? How accurate was the information provided by Russian authorities about the child's needs? Why were no post-placement supports available to this family to help stave off such a crisis?

Experts agree that the factors influencing an adoption disruption are multi-faceted, complex, and sometimes systemic (see Chapter 21). Among these factors is the need for adequate home study assessments to screen and prepare families for adoption. Ruggiero and Johnson (2009) outlined three major risks to successful adoptive child and family functioning: (1) Inadequate pre-adoption preparation; (2) Receiving inadequate or false information about the children and their pre-adoption histories; and (3) The lack of appropriate post-adoption services and support. Among the practice recommendations to ameliorate these risk factors, Ruggiero and Johnson (2009) suggest that home study assessments of pre-adoptive families should be revamped to include more thorough family preparation. In fact, the variability of home study assessments across agencies and jurisdictions has been the topic of recent research and discussions (Crea, Barth, and Chintapalli, 2007; Crea, Barth, Chintapalli, and Buchanan, 2009a; Rotabi, 2010a) which

1 This chapter is, in part, based on Crea, T.M. (2009). Brief Note: Intercountry adoptions and domestic home study practices: SAFE and the Hague Adoption Convention.. *International Social Work*, 673-8. © Sage.

suggest that that lack of uniformity in home study practices may contribute to less thorough assessment and preparation of families.

The purposes of this chapter are: (a) to explore how USA domestic home study practices are integrated within The Hague Adoption Convention regulations; (b) to explore deficiencies in the home study processes often employed within the USA and abroad; and (c) to present recent research findings related to the Structured Analysis Family Evaluation (SAFE) home study methodology, the first standardized home study process widely implemented in the USA and Canada.

Home Studies and the Hague Adoption Convention

In April of 2008, the United States began implementation of the Convention on Protection of Children and Co-Operation in Respect of Intercountry Adoption (Hague Conference on Private International Law [HCPIL], 1993). As in domestic adoptions, a key component of intercountry adoptions through the Hague Convention involves the approval of a family through a formal home study process to assess the family's suitability (U.S. Department of State [U.S. DOS], 2010c). Hague Convention regulations, however, specify a central authority by which adoption agencies are approved to conduct home studies. The formalization of processes for intercountry adoptions to ensure ethical and professional practices in the USA has further highlighted the variability of home study practices across agencies, states, and jurisdictions (Rotabi, 2008; Rotabi, 2010a; U.S. DOS, 2010c).

The Hague Convention was established in 1993 to develop safeguards to protect the rights of children involved in intercountry adoptions. The Convention sought to streamline the ethical and legal complexities introduced by intercountry adoption arrangements (HCPIL, 2008a). With regard to the approval of adoptive families, the Convention specifies that home studies must be conducted by an accredited agency, or that an accredited agency must approve a home study conducted by a contracted provider (Rotabi, 2008; U.S. DOS, 2010c). Agencies are accredited by a Central Authority, which "shall co-operate with each other and promote co-operation amongst the competent authorities in their States to protect children and to achieve the other objects of the Convention" (Chapter III, Article 7, HCPIL, 1993). The purpose of these regulations is to ensure both that adoption practices are ethical, and that "prospective adoptive parents are eligible and suited to adopt" in the country in which they wish to locate a child (Chapter II, Article 5, HCPIL, 1993).

Yet, these regulations are only recently being articulated clearly. The U.S. Citizenship and Immigration Services (U.S. CIS, 2009) acknowledged receiving many questions about the types of material to be included in the home study. In response, the agency created a Hague Home Study Tip Sheet to help guide home study practices to align with Hague regulations. This document provides practice examples and sample wording of home studies to avoid processing delays. While these guidelines are likely helpful to workers in negotiating the complex regulatory changes introduced by the Hague Convention, it seems unlikely that such a brief outline, in the absence of training, will help improve the thoroughness and quality of home study practices across jurisdictions.

The Variability of Home Study Practices

In the interim between the establishment of the Hague Adoption Convention in 1993 and its entry into force in the U.S. in 2008, scholars have identified weaknesses in the assessment of prospective adoptive families. Triseliotis (2000) provided the illustration of a family who was approved for intercountry adoption in the USA based on one home visit around "coffee and carrot cake" (p. 51), and mentioned other scenarios in which home study assessments were conducted by telephone. Triseliotis concluded that the blame for such weak practices lies in the absence of "suitable structures to provide confidence that the best interests of those involved, including the children, will be safeguarded" (p. 51). Similarly, Chou, Browne and Kirkaldy (2007) call for tightened restrictions in the Hague Convention around home study assessments, especially given the wide variability of practices internationally and even across jurisdictions in the United States.

In the United States, the quality and variability of domestic home study practices has been the subject of increasing scrutiny in the media, which in turn has placed pressure on policy makers to change adoption practices. The Artyem Savelyev case has precipitated new intercountry adoption agreements between the U.S. and Russia which, in part, will mandate specialized training for prospective applicants (e.g., characteristics of institutionalized children) and strengthen requirements for social workers conducting home visits (Kralnova, 2010), possibly by increasing the number of visits. These improvements would make the criteria similar to those for adopting from foster care. but still do not address the problems inherent in conducting inadequate assessments of families' suitability to adopt.

The risks involved with deficient home study practices in the USA can lead to dire consequences. In an earlier adoption scandal, a child predator in Pennsylvania was allowed to adopt a girl from Russia and subject her to brutal abuse and exploitation (ABC News, 2005). Once the abuse was discovered, the ensuing investigation determined that the abuser had similarly abused an adult daughter in childhood. Yet, during the home study, this daughter was never interviewed, nor did the adoption placing agency make any post-placement visits to the home to ensure the adopted girl's safety (ABC News, 2005; Rotabi and Heine, 2010). According to the home study agency, workers were not required under Pennsylvania regulations to contact adult children, nor was doing so a common practice among adoption agencies in their region (U.S. House of Representatives, 2006b). The director of the agency stated that he "firmly believed that our home study was conducted in accordance with all applicable requirements and standards and that there were no red flags to indicate this man's true intentions" (U.S. House of Representatives,

2006b, p. 28). Yet, clearly red flags did exist but remained uncovered in the course of the home study assessment. As the Chairman of the Senate Subcommittee on Oversight and Investigation stated during a hearing before the U.S. House of Representatives, "Calling references, ensuring there are in-person follow up visits with the child, and speaking to the children of the prospective adoptive parent rise to the level of minimal diligence in my book" (U.S. House of Representatives, 2006b, p. 5). In this case, the lack of a thorough home study investigation—and of rigor in statutory requirements for home studies—allowed a known pedophile to adopt and continue abusing.

The quality and consistency of home studies in the USA is also becoming a focus of attention in the scholarly literature. Freundlich, Heffernan, and Jacobs (2004) point to the absence of clear home study assessment standards as undermining the effectiveness of domestic interjurisdictional adoptions through the Interstate Compact for the Placement of Children. This problem was confirmed in interviews with leading experts in the field of adoption, who pointed to inconsistencies in home studies across jurisdictions as the source of slowed adoption placements (Crea et al., 2007).

Problems in home study practices have also emerged in Europe. Selinske, Naughton, Flanaghan, Fry, and Pickles (2001) cited two cases in which home studies conducted in the UK, for an intercountry adoption from the USA, were completed by an unqualified and unlicensed worker. In both cases, British authorities raised "serious questions regarding (the) suitability of the families" (Selinske et al., 2001), and legislation introduced following these cases prohibited home studies' being completed by independent social workers. These authors concluded that "the parental home study is central to ensuring the safety of an adoptive child in a domestic or international adoption" (Selinske et al., 2001, pp. 662-3), and that "intercountry adoption requires formalized mechanisms to ensure universally implemented ethical and legal practices" (p. 665).

Similarly, a study of disrupted intercountry adoptions in Spain (N=22) revealed that 60 percent of these disruptions included problems related to the original home study (Palacios, Sánchez-Sandoval, and León, 2005). A common problem involved a lack of exploration into the child-rearing capabilities or coping strategies used by prospective parents. The authors cited a specific example of a family who wanted to adopt a ten year-old girl from Ecuador. While this family was repeatedly informed of the potential challenges in adopting an older child, the home study report recorded that "the applicants however have not paid attention to our recommendations" (Palacios et al., 2005, p. 42). Despite having to enroll in a pre-adoptive education program, the family was not subject to further professional assessments of their capacity to adopt an older child. Little additional information was provided about the family's suitability even after requests for further information from authorities in Ecuador. Clearly, however, the heightened risks presented by this family were likely related to the adoption's eventual disruption (Palacios et al. 2005).

The above scenarios point to serious deficiencies in home study practices, but rely mainly on anecdotal evidence. However, further research suggests that the content of many home studies often lacks critical information, or contains biased information. Using a national sample of child specific recruiters (workers identifying prospective adoptive families for specific children in foster care), a recent study examined perceptions of home studies as they pertained to general family functioning and expectations for children's functioning (N=78; Crea, Griffin, and Barth, 2011). This study found that while recruiters perceive that home studies tend to function well in gathering basic information about families, these studies perform much less well in gathering sensitive information about applicants' backgrounds. Furthermore, home studies generally do not adequately cover parents' understanding and ability to deal with children's behavioral and medical issues, critical areas for which prospective applicants should be prepared (Crea et al., 2011). Another study involving a review of home study records found that among families' home study autobiographies, applicants tended to portray themselves as having normal backgrounds and experiences. Yet, workers tended to overlook or downplay existing risks identified through the home study process by not including an assessment of these risks within the written home study (Noordegraaf, van Ninjnattan, and Elders, 2009).

Home study practices also vary in both the quality of their assessment practices and procedures for training parents. Ruggiero and Johnson (2009) identified inadequate pre-adoption preparation of parents as one of the major risk factors impeding successful adjustment of adoptive families. One contributing issue is that some home study agencies may believe the child placing agency should be responsible for training and preparing families. This apparent dichotomy between assessing families' appropriateness to adopt, and preparing them for the potential challenges of adoption, highlights an additional issue to be considered in pre-adoption preparation. Most home study methods include a parallel component of parent training (Crea et al., 2007) but in the context of intercountry adoptions, this component frequently seems to be absent (Ruggiero and Johnson, 2009). With the rapid policy and practice changes now in effect, including the United States' entry into The Hague Convention, the enduring issue of variability in home study assessments has come to the forefront of adoption practice.

Structured Analysis Family Evaluation (SAFE)

The Structured Analysis Family Evaluation (SAFE) holds promise as a means of standardizing the quality of assessments. The forerunner to SAFE was originally developed in 1989 in the California Department of Social Services Adoptions Branch. In 2004, the Consortium for Children received a Federal grant to expand SAFE to multiple sites and evaluate its performance. To date, SAFE has been implemented in 20 states and five Canadian provinces, with over 4,000 practitioners and over 1,000 supervisors being trained in its use (Consortium for Children, 2008).

SAFE's purposes are fourfold: (1) to create a standardized home study methodology across sites; (2) to promote greater worker efficiency and effectiveness; (3) to conduct a thorough psychosocial evaluation of families within the home study; and (4) to promote more thorough assessments of families compared with conventional formats. The structured SAFE format provides a means by which workers collect sensitive information about families' backgrounds and current functioning. Practitioners rely on social work interviews that draw on information collected from structured questionnaires. These structured tools include two questionnaires completed by applicants that review their past and current functioning, as well as a reference letter in questionnaire format. SAFE also provides a Psychosocial Inventory and Desk Guide to assist the worker in completing the psychosocial inventory based on information gathered during the unscripted interview process. Workers are instructed to use a mitigation process that examines past issues of concern in light of current functioning (see Crea et al., 2009a, for more information, or http://www.safehomestudy.org). In order to reflect Hague regulations, SAFE Home Study templates are modified for each jurisdiction consistent with the site's unique culture and traditions. Outside of the United States, the Desk Guide and Work Books/Questionnaires are also modified to reflect the terminology, regulations and culture of the implementing jurisdiction.

SAFE also includes an optional Compatibility Inventory. This Inventory guides an assessment of a child's needs, characteristics and vulnerabilities in 112 potential areas (as applicable to the specific child), linked to a parallel evaluation of a family's ability and willingness to deal with these issues. The need to explore families' expectations and capabilities to meet children's needs is an important, but often overlooked, aspect of the pre-adoption process (Cowan, 2004; Reilly and Platz, 2003; Ruggerio and Johnson, 2009). The ability to match families and children based on parents' expectations and capacities may be an important area for future research.

Research on the SAFE Methodology

The existing research has shown that practitioners are generally favorable towards SAFE in its ability to improve home study practices (Crea et al., 2009a; Crea et al., 2009b). In one study, workers and supervisors who had received training in SAFE (N=145) found that respondents generally preferred SAFE over conventional home study methods (Crea et al., 2009a). When compared to conventional methods, practitioners tended to favor the use of SAFE overall, and especially in its ability to improve aspects of professional practice and parent selection. Many respondents stated that SAFE represented a more thorough and more equitable means of decision-making within the home study process. Less experienced workers are especially positive about SAFE while more experienced workers and supervisors tended to be less positive (Crea et al., 2009a).

Yet, despite the positive ratings of SAFE within the quantitative survey results, open-ended comments in this study uncovered some potential limitations which some respondents missed in conventional methods (Crea et al., 2009a). For example, those with greater experience in the field felt that family autobiographies should be included in a home study; that the quality of a home study is mostly dependent on the quality of an individual investigator's work; and that the increased structure is too limiting for workers and families. The discrepancy between these generally negative qualitative findings, and the positive quantitative findings, may in part be explained by the field experience of the respondent. Previous research has shown that experienced practitioners often resist external increases in the structure of their decision-making (Chapman and Zweig, 2005) despite findings which show that the validity of collected information increases as the structure of the interview process increases (Campion, Palmer, and Campion, 1997). Nevertheless, respondents in this study overall tended to agree that SAFE represented a more valid home study process than more unstructured, conventional methods. SAFE program developers have also been quick to implement improvements in the design and structure of the method, based on research and evaluation findings (Crea et al., 2009b).

A second study of SAFE surveyed practitioners trained in the SAFE method and who had completed at least three SAFE studies and at least three conventional studies (N=220; Crea et al., 2009b). This study found that practitioners report SAFE to be superior to conventional home study methods in identifying and exploring sensitive issues with families, and in particular, "red flag" issues there might relate to serious concerns. The study also found that SAFE is a useful means of exploring family issues across a range of family structures and practice situations. Respondents, and especially frontline workers, tended to prefer SAFE over unstructured methods for issues related to families' medical and mental health histories, illicit activities, and issues related to problems within relationships. Those without a degree in social work tended to rate SAFE higher, a finding which suggests that SAFE's increased structure may provide needed direction to those workers lacking a formal social work education. Some respondents indicated that particular areas are beyond the reach of any home study method, such as the honesty of applicants. However, the positive responses towards SAFE in this study added to evidence that SAFE represents a needed improvement in adoption practice.

SAFE and Intercountry Adoptions

SAFE is not currently being widely used in intercountry adoptions but it is poised to do so. To comply with Hague Convention regulations, the Consortium for Children has developed a new SAFE template for use in the United States, which specifies instructions for workers to report all parent preparation activities, plans for post-placement counseling and supervision, and discussions regarding fees and general processes related to intercountry adoptions. This template has received favorable reviews by representatives of the U.S. Department of State and the Department of Homeland Security, and a version of this template is currently being used for all intercountry adoptions in the state of Colorado (Consortium for Children, 2008). In Canada, integrated domestic/intercountry home study templates are currently being used in British Columbia, Nova Scotia, Ontario, and Alberta (Kate Cleary, personal communication, June 18, 2010).

As the first standardized home study process currently implemented in multiple USA states, SAFE has potential to increase the standardization, and quality, of home study assessments across jurisdictions. The quality of home studies is a critical piece of adoption practice and one that is under increasing scrutiny with the Hague Convention fully in effect for intercountry adoptions in the United States. Future research should track the usage of SAFE for intercountry adoptions and its ability both to streamline the Hague adoption process. While the existing satisfaction research on SAFE is promising, future research on outcomes is needed, with a focus on improving children's safety and placement stability for domestic and international adoptions.

Chapter 21
Understanding and Preventing Intercountry Adoption Breakdown

Jesús Palacios[1]

The addition of a new child to the family through adoption changes the family system forever, and is an outstanding milestone in the family life cycle. Like any other form of parenting, adoption begins with the hope and expectation of a long and positive adventure. Certainly difficulties will appear along the way, but there will be many rewarding aspects and experiences. In the vast majority of cases, the parent-child relationship will not be at issue and the family will continue its development over time.

The adventure that for many is marked mainly by satisfaction becomes more problematic in other cases. The difficulties may be much greater than expected, and the relationship may have considerable elements of frustration. The crisis does not bring into question the relationship between adopters and adoptees, which will continue its development in the midst of unexpected problems.

There is a third group of adoptive families in which what began as an exciting adventure becomes a frustrated undertaking. The family that was assembled through adoption is disassembled by the departure of the adoptee. These are the adoptions that break down. In the cases of intercountry adoption, the long journey takes an unexpected turn, undoubtedly frustrating and painful for everyone involved, but especially for the children affected, who have to add the loss of their new family to their many previous losses (including their original family, country, and culture). It is these cases that are dealt with in this chapter. A discussion of the various terms used to refer to this failed undertaking is followed by some statistics on its incidence. The factors that tend to be involved in this painful experience are then analyzed. Finally, some thoughts are offered on its prevention.

It should be noted that while there is relatively abundant research on adoption breakdown in cases of domestic adoptions (particularly in special needs adoptions), research on this phenomenon in intercountry adoption is much more limited, for reasons that will be discussed later. This is why many of the arguments used must assume that the main findings of research on adoption breakdown in domestic adoptions are also applicable to intercountry adoption.

---

1 This chapter is based, in part, on: Palacios, J., Román, M., Moreno, C. and Esperanza, L. (2009). Family context for emotional recovery in internationally adopted children. *International Social Work*, 52, 609-20. © Sage.

Disruption, Dissolution, Displacement, Breakdown, Termination

To begin with, the problem that we address is surrounded by considerable confusion in terminology. The term *adoption disruption* is used to refer to the termination of a placement before the final legalization of the adoption. However, if the adoption fails after it was legally completed and constituted, the term *adoption dissolution* is used. The term *adoption displacement* refers to cases in which, once the adoption is legally formalized, there is a temporary return (of varying length) to public custody. The terms *adoption breakdown* and *adoption termination* are used as generic terms to refer to the failure of the adoption at any stage of the process. As indicated below, this diversity of terms is an obstacle for obtaining statistical data.

Some of the earlier terminological distinctions are more meaningful in the case of domestic adoptions, than in intercountry adoptions. Very often, intercountry adoptions are completed totally or to a great extent in the country of origin of the adoptee, after a short stay by the adoptive parents. In many countries legal formalization of adoption takes place just days or weeks after the arrival of the adoptive parents. Contrary to what is often the norm in cases of domestic adoption, in those of intercountry adoption pre-adoption contact is often reduced to a minimum, and in some cases, virtually nonexistent.

Finally, with regard to the conceptual problems, the definition of adoption breakdown is problematic. Should adoption breakdowns be considered to be only those in which there is a departure from the home certified by a court decision? If a girl of 14 is admitted to a boarding school by her parents, who are responsible for her maintenance but have almost no contact with her thereafter, should this be considered an adoption breakdown? Does the situation fall outside of our definition where an 18-year-old adoptee, legally of age, leaves the parental home and after which neither party has anything to do with the other? None of these situations are taken into account statistically, due to, among other things, the enormous difficulty involved in the quantification of issues that occur within the family and which do not become known to judges or child protection authorities.

Adoption Breakdown Statistics

Statistical information on intercountry adoption breakdowns is inadequate. This is due, first, to the terminological confusion referred to above, and difficulties in determining when an adoption should be considered as a breakdown. Second, while all Western countries keep statistics on the number of adoptions, there is no system for the collection of information about adoption breakdowns. Information on the number of children adopted can be obtained through the consulates and embassies of the countries in which the procedures are carried out, but what happens later is much more poorly documented. The multiplicity of actors involved in intercountry adoption complicates the collection of such information.

The limited information available suggests that the adoption breakdown rate is very low in intercountry adoptions. For example, a recent report of the Bureau of Consular Affairs of the U.S. Department of State indicated that in 2010 there were 11,059 intercountry adoptions in the USA and 22 breakdowns, including adoption disruptions and dissolutions (U.S. Department of State, 2010b). The Dutch data of Hoksbergen (1991b) estimated a rate of adoption dissolutions of around 2.5 per cent. In Spain, data from Berástegui (2003) estimated a total of 1.5 per cent for the combined total of disrupted and high risk adoptions.

Although intercountry adoption figures have declined in Western countries since 2004, previous decades had seen a very significant increase in the number of inter-country adoptions. According to the estimate of Selman (2009a), nearly one million children were adopted internationally in Western countries between the end of the Second World War and the present (See Chapter 1). It may be supposed that the substantial increase in the total numbers of intercountry adoption would have been accompanied by a parallel increase in the numbers of adoption breakdowns, but the few available figures do not seem to reflect this trend.

A similar phenomenon has been observed in some countries in relation to domestic adoptions. In the USA, the Adoption and Safe Families Act (ASFA; PL 105-89) was passed by Congress in 1997, with a mandate to the states to be more active in seeking permanency for children in the foster care system. A faster permanency plan for children and a more rapid termination of parental rights were set in place, and financial incentives were introduced for the states to increase the number of adoptions from foster care. According to data from the U.S. Children's Bureau, compared with 24,000 children adopted from the foster care system in 1996, in the year 2000 (after the implementation of ASFA), the figure had doubled, to 51,000 cases. The question of whether adoption breakdowns would increase proportionally was therefore important. According to data from the analysis of Smith, Howard, Garnier, and Ryan (2006), the total number of post-ASFA adoption disruptions increased, but the total number of adoptions had increased much more, so that the rate of adoption disruptions actually declined, with a 12 percent higher risk of disruption in the pre-ASFA period than following its implementation.

Factors Associated With Adoption Breakdown

Irrespective of the domestic or international context, research on adoption breakdown has identified very similar associated factors, although some have special relevance in the case of intercountry adoptions. Generally, these factors are grouped into three clusters identified both in our own analysis of intercountry adoption disruptions in Spain (Palacios, Sánchez-Sandoval and León, 2005), and in the analysis of adoption terminations in domestic adoptions (Evan B. Donaldson Adoption Institute, 2004). The three groups of factors relate to the adoptee, to the adopters and to the professional intervention in the adoption.

Characteristics of the Adoptee

Without a doubt, the *age* at the time of adoption is the single indicator for the child most clearly associated with serious difficulties. According to a study by Goerge, Howard, Yu, and Radomsky (1997), relating to domestic adoptions, and controlling the other factors involved, compared with those adopted at less than one year of age, the risk of breakdown is multiplied by three in those adopted between five and nine years, by four in those adopted between 10 and 14 years, and by nine in those adopted at 15 years or more. In our analysis of intercountry adoptions in Spain, 75 percent of adoption breakdowns affected adopted children over six years. It must be stressed here that the vast majority of adoptions of older children are successful, but it should also be noted that the difficulties increase with the age at the time of arrival.

Some factors that have been associated with serious difficulties in the adoption must be interpreted in light of the influence of the child's age at the time of arrival. For example, in our study in Spain, the breakdown rate was significantly higher for the adoptions made in Russia than for those carried out in China. However, the average age of the adoptees at the time of their arrival was 1.8 years in the case of China and 4.8 years in that of Russia (Palacios et al., 2005). Moreover, the age at the time of arrival cannot be considered alone, since, as shown by Barth and Miller (2000), the older the children are on arrival, the more likely they are to have accumulated more adversity, present more problems, have less malleable characteristics, have experienced more separations, and desire more independence.

Together with increasing age (and often in relation to it), the presence of serious *behavioral and emotional problems* should be mentioned in second place for their frequent association with cases of adoption breakdown. Among behavioral problems, aggressive and acting-out behaviors (including cruelty, physical aggression, defiance, stealing, sexual acting-out, suicide attempts) are those most frequently associated with serious difficulties, both in domestic (McRoy, 1999; Rosenthal, 1993) and intercountry adoptions (Berástegui, 2003, Palacios et al., 2005). For its part, emotional problems can include both the presence of strong links with figures prior to adoption, including the birth parents (Rosenthal, 1993; Smith and Howard, 1991), and difficulties in bonding with the adopters, which will be discussed later when referring to their associated factors.

Regarding the *history of adversity* prior to adoption, while some characteristics may play a similar role in cases of national and intercountry adoption, others may have a different profile. For example, if children with pre-adoptive histories of sexual abuse are at greater risk of more complex adoption difficulties than adopted children without such histories (Nalavany, Ryan, Howard, and Smith, 2008), this factor should apply to both domestic and intercountry adoptions. However, other factors traditionally associated with breakdown in domestic adoption, such as the number of different placements before adoption (e.g., Rosenthal, 1993), may be less significant in the case of intercountry adoption, where the institutionalization is more common than family foster care. In these cases, the quality of care provided in institutions can play a greater role. The influence that other pre-adoptive risk factors play in later difficulties is less clear; for example, prenatal drug and alcohol exposure, co-varies with other factors, such as younger age at adoption.

The role of the simultaneous *adoption of siblings* versus that of one child probably does not differ in importance between domestic and intercountry adoption. However, the role that sibling adoptions play in adoption breakdown is far from clear. As indicated by the Evan B. Donaldson Adoption Institute (2004) report on adoption breakdown, researchers have cited conflicting and ultimately inconclusive evidence as to whether sibling placement constitutes a risk factor or a benefit to placement success.

Characteristics of the Adopters

The personal and socio-economic characteristics of the adopters, their parenting skills, and the issues related to the adoption process are all important because of their relationship with the presence of difficulties. Among the former, some research, but not all, has found a higher incidence of severe hardship among single mothers than among couples, both in domestic (McRoy, 1999) and intercountry adoption (Palacios et al., 2005). However, in these two studies it was shown that single mothers were more likely to be matched with children with a more problematic background and who were older at arrival, so that the relevant factor may not be marital status per se. In fact, the majority of adoptions by single mothers develop successfully.

Regarding other personal characteristics, educational level is one of the factors most associated with adoption difficulties. In research on domestic adoption, a classic example is found in the data of Barth and Berry (1988), which showed that, although it was less likely that they had adopted children with special needs, adoptive parents with a college degree were twice as likely to be involved in an adoption breakdown as those with only a high school degree. Among the first, the presence of higher expectations in relation to their adopted children has typically been considered one of the key factors. For example, the study of Welsh, Viana, Petrill, and Mathias (2008) on a sample of typical parents in intercountry adoption, relatively affluent and well-educated, found that virtually all parents expected a bright future for their children, with good academic performance and social adjustment. Although some expected minor difficulties in the adoptees upon arrival (typically referring to problems in adapting to food or sleep, and mild health and developmental problems), the parents who expected emotional or behavioral problems were far fewer. Since the majority would have to face more complicated realities, the risk of these parents having difficulty in bridging the gap between expectations and reality is logically higher.

Regarding factors related to the adoption process, it is worth referring to issues related to the *motivation* to adopt. In our study, some risk factors were motivations classically considered unsuitable (such as replacement of a lost child with an adoptee), as well as serious disagreements between the motivations of each adopting partner (for example, where the motivation to adopt is only on the part of the woman, with the man simply assisting in the process without conviction; Palacios et al., 2005). Regarding motivation to adopt, the analysis of Zhang and Lee (2011) shows that the USA families in their sample perceive American children in need of adoption as presenting "problems that are difficult to resolve," while foreign children are seen as viable alternatives, perhaps presenting "interesting challenges." In reality, however, parents will face challenges and problems (and rewards) that are very similar in either case.

A final aspect to be mentioned among the risk factors in the adopters is related to their *parenting skills*. When children's behavior is simple and poses no particular challenges, the possession of special parenting abilities is not crucial. However, when children's behavior is more difficult, parents' response is critical. Discipline, the ability to adapt the parenting style to the changing needs of the children, tolerance to frustration, the ability to feel satisfied with small advances, and the ability to establish proper boundaries are some of the qualities that have been associated with greater stability in the placements, both in foster care and adoption (e.g., see Crum, 2010). The greater presence of behavioral problems in children is associated with the parents' reduced feeling of closeness to the child (Howard and Smith, 2003), so it is essential that adopters are able to respond adequately to these problems.

Characteristics of the Professional Intervention

In the ecology of adoption (Palacios, 2009), professional intervention is an important factor, the degree of stability of placements being related to professional practice. Some of the main aspects identified by the research are discussed briefly below.

Adequate *preparation* is a prerequisite for successful adoption (Brodzinsky, 2008). As noted above, prospective adopters often approach the adoption with some ideas that do not correspond with reality. The role of education is to help form appropriate motivations and expectations, as well as providing advice for a more successful response to the challenges of adoption. Our own data showed how lack of preparation or inadequate preparation (e.g., focusing only on legal aspects or those relating to travel and the stay in the country of origin) were a frequent characteristic in intercountry adoptions that ended in breakdown. The same is true of other professional interventions such as the assessment for suitability to adopt: the more superficial the home study assessment (for example, focusing mainly on income or housing characteristics), and the less informed by professional knowledge about adoption, the more likely it is for the suitability decision to be inappropriate (Palacios et al., 2005; see Chapter 20).

An essential aspect of professional practice lies in the adopters-adoptees *matching*. Logically, the more complex the behavior of the adoptee, the more crucial is the matching with adopters that are able to deal with that complexity. In fact, the research by McRoy (1999) on special needs adoptions identified poor matches as one of the most important risk factors for the stability of the adoption. Our own data on intercountry adoption breakdowns identified specific characteristics such as large discrepancies between the child profile originally requested and that which was later accepted, the concealment (perhaps in ignorance) of important problematic characteristics of the child from the future adopters, and the assignment of a child of the same age as another already in the adoptive home (Palacios et al., 2005). In connection with the matching, the simultaneous presence of two facts must be understood as an important risk factor: first, the professionals try stretching the motivation of the prospective adopters, so that they would accept more complex realities than they initially envisaged. Second, adopters often downplay the problems of the child they are told about and are overly optimistic about their ability to cope with any difficulties.

Once problems arise, *post-adoption support* is essential, whether in the form of advice and guidance, or in the form of therapeutic activities (Hart and Luckock, 2004). The closeness of professionals to the adopters is a critical element, as very often the latter take too long to become aware of the seriousness of the difficulties, too often reporting problems when an accumulation of difficulties and emotional distancing have already occurred and which are then much more difficult to repair (Palacios et al., 2005).

Finally, together with the shortages or lack of professional interventions, it should also be mentioned that their excessive fragmentation constitutes a negative characteristic. It frequently happens that the adopters deal with different professionals for each stage of the adoption process; also, the caseworkers change too often and tend to be scattered among various agencies and organizations. The existence of this "disorganized army" of professionals (Palacios, 2009) is very inefficient in helping adopters who are overwhelmed by problems and difficulties.

Accumulation of Risk Factors

The presence of some of the aforementioned indicators occurs too often. Thus, it is common for children to arrive at an age later than infancy, for adopters to have overly optimistic expectations, and for the assessment of suitability to be superficial and the matching to be unwise. It is frequently found in adoption breakdowns that several of these elements are present at the same time. The critical accumulation of risk factors becomes a powerful predictor of serious difficulties much more than the presence of any single factor. When the motivation to adopt presents elements of risk, when there is inadequate preparation for the adoption, and the assessment of suitability is superficial, when the parents also have poor parenting skills or excessively optimistic expectations, when they are matched with children who are very different from what they expected and with a behavioral or emotional complexity that far exceeds their parenting abilities, when, in addition, there is no professional support for those relationships, there is a very high likelihood that serious difficulties will arise and that eventually the adoption will breakdown.

The accumulation of risk factors can be illustrated with one of the cases in our study of intercountry adoption disruptions in Spain (the name of the child and the country of origin have been purposely altered). A couple whose biological son died, considered adopting a young boy and started the adoption proceedings in Peru where they knew several people who could help them in the process. After applying for adoption and contacting Cristina, who would eventually become their daughter, the couple were assessed and deemed suitable by professionals with no expertise in adoption. It was later revealed that the desire to adopt was held solely by the mother, and that her husband had accepted the adoption just to spare his wife any further ordeal after having gone through the hardship of losing her child. The couple did not go through any pre-adoption educational program. Cristina was nine years old when she arrived in her new family. Her childhood had been very complicated, she had lived with her mother and then with her siblings in an institution. Shortly after arriving in Spain, subsequent to a week spent with her adoptive parents in Lima, the girl began displaying a highly sexualized behavior which strongly offended her parents who had very strict religious beliefs and who were strongly prejudiced against "bad behaviors." The girl rejected her adoptive mother as much as she was rejected by her. The records show at least one episode in which she assaulted her mother. After running away from home, the girl was placed in an institution where she had severe problems, and from which she escaped a few days after her arrival to go back to her adoptive parents' home. However, the strong mutual rejection that existed between them made living together impossible and the adoption was finally and definitely terminated.

Preventing Adoption Breakdown

The examination of the characteristics and traits that are most frequently associated with serious difficulties in adoption (leading or not to a final breakdown) suggests some of the ways to avoid the painful experience for all involved in an adoption breakdown. We cannot but agree with the two ideas expressed by Coakley and Berrick (2008). First, it would be unrealistic to expect that any policy or practice could eliminate the chance of serious difficulties in adoption. Second, it is not unrealistic to attempt to reduce the frequency of breakdown "through enlightened policy and practice" (Coakley and Berrick, 2008, p. 110).

Of all the factors considered in the above analysis, the only one that cannot be changed is that which refers to the characteristics of the adoptees. Particularly in the case of intercountry adoption, it is unrealistic to think that any policy in the country of the adopters could easily change the conditions under which children are declared adoptable, the quality of institutional experiences, or the age at which children are adopted. Of course, the recipient countries and agencies involved can take steps to ensure the *clarity and transparency of the processes and procedures*, choose the countries with which they relate, and ensure that adoptions are handled following principles of strict professional ethics. A basic starting point should be adherence to the Hague Convention and the application of its principles and agreements. Making adoptions in countries whose practices are questionable or directly improper, using obscure or shameful procedures, is an inappropriate start to a process fraught with complexity.

Adopters need *proper information and preparation.* Sometimes, those who decide to adopt may do with as much goodwill as lack of information. They may believe, for example, that international adoptees have no major problems and only have "interesting challenges" (Zhang and Lee, 2011). They may believe that there is no problem that love and stimulation cannot solve. They may believe that the best that can happen to a child with very adverse early experience is to forget the past and live only in the present, or that ethnic differences are irrelevant in a world of increasing multiculturalism. It is understandable that some people think in these ways, but the lack of professional intervention that puts prospective adopters before the reality of adoption, before its complexity and difficulty, is less understandable. The mission of the preparation for adoption is not to scare or discourage. It is, rather, to provide adoptive parents with a better understanding of adoption and improve their skills to deal with the typical challenges of adoption (e.g., communication about adoption). Pre-adoption preparation should not be voluntary, nor done exclusively through the very abundant (but of very variable quality) information available online. It should be part of the basic procedures required for all people who are considering adopting. In fact, educational preparation for adoption is mandatory in many countries (e.g., USA), and strongly recommended in the Hague Conference *Guide to Good Practice* (The Hague Conference on Private International Law, 2008b).

Professionals involved in working with prospective adopters need *training and appropriate professional skills* to carry out their important work. The problems that arise in adoptive families are often based on a lack of adoption-specific knowledge and training among professionals who serve adopted children and adoptive families (Casey Family Services, 2003). Neither the children nor the families involved can afford what Rycus, Freundlich, Hughes, Keefer, and Oakes (2006) describe as "the high cost of ignorance" (p. 218) or the professional "unconscious incompetence" (p. 220). It is critical that important decisions such as the declaration of suitability to adopt, or the matching, are left in the hands of well-trained professionals, with the specific skills and working conditions (e.g., time) to implement them properly.

But neither the needs of those who adopt nor professional intervention ends once the adoption is legally formalized. That is not the moment when it is all over, but rather one in which everything begins. *Post-adoption support* is therefore crucial, particularly when problems or difficulties arise that are beyond the adopters' capabilities. Ideally, in the preparation for the adoption, the prospective adopters should be familiarized with the possibility that problems may arise as well as the need to establish a good partnership with professionals in order to address them. Occasionally problems start out small and manageable, but if they are not addressed properly and in time, they accumulate and become more complex, compromising the success of the process. As the adopters often have difficulty being aware of some problems or of gauging their importance, a proactive approach by the professionals is essential, particularly, but not solely, in those cases where circumstances give rise to concern.

Once problems are identified, the training of those providing support is again crucial. If a child has language problems, for example, perhaps any professional speech therapist could intervene successfully. However, other problems can only be understood and adequately addressed when interpreted and dealt with through a specifically adoption-focused approach. For example, to understand what the losses mean for the adoptee, to help deal with them in the most appropriate way within family relationships or in a therapeutic context, requires professionals with specific knowledge to address adoption-related issues.

If an adoption breaks down, it is not usually just a failure of the adopters. It is also, and perhaps above all, a systemic failure of all persons and entities involved, as well as a failure of the procedures and professional interventions concerned with the case. Prevention therefore should also be systemic and approached by the various actors and elements involved in the ecology of the adoption.

Finally, we obviously need to *improve our knowledge about adoption breakdown*. This includes better statistics, of course, but also a better knowledge of the circumstances under which adoptions are at serious risk, as well as the most effective way of preventing this painful experience for the individuals and the professionals involved. Up until now, research on intercountry adoption breakdown has been very limited. Having a more detailed and thorough knowledge will be one of the starting conditions to enhance our ability to improve the response to the problem addressed in this chapter.

Chapter 22
Openness and Intercountry Adoption in New Zealand

Rhoda Scherman

Intercountry adoption and open adoption are both highly topical, complex, and contentious forms of adoption. Both types of adoptive practice have ever-growing bodies of empirical research and literature, as well as multiple discourses that drive their respective debates. Yet, despite both being focal and long-standing research areas in the broad field of adoption, and being key features of current adoption policy and practice in most Western countries, they are rarely considered in tandem. In other words, can an intercountry adoption be open? Can openness be achieved in intercountry adoptions? To better consider this issue, let us first look at the different ways that we can describe and conceptualize adoptive relationships.

Adoptive Relationships Based on Nationality, Race or Culture

As has been thoroughly described in this volume, *intercountry adoption* (ICA) is a form of adoption whereby children from one country are adopted into the homes of another country. Within the literature, this practice goes by many other names including *international*, *foreign, overseas, trans-national, cross-cultural, trans-cultural, inter-cultural* and *cross-national.* The terminology reflects the nature of the adoptive child-parent relationship as involving more than one country, ethnicity, or culture (Scherman, 2010a).

For instance, if a child is from a different racial group but born into the same country as the adopters, this is usually referred to as a *transracial adoption.* If the adopters and children are culturally or ethnically different, regardless of race, then we would say the adoptions are *transcultural* or *transethnic* (respectively). A transracial adoption can be international (e.g., USA parents adopting Korean children) or it can be domestic (e.g., White American parents adopting an African American child). The same is true of transcultural and transethnic adoptions—these also can be either international or domestic. Likewise, an intercountry adoption can be transracial, transcultural or transethnic, whereby the child is from another country as well as being racially/culturally/ethnically different (Freundlich, 2000a). Yet, intercountry adoptions can also be in-racial; for instance, when the child is from another country but is the same race as the adopters (e.g., European parents adopting Eastern European children), meaning that not all international adoptions are transracial, despite the fact that the vast majority of research on intercountry adoption pertains to transracial relationships (Scherman and Harré, 2004).

Adoptive Relationships Based on Contact and Shared Knowledge

In addition to considering the race, culture or nationality of the parties in adoption, adoptive relationships are also described in terms of how *open* or *closed* they are. These terms refer to the adoptive family and birth family relationships and how much contact and/or knowledge about one another is shared at the time of placement and throughout the adoptee's life (Wolfgram, 2008). Below is a fuller description of both types of adoptive relationships.

Closed Adoption

Marked by secrecy, anonymity, and confidentiality, *closed* adoptions are characterized by closed or 'sealed' records, whereby birth and adoptive parents are prevented from meeting or sharing identifying information with one another (Rosenberg and Groze, 1997). In most countries, the adopted person is issued an amended birth certificate, showing the adopters as parents, thereby creating the appearance that the adoptee was "born" to the adoptive parents (Shawyer, 1979). The original birth certificate, along with all other 'identifying' information from both sets of parents, is sealed away from all parties by the social welfare agency facilitating the adoption. Initially, this secrecy was considered necessary to protect the child from the negative stigma of being born (often) out of wedlock, as well as to protect the birth mother, allowing her to "move on with her life" (Wolfgram, 2008, p. 134). Over time, secrecy became a standard theme in adoption, as it was considered necessary for the adopted child's psychological adjustment and integration into the adoptive family. Throughout much of the twentieth century, closed adoptions dominated the social welfare practices of most Western countries, and are still common-place in many countries including the USA.

Open Adoption

In contrast to closed placements, *open* adoption is best understood as a type of family *structure*; a set of adoptive family relationships characterized by varying degrees of contact, communication and identifying knowledge shared among the adopted child, birth parents, and adopting parents (e.g., Townsend, 2003). These structurally open adoptions sit on a continuum. At the lesser-open end, the adoptive and birth parents may exchange identifying information prior to the placement, or they may share occasional letters and pictures throughout the adoptee's childhood, all of which may be done directly or with an intermediary. At the more-open end of the continuum, birth and adoptive parents might spend time together during the pregnancy, and the adoptive parents may be present at the birth, all of which may lead to both parties having continued visits throughout the child's life. Between these extremes, there are an almost limitless number of permutations, each designed to suit the parties involved (e.g., Logan and Smith, 2005; Townsend, 2003). After years of research into the efficacy of both closed and open adoptions it has been established that open adoptions can confer benefits for all members of the adoption triad (e.g., Grotevant et al., 2007).

Looking at the many features of adoptive relationships, the question at the heart of this chapter is whether or not an *intercountry* adoption can also be an *open* adoption. In other words, can a family adopting from overseas achieve some degree of contact or communication with the child's biological family residing in the sending country? To answer this question, I'm going to use New Zealand's unique adoption environment to more fully conceptualize *openness* in adoption. I will then describe the outcomes of a review of the empirical literature, which will include a brief summary of the preliminary findings of our own New Zealand study. Finally, I will conclude with a discussion of the intersection of ICA and open adoption.

The New Zealand Context: From Open to Closed to Open

New Zealand has had a long and prolific history of adoption practices. The Adoption Act of 1881 was the country's first legislative act governing this institution. By legally regulating adoptive relationships, its aim was to promote the practice of adoption, thereby providing homes for deserted or neglected children (Rockel and Ryburn, 1988). Adoption was not yet a means of providing children for infertile couples, nor was it a practice requiring secrecy. It would be several more decades before either of those concepts would manifest in law or practice.

After World War II, a growing number of people, unable to conceive children of their own, began to see adoption as a way of creating much-wanted families. For these people, pressured by society's emphasis on the importance of the *nuclear family*, and the shame and stigma surrounding illegitimate births, secrecy was a dominant theme, and clearly seen in the Adoption Act of 1955 (Rockel and Ryburn, 1988). Under this legislation, and influenced by the "Clean Break Theory" (Griffith, 1996; Iwanek, 1997), ties to the birth family were permanently severed, records were sealed, and new birth certificates were issued. These *closed* adoption practices embodied an ideology common throughout the Western world at the time.

Today, the domestic adoption atmosphere in New Zealand is much more open, despite the fact that no new legislation has yet replaced the 1955 Adoption Act. This can be seen in the facilitation of structurally open adoptive placements and openness achieved through access to formerly closed records, each described in turn below.

Open Placements

In the 1970s and 1980s, research began emerging from overseas and locally, which suggested that many of the children brought up in the traditional *closed* adoptions were at risk for possible psychological problems (Triseliotis, 1973). The nature of the closed placement meant that the adoptees were missing out on the most basic of childhood experiences: the stories of their birth; ruminations about who they looked like; even basic medical histories (Scherman, 2010b). Much of this research had been precipitated by early clinical reports of adoptees being over-represented within mental health services (Schechter, 1960), resulting in a robust body of literature showing a multitude of negative psychological effects from the secrecy on which closed adoptions were formed (e.g., Baran and Pannor, 1990; Else, 1991; Mullender, 1991a). Around the same time, the concept of an *open* adoption was emerging and gaining empirical support in New Zealand and elsewhere in the world (e.g., Borgman 1982; Gross, 1993; Iwanek, 1987).

In light of the negative outcomes associated with closed adoption, and the growing body of work promoting open placements, in the 1980s New Zealand's adoption practices also began to change. Despite the fact that the 1955 Adoption Act called for closed arrangements, the Adoption Unit of Child, Youth and Family Services (CYFS)—the country's national social welfare organization—began an *unlegislated* policy of placing children into *open* adoptive arrangements. According to Iwanek, former head of the Adoption Unit of CYFS, by 1997, 90 percent of domestically-placed non-relative adoptions in New Zealand were open[1] (Iwanek, 1997).

Open Access to Formerly Closed Records

In response to their own negative experiences, as well as the mounting body of research on the detrimental effects of closed adoptions, throughout the 1970s and 1980s, adult adoptees in New Zealand and elsewhere in the world, actively fought to *open* their sealed records, asserting that knowledge of one's history was an inherent human need and right (Griffith, 1996; Sorosky, Baran, and Pannor, 1974; Triseliotis, 1973). In New Zealand, this movement resulted in the passage of the

1 After more than 30 years of open adoption practice in New Zealand, there still exists no legal difference between open and closed adoptions, because under the 1955 Adoption Act, which has not yet been updated, openness is voluntary and so provides no protection in law (Ludbrook, 1990; Rockel and Ryburn, 1988). Nonetheless, even though the open adoption policy has not yet been formally recognized in legislation, it appears to have become the standard practice (Child, Youth, and Family, 2007).

1985 Adult Adoption Information Act. For the first time since adoptions became 'closed' in 1955, this legislation allowed access to formerly sealed records. Both adoptees and birth parents from past *closed* adoptions were legally entitled to seek out and reunite with one another (Corcoran, 1991; Mullender, 1991b).

Openness in Assisted Reproductive Technologies

It is worth noting that the philosophy of openness underlying New Zealand's open adoption practices seems to have also influenced laws, policy and practices beyond its child welfare systems, as can be seen in legislation governing the human-assisted reproductive technologies. Here again, New Zealand is unique with its legislation requiring that identifying information be collected and made available to any offspring to come from embryo, egg, and even sperm donations (Daniels and Taylor, 1993; Goedeke and Payne, 2010).

What Makes New Zealand So Unique?

Collectively, the features described above make New Zealand stand apart from other Western countries—demonstrating its long-standing experience with adoption practice and an unusual amount of openness when it comes generally to adoption laws and practices. In looking at why New Zealand embodies this ethos of openness, one likely influence is the Māori notions of family and the concomitant beliefs in the rights of every child to access information about his/her origins.

Influences of the Māori Concept of Family and Birthright

The institution of adoption is essentially a Western practice. Māori—New Zealand's indigenous population—like most indigenous cultures, have traditionally engaged in less formal mechanisms when considering with whom a child should be raised. Before European colonization and the introduction of adoption legislation, Māori had for years practiced what is called *tamaiti whangai* (pronounced *taw-maw-ee-tee faw-ng-eye)*. From the words *tamaiti* meaning 'child' and *whangai* meaning 'to feed or nourish[2]', *tamaiti whangai* is a child who is nurtured or raised by someone other than the child's biological parents (McRae and Nikora, 2006). Yet, unlike Western adoption practice where children are often seen as parental possessions (Griffith, 1996), with laws enacted to legitimize that sense of ownership, for Māori, children are not possessed but considered 'assets' of the *whanau* (larger extended

2 In this context, to nourish is meant in the fullest sense of the word; not only with food but with affection and instruction (Griffith, 1996).

family; pronounced *faw-naw-o*; Bradley, 1997, p. 7). They are considered *taonga* (highly-valued treasures; pronounced *taw-o-ng-aw*) to be held collectively and in trust for future generations (Griffith, 1996). Whangai, therefore, are 'gifted' to the whangai parent whose role it is to look after the children and nurture them through to adulthood.

Moreover, to Māori, the concept of adoption would offer children an *additional* family—not disconnect them from their original one. In fact, whangai children will gain ties and commensurate rights to both families (Bradley, 1997). Likewise, this relationship is completely open; the child knows both sets of parents, and so is not made to relinquish his/her heritage. As such, the traditional Western closed adoption practice, with its complete severing of ties to not only the birth family but to the birth culture and genealogical line, is inconsistent with Māori concepts of whanau and *whakapapa* (genealogical information; pronounced *faw-kaw-paw-paw*) in the extreme. "Secrecy impacts upon a child's well being by disconnecting them from their whakapapa. They lose their identity, sense of belonging, history, connection to land, extended family and ancestors and knowledge of their place in the world" (Dyhrberg, 2001, p. 10). "Adopted children who are denied access to knowledge of their whakapapa through natural parents are deprived of an important aspect of their birthright" (Judge Metge, 1991, as cited in Griffith, 1996, p. 224).

While it would be incorrect to see whangai as simply the Māori version of adoption, it is not unlike the open adoption practices currently promoted by CYFS. Similar to open adoption, whangai also has no legal standing (Dyhrberg, 2001). Nevertheless, like open adoption, it is still regularly practiced, and the influences of the cultural ideology of openness underpinning this practice can be clearly seen in the country's child welfare and family formation laws and policies.

Growth of Intercountry Adoption in New Zealand

In the late 1960s to early 1970s, New Zealand had the distinction of having one of the highest rates of domestic adoptions in the Western world, whereby more than 6 percent of our children were being placed for adoption (Iwanek, 1997). Since then, domestic adoption rates have been steadily declining; where once there were too many children with too few homes to accommodate them, now the number of couples desiring children far exceeds the number of children available for adoption.

A combination of factors are at the heart of the decline: the global rise in infertility rates (responsible for not only the increased demand but also the diminished supply of children); increases in contraception use; legalization of abortions; relaxed social attitudes towards out-of-wedlock births and single-parenting; and finally, the introduction in 1973 of the Domestic Purposes Benefit, allowing unmarried mothers to parent their children, rather than relinquish them as they once did (Scherman, 2010b). All of this translates to fewer children available domestically, leading New Zealanders to look overseas for adoptable children.

However, unlike our Western contemporaries, New Zealanders did not take a strong interest in adopting from overseas until 1990 when local media began airing video footage of over-crowded Romanian orphanages (See Chapter 7; Dominion, 1990). Since then, in addition to providing homes for orphaned and abandoned children, ICA has become the primary means for potential adopters to form their families. Currently in New Zealand, the total number of intercountry adoptions surpasses the number of domestic adoptions taking place each year (Selman, 2006).

Where Open Adoption and Intercountry Adoption Intersect

In 1985 New Zealand passed the Adult Adoption Information Act, bringing post-placement openness to the adoptees and birth parents from formerly closed adoptions (Mullender, 1991a). Around the same time, the Adoption Unit of CYFS began an unlegislated policy of placing children in open adoptive relationships—a practice that continues today (Iwanek, 1997). In 2004, the Human Assisted Reproductive Technologies Act was passed (New Zealand Parliamentary Counsel Office, 2010), legally requiring that donors remain identifiable, and ensuring that donor offspring can access information regarding their genetic origins. These three events strongly reflect the influence of Māori and the value they place on family, culture, and genealogical integrity, all of which underpins New Zealand's strong ideology of openness.

Intercountry adoption, on the other hand, while not precluding the possibility of being structurally open, is more than likely to be closed. This will be due to the distance between countries, language barriers, poor record-keeping in institutions, etc., thereby reducing the chance of making or maintaining ongoing contact with birth family. Does the ostensibly closed nature of ICA make it a practice potentially at odds with New Zealand's openness attitudes? Can intercountry adoptions involve openness? And how open are New Zealand's existing intercountry adoptions? These are the questions central to the issues being raised in this chapter.

The Empirical Evidence

In an effort to see what research has been previously conducted, a thorough search of the literature was undertaken. The intercountry adoption articles were reviewed for any reference to openness. Likewise, the open adoption studies were reviewed for any reference to international contexts. In brief, research on structural openness and contact in adoption seems firmly linked to domestic contexts with one notable exception (i.e., Roby, Wyatt, and Pettys, 2005), discussed below. On the other hand, numerous ICA studies described adoptees 'returning' to the birth country in search of birth family/origins (e.g., Irhammar and Cederblad, 2000; Tieman, van der Ende, and Verhulst, 2008). This after-the-fact openness is seen in the domestic adoption literature as an act of search and reunion; whereas in the international context, it is more often described as a 'heritage' trip (Ponte, Wang and Fan, 2010) since the search involves aspects of culture and nationality that go beyond birth family.

Openness as a form of communication style within adoptive families has also been investigated (Brodzinsky, 2006). A relatively new construct in the adoption literature, *communicative openness,* as it is termed, describes a willingness to explore the meaning in adoption for all involved; to acknowledge and foster birth connections; and to discuss the full range of issues (positive and negative) related to adoptive family life (e.g., Brodzinsky, 2006; Wrobel, Kohler, Grotevant, and McRoy, 2003). Here, several studies were found that discussed communicative openness within an ICA context (e.g., Beckett et al., 2008; Hawkins et al., 2007). In terms of structurally open intercountry adoptions, at the end of the search, only one empirical study was located.

Roby, Wyatt, and Pettys (2005) surveyed 44 USA adoptive families about their experiences in open international adoptions from the Marshall Islands. The adopters were asked about their attitudes towards openness generally; factors that influenced their decisions to go into an open ICA; the development of openness arrangements; and the mechanisms and challenges for maintaining contact with birth families. Across all of the primary areas of inquiry, there was evidence of positive experiences, motivated by concern for birth family, and the desire that the adopted children maintain ties to the birth family and culture. The greatest frustrations for most were related to the decreases in contact that occurred over time, and the challenges arising when trying to maintain contact. Overall, Roby and her colleagues demonstrated that structural openness could be achieved in an ICA context, and while not without its challenges, that it can offer adopters a positive experience (Roby et al., 2005).

Finding no other empirical studies linking structural openness with ICA; knowing the value placed on openness in New Zealand; and guided by the preceding review, my colleague and I embarked on our own investigation into the degree of information-based, communicative, and structural openness being achieved in New Zealand intercountry adoptions (Scherman and Hawke, 2010). Still in progress, initial findings from the 73 adoptive parent surveys collected so far shows that the majority of families are:

- seeking and obtaining identifying information about the adopted children and birth families;
- finding it easy to regularly communicate with their adopted children about a full range of adoption issues;
- attempting to make contact with birth family members still living in the birth country (half of the current sample), often when the children are still young; and for a small percentage (half of those who attempted or approximately 25 percent of sample), actually making face-to-face contact with family members in the birth country.

Unlike the intercountry adoptions in the study by Roby et al. (2005), the New Zealand adoptions began closed, so the greatest challenges for adoptive families was finding, and then making initial contact with, overseas birth families (Scherman and Hawke, 2010). Overall, however, early findings suggest that not only is openness in ICA possible, but that many New Zealand intercountry adoptions are achieving openness across a full range of contexts.

Summary: Where to From Here?

Despite their parallel socio-historical paths, ICA and open adoption have not had much empirical or theoretical consideration as a dual process. The idea of intercountry adoptions also being open adoptions is clearly an idea in its infancy. Adding a layer of complexity is the fact that *openness* is a term with multiple meanings in the adoption literature. It is used to describe adoptive relationships that encompass contact between birth and adoptive family members; shared knowledge about family, history and culture; after-the-fact access to formerly closed records; and more recently, a communication style within the adoptive family. Clearly, openness is a concept that takes many forms, which are not mutually exclusive.

Intercountry adoption, on the other hand, comes with numerous natural barriers to openness including multiple languages, geographic distance, international politics, bureaucratic hurdles, lost or non-existent records, limited technology in sending nations, and poverty (or even family deaths) that may have led to the child being relinquished in the first place—to name only a few of the barriers. In truth, the lack of explicit openness in ICA may be the very reason why some people choose it as a means of family formation.[3] Nevertheless, it seems clear that we are at a point in adoption's long history when we should further broaden our definition of what *open* adoption actually means. Seeing it as a multi-faceted concept that is not restricted to just domestic placements, face-to-face contact, or after-the-fact access to identifying information, is the first step.

Once that happens, we will begin to see that even intercountry adoptions, with all of their hindrances to contact and identifying information, can also be *open.* A fledgling body of work is emerging showing that openness in ICA is already being achieved in creative ways, driven in large part by a generation of conscientious adoptive parents who value not only the birth culture, but the birth family itself (Roby et al., 2005; Scherman and Hawke, 2010). The next step will be to empirically determine how beneficial openness in ICA is for adopted children, as well as for birth and adoptive parents.

---

3 Harré and I found that 18 percent of the 112 adoptive parents in an earlier study reported choosing ICA as a means of avoiding New Zealand's open adoption practices (Scherman and Harré, 2004).

Chapter 23
All Grown Up: Rise of the Korean Adult Adoptee Movement and Implications for Practice

Hollee McGinnis

On a hot day in July 1996, I stood outside of a Korean restaurant in New York City's Korea town, anxiously waiting for people to arrive for the launch of an organization that a few other Korean adoptees and non-adopted Korean-Americans and I had begun planning six months earlier. I was 24-years-old and had grown up with only sporadic contact with other people who had, like me, been adopted from South Korea. My anxiety stemmed both from a concern that no one would show up, but also the realization that there were no visual markers that distinguished a Korean who had been adopted from those who had not. Despite my concerns, we found each other Korean faces with last names like Savasta, Glick, and Nelson—and for the first time approximately 40 Korean-born adult adoptees, adoptive parents, and supporters gathered in the heart of New York City.

The name of the organization, *Also-Known-As, Inc.*, reflected the desire to create a space in which transnational adoptees could explore and embrace their complex identities and give back to the international adoptive community. As a woman who had been adopted from South Korea at the age of three and a half and raised in a white, Irish Catholic family, I personally understood the struggle of trying to understand where I 'fit' within societal constructions of race and biological norms of family. The fact was that I loved and fully embraced my life within my adoptive family; it was the only family I knew. I was a McGinnis; but I knew that I was also-known-as Lee Hwa Yeong, the name my Korean birth father had given me, a constant reminder in the face I saw reflected in the mirror every day.

Recently, *Also-Known-As* celebrated its 15th anniversary, a milestone I could never have imagined that day in July 1996. Today the leaders in the organization are once again young adults in their twenties and early thirties—predominantly adopted from South Korea but also including adoptees from China, Vietnam, and the Philippines—committed to making a difference in the lives of young adoptees through mentorship and post-adoption services, and sustaining an international community of adopted adults. Unlike my generation, many of these young adult adoptees grew up knowing other adoptees, either through summer 'heritage camps' or adoptive parent associations. And most of them affirmed that those experiences had helped them and instilled their desire to provide services to the next generation of transnational adoptees. At the 15th anniversary, a Korean adopted woman came up to me and shared how a South Korean consulate official told her of his surprise to meet adult adoptees. We laughed wryly together, "Yup, we grow up!"

The purpose of this chapter is to describe the rise of the adult Korean adoptee movement since the late 1990s. Adult transnational adoptees from South Korea have been at the forefront of establishing formal organizations, and in absolute numbers represent the largest number of adoptees from any single country in the United States. In addition, a growing body of work, led by adult adopted Koreans, such as Kathleen Ja Sook Bergquist (Bergquist, Vonk, Kim and Feit, 2007), Tobias Hübinette (Hübinette, 2005), John D. Palmer (Palmer, 2010), as well as non-adopted Asian-American scholars, such as Eleana J. Kim (Kim, 2010), Mark C. Jerng (Jerng, 2010) and Mia Tuan and Jiannbin Lee Shiao (Tuan and Shiao, 2011), have recently focused their analysis on adult Korean adoptees. These scholars and others are carving out a new field of Korean Adoption Studies, which recently included the launch of the *Journal of Korean Adoption Studies* in 2009. Finally, implications for intercountry adoption policy and practice will be discussed.

Intercountry Adoptions from South Korea: Brief History

Since the Korean War (1950-1953) over one million South Korean nationals have emigrated abroad, of whom significant portions—15 percent—have been children adopted by families overseas (Hübinette, 2005). According to official statistics from the South Korean Ministry for Health, Welfare, and Family Affairs (MIHWAF) between 1955 and 2008 a total of 163,705 South Korean children were sent to predominantly Western nations for adoption (Kim, 2010). Of this total 109,242 were adopted by USA citizens, with half of those adopted into European families placed in Sweden, Norway, and Denmark. Although intercountry adoptions were initiated in response to the plight of war orphans, many of whom were born to white American soldiers and Korean mothers, the practice continued long after the war as the problem of child abandonment persisted throughout the decades of South Korea's rapid economic development (Hübinette, 2005; Kim, 2010; McGinnis, 2006a).

Policies implemented under the military dictatorships of Park Chung-hee (1961-1979) and Chun Doo-hwan (1981-1987) promoted intercountry adoption as part of a national family planning strategy that included a one child policy, sex education, contraception, legalized abortion (in 1973), and economic incentives to reduce family size (Hübinette, 2005; Sarri, Baik and Bombyk, 1998;). Hence, the decades of the 1970s and 1980s mark the largest cohorts of orphans to leave the country for intercountry adoption (Table 23.1), peaking in 1985 at an all-time high of 8,837 children to leave in a single year (Hübinette, 2004a). While the circumstances for adoption in the 1960s were largely due to child abandonment attributable to poverty and social stigma, by the 1980s and the 1990s the majority of children being relinquished for overseas adoption had been born to single, unwed,

Table 23.1 Total Number of Overseas Adoptions and Circumstances of Relinquishment 1955-2008

	No. of Children	Abandoned (%)	Divorce (%)	Single (%)
1955-1960	3,748			
1961-1970	7,275	55.16	26.91	17.92
1971-1980	48,247	35.77	27.69	36.53
1981-1990	65,321	10.36	17.45	72.19
1991-2000	22,129	1.02	6.53	92.46
2001-2009	16,985	0.21	1.04	98.75

Sources: Kim, 2010: South Korean Ministry for Health, Welfare and Family Affairs, 2009.

middle-class and working-class young women and teenage girls (Hübinette, 2005; Kim, 2010).

Rise of the Korean Adult Adoptee Movement

Although some adoption agencies and adoptive parents' groups hosted picnics and small gatherings for adoptive families in the 1970s, the first associations organized by young adult Korean adoptees occurred in Europe in the 1980s. The first organization, *Adopterade Koreaners Förening* (Association of Adopted Koreans, AKF) was created in 1986 in Stockholm, Sweden followed by two sister organizations established in 1988 in the cities of Malmö and Gothenburg (Kim, 2010). In 1989, the South Korean government sponsored a three-week 'homecoming' program for adoptees from Europe, including the founder of AKF who inspired others to start groups in their respective adoptive countries. In 1991, a group of Korean adoptees in Denmark formed the group *Korea Klubben* and that same year another adoptee started the group *Euro-Korean League* (EKL) in Brussels. In 1993, the Swiss Korean adoptee group, *Dongari*, was created and one year later the first conference to network adoptees in Europe was held in Dusseldorf, Germany (Kim, 2010).

In the USA the first association for Korean young adult adoptees was established in 1991 in Minnesota, which has the highest per capita of adoptees in the USA (Meier, 1998). Following the 1992 Rodney King riots in Los Angeles, a group of adoptees decided to formalize their contacts and established the *Association of Korean-Adoptees-Southern California* (AKA-SoCal) in 1994 (Kim, 2010). In 1996, the organization *Also-Known-As, Inc.* was started in New York City on the east coast and the *Asian Adult Adoptees of Washington* (AAAW) on the west coast, followed by the formation of *Boston Korean Adoptees* (BKA) in 1998 (Kim, 2010). The first conference to network adult Korean adoptees in the USA occurred at the 1997 Global Korean Network meeting in Los Angeles; however, the Gathering of the First Generation of Adult Korean Adoptees (the Gathering) held in September 1999, is largely acknowledged as the beginning of the international adoptee community (Kim, 2010).

The Gathering was sponsored by Holt International Children's Services, the New York based adult adoptee organization *Also-Known-As*, the *Korea Society*, and the *Evan B. Donaldson Adoption Institute*. It was the first conference to bring together nearly 400 adult Koreans who had been adopted between 1955 and 1985, representing over 30 USA states and several European countries (Freundlich and Lieberthal, 2000). This conference was unique in its purpose to provide an opportunity for the first generation of adopted Koreans—who ranged in age from 21 to 50 and who shared the common experience of growing up when assimilation was promoted—to share their experiences and connect as a community. To gain greater insight into the experiences of adult adopted Koreans, the *Evan B. Donaldson Adoption Institute* surveyed participants and published one of the first reports to examine intercountry adoption from the adult adopted persons' perspective (Freundlich and Lieberthal, 2000). Both the USA and South Korean media covered the conference widely, propelling recognition of these pioneers in intercountry adoption and shared experiences as a community.

Since the 1999 Gathering, adopted Koreans in the USA have continued to meet at 'mini-gatherings' throughout the country, new organizations for adopted Koreans have sprung up in several other states, and a plethora of websites, blogs, and Facebook pages connect adopted Koreans throughout the world. A second Gathering, organized by adopted Korean associations in Europe, occurred in Oslo, Norway, in July 2001, and in 2004, a third Gathering of adopted Koreans occurred in Seoul, South Korea. Following the 2004 Gathering in Seoul, a new umbrella organization, *International Korean Adoptee Association* (IKAA), was launched which has sponsored two other Gatherings in Seoul in 2007 and 2010, and is planning for another Gathering in 2013. IKAA's mission is to facilitate the exchange of information and provide a 'permanent forum' for the international network of Korean adoptee associations (IKAA, 2011).

The Return: Korean Adoptees in the Motherland

The first generation of Korean born adult adopted people began to return to their birth country by the late 1970s as participants in motherland tours organized by adoption agencies and associations in South Korea or independently (Hübinette, 2005). As Kim (2010) notes, the South Korean government and adoption agencies were largely surprised and unprepared for adoptees' return. In some respects, adoptees' return to their country of birth was counter intuitive to the notion that overseas adoption would provide a 'better life' and that adoptees would assimilate into their new adoptive families and nations. By the end of the 1980s advertisements submitted by adopted Koreans searching for birth parents began to appear in the South Korean media as a growing number of adoptees began to return to learn more about their birth culture or to search for biological kin (Hübinette, 2005).

In 1993, the Ministry of Health and Welfare began to track the number of adopted Koreans returning to visit their adoption agencies in South Korea; this number more than doubled from 1,236 visitors in 1993 to 2,760 visitors in 2001 (Hübinette, 2004a). In addition, the provision of post-adoption counseling for birth family search—including face-to-face interviews, emails, letters and phone conversations with adoptees, birth and adoptive family members—has risen exponentially from 1,269 in 1995 to 13,068 in 2005 (Overseas Korean Foundation, 2006). By 1995 the South Korean government began to address returning adoptees by including provisions in the Special Act Regarding Adoption Promotion and Procedure for services; in 1996 these services were specified to include cultural education, language, preferential job recruitment, and birth family reunions for returning adoptees (Kim, 2010).

The first adult Korean adoptee association was established in South Korea by the founder of the Brussels adoptee association *Euro-Korean League* (Kim, 2010). This organization was established specifically in response to the nominal services provided by adoption agencies at the time in assisting adoptees in their search for birth family; this group would later become the non-governmental organization *Global Overseas Adoptees' Link* (GOA'L) in 1998 (GOA'L, 2011). In the wake of the 2004 Gathering in Seoul, a new organization was started by a politically-oriented group of adult adoptees living in South Korea called *Adoptee Solidarity Korea* (ASK) who envision "an end to intercountry adoption out of Korea"(ASK, 2011). And in 2007, the organization *Truth and Reconciliation for the Adoption Community of Korea* (TRACK) was formed to advocate for "full knowledge of past and present Korean adoption practices to protect the human rights of adult adoptees, children, and families" (TRACK, 2011).

Adoption Politics and the Specter of the 'Angry Adoptee'

The political activism of adult Korean adoptees residing in South Korea has raised considerable alarm among adoption practitioners. I personally recall being asked by an adoption agency worker in the USA if I could find out what those "angry adoptees" were up to in South Korea. More notable was an email forwarded to a number of Korean adoptee LISTSERVs in 2006 from Children's Home Society of Minnesota. In response to the announcement that a South Korean National Assembly member had proposed legislation to end overseas adoption, the email requested adult adoptees to write letters in support of intercountry adoption.

As the email explained, "One of the driving forces behind this legislation is the fact that Korean officials are only hearing from adopted Korean adults living in Korea currently who had negative adoption experiences and who support ending international adoption in Korea." One adoptee who provided testimony to the National Assembly when the legislation was proposed shared on the listserv, "Incidentally, they had already decided to make that action completely independent of the adoptees—we don't actually have that much power because we are not Korean political constituents!" (Trenka, 2006 Aug 19).

Indeed, the return of adopted Koreans coincided with major social and political changes in South Korea. Specifically under the presidency of Kim Dae-jung (1998-2003), whose democratic election marked the first peaceful transfer of power in South Korean history, overseas adoptees were actively incorporated into Korea's state-sponsored globalization drive (Kim, 2010). During his inauguration in early 1998, Kim Dae-jung, who had met overseas-adopted Koreans during his time in exile as an opposition leader, stated that international adoption would be one of the main issues during his presidency (Hübinette, 2005).

By the late 1990s a number of adult Korean adoptees who had returned to South Korea in the early part of the decade had decided to make South Korea their permanent home. In response, the adult adoptee organization GOA'L sought to meet the needs of this unique expatriate community as well as to be a home base for adoptees returning for shorter stays. When the Korean government proposed legislation that was approved in 1999 that would expand privileges to overseas ethnic Koreans, GOA'L played an active role in ensuring overseas adoptees were included as part of the Korean diaspora (GOA'L, 2001).

The controversial Overseas Koreans Act (OKA) allowed overseas ethnic Koreans—including adoptees who could provide proof of their Korean birth—to obtain a special F-4 visa allowing them to live in the country for up to two years, to work, to make financial investments, to buy real estate, and to obtain medical insurance and pensions—which would greatly assist those adoptees who were trying to make Korea their home (Kim, 2010). Most recently, GOA'L has worked with Korean legislators, some of whom serve on GOA'L's board of directors, to pass the Nationality Law Revision of 2010, which will permit certain individuals—including overseas adoptees—to hold dual citizenship with South Korea (GOA'L, 2011 January).

The expatriate adoptee community in South Korea has been helped greatly by the proliferation of civil society organizations and NGOs that developed in South Korea, as it shifted from an authoritarian to a civilian government in the early 1990s (Kim, 2010). Because adoptees in South Korea were hindered by their lack of Korean language abilities and political standing, groups like GOA'L and other adoptee organizations have relied heavily on partnerships with native Koreans and advocacy NGOs (Kim, 2010). At the same time, by the mid-2000s, South Koreans had become increasingly critical of its overseas adoption program. Specifically, the continued reliance on intercountry adoption has been framed as being contradictory to South Korea's standing as an advanced nation (Kim, 2010). Thus, criticisms raised by adoptees living in South Korea have gained status in light of the discontent among native Koreans, resulting in a 'perfect storm' that threatens Korea's long-standing overseas adoption practice.

International Adoptees Movement: Implications for Practice

The anthropologist Kim (2010), who embedded herself within the Korean adoptee network from 1999 to 2004, provides a cogent analysis of the development and motivation behind the formation of adult Korean adoptee associations. Kim writes, "What I found was that most adoptees were engaged in journeys of self-exploration rather than in activism per se, but that there was a latent tension around the politics of adoption, notably its pros and cons" (2010, p. 23). Kim elegantly illustrates this journey as a relational process between adult adoptee agents and the broader historical, social, and political processes in which their lives have been intimately entwined.

I regard the rise of the adult Korean adoptee movement and adoptee political activism in South Korea as part of the normative process of adoptive identity formation. Grotevant, Dunbar, Kohler and Esau (2000) have defined adoptive identity development as "how the individual constructs meaning about his/her adoption" (p. 381). In essence, the work of adoptive identity formation is coming to understand one simple question: Why was I adopted?

For most adoptees and adoptive parents, the answer begins with the individual: the decision of the birth mother to give up a child born to her. Eventually, though, an adoptee may want to know: Why would a birth mother give up a child? This explanation may come to include her family (e.g., poor), her culture (e.g., stigma toward unwed mothers), or government policy (e.g.. promotion of overseas adoption policy) or geopolitics (e.g., imperialism). Particularly for adoptees who may never be able to meet and ask their biological family why they were given up, cultural, governmental, or geopolitical explanations maybe the only way to understand the circumstances of their relinquishment. For those adoptees who have been reunited with biological family, inconsistencies in the stories provided by adoption agencies and their families raise significant questions on the ethics of their relinquishment.

The self-conscious efforts to form a distinct identity and community of KADs (Korean ADoptee) coalesced with the coming of age of a critical mass of young adoptees and the advent of new technologies such as the Internet. For the early adult adoptee community organizers, the concern was how to establish a community that shared no geographical boundary and what exactly defined a Korean adoptee community (Kim, 2010). Thus, adoptee associations grew out of adoptees' desire to create spaces for adults to socialize and explore what adoption had given them and taken away (McGinnis, 2003). However, the ability to reconcile the losses and gains of adoption are often impeded by laws and practices that do not reflect transnational adoptees' realities: that their lives span two families and two nations (McGinnis, 2006b). GOA'L's press release announcing the passage of the dual citizenship poignantly reflects the fact that the law "will give Korean adoptees the *right* to re-gain their Korean nationality *in addition* to their adoptive nationality" [emphasis added] (GOA'L, 2011 January).

Grotevant and colleagues (2000) write that for adopted people, "most aspects of the adoption did not concern things that the person has chosen" (p. 382). The ability to assert agency and ownership over their own histories and journeys has been at the heart of the adult Korean adoptee movement and thus adoption politics have always been at work. The self-conscious use of the adjective *adult* to modify 'adoptee' within the community has been a form of resistance to the infantilization of adoptees as forever children (Kim, 2010). I also know from my personal relationships with adult adoptee organizers of the 1999 and 2004 Gathering that their effort to show adoptees as successful adults was also a strategy to resist the pathologizing of adopted persons. However, for some adoptees there is a desire to do more to change and inform practice. Some have chosen to become social workers and work at adoption agencies, or have become scholars and are researching adoption, while others have become involved in political activism framing their work within a social justice and human rights perspective.

What then are the implications of the adult Korean adoptee movement for transnational adoption practice? First, it is not limited to adoptees from South Korea. Since the late 1990s young adult adoptees from Vietnam, the Philippines, India, and Colombia—many whom I know personally—have been organizing associations and conferences and connecting through the Internet, and it is highly anticipated that the adoptees from China, who are already connected through strong adoptive parent associations such as *Families with Children from China*, will similarly organize as they come of age. Second, the rise of the adult Korean adoptee movement speaks to the necessity of adoption practices to recognize the life-long impact of adoption and to provide services that meet the life-course needs of the adoptee. Third, adopted adults should be seen as partners in both exposing the benefits and limitations of intercountry adoption and achieving ethical adoption practices. Critical to this aim of ethical adoption practices is contextualizing intercountry adoption within the political, social, and economic processes and structures in which it is embedded. Adoptees, who must negotiate these processes as part of their journey of self-exploration may be able to offer insights into how adoptions, when necessary, may be conducted in the best interest of children—young and old.

Chapter 24
Truth, Reconciliation, and Searching for the Disappeared Children of Civil War: El Salvador's Search and Reunion Model Defined

Carmen Mónico and Karen Smith Rotabi[1]

No Future without Forgiveness was the title of Archbishop Desmond Tutu's (2000) book about the truth and reconciliation process in South Africa. The importance of honesty and forgiveness as a nation moves to build peace and emerge into a more just society is further underscored by the sentiments of Monsignor Juan Gerardi who spoke of the documentation of atrocities in Guatemala stating that it requires a reconstruction of history "… of pain and death, understanding the reasons for it, the why and how" (Recuperación de la Memoria Histórica, 1999, p. xxiii). As a leader, Gerardi understood that the truth was essential in order for a society to democratize and ultimately realize freedom for its citizens. "To open ourselves to truth and to face our personal and collective reality are not options that can be accepted or rejected. They are indispensible requirements for all people and societies that seek to humanize themselves and to be free" (Recuperación de la Memoria Histórica, 1999, p. xxiv).

In addressing trauma in the post-conflict society, a group that is important to consider are the children of the disappeared—those children who became the "living disappeared" (Avery, 2004) as a result of non-relative adoption. These are the children who were forcibly removed from their families during conflict or chaos. The 1948 Genocide Convention (United Nations, 1948a), resulting from crimes against humanity in Nazi Germany, specifically identifies the forcible removal of children from one group to another as a form of genocide (January, 2007).

Even so, forcible removal of children and adoption was repeated in subsequent conflicts, especially in Latin America. During Argentina's Dirty War (1976-1984) a mass group of intellectuals and others determined to be undesirable or dissident were put to death and some of their children were forcibly removed from biological family life and placed into adoptive families (Avery, 2004; Brysk, 1994). Other

1 The authors would like to thank Ester Alvarenga of *Pro-Búsqueda* for her invaluable help with this chapter.

nations share a history of illegal adoptions during conflict, including Guatemala (Recuperación de la Memoria Histórica, 1999) and El Salvador (Sprenkles, Carrillo Hernandez and Villacorta, 2001).

When ICA is mis-used during war and is characterized as "child rescue" (Bergquist, 2009, see Chapter 3), the idea of being "set free" in a truth and reconciliation process requires careful attention to the details. Echoing Gerardi's sentiments, the process includes identifying the causes and consequences of conflict, recording the histories of communities and family life, and determining the details of individual cases. Therefore an essential part of the process involves searching practices that may reunite families with their 'forcefully disappeared' children.

Argentina's Dirty War and History of Child Adoption

The Dirty War of Argentina (1976-1984) is an important starting place in exploring the phenomena of child separation and adoption carried out as an act of reprisal against those resisting the government and military forces during civil conflict (Brysk, 1994; Horwitz and Catherwood, 2006). The seven-year conflict involved grotesque human rights violations including torture, mass murder, and disappearance of tens of thousands of people under the guise of "national security" (Avery, 2004; Brysk, 1994). Some 30,000 people died in the war and among the crimes against humanity were the non-relative adoptions of children born to dissident "pregnant women [who] were detained, tortured, and mistreated until they gave birth. The mothers were killed, while the children were taken and illicitly adopted by friends and relatives of the torturers" (Brysk, 1994, p. 679). President and founding member of the *Abuela's* (grandmother's) activist group Ester Barnes de Carlotto reflects on the crime of child abduction and its psychological impact "… even though the crime of child stealing affects this child … the real family of the child is also a victim with rights… . It is also a crime which affects the whole society" (quoted in Avery, 2004, p. 237). As a result, family search and reunion is an essential part of healing.

Reunion of adoptees with their biological families is emotionally difficult, even in the best of circumstances (Kirton, Feast, and Howe, 2000). In the case of child abduction for intercountry adoption during war, reunion is complicated as it occurs across vast geographic space and further distance that emerges when language and culture must be navigated. Reconstruction of details with varying perspectives on causes and consequences is also a part of the process. Methodologically, it means sorting through the small and known details or 'the truth' retrospectively to determine identity and history on a case-by-case basis, almost like reconstructing a family and community puzzle. An organization dedicated to 'searching' in El Salvador has extensively documented its processes and methodologies of investigation and we turn to their experience to explore the search and reunion process, beginning with a historical overview of war and peace and reconciliation in El Salvador.

El Salvador: Brief History of War, Child Abduction and Adoption, and the Peace Process

A long-standing military dictatorship and widespread human rights violations were pervasive during the 1970s and 1980s and led to mass chaos in this smallest Central American nation (Armstrong and Shenk, 1982). Individuals and families suspected of sympathizing with the opposition became objects of political and military repression and an estimated 75,000 Salvadorans were killed, a half million were internally displaced, and nearly one million Salvadorans sought refuge outside of the country (Studemeister, 2001). By the end of the conflict, the U.N. High Commission on Refugees estimated that about half a million Salvadorans had sought refuge in the USA, and 200,000 had fled to other Central American nations and Mexico, with the total accounting for approximately 20 percent of the country's population (United States Institute for Peace, 2001). An unknown number of forced separations and disappearances of children took place during the war and some children were sent overseas as adoptees to families mainly in the USA, Italy, France, and Honduras (Steiner, 2007).

After a cease fire ended the two-decade conflict in December 1991, the Truth Commission registered a total of 22,000 complaints of gross violations that occurred between January 1980 and July 1991. The 1993 report titled *From Madness to Hope* documents that 85 percent of the registered cases were attributed to government forces and paramilitary groups. Although the Truth Commission did not explicitly identify illegal adoptions in its report, it recommended a thorough investigation of the documented violations of human rights (United States Institute for Peace, 2001).

Investigations with Search and Reunion when Possible: *Pro-Búsqueda*

The Salvadoran Association in Search of Disappeared Children (Asociación Pro-Búsqueda de Niñas y Niños Desparecidos hence forth referred to as *Pro-Búsqueda*) is a small non-government organization which has taken on the charge of documenting and restoring social justice for those affected by illegal adoptions during the civil war. *Pro-Búsqueda* engages in political advocacy, investigations, and the search and reunion process. Their practice for bringing together families after years of separation is an important model, having yielded results in hundreds of cases. Their investigative work, which includes extensive review of documents found at child institutions, interviews, and other documentation sheds light on the separation of children from families and their alternative care during the war years.

Family Separation and Alternative Care Strategies During the War

According to *Pro-Búsqueda* (2002), forcibly disappeared children are those who were removed or kidnapped from their birth families during military operations, via direct assault or other means of coercion, such as threats. There is no exact record of how many military operations took place during the civil war in El Salvador or exactly how many children were disappeared/abducted in this manner. However, from its founding in 1994 through December 2010, *Pro-Búsqueda* has documented 811 cases of disappeared children and helped to locate 363 such individuals (*Pro-Búsqueda*, 2011a).

Pro-Búsqueda has made attempts to document the number of children 'forcefully disappeared' and subsequently reunited at the community level of analysis. For example, the organization documented at least 38 disappeared children during a single military operation; of those cases, only 18 biological children have been found or have been reunited with their birth families. By reviewing those cases, the organization found that in most cases, children who survived the military operations were turned over to the national Red Cross. In turn, Red Cross workers placed them in institutions, often referred to as "orphanages," or in other alternative care arrangements (Sprenkles et al., 2001).

Sprenkles and colleagues (2001) identify the different care options that were exercised and classify those arrangements into five categories: (1) children reared in state or privately run residential institutions, (2) children adopted *de facto* through traditionally non-legal agreement by the adoptive family to care for the child, (3) children fostered within El Salvador, (4) children taken to a military base and raised there, and sometimes militarized and conscribed to serve as soldiers, and (5) children adopted within El Salvador or internationally. The most common formal care was placement into residential institutions (Sprenkles et al., 2001). As many as 50 such organizations operated during the civil war (*Pro-Búsqueda*, 2004) and they functioned without government oversight.

With limited documentation, reconstructing a child's history is difficult. Many of the children brought to institutions carried no personal documents and, as a result, they were registered with fictitious identities (falsified names, dates of birth, and record of parents) in order to attend school and to have access to health care (*Pro-Búsqueda*, 2009). Smolin (2006) calls this change of identity "child laundering" (see Chapter 18) and the term "paper orphans" (*Terre des Hommes and UNICEF, 2010*), has also been used to capture the idea of new personal documents (e.g., birth certificates) being constructed. This loss of identity is obviously a serious human rights abuse related to identity and citizenship (Lister, 2003) and to the inherent right to family and kinship. However, given the nature of war and the need to respond to child welfare needs, the practice of 'creating' an identity is not entirely surprising. This practice likely originated innocently in the early days of conflict out of the need for efficiency, rather than as a conspiracy to traffic children for intercountry adoption. However, in time, a child trafficking dynamic emerged in El Salvador and, at some point, unscrupulous lawyers, corrupt military institutions and justice system, and government officials actively engaged in falsification of identity documentation for ICA. In its case investigations, *Pro-Búsqueda* uncovered an articulated chain, including the aforementioned false documentation, for the abduction and trafficking of children for ICA (*Pro-Búsqueda*, 2002).

The intersection with child trafficking assertion is bolstered by *Pro-Búsqueda's* (2002) documented evidence of lawyers having charged upwards to $10,000 US dollars for the adoption of a child—an exceptionally high sum of money given the extreme poverty in El Salvador. Also, there is evidence of 'casas de engorde' (fattening houses) and foster homes that were specifically set-up for the purpose of adoption, including ICA (*Pro-Búsqueda*, 2004; Steiner, 2007).

The compilation and review of documentation and testimony led to the first reunion facilitated by *Pro-Búsqueda* in 1994. Taking place in Guarjila, a community that was war-torn due to its perceived involvement in and support for resistance forces, the reunion event marked an important shift in the lives of reunified birth parents and disappeared children (*Pro-Búsqueda*, 2002). It was inevitably an emotional moment in the peace and reconciliation process, bringing justice and healing to individuals, families, and communities. Since then, many reunions have taken place, shedding more light on the atrocities of war.

The story of Suzanne, an adoptee living in the USA and originally from the village of Morazán, is one example. As a result of her reunion, Suzanne learned from her biological family that she had been 'snatched' by soldiers from a hammock at her family's home in the rural village. With falsified identity documents, Suzanne became a disappeared child who was taken to a home as she awaited adoption to the USA (Steiner, 2007). As an adult, Suzanne was reunited with her biological family after a long search and reunion process facilitated by *Pro-Búsqueda*. At the time of reunion, she learned the details of her abduction and her biological family's distress and desire to be reunited (Steiner, 2007).

Search and Reunion Activities of *Pro-Búsqueda*: A Seven-Stage Process

In this chapter we identify the seven-stage model used by *Pro-Búsqueda*. The model was constructed using previous reports, research,[2] and discussions with *Pro-Búsqueda* staff. After the model was identified, the *Pro-Búsqueda* staff verified its accuracy.

2 The research initiative "Care and Protection of Separated Children in Emergencies" (CPSC) of Save the Children Alliance assisted *Pro-Búsqueda* in the development of a study involving interviews, surveys and focus group discussion among reunited families. The project summarizes *Pro-Búsqueda's* work between 1994 and 2002 and resulted in two published books. One is a collection of birth parent testimonies involved in a search for their children and the other book brings together stories of young adult adoptees now reunited with their birth families.

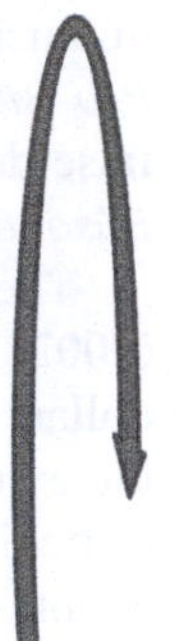

1. Case intake (birth parents or other sources)
2. Gather testimonies of child loss/abduction event (recorded interviews)
3. Investigate context (oral history, legal and other historical documents)
4. Follow leads (interviews with those directly involved in event context)
5. Follow more leads (interviews with relevant higher authorities)
6. Report to birth relatives on findings of investigations
7. If successful, provide psychosocial services to families prior and after reunion; if not, start again at stages 2 or 3

Figure 24. 1 Pro-búsqueda Search-and-Find Approach

Figure 24.1 depicts the search process that *Pro-Búsqueda* uses as a case management model. It is a dynamic and a collaborative approach to investigative work.

The first step of the search-and-find approach that *Pro-Búsqueda* developed involves case intake, similar to a process found in any case management and human services organization (Rothman and Sager, 1997). In most cases, birth parents provide an account of the events that led to their child's disappearance, including preliminary clues about the potential whereabouts of the child. Information may also come from third parties such as relatives, members of the community, non-profit organizations, public officials, and other sources. Then, gathering information of greater depth for case assessment (Rothman and Sager, 1997), *Pro-Búsqueda* documents testimonies about the event related to abduction. This step involves conducting more intensive interviews, including recording of such interviews, and other document collection if and when information is available. The sources of information vary according to the case, opportunity, and contextual factors.

With more in-depth information, *Pro-Búsqueda* engages in the investigation of the context or social environment in which the abduction took place. Staff again uses methods of oral history, historical documentation, obtaining legal documents, and any other evidence that may be available as the case unfolds. One data point, when possible, is the use of DNA testing, which is carried out in collaboration with international organizations specializing in forensic evidence (*Pro-Búsqueda*, 2011a). Tissue samples are collected to confirm genetic relationships. As data are collected, new leads are developed, and evidence is strengthened with new layers of information that may generate sufficient leads to finding the disappeared child, or may lead to a dead end for some cases. A case status report is produced and this is communicated to the searching family or relatives. The communication of disappointing news to members of the adoption triad requires sensitivity in debriefing a traumatized individual or family.

In the event that the search is successful, assessment for reunion readiness is made and a reunion is organized by *Pro-Búsqueda* staff. As a part of this assessment and prior to the reunion meeting, *Pro-Búsqueda* staff begins to provide services to assist the affected members of the triad, especially biological families and adoptees, so that they receive adequate and professional support for this emotional process. In most cases, this process involves other organizations which may have collaborated in the investigation, and other individuals involved in the search, including members of the community.

If the disappeared child is not found during a first round of investigations, staff members gather more information about the case. In continuing cases, psychosocial services are still provided to those involved in and most affected by the search. This process is ended when the whereabouts of the disappeared child are determined and a satisfactory degree of 'closure' is brought to the case.

A Case Example of *Pro-Búsqueda:* Search and Reunion

While she was living in a refugee camp in Honduras during the civil war, Francisca tried to obtain information about her missing daughter Elsy (*Pro-Búsqueda*, 2002). She reported the case to the International Committee of the Red Cross, the Catholic Church and the U.N. High Commissioner of Refugees with no results. When she returned to her hometown of El Rancho in Chalatenango, El Salvador, Francisca continued to search for Elsy. She checked with distant-relatives and inquired with non-governmental organizations. During the search process, Francisca met Mayda, who was also in search of her baby son, Juan Carlos. They shared the fact that both missing children had disappeared during the same military operation and they formed a powerful bond in mutual support. They approached a local priest, Father Jon Cortina and he promised to help find their missing children. That promise became a reality several years later when a delegation of the Truth Commission visited Guarjila soon after the Peace Accords (*Pro-Búsqueda*, 2002).

The Healing and Reunion Experience of Francisca and Mayda

Through their testimony to the Truth Commission, both Francisca and Mayda had a therapeutic experience (*Pro-Búsqueda,* 2002). Their hearts were lightened and they felt "… almost happy. The pain that had kept them captive for ten years was alleviated, and they felt that by taking this step they had officially initiated the search for their children" (p. 43, translated by Mónico). The case of Elsy was included in the final report of the Truth Commission (*Pro-Búsqueda*, 2002). A month after the Truth Commission report was released, Francisca and Mayda submitted formal claims in the Court of First Instances in Chalatenango, eventually with the support of the Human Rights Commission in El Salvador. They also presented a similar claim to the General Attorney's Office (*Pro-Búsqueda*, 2002).

Only years after the Peace Accords, Francisca and Mayda located their children with the help of *Pro-Búsqueda*. The disappeared children had been part of a group of six children "rescued" by the Salvadoran Red Cross after a military operation in Los Ranchos in 1982, and taken to the Aldeas Infantiles (Children's Communities), where they remained until found by their families. The reunion of Francisca and Mayda with their biological children (young adults at the time of reunion) involved at least 1,000 people, and it was occasion of celebration not only for their individual families but for the entire community who fully supported the search process (*Pro-Búsqueda*, 2004).

Beyond Reunions: *Pro-Búsqueda*, Legal Actions, and Policy Advocacy

Since inception, *Pro-Búsqueda* has become known and respected for its work "culling through orphanage and adoption records, collecting witness testimony, and using DNA tests to confirm suspected matches" and reunite families (Popkin, 2001, p. 13). *Pro-Búsqueda* has also collaborated with specialized organizations to exhume the dead bodies of suspected disappeared children to carry out DNA testing (*Pro-Búsqueda*, 2011a).

From an advocacy prospective, *Pro-Búsqueda* has also been strategic in bringing the facts forward as evidence to address system failures. For example, documentation gathered about the disappeared sisters Ernestina and Erlinda Serrano Cruz led to this case being favorably resolved in the Inter-American Human Rights Court (Inter-American Commission on Human Rights [IACHR], 2001). *Pro-Búsqueda* has brought several other claims to both national and international courts, further highlighting problems in the process. Since October 2007, *Pro-Búsqueda* has filed Habeas Corpus recourses (constitutional right of protection of rights and liberty) for 14 cases in national courts. The IACHR has indicated that this is the ideal recourse for resolving cases of disappeared children and also to improve the country's judicial system (*Pro-Búsqueda*, 2011b). The policy advocacy work of *Pro-Búsqueda* has resulted in major steps forward when, during the 137 Period of Sessions of the IACHR (November, 2009), the Salvadoran government committed to establishing a special commission to search for the disappeared children including the creation of a publically-funded DNA bank to support investigations. In January 2010, on occasion of the Peace Accords anniversary, besides asking for forgiveness for human right violations, the government announced the establishment of a commission to investigate the disappeared children. It was also announced publically, in El Salvador, that a DNA database would be developed and that an identified government office would be responsible for oversight of the database and related processes (*Pro-Búsqueda,* 2011c). At the time of this writing, this mandate is unfunded and the promise is unfulfilled.

Conclusion

On January 16, 2010, on occasion of the anniversary of signing the Peace Accords in El Salvador, Salvadoran President Mauricio Funes declared: "I ask forgiveness of those who have been unable to move beyond their grief because they do not know where their loved ones lie" (Funes, 2010, p. 1). Father Cortina, a catalyzing force in *Pro-Búsqueda's* work, always said that forgiveness and searching for loved ones was a requirement for national reconciliation in El Salvador (*Pro-Búsqueda*, 2011d). These sentiments and actual acknowledgement of the crimes against humanity in the nation, specifically the forcible removal of children from their families, are critically important in healing the emotional wounds. Today *Pro-Búsqueda* recognizes that the Salvadoran government has not yet demonstrated due diligence in bringing about truth and reconciliation, and as a result a 'historical debt' or moral and material reparation to affected families is long overdue (*Pro-Búsqueda*, 2011d). *Pro-Búsqueda* investigations continue on and case outcomes continue to confirm that the human rights violations and abuses of power were gross; these included using ICA as a separation and alternative care strategy for children of those persecuted and massacred.

As war and violence continue to plague our existence globally, there will inevitably be more instances of such abuses and requirements for ethical alternative care strategies (United Nations, 2009). The Hague Convention on Intercountry Adoption (The Hague Conference on Private International Law, 1993) holds some promise, but as Bergquist points out in chapter 3, the agreement does not explicitly address disaster and war conditions. El Salvador's neighboring country, Guatemala, as well as other post-conflict countries, like Vietnam, serve as important reminders of the vulnerabilities related to war, both during armed conflict and post-conflict (see Chapters 3, 5, and 9).

Searches for families are very complex, especially when the search is global, involving families in other nations. The discoveries about the circumstances under which children were abducted certainly stir anger, anxiety and despair, as well as joy and happiness in the case of successful reunions. The truth touched not only the families involved but entire communities and the nation.

The search and find process of *Pro-Búsqueda* is presented to both describe the practice, including social work case management intake and assessment, and also to identify the practice as essential in truth and reconciliation. The activities of *Pro-Búsqueda* serve as a model and the organization's general approach may be applied to other cultural contexts and circumstances of family-child separation and reunion. While this diffusion of intervention has not yet been tested, it is a worthwhile endeavor.

An example opportunity for diffusion is in neighboring Guatemala, where post-conflict adoptees are beginning searches for their biological families. In Guatemala the search and find activities require the same careful attention to community and family context as well as to traumatic experiences of biological families. At this time in Guatemala search activities are largely carried out by for-profit businesses. Search activities do not include attention to formal case management, including the psychological or healing dimensions of the process. This approach has inherent problems because an unknown number of Guatemalan adoptees will be faced with difficult realties, ranging from extreme poverty to issues of child sales and abduction. The lessons from *Pro-Búsqueda's* attention to the psychological process are critically important as services for these adoptees emerge. Also, the non-profit nature of *Pro-Búsqueda*, funded by donations and grants, is the ethically sound and just way forward.

Chapter 25
Looking to the Future

Judith L. Gibbons and Karen Smith Rotabi

The authors of this book express a variety of viewpoints on the issue of intercountry adoption of children. The majority, however, endorse the pragmatic approach—that ICA is acceptable, but that there must be additional safeguards to eliminate abuses and improve standards (Masson, 2001). Several authors describe how policies about child welfare and intercountry adoption are shaped by underlying pervasive beliefs about what is best for children (see Chapters 2 and 6). The actual practices of intercountry adoption, especially as social workers are involved, are outlined as well (see especially Chapters 3, 4, 6, 7, 9, 10, 12, 20, 21, 22, and 24). Sending countries' perspectives are represented in Chapters 7, 8, 9, 10, 11, and 12. Finally, the outcomes for internationally adopted children are addressed in Chapters 13, 14, 15, 16, 17, and 23. In intercountry adoption research, the voices of those most affected by adoption—the adoption triad—are rarely heard. A strength of this book is that the perspectives of adult adoptees (see Chapters 17 and 23), and especially birth parents (see Chapters 8 and 11) are highlighted, as a corrective to their frequent silencing.

The sincere differences of opinion about ICA are brought into sharp contrast in the debate between Elizabeth Bartholet and David Smolin, eloquently articulated in Chapter 18. The dilemma is clearly revealed. Who would pit the unparalleled physical, emotional, and cognitive catch-up of children placed internationally against their cultural and racial identities? Does the well-being of a single child outweigh the needs of many? How should the wishes of birth families be incorporated into the child's "best interests" principle? Does the authorization and instantiation of intercountry adoption inevitably promote child trafficking? Those questions are impossible to answer.

The wisdom of Solomon would be needed to ethically resolve the heart-breaking case of a child allegedly abducted in Guatemala and adopted to the USA in 2008. Recently a Guatemalan court ordered that the adoptive parents return the six-year-old girl because the adoption was fraudulent (Perez, 2011). It appears that the adoptive parents did not know their child had been illegally adopted at the time of the adoption decree, and it is unlikely that the Guatemalan court ruling will be enforced in the United States (Kirpalani and Ng, 2011). But determining what is in the best interests of the child in this situation is problematic, and this case may well be a test of the "best interests" value system for child custody determinations in fraudulent ICAs.

An issue that is oft-repeated within these chapters is that abject poverty in countries of origin is a root cause of intercountry adoption. Article 25 of the Declaration of Human Rights states:

> Everyone has the right to a standard of living adequate for the health and well-being of himself and of his family, including food, clothing, housing and medical care and necessary social services, and the right to security in the event of unemployment, sickness, disability, widowhood, old age or other lack of livelihood in circumstances beyond his control. Motherhood and childhood are entitled to special care and assistance. All children, whether born in or out of wedlock, shall enjoy the same social protection (United Nations, 1948b).

The argument that freedom from poverty is a basic human right has been made by scholars as well (e.g., Mbonda, 2004). Mbonda further argues that globalization requires a broad perspective on the alleviation of poverty, not just leaving that task to individual developing countries. "Poverty is a global or international problem, and ... there is a global duty to root it out, making it possible for everyone to enjoy the right to non-poverty" (p. 287). A human rights perspective for practical steps that can be taken to eliminate poverty are listed by Leisinger (2004), and Amnesty International has placed poverty on its agenda for social change (Khan, 2009). All cultures consider children as precious and valuable treasures. Given adequate resources many extended families and communities could and would step in to care for unparented children, making finding an outside alternative family for a child unnecessary.

Within these chapters are multiple suggestions for improving the intercountry adoption process through changes at all levels. Attention to ethics is especially important for the field of social work because during some historical periods social workers have been complicit in the unwarranted removal of children from their families. For example, in Canada during the 1960s, social workers were known as "baby snatchers" for their roles in scooping Aboriginal babies from their homes (Faith, 2010). This represents an unfortunate reality throughout the history of social work in which often well-meaning professionals intervene in impoverished children's lives and make "best interests" decisions counter to family support and the basic human right of a child to remain in her family group, retain his family name, culture, and in the case of ICA—citizenship and often language rights. The removal of children often ignores the strengths of biological family and kinship systems and, in some cases, even exploits women and children living in poverty (Hollingsworth, 2003). The critical and difficult decision to terminate parental rights must be made with due diligence and adherence to human rights before, during, and after adoption (Roby, 2007; see Chapter 4).

Recommendations for change and reform of the ICA system globally include training social workers and other actors for this sensitive work on both sides of the ICA transaction. The capacity building approach also includes providing more effective service regulation in both sending and receiving nations, specifically financial transparency to counter graft and corruption in many impoverished nations (see Chapters 7 and 8). Greater cooperation between interacting nations must occur to set ranges for reasonable and professional fees for ICA services, as required by the Hague Convention (Hague Conference on International Private Law, 1993, 2008b). Also, when laws are broken, prosecution must be swift with appropriate penalties for child trafficking, not only to send a strong message to unscrupulous entrepreneurs, but also to remove bad actors from the ICA process (Bromfield and Rotabi, 2012; see Chapters 3, 4, 5, 18, and 19).

System strengthening strategies to deal with poor practices must include a sharpening of the adoption agency accreditation process, as per HCIA requirements, including more aggressive and transparent investigation of complaints (Rotabi and Gibbons, 2012; see Chapter 21). Evaluation of the social and economic forces influencing activities of agencies in high resource nations and their partners and/or intermediaries in low resource nations is essential (see Chapter 6). The inherent market pressures in this transaction must be considered and ultimately accountability requires active assessment by and collaborative engagement between Central Authorities as oversight entities. Adequate domestic laws and strong policy and administrative procedures must support Central Authorities to intervene as necessary (Chapters 4, 5, and 18).

Biological family support is an absolute imperative. Using a rights-based approach, children may be considered "at risk" for ICA, rather than being viewed as "available" for ICA (Fronek and Cuthbert, 2012; see Chapter 21). If and when adoption is considered, appropriate birth parent counseling and processes of informed consent are essential (Wiley and Baden, 2005; see Chapter 11) to preserve the rights of the entire family system (see Chapter 6). Sensitivity to open adoptions is an area for improvement and the model in New Zealand is important for global consideration as we strive for more ethical adoptions (see Chapter 22). Growth in this area will require us to consider how the Hague Convention helps or hinders open adoptions and the barriers identified need to be considered to determine if they are truly necessary to prevent child trafficking.

Services for prospective adoptive families include better screening of prospective families and assessment. SAFE home studies hold promise for improvement in this practice area (Chapters 20 and 23), especially in preventing later adoption disruption (see Chapter 21) Pre-placement activities include training families to effectively integrate a child or children into the family system, tailored to meet the specific needs of the internationally adopted child; these might include issues of race, racism, and transracial parenting (see Chapter 16). Pre-placement training is essential for families adopting older and institutionalized children, who may have social, emotional, educational, and medical special needs (see Chapters 13, 14, and 15). Adoption agencies must be required to improve their post-placement services to support families, most especially during adoption disruption and ultimately to prevent adoption dissolution (see Chapter 23).

Although it is impossible to predict the future with certainty, we see several trends in the intercountry adoption arena. In Chapter 1, Selman has documented the decline in the numbers of intercountry adoptions. We predict that the numbers will continue to decline as more countries sign and implement the Hague Convention, and some nations initiate moratoriums on ICA. Several countries of origin are striving to institute more effective child welfare strategies within their borders (see Chapters 4, 7, 8, and 10). In addition, intercountry adoption is increasingly seen as a flawed response for the humanitarian 'rescue' of children during emergencies (see Chapter 3; Doyle, 2010).

We also predict that social workers within countries of origin will explore a full range of options for unparented or separated children, taking into account children's individual needs and circumstances. They might engage in family preservation efforts, using processes such as Family Group Conferencing (see Chapters 9 and 10). Governments or NGOs might more often provide support to family members or close friends caring for orphans. However, we expect that efforts will come under critical scrutiny as no option is a panacea for all unparented or separated children (see Chapter 19; Cheney, 2010). Using the results of research on what makes institutions work for children (e.g., James, 2011), small residential facilities with appropriate caregiver-child ratios might be good placements for some children. And foster care and domestic adoption will be part of the full range of services available, as the sheer number of orphaned and vulnerable children globally can only be served by the development of additional family-setting placements.

In the future there are likely to be additional safeguards to prevent the trafficking of children under the guise of intercountry adoption. Many of the recommendations, such as creating financial transparency, limiting cash transfers, instituting controls over humanitarian giving, and providing non-biased counseling for birth mothers, have been mentioned previously.

A nascent trend that may continue is that of increasing openness in intercountry adoption. Openness appears to confer advantages for all members of the adoption triad (Roby, Wyatt, and Pettys, 2005). Although openness may be difficult to achieve given geographic and cultural distance and language differences, there is the likelihood that greater efforts will be made. There is evidence that most birth mothers would prefer some contact with their relinquished children (Chapters 4 and 11; Bos, 2007; Roby and Matsumura, 2002), and as they are more empowered they may demand a continuing relationship with their children.

As the numbers of healthy infants available for intercountry adoption continue to decline, there may be a greater proportion of special needs adoptions and adoptions of older children (See Chapter 1). For social workers, psychologists, pediatricians, and others invested in ICA, this is a critical area for practice advances that emphasize family support before, during, and after adoption. Greater emphasis must be placed on 'after' adoption, even though those services may be costly to provide. Adoption agencies that are not currently able to provide or effectively link families to high quality post-adoption support services should either make programmatic improvements or cease engagement in ICA.

We predict that the demand for young healthy babies will continue to grow (Goodwin, 2010) and that markets for enhanced fertility technologies and global surrogacy will create new challenges related to rights, responsibilities, and regulation (Carney, 2010; Pande, 2009; Rotabi and Bromfield, 2010). Whether it is ICA, surrogacy, or some other form of building families, issues related to exploitation and self-determination of marginalized people will persist as problems, while global markets continue to define humanity (Green, 2010).

There is an emerging movement in the study of child development to acknowledge and foster children's agency (Dockett and Perry, 2011). That is, instead of viewing children as helpless and vulnerable (a portrayal that may not serve their needs, see Dubinsky, 2010), researchers and practitioners are acknowledging that children have "the power to make decisions that impact on self and others and [to] act on them" (Sancar and Severcan, 2010, p. 277). Within the Hague Convention, children's agency is recognized in two clauses from Chapter II, Article 4 that discuss eligibility for adoption: (1) "consideration has been given to the child's wishes and opinions," and (2) "the child's consent to the adoption, where such consent is required, has been given freely" (Hague Conference on Private International Law, 1993). However, to our knowledge there are no specific guidelines or suggestions as to how and under what circumstances children might express their wishes about intercountry adoption. The *Guide to Good Practice* notes only that Norway requires consent for intercountry adoption for children over the age of 12, and recommends that during implementation of the Hague countries address "how [they are] to take into consideration the child's wishes and opinions" (Hague Conference on Private International Law, 2008b, Annex 8-3).

In order to explore the possibilities for child agency in intercountry adoption, we need to turn to two areas in which children's wishes have been taken into account (1) in assent for research participation (Mason and Hood, 2011) and (2) in custody disputes (Raitt, 2007). In both of those areas, it is clear that even very young children can express their preferences. For example, Anthy, aged 4, turned away and avoided a researcher who came to a pre-school to recruit participants. By her nonverbal behavior she indicated her dissent (Dockett and Perry, 2011). Critical issues include presenting information in a form that children can understand, responding to children's verbal and nonverbal expressions of their wishes, and developing a trusting relationship with the child (Bell, 2002; Dockett and Perry, 2011).

With respect to custody cases, a judge said, "I have been amazed at the way in which children can articulately state their preference" (Raitt, 2007, p. 4). Another judge reported that he had obtained useful information about children's wishes from children as young as four-years-old (Raitt, 2007). Yet another judge said, "ultimately you can't force a child, you can't have a child taken kicking and screaming" (Raitt, 2007, p. 7). Yet that is exactly what foster mothers report—that children are often torn away crying when they are handed over to international adoptive parents (Gibbons, Wilson, and Schnell, 2009). Social workers should be at the forefront in working competently and sensitively with children to understand children's own wishes on adoption, and to assist with child-family adjustment when adoption is the chosen path (O'Loughlin and O'Loughlin, 2011). Countries of origin might mandate visits by prospective adoptive parents, allowing children to choose their parents (or choose not to be adopted) rather than the other way around. This would have to take place in a very guarded manner to avoid the 'child shopping' dynamics that emerged in problematic nations like Romania (Post, 2007; see Chapter 10). Nevertheless, taking into account the child's wishes might be a way out of the conundrum of the Guatemalan child illegally adopted to the USA. If she were re-introduced to her biological parents and then offered a choice, what would she choose?

Of course, the future will bring even more difficult issues for consideration. For example, with more openness and increased children's agency, could children choose to return to their country of origin? When adoptees return, often finding extreme poverty, how might we help them cope and develop long-term relationships with biological families (Hayes and Kim, 2007)? When there is openness, what sort of financial transactions are appropriate and ethical? For example, adoptive families and adoptees have found deeply impoverished birth families in nations like Guatemala and Cambodia. Confronted with the human need to give, adoptive families sometimes offer to replace sub-standard or slum housing with a concrete block home or to provide monies/scholarships to educate other children in the biological family. While this is an obvious human connection and the nature of reciprocity, it does complicate the issue of financial transactions and the prevention of child sales. When a biological family receives a new home or other resources in an impoverished area, the message is clear to other community members who may be enticed to also relinquish a child for ICA. This is currently a concern in Ethiopia where gift giving has been documented during and after ICA (Rotabi, 2010b; see Chapter 8).

There is a disagreement about just how many orphaned and vulnerable children there are in the world (see Chapter 18), but we can all agree that millions of children are suffering and the number is growing in the context of HIV/AIDS (Roby and Shaw, 2006; Zimmer and Dayton, 2005). Intercountry adoption is an important and life-changing intervention for a small number of those children and it should not be dismissed, even with the tremendous reform challenges identified. However, as an intervention, we must remember that ICA is not truly the answer to child and family needs on a global basis.

That child welfare systems must be strengthened is a position that we can all agree upon. The disagreements will be in *how* to move forward, including how to find loving and healthy environments for children that take into account their individual needs and the cultural and contextual conditions of their lives. Social workers are well-positioned to effect changes in child welfare, given their roles as policy makers and implementers. That they should take up those challenges, jumping into the fray with energy and sensitivity, is the fervent wish of these authors.

References

26 orphans escape harm in earthquake, all get adopted. (2010, April 6). *Huffington Post.* Retrieved from http://www.huffingtonpost.com/2010/02/04/26-orphans-escape-harm-in_n_449357.html.

Abebe, T. (2009). Orphanhood, poverty and the care dilemma: Review of global policy trends. *Social Work and Society*, 7(1), 70-85.

Abebe, T. and Aase, A. (2007). Children, AIDS and the politics of orphan care in Ethiopia: The extended family revisited. *Social Science and Medicine*, 64, 2058-69.

Abrahamson, P. (1999). The welfare modeling business. *Social Policy and Administration*, 33, 394-415.

Abrams, T. (2010, April 9). Artyom Savelyev: To Russia without love. *Huffington Post.* Retrieved from http://www.huffingtonpost.com/tamar-abrams/artyom-savelyev-to-russia_b_532621.html.

Abreu, D. (2009). Baby-bearing storks: Brazilian intermediaries in the adoption process. In D. Marre and L. Briggs (eds), *International Adoption: Global Inequalities and the Circulation of Children* (pp. 138-53). New York, NY: New York University Press.

Accreditation of Agencies and Approval of Persons under the Intercountry Adoption Act of 2000, 22 C.F.R. pt. 96. (2000). Retrieved from http://ecfr.gpoaccess.gov/cgi/t/text/text-idx?c=ecfr;sid=fe1c7d6d975740e4baa264038fb3c436;rgn=div5;view=text;node=22%3A1.0.1.10.52;idno=22;cc=ecfr.

Adams, G. (2010, January 19). Adoption agencies warned off Haiti's orphans. *The Independent.* Retrieved from http://www.independent.co.uk/news/world/americas/.

Adoption History Project. (2007). *International Adoptions.* Retrieved from http://darkwing.uoregon.edu/~adoption/topics/internationaladoption.htm.

Adoptee Solidarity Korea. (2011). *About ASK.* Retrieved from http://www.adopteesolidarity.org/indexH.html.

Agence France-Presse. (2005, January 3). *France may Streamline Adoption of Tsunami Orphans.* Retrieved from http://www.laborlawtalk.com/archive/index.php/t-12711.html.

Agence France-Presse. (2009, May 29). L'Arche de Zoé inculpée pour 'escroquerie.' [Zoe's Ark charged with 'fraud'] *Le Figaro.* Retrieved from http://www.lefigaro.fr/flash-actu/2009/05/29/01011-20090529FILWWW00504-l-arche-de-zoe-inculpee-pour-escroquerie.php.

Agence France-Presse. (2010a, September 13). Arche de Zoé: Renvoi devant le tribunal. *Le Figaro.* Retrieved from http://www.lefigaro.fr/flash-actu/2010/09/14/97001-20100914FILWWW00572-arche-de-zoe-renvoi-devant-le-tribunal.php.

Agence France-Presse. (2010b, October 22). Six membres de l'Arche de Zoé renvoyés en process [Six members of Zoe's Ark returned to process]. *Le Monde*. Retrieved from http://www.lemonde.fr/afrique/article/2010/10/22/six-membres-de-l-arche-de-zoe-renvoyes-en-proces_1430109_3212.html.

Agency for International Development. (1975). *Operation Babylift Report.* Retrieved from http://www.uoregon.edu/~adoption/archive/AIDOBR.htm.

Albers, L.H., Johnson, D.E., Hostetter, M.K., Iverson, S., and Miller, L.C. (1997). Health of children adopted from the former Soviet Union and Eastern Europe. Comparison with preadoptive medical records. *Journal of the American Medical Association*, 278, 922-4.

Aldeas SOS and Red Latinoamericana de Acogimiento Familiar. (2010). *Informe Latino Americano situación de la niñez sin cuidado parental o en riesgo de perderlo en America Latina: Contextos, causas y respustos* [Report on the situation of children without parental care or at risk of losing it in Latin America: Context, causes and responses]. Retrieved from http://www.relaf.org/www.relaf.org/index_engl.html.

Alexander, P. (2006). Globalisation and new social identities: A jigsaw puzzle from Johannesburg. In P. Alexander, M.C. Dawson and M. Ichharam (eds), *Globalisation and New Identities: A View from the Middle* (pp. 13-66). Johannesburg: Jacana Media.

Alexander, R. and Curtis, C.M. (1996). A review of empirical research involving the transracial adoption of African American children. *Journal of Black Psychology*, 22, 223-35.

Altstein, H. (1984). Transracial and inter-country adoptions: A comparison. In P. Sachdev (ed.), *Adoption: Current Issues and Trends* (pp. 195-203). London: Butterworth.

Altstein, H. and Simon, R.J. (1991). *Intercountry Adoption: A Multinational Perspective.* New York, NY: Praeger.

Ambrose, M. and Coburn, A. (2001). *Report on Intercountry Adoption in Romania.* Retrieved from USAID website: http://pdf.usaid.gov/pdf_docs/PNACW989.pdf.

American Broadcasting Company News. (2005, December 1). Heroic young girl tells of her child porn ordeal. *ABC News Online.* Retrieved from http://abcnews.go.com/Primetime/LegalCenter/story?id=1364110.

Amoateng, A.Y., Heaton, T.B., and Kalule-Sabiti, I. (2007). Living arrangements in South Africa. In A.Y. Amoateng and T.B. Heaton (eds), *Families and Households in Post-apartheid South Africa: Socio-demographic Perspectives* (pp. 43-59). Cape Town: Human Sciences Research Council. Child, Youth, Family and Social Development Research Programme.

Andersen, T.M. (ed.). (1999). *Social Implications for Institutionalised Children.* Oslo, Norway: University of Oslo.

Andersson, G. (1986). The adopting and adopted Swedes and their contemporary society. In R. Hoksbergen (ed.), *Adoption in Worldwide Perspective* (pp. 23-36). Lisse: Swets and Zeitlinger.

Archdiocese of Guatemala. (1999). *Guatemala Never Again!* London: Catholic Institute for International Relations CHR.

Armstrong, J. (2005, October 1). A Canadian haven for black U.S. black babies. *The Globe and Mail,* p. A7.

Armstrong, R. and Shenk, J. (1982). *El Salvador: The Face of Revolution.* Boston, MA: South End Press.

Aronson, J. (2000). Medical evaluation and infectious considerations on arrival. *Pediatric Annals*, 29, 218-23.

Aronson, J. (2002). HIV in internationally adopted children. Joint Council for International Children's Services. Washington, D.C.

Associated Press. (2005, January 7). Agencies warn against speedy adoptions of tsunami orphans. Retrieved from http://www.family-source.com/cache/282315/idx/0.

Associated Press. (2007, December 21). Chad kidnap trial begins for French aid workers. *MSNBC.* Retrieved from http://www.msnbc.msn.com/id/22361183/.

Associated Press. (2008a, July 24). DNA tests confirm first stolen baby in troubled Guatemalan adoption system. *Los Angeles Times.* Retrieved from www.msnbc.msn.com/id/25821096/ns/world_news-americas/t/dna-tests-confirm-first-stolen-guatemalan-baby/.

Associated Press. (2008b, July 24). Stolen Guatemalan baby found just before adoption by U.S. couple. *Fox News*. Retrieved from http://www.foxnews.com/story/0,2933,390044,00.html.

Associated Press. (2010a, April 7th). Haitian orphans' quick entry to US to end. *Institute for Justice and Democracy in Haiti.* Retrieved from http://www.signonsandiego.com/news/2010/apr/07/haitian-orphans-quick-entry-to-us-to-end/.

Associated Press. (2010b, April 28). Lesser charge for missionary. *New York Times.* Retrieved from http://query.nytimes.com/gst/fullpage.html?res=9F01E3D61F38F93BA15757C0A9669D8B63.

Associated Press. (2010c, June 6). U.S. missionary convicted in orphanage case is freed. *New York Times.* Retrieved from http://www.nytimes.com/2010/05/18/world/americas/18briefs-HAITI.html.

Astley, S.J. and Clarren, S.K. (1996). A case definition and photographic screening tool for the facial phenotype of fetal alcohol syndrome. *Journal of Pediatrics*, 129, 33-41.

Atkinson, W.L., Pickering, L.K., Schwartz, B., Weniger, B.G., Iskander, J.K., and Watson, J.C. (2002, February 15). General recommendations on immunization: Recommendations of the Advisory Committee on Immunization Practices (ACIP) and the American Academy of Family Physicians (AAFP). *MMWR Recommendations and Reports*, 51, 1-35.

Australian Intercountry Adoption Network. (n.d.). *International Adoption Statistics*. Retrieved from http://www.aican.org/statistics.php?region=0andtype=birth.

Avery, L. (2004). A return to life: The right to identify Argentina's "living disappeared." *Harvard Women's Law Journal*, 27, 235-58.

Avitan, G. (2007). Protecting our children or our pride? Regulating the intercountry adoption of American children. *Cornell International Law Journal*, 40, 489.

Babb, L.A. (1999). *Ethics in American Adoption*. New York, NY: Praeger.

Baden, A.L. (2002). The psychological adjustment of transracial adoptees: An application of the Cultural–Racial Identity Model. *Journal of Social Distress and the Homeless*, 11, 167-91.

Baden, A.L. (2010, July). *Forcing the Conversation: Racial and Cultural Issues in Adoption*. Keynote lecture presented at the third International Conference on Adoption Research (ICAR3), Leiden, Netherlands.

Baden, A.L. and Steward, R.J. (2000). A framework for use with racially and culturally integrated families: The cultural-racial identity model as applied to transracial adoption. *Journal of Social Distress and the Homeless*, 9, 309-37.

Bagley, C. (1993). *International and Transracial Adoptions: A Mental Health Perspective*. Aldershot: Avebury.

Bagley, C. and Young, L. (1980). The long-term adjustment and identity of a sample of inter-country adopted children. *International Social Work*, 23, 16-22.

Bailey, J.D. (2009). Expectations of the consequences of new international adoption policy in the US. *Journal of Sociology and Social Welfare*, 36(2), 169-83.

Bainham, A. (2003). International adoption from Romania—Why the moratorium should not be ended. *Child and Family Law Quarterly*, 15, 223-36.

Bajak, F. (2010, February 21). AP finds all Baptist group's 'orphans' had parents. *Associated Press*. Retrieved from http://www.blnz.com/news/2010/02/15/Power_outage_delay_release_Americans_4229.html.

Bajak, F. and Dodds, P. (2010, January 31). Haiti detains Americans taking kids across border. *Associated Press*. Retrieved from http://www.chron.com/disp/story.mpl/world/6844384.htmlhttp://abcnews.go.com/International/wireStory?id=9709437.

Baker, J. and Bouillon, J. (1995). *Josephine*. New York, NY: Marlowe.

Bakermans-Kranenburg, M.J., Van IJzendoorn, M.H., and Juffer, F. (2008). Earlier is better: A meta-analysis of 70 years of intervention improving cognitive development in institutionalized children. *Monographs of the Society for Research in Child Development*, 73(3), 279-93.

Balcom, K., (2011). *The Traffic in Babies: Cross-border Adoption and Baby-selling between the United States and Canada, 1930-1972*. Toronto: University of Toronto Press, Scholarly Publishing Division.

Balcom, K. and Dubinsky, K.B. (2005, October 13). Babies across borders; Canadians like to think that adopting Black U.S. infants is an act of rescue. Others call it 'kidnap.' Let's outgrow both terms. *The Globe and Mail*, p. A21.

Ball, P., Kobrak, P., and Spirer, H.F. (1999). State violence in Guatemala, 1960-1996: A quantitative reflection. *Advancing Science Serving Society Science and Human Rights Program.* Retrieved from http://shr.aaas.org/guatemala/ciidh/qr/english/index.html.

Balsari, S., Lemery, J., Williams, T.P., and Nelson, B.D. (2010). Protecting the children of Haiti. *New England Journal of Medicine*, 362, e25.

Baran, A. and Pannor, R. (1990). Open adoption. In D.M. Brodzinsky and M.D. Schechter (eds), *The Psychology of Adoption* (pp. 316-31). New York, NY: Oxford University Press.

Barth, R.P. and Berry, M. (1988). *Adoption and Disruptions: Rates, Risks and Responses.* New York, NY: Aldine de Gruyter.

Barth, R.P. and Miller, J.M. (2000). Building effective post-adoption services: What is the empirical foundation? *Family Relations*, 49, 447-55.

Bartholet, E. (1991). Where do Black children belong? The politics of race matching in adoption. *University of Pennsylvania Law Review*, 139, 1163-711.

Bartholet, E. (1993a). Family bonds: Adoption and the politics of parenting. Boston, MA: Houghton Mifflin.

Bartholet, E. (1993b). International adoption: Current status and future prospects. *The Future of Children*, 3(1), 89-103.

Bartholet, E. (2000). Whose children? A response to Professor Guggenheim. *Harvard Law Review*, 113, 1999-2008.

Bartholet, E. (2005). International adoption. In L. Askeland (ed.), *Children and Youth in Adoption, Orphanages and Foster Care* (pp. 107-30). Westport, CT: Greenwood Publishing Group Inc.

Bartholet, E. (2007). International adoption: Thoughts on the human rights issues. Buffalo *Human Rights Law Review*, 13, 151-203.

Bartholet, E. (2009). *Inter-American Commission on Human Rights Organization of American States Hearing on Human Rights of Unparented Children and Related International Adoption Policies.* Retrieved from http://www.law.harvard.edu/programs/about/cap/ia/testimonyfullnov09.pdf.

Bartholet, E. (2010a). International adoption: The human rights position. *Global Policy*, 1(1), 91-100.

Bartholet, E. (2010b). International adoption: The human rights issues. In M.B. Goodwin (ed.). *Baby Markets: Money and the New Politics of Creating Families* (pp. 94-117). New York, NY: Cambridge University Press.

Bartholet, E. (2010/11). International adoption: A way forward. *New York Law School Law Review*, 55, 687-99.

Bartholet, E. (2011). Ratification by the United States of the Convention on the Rights of the Child: Pros and cons from a child's rights perspective. *Annals of the American Academy of Political and Social Science*, 633, 80-101.

Barth, R.P. and Miller, J.M. (2000). Building effective post-adoption services: What is the empirical foundation? *Family Relations*, 49, 447-55.

Bascom, B.B. and McKelvey, C.A. (1997). *The Complete Guide to Foreign Adoption: What to Expect and How to Prepare for your New Child.* New York, NY: Pocket Books.

Beck-Gernsheim, E. (2011). Families in a globalized world. In R. Jallinoja and E.D. Widmer (eds), *Families and Kinship in Contemporary Europe: Rules and Practices of Relatedness* (pp. 192-200). Basingstoke, Hampshire and New York, NY: Palgrave MacMillan.

Beckett, C., Castle, J., Groothues, C., Hawkins, A., Sonuga-Burke, E., Colvert, E., Rutter, M. (2008). The experience of adoption: The association between communicative openness and self-esteem in adoption. *Adoption and Fostering*, 32(1), 29-39.

Becket, C., Maughan, M. Rutter, M., Castle, J., Colvert, E., Groothues, C., Sonuga-Barka, E.J.S. (2006). Do the effects of early severe deprivation on cognition persist into early adolescence? Findings from the English and Romanian adoptees study. *Child Development*, 77, 696-711.

Beckstrom, J.H. (1972). Adoption in Ethiopia ten years after the civil code. *Journal of African Law*, 16, 145-68.

Behr, E. (1991). *Kiss the Hand you Cannot Bite: The Rise and Fall of the Ceausescus.* New York, NY: Villard Books.

Bell, M. (2002). Promoting children's rights through the use of relationship. *Child and Family Social Work*, 7, 1-11.

Bellinger, D.C., Stiles, K.M., and Needleman, H.L. (1992). Low-level lead exposure, intelligence and academic achievement: A long-term follow-up study. *Pediatrics*, 90, 855-61.

Bellock, P. and Yardley, J. (2006, December 20). China tightens adoption rules for foreigners. *New York Times.* Retrieved from www.nytimes.com/2006/12/20/us/20adopt.html?emandex=1166850000anden=015f107024876060and ei=5087.

Benoit, T.C., Jocelyn, L.J., Moddemann, D.M., and Embree, J.E. (1996). Romanian adoption: The Manitoba experience. *Archives of Pediatrics and Adolescent Medicine*, 150, 1278-82.

Berástegui, B. (2003). *Las adopciones internacionales truncadas y en riesgo en la comunidad de Madrid* [Broken-down and at-risk international adoptions in Madrid]. Madrid: Consejo Económico y Social.

Bergquist, K. (2009). Operation Babylift or Babyabduction? Implications of the Hague Convention on the humanitarian evacuation and 'rescue' of children. *International Social Work*, 52, 621-33.

Bergquist, K., Vonk, M.E., Kim, D.S., and Feit, M.D. (2007). *International Korean Adoption: A Fifty-year History of Policy and Practice.* New York, NY: Haworth Press.

Berry, M. and Barth, R. (1990). A study of disrupted adoptive placements of adolescents. *Child Welfare*, 69, 209-25.

Bhargava, V. (2005). *Adoption in India: Polices and Experiences.* New Delhi, India: Sage Publications.

Birth planning methods … the toughest in history. (2009). Retrieved from http://laiba.tianya.cn/laiba/CommMsgs?cmm=16384andtid=270962866013968812 9andref=commmsgs-next-topic.

Bistransky, D. (2010). A guide for judges in outgoing cases under the Hague Adoption Convention. *Judges' Page Newsletter.* Retrieved from http://www.casaforchildren.org/site/c.mtJSJ7MPIsE/b.5720885/k.4071/Hague_Convention_Requirements.htm.

Bohman, M. (1970). *Adopted Children and their Families: A Follow-up Study of Adopted Children, their Background, Environment and Adjustment.* Stockholm, Sweden: Propius.

Bohman, M. and Sigvarsson, S. (1980). Negative social heritage. *Adoption and Fostering*, 3, 25-31.

Boivin, M.J. and Giordani, B. (1993). Improvements in cognitive performance for schoolchildren in Zaire, Africa, following an iron supplement and treatment for intestinal parasites. *Journal of Pediatric Psychology*, 18, 249-64.

Bond, P. (2006). Reconciliation and economic reaction: Flaws in South Africa's elite transition. *Journal of International Affairs*, 60(1), 141-56.

Borgman, R. (1982). The consequences of open and closed adoption for older children. *Child Welfare*, 61, 217-26.

Bornstein, D. (2004). *How to Change the World: Social Entrepreneurs and the Poser of New Ideas.* New York, NY: Oxford University Press.

Bos, P. (2007). Once a mother. Relinquishment and adoption from the perspective of unmarried mothers in south India. (Doctoral dissertation, Nijmegen University). Retrieved from http://dare.ubn.kun.nl/bitstream/2066/73643/1/73643.pdf.

Bowlby, J. (1982). *Attachment and Loss. (Vol. 1): Attachment* (2nd ed.). New York, NY: Basic Books.

Bowring, B. (1999). The children of Russia: Victims of crisis, beneficiaries of international law. *Child and Family Law Quarterly*, 11, 125-38.

Bradley, J. (1997). Kei konei tonu matou [We are still here]. In K. Sprengers (ed.), *Adoption and Healing: Proceedings of the International Conference on Adoption and Healing, Wellington, Aotearoa New Zealand, 1997* (pp. 37-44). Wellington: New Zealand Adoption Education and Healing Trust.

Breuning, M,. and Ishiyama, J. (2009). The politics of intercountry adoption: Explaining variations in the legal requirements of sub-Saharan African countries. *Perspectives on Politics*, 7, 89-101.

Briggs, L. (2009). Somebody's children. *Utah Law Journal*, 2. Retrieved from http://epubs.utah.edu/index.php/ulr/issue/view/23/showToc.

BBC News. (2000, November 14). *Rwanda Accuses Italy over Orphans.* Retrieved from http://news.bbc.co.uk/1/hi/world/africa/1022875.stm.

BBC News. (2001, April 12). Rwanda's tug-of-war children. Retrieved from http://news.bbc.co.uk/1/hi/programmes/crossing_continents/africa/1271890.stm.

BBC News. (2007, October 29). *Profile: Zoe's Ark.* Retrieved from http://news.bbc.co.uk/2/hi/europe/7067374.stm.

Brodzinsky, D.M. (1990). A stress and coping model of adoption adjustment. In D.M. Brodzinsky and M.D. Schechter (eds), *The Psychology of Adoption* (pp. 3-24). Oxford: Oxford University Press.

Brodzinsky, D.M. (2006). Family structural openness and communication openness as predictors in the adjustment of adopted children. *Adoption Quarterly*, 9(4), 1-18.

Brodzinsky, D.M. (2008). *Adoptive Parent Preparation Project. Phase 1: Meeting the Mental Health and Developmental Needs of Adopted Children.* New York, NY: Evan B. Donaldson Adoption Institute.

Brodzinsky, D.M., Schechter, M.D., and Henig, R.M. (1992). *Being Adopted: The Lifelong Search for Self.* New York, NY: Anchor Books.

Brodzinsky, D.M., Singer, L.M., and Braff, A.M. (1984). Children's understanding of adoption. *Child Development*, 55, 869-78.

Bromfield, N.F. and Rotabi, K.S. (2012). Human Trafficking and the Haitian Child Abduction Attempt: Policy Analysis and Implications for Social Workers and NASW. *Journal of Social Work Values and Ethics*, 9, 13-25.

Brooks, G. (1998). *The International Law on the Rights of the Child.* Leiden: Martinus Nijhoff Publishers.

Brottveit, Å. (1999). *"Jeg ville ikke skille meg ut!" Identitetsutvikling, ekstern kategorisering og etnisk identitet hos utenlandsadopterte fra Colombia og Korea* [Identity development, external categorization and ethnic identity among foreign-born adoptees from Colombia and Korea]. Universitetet i Oslo: Diakonhjemmets høgskolesenter.

Brysk, A. (1994). *The Politics of Human Rights in Argentina: Protest, Change, and Democratization.* Stanford, CA: Stanford University Press.

Bunkers, K.M. (2006). Guatemala: Fostering children prior to adoption. *Early Childhood Matters*, 105, 42-4.

Bunkers, K.M. (2010). *Informal Family-based Care Options: Protecting Children's Rights? A Case Study of Gudifecha in Ethiopia.* Geneva, Switzerland: Institut Universitaire Kurt Bosh and Universite de Fribourg.

Bunkers, K.M., Groza, V., and Lauer, D. (2009). International adoption and child protection in Guatemala: A case of the tail wagging the dog. *International Social Work*, 52, 649-60.

Bureau, J.J., Maurage, C., Bremond, M., Despert, F., and Rolland, J.C. (1999). Children of foreign origin adopted in France: Analysis of 68 cases during 12 years at the University Hospital Center of Tours. *Archives Françaises de Pédiatrie*, 6, 1053-8.

Burrow, A., Tubman, J. and Finley, G. (2004). Adolescent adjustment in a nationally collected sample: Identifying group differences by adoption status, adoption subtype, developmental stage and gender. *Journal of Adolescence*, 277, 267-82.

Buser, P.J. (1993). Habeas corpus litigation in child custody matters: An historical mine field. *Journal of American Academic Matrimonial Lawyers*, 11, 1-42.

Campion, M.A., Palmer, D.K., and Campion, J.E. (1997). A review of structure in the selection interview. *Personnel Psychology*, 50, 655-702.

Cantwell, N. (2003). Intercountry adoption. A comment on the number of 'adoptable' children and the number of persons seeking to adopt internationally. *Judge's Newsletter*, 5, 70-72.

Cardarello, A. (2009). The movement of the mothers of the Courthouse Square: "Legal child trafficking," adoption and poverty in Brazil. *Journal of Latin American and Caribbean Anthropology*, 14, 140-61.

Carlberg, L.K. (2006). The agreement between the United States and Vietnam regarding cooperation on the adoption of children. *Indiana International and Comparative Law Review*, 17, 119-25.

Carlberg, M. and Nordin Jareno, K. (eds), (2007). *Internationellt adopterade i Sverige. Vad säger forskningen?* [International adoptees in Sweden. What does research say?]. Stockholm: Gothia förlag.

Carlson, R. (2011). Seeking the better interests of children with a new international law of adoption. *New York School Law Review*, 55(1), Retrieved from http://papers.ssrn.com/sol3/papers.cfm?abstract_id=1788685.

Carney, S. (2010, March/April). Inside India's rent-a-womb business: Gestational dormitories, routine c-sections, quintuple embryo implants. Brave new world? Nope, Surrogacy tourism. *Mother Jones*, 69-73.

Carozza, P.G. (2003). Subsidiarity as a structural principle of international human rights law. *American Journal of International Law*, 97, 38-79.

Casa Alianza, Myrna Mack Foundation, Survivors Foundation, the Social Movement for the Rights of Children and Adolescents, Human Rights Office of the Archbishop of Guatemala and the Social Welfare Secretariat. (2007). *Adoptions in Guatemala: Protection or business?* Guatemala City, Guatemala: Author.

Casey Family Services. (2003). *Promising Practices in Adoption-competent Mental Health Services.* New Haven, CT: The Casey Center for Effective Child Welfare Practice.

Cavada, J., Gibault, C., and de Boer-Buquicchio, M. (2008). *A European Adoption Procedure.* Retrieved from http://www.coe.int/t/DC/Files/Source/FS_children_adoption_en.doc.

Cederblad, M., Irhammar, M., Mercke, A.M., and Norlander, E. (1994). *Identitet och anpassning hos utlandsfödda adopterade ungdomar* [Identity and adjustment among foreign-born adopted youth]. Lund University: Institutionen för barn- och ungdomspsykiatri.

Center for Constitutional Rights. (n.d.). Nguyen Da Yen, et al. v. Kissinger. Retrieved from http://ccrjustice.org/ourcases/past-cases/nguyen-da-yen%2C-et-al.-v.-kissinger.

Central Intelligence Agency. (2008). *World Factbook.* Retrieved from http://indexmundi.com/g/g.aspx?c=gtandv=24.

Central Intelligence Agency. (2011). *World Factbook.* Retrieved from https://www.cia.gov/library/publications/the-world-factbook/index.html.

Chang, C. (Producer and Director). (2008). *Long Wait for Home* [DVD]. Retrieved from http://www.lovewithoutboundaries.org/lwfh/index.html.

Chapman, D.S. and Zweig, D.I. (2005). Developing a nomological network for interview structure: Antecedents and consequences of the structured selection interview. *Personnel Psychology*, 58, 673-702.

Charlton, A. and von Derschau, V. (2007, December 12) French Group's methods raise questions. *Associated Press.* Retrieved from http://www.usatoday.com/news/world/2007-12-12-3137155544_x.htm.

Cheney, K. (2010). Expanding vulnerability, dwindling resources: Implications for orphaned futures in Uganda. *Childhood in Africa*, 2, 8-15. Retrieved from http://www.afrchild.ohio.edu/CAJ/articles/CheyneyCAJ2010.pdf.

Cheney, K. (2011, February). *Whose "Best Interests"? Revisiting African Orphan Circulation and Children's Rights in the Age of HIV/AIDS.* Paper presented at the meeting of the American Anthropological Association Child Interest Group, Charleston, SC.

Child Advocacy Program. (2008). *International Adoption Policy Statement.* Retrieved from http://www.law.harvard.edu/programs/about/cap/ia/iapolicystatementreport.pdf.

Child Welfare Information Gateway. (2004). *U.S. Children Placed for Adoption with Non-U.S. Citizens.* Retrieved from www.childwelfare.gov/pubs/four.cfm.

Child Welfare Information Gateway. (2010). *Court Jurisdiction and Venue for Adoption Petitions.* Retrieved from http://www.childwelfare.gov/systemwide/laws_policies/statutes/jurisdiction.cfm.

Child Welfare League of America. (2005, January 24). *CWLA Statement on the Adoption of Tsunami Orphans.* Retrieved from https://www.cwla.org/newsevents/tsunami050124.htm.

Child, Youth, and Family. (2007). *Adoption in New Zealand: Some Questions and Answers.* Wellington, New Zealand: Author.

ChildONEurope. (2009). *International Adoption in the EU: Report to the European Parliament.* Florence: Istituto degli Innocenti. Retrieved from http://www.scribd.com/doc/22984065/International-Adoption-in-the-European-Union.

Children taken by Zoe's Ark go home. (2008, March 15). *Gulf Times.* Retrieved from http://www.gulf-times.com/site/topics/printArticle.asp?cu_no=2anditem_no=207287andversion=1andtemplate_id=39andparent_id=21.

Children's Home Society and Family Services. (n.d.) *About Us.* Retrieved from http://www.chsfs.org/about-us/about-us.

China's sex ratio at birth: From disbelief to solving the problem. (2006). *Population Research*, 1.

Chou, S. and Browne, K. (2008). The relationship between institutional care and the international adoption of children in Europe. *Adoption and Fostering*, 32(1), 40-48.

Chou, S., Browne, K., and Kirkaldy, M. (2007). Intercountry adoption on the internet. *Adoption and Fostering*, 31(2), 22-31.

Coakley, J.F. and Berrick, J.D. (2008). In a rush to permanency: Preventing adoption disruption. *Child and Family Social Work*, 13, 101-12.

Cobelens, F.G.J., van Schothorst, H.J., Wertheim-Van Dillen, P.M.E., Ligthelm, R.J., Paul-Steenstra, I.S., and van Thiel, P.P.A.M. (2004). Epidemiology of hepatitis B infection among expatriates in Nigeria. *Clinical Infectious Diseases*, 38, 370-76.

Cohen, J. (1988). *Statistical Power Analysis for the Behavioral Sciences* (2nd ed.). New York, NY: Academic Press.

Cojocaru, S. (2008a). Child rights based analysis of children without parental care or at risk of losing parental care in Romania. *Revista de Cercetare si Interventie Sociala*, 24, 41-72.

Cojocaru, S. (2008b). Child protection in Romania after the fall of communism: Challenges for the development of community social services. *International Journal of Environmental Studies*, 55, 515-27.

Colen, S. (1995). 'Like a mother to them': Stratified reproduction and West Indian childcare workers and employers in New York. In F. Ginsburg and R. Rapp (eds), *Conceiving the New World Order* (pp. 78-102). Berkeley, CA, Los Angeles, CA and London: University of California Press.

Comisión Internacional Contra la Impunidad en Guatemala. (2010). *Informe sobre actores involucrados en el proceso de adopciones irregulares en Guatemala a partir de la entrada en vigor de la Ley de Adopciones Decreto 77-2007* [Report on actors involved in the irregular adoption process in Guatemala after the entry into force of the Adoption Law 77-2007]. Guatemala. Retrieved from www.cicig.org/uploads/documents/adopciones_presentacion.pdf.

Congreso de la República de Guatemala. (2007a). *Decreto Número 31-2007.* Retrieved from http://www.lexdelta.com/pdf/5848.pdf.

Congreso de la República de Guatemala. (2007b). *Decreto Número 77-2007.* Retrieved from http://www.cna.gob.gt/doc/58267%20DECRETO%20DEL%20CONGRESO%2077-2007.pdf.

Consejo Nacional de Adopciones. (2011). *Comunicado sobre el plan piloto* [Communication about the pilot plan]. Retrieved from http://www.cna.gob.gt/portal/adopcionesinterncionales.

Consejo Nacional de Adopciones (n.d.). *La adopción, otra forma de hacer familia* [Adoption, another way of making a family]. Retrieved from http://www.cna.gob.gt/portal/.

Consortium for Children. (2008). *Final Report to Department of Health and Human Services, Administration for Children and Families, Administration on Children Youth and Families.* San Rafael, CA: Author.

Convention on the Rights of the Child. *UNICEF.* Retrieved from http://www.unicef.org/crc/.

Cook, L. and Snider, S. (2010, March 17). Haitian kids allegedly taken by Americans reunited with families. *CNN.* Retrieved from http://articles.cnn.com/2010-03-17/world/haiti.baptists.children_1_laura-silsby-haitian-officials-orphanage?_s=PM:WORLD.

Corbett, S. (2002, June 16). Where do babies come from? *New York Times*, p. E42.

Corcoran, A. (1991). Opening of adoption records in New Zealand. In E. Hibbs (ed.), *Adoption: International Perspectives* (pp. 223-7). Madison, CT: International Universities Press.

Corley, C. (Reporter) and Ludden, J. (Host). (2005). Increasing number of black American children being adopted by families from other countries [Radio program episode]. In J. Ludden (Host), *All Things Considered.* Boston: WBUR. Retrieved from http://www.wbur.org/npr/4726046/foreign-adoption-of-african-american-babies-grows.

Costantino, R. (2006). Femicide, impunity, and citizenship: The old and new in the struggle for justice in Guatemala. *The Journal of Mujeres Activistas en Letras y Cambio Social*, 6(1), 107-21.

Council on Accreditation. (2007). *Hague Accreditation and Approval Standards.* New York, NY: Author. Retrieved from http://www.coanet.org/files/Hague_Accreditation_and_Approval_Standards.pdf.

Court Appointed Special Advocates for Children. (2010, January). International solutions for connecting US foster care children with families. *Judges' Page Newsletter*. Retrieved from http://www.casaforchildren.org/site/c.mtJSJ7MPIsE/b.5720841/k.1EB7/January_2010.htm.

Cowan, A.B. (2004). New strategies to promote the adoption of older children out of foster care. *Children and Youth Services Review*, 26, 1007-20.

Crea, T.M. (2009). Brief Note: Intercountry adoptions and domestic home study practices: SAFE and the Hague Adoption Convention.. *International Social Work*, 673-8.

Crea, T.M., Barth, R.P., and Chintapalli, L. (2007). Home study methods for evaluating prospective resource families: History, current challenges, and promising approaches. *Child Welfare*, 86, 141-59.

Crea, T.M., Barth, R.P., Chintapalli, L.K., and Buchanan, R.L. (2009a). Structured home study evaluations: Perceived benefits of SAFE vs. conventional home studies. *Adoption Quarterly*, 12, 78-99.

Crea, T.M., Barth, R.P., Chintapalli, L., and Buchanan, R.L. (2009b). The implementation and expansion of SAFE: Frontline responses and the transfer of technology to practice. *Children and Youth Services Review*, 31, 903-10.

Crea, T.M., Griffin, A., and Barth, R.P. (2011). The intersection of home study assessments and child specific recruitment: The performance of home studies in practice. *Children and Youth Services Review*, 33, 28-33.

Cross, R. (2005, April 15). *Operation Broken Hearts: Transcript of Richard Cross Video.* Lecture given at Samford University, Birmingham, Alabama. Retrieved from http://cumberland.samford.edu/files/rushton/Richard_Cross_transcript.pdf.

Crum, W. (2010). Foster parent parenting characteristics that lead to increased placement stability or disruption. *Children and Youth Services Review*, 32, 185-90.

Crumley, B. (2007, October 29). Charges made in Darfur 'Adoptions.' *Time.* Retrieved from http://www.time.com/time/world/article/0,8599,1677231,00.html.

Cruz, N. (2011). An open letter from Norma Cruz to Senator Mary Landrieu. Retrieved from http://pear-now.blogspot.com/2011/05/open-letter-from-norma-cruz-to-senator.html.

Cruz, N., Smolin, D., Dilworth, A., Rotabi, K.S., and DeFilipo, T. (2011, April 4). *Stolen Children: Illegal Practices in Intercountry Adoption and the Need for Reform*. Invited presentation for the Human Rights Impact Litigation Clinic of the American University Washington College of Law, Washington, DC.

Curtis, C.M. (1996). The adoption of African American children by Whites: A renewed conflict. *Families in Society*, 77, 156.

Curtis, A., Ridzon, R., Vogel, R., McDonough, S., Hargreaves, J., Ferry, J., andOnorato, I. (1999). Extensive transmission of Mycobacterium tuberculosis from a child. The *New England Journal of Medicine*, 341, 1491-5.

Dalen, M. (1995). Learning difficulties among inter-country adopted children. *Nordisk Pedagogik*, 15(4), 195-208.

Dalen, M. (2001). School performances among internationally adopted children in Norway. *Adoption Quarterly*, 5(2), 39-58.

Dalen, M. (2005). International adoptions in Scandinavia: Research focus and main results. In D.M. Brodzinsky and J. Palacios (eds), *Psychological Issues in Adoption* (pp. 211-31). Westport, CN: Praeger.

Dalen, M., Lindblad, F., Odenstad, A., Rasmussen, F., Vinnerljung, B., and Hjern, A. (2008). Educational attainment and cognitive competence in adopted men—A study of international and national adoptees, siblings and a general Swedish population. *Children and Youth Services Review*, 30, 1211-19.

Dalen, M. and Rygvold, A.L. (2006). Educational achievement in adopted children from China. *Adoption Quarterly*, 9(4), 45-58.

Dambach, C. and Baglietto, C. (2010). *Haiti: "Expediting" Intercountry Adoptions in the Aftermath of a Natural Disaster.* Geneva: ISS, Retrieved from http://www.iss-ssi.org/2009/assets/files/Haiti%20ISS%20final-%20foreword.pdf.

Daniels, K. and Taylor, K. (1993). Secrecy and openness in donor insemination. *Politics and the Life Sciences*, 12, 155-70.

Davenport, D. (2004, October 27). Born in America, adopted abroad. *The Christian Science Monitor.* Retrieved from http://www.csmonitor.com/2004/1027/p11s01-lifp.html.

Deacon, B. (2000). *Globalization and Social Development: The Threat to Equitable Development.* Retrieved from United Nations Research Institute for Social Development website: http://www.unrisd.org/unrisd/website/document.nsf/0/815BC5D09E74323A80256B67005B740A?OpenDocument.

Deacon, B. (2007). *Global social policy and governance.* London: Sage.

Defence for Children International, and International Social Services. (1991). *Romania: The Adoption of Romanian Children by Foreigners.* Geneva: DCI and ISS.

Degeling, J. (2010a). *Intercountry Adoption Technical Assistance Programme: Report of Mission to Nepal, 23-27 November 2009*. Hague: Hague Conference on Private International Law. Retrieved from http://www.hcch.net/upload/wop/nepal_rpt09.pdf.

Degeling, J. (2010b, September). *The Special Commission on the 1993 Hague Intercountry Adoption Convention*. Presented at the Intercountry Adoption Summit, Waterloo University, Canada. Retrieved from http://adoptionsummit.uwaterloo.ca/documents/TheSpecialCommissionmeetingonthe1993HagueIntercountryAdoption.pdf.

Deletant, D. (1995). *Ceauşescu and the Securitate: Coercion and Dissent in Romania, 1965-1989*. Armonk, NY: M.E. Sharpe, Inc.

De Luca, P. (2009, November). *Results of the European Commission Study of Adoption in Europe*. Presentation at Joint Council of Europe and European Commission Conference, Strasbourg. Retrieved from http://www.coe.int/t/dghl/standardsetting/family/adoption%20conference/Presentation%20DE%20LUCA.pdf.

Demick, B. (2009, September 20). Some Chinese parents say their children were stolen for adoption. *Los Angeles Times*. Retrieved from http://articles.latimes.com/2009/sep/20/world/fg-china-adopt20.

Dennis, W. (1973). *Children of the Creche*. New York, NY: Appleton-Century-Crofts.

Department of Homeland Security. (2010). *Secretary Napolitano Announces Humanitarian Parole Policy for Certain Haitian Orphans*. Retrieved from http://www.dhs.gov/ynews/releases/pr_1263861907258.shtm.

Diamond-Smith, N., Luke, N., and McGarvey, S. (2008). "Too many girls, too much dowry": Son preference and daughter aversion in rural Tamil Nadu, India. *Culture Health and Sexuality*, 10, 697-708.

Dickens, J. (1999). Protecting the rights of the child in Romania: Children's rights perspectives on Romania's 1997 child care reforms. *European Journal of Social Work*, 2, 139-50.

Dickens, J. (2002). The paradox of inter-country adoption: Analyzing Romania's experience as a sending country. *International Journal of Social Welfare*, 11, 76-83.

Dickens, J. (2009). Social policy approaches to intercountry adoption. *International Social Work*, 52, 595-607.

Dickens, J. (2010). *Social Work and Social Policy: An Introduction*. London: Routledge.

Dickens, J. and Groza, V. (2004). Empowerment in difficulty: A critical appraisal of international intervention in child welfare in Romania. *International Social Work*, 47, 469-87.

Dillon, S. (2003). Making legal regimes for intercountry adoption reflect human rights principles: Transforming the United Nations Convention on the Rights of the Child with the Hague Convention on Intercountry Adoption. *Boston University International Law Journal*, 21, 179.

Dobbs, J.K. (2011, June 23). Ending South Korea's child export shame. *Foreign Policy in Focus*, Retrieved from www.fpif.org/articles/ending_south_koreas_child_export_shame.

Dobrova-Krol, N.A., Van IJzendoorn, M.H., Bakermans-Kranenburg, M.J., Cyr, C., and Juffer, F. (2008). Physical growth delays and stress dysregulation in stunted and non-stunted Ukrainian institution-reared children. *Infant Behavior and Development*, 31, 539-53.

Dockett, S. and Perry, B. (2011). Researching with young children: Seeking assent. *Child Indicators Research*, 4, 231-47.

Dohle, A. (2008). Inside story of an adoption scandal. *Cumberland Law Review*, 39, 131-85.

Dolgin, G. (Producer), and Dolgin, G., and Franco, V. (Directors). (2002). *Daughter from Danang.* [Documentary film.] United States: American Experience and the Independent Television Service in association with the National Asian American Communication Association.

Dominion. (1990, January 8). Shortage of babies drives adoptive parents overseas. *Dominion*, 2.

Dorow, S. (1999). *I Wish for You a Beautiful Life: Letters from the Korean Birth Mothers of Ae Ran Won to their Children.* St. Paul, MN: Yeong and Yeong Book Company.

Dorow, S. (2006a). Racialized choices: Chinese adoption and the `White noise" of Blackness. *Critical Sociology*, 32, 357-79.

Dorow, S. (2006b). *Transnational Adoption: A Cultural Economy of Race, Gender and Kinship.* New York, NY: NYU Press.

Dowling, M. and Brown, G. (2009). Globalization and intercountry adoption from China. *Child and Family Social Work*, 14, 352-61.

Doyle, J. (2010). *Misguided Kindness: Making the Right Decisions for Children in Emergencies.* Retrieved from Save the Children website: http://reliefweb.int/sites/reliefweb.int/files/resources/1481589D74C062C4C12577FF003BCCFC-Full_report.pdf.

Drennan, D. (2007, December 26). Re-evaluating adoption: Validating the local. *MRzine.* Retrieved from http://mrzine.monthlyreview.org/2007/drennan261207.html.

Dubinsky, K. (2008). The fantasy of the global cabbage patch: Making sense of transnational adoption. *Feminist Theory*, 9, 339-45.

Dubinsky, K. (2010). *Babies without borders: Adoption and Migration Across the Americas.* New York, NY: NYU Press.

Duflo, E. (2003). *Grandmothers and Granddaughters: Old Age Pensions and Intrahouse Allocation in South Africa.* Retrieved from http://obssr.od.nih.gov/pdf/wberduflofinal.pdf.

Duressa, A., (2002). Guddifachaa: Adoption practice in Oromo Society with particular reference to the Borana Oromo. (Unpublished Master's Thesis). Retrieved from http://etd.aau.edu.et/dspace/bitstream/123456789/1099/1/AYALEW%20DURESSA.pdf.

Duval Smith, A. and Rolley, S. (2007, November 4). Did they plot to steal Africa's orphans of war? *The Observer.* Retrieved from www.guardian.co.uk/world/2007/nov/04/france.sudan.

Duyme, M. (1990). Antisocial behavior and postnatal environment: French adoption study. *Journal of Child Psychology and Psychiatry*, 31, 699-710.

Duyme, M., Dumaret, A-C., and Tomekiewicz, S. (1999). How can we boost IQs of "dull children"? A late adoption study. *Proceedings of the National Academy of Sciences USA*, 96, 8790-94.

Dyhrberg, M. (2001, October/November). *Intercountry Adoptions, Pacific Rim Adoptions: The Impact of European Law on Customary Adoption Practices in Aotearoa.* Presented at the International Bar Association Conference, Cancun, Mexico. Retrieved from http://mariedyhrberg.co.nz/showfile.php?downloadid=417.

Ebenstein, A. (2010). The "Missing Girls" of China and the unintended consequences of the one child policy. *Journal of Human Resources*, 45, 87-115.

Ebenstein, A., and Leung, S. (2010). Son preference and access to social insurance: Evidence from China's rural pension program. *Population and Development Review*, 36, 47-70.

Ehrenreich, B., and Hochschild, A. (2003). Introduction. In B. Ehrenreich and A. Hochschild (eds), *Global Woman: Nannies, Maids, and Sex Workers in the New Economy* (pp. 1-13). London: Granta Books.

Else, A. (1991). *A Question of Adoption: Closed Stranger Adoption in New Zealand 1944-1974.* Wellington, New Zealand: Bridget Williams Books Ltd.

El-Serag, H.B., and Mason, A.C. (1999). Rising incidence of hepatocellular carcinoma in the United States. *The New England Journal of Medicine*, 340, 745-50.

Elisofon, S.A., and Jonas, M.M. (2006). Hepatitis B and C in children: Current treatments and future strategies. *Clinics in Liver Disease*, 10, 133-48.

Emerson, G. (1978). *Winners and Losers.* New York, NY: Harcourt Brace Jovanovich. Retrieved from http://darkwing.uoregon.edu/~adoption/archive/EmersonOB.htm.

Eng, D.L. (2003). Transnational adoption and queer diasporas. *Social Text*, 21(3), 1-37.

Eng, D.L., and Han, S. (2006). Transnational adoption, racial reparation, and racial transitional objects. *Studies in Gender and Sexuality*, 7, 141-72.

Englander, B. (2010). Oregon DHS develops policy and procedures for international relative placement adoptions. *Judges' Page Newsletter*. Retrieved from http://www.casaforchildren.org/site/c.mtJSJ7MPIsE/b.5720883/k.3EB4/Oregon_DHS_Policy__Procedures.htm.

Esping-Andersen, G. (1990). *The Three Worlds of Welfare Capitalism.* Cambridge: Polity Press.

Estrada Zepeda, B.E. (2009). *Estudio jurídico-social sobre trata de personas en Guatemala* [Socio-judicial study on human trafficking in Guatemala]. Cuidad de Guatemala, Guatemala: Fundación Red de Sobrevivientes de Violencia Domestica.

Ethica. (2006). *Comments on the Final Regulations Implementing the Hague Adoption Convention.* Retrieved from www.ethicanet.org/HagueRegComments.pdf.

Ethiopian Federal Ministry of Health. (2007). *Single-point HIV Prevalence Estimate Report.* Retrieved from http://www.etharc.org/aidsineth/publications/singlepointprev_2007.pdf.

Evan B. Donaldson Adoption Institute. (2004). *What's Working for Children: A Policy Study of Adoption Stability and Termination.* New York, NY: Author.

Fager, J. (Producer) and Stahl, L. (Host). (2005, July 24). *Born in USA; Adopted in Canada* [Television series episode]. CBS.

Faith, E. (2010). Indigenous social work education: A project for all of us? In M. Gray, J. Coates, and M. Yellow Bird (eds), *Indigenous Social Work around the World: Towards Culturally Relevant Education and Practice* (pp. 245-55). Surrey, UK: Ashgate.

Family Health International, Children's Investment Fund Foundation, and United Nations Children's Fund. (2010). *Improving Care Options for Children in Ethiopia through Understanding Institutional Childcare and Factors that Drive Institutionalizations.* Retrieved from www.fhi.org/en/CountryProfiles/Ethiopia/res_eth_institutional_care.htm.

Federal National Gazetta of the Federal Democratic Republic of Ethiopia. (2000). No. 1/2000. *The Revised Family Code Proclamation 213/2000.* Retrieved from www.lexadin.nl/wlg/legis/nofr/oeur/arch/eth//RevisedFamilyCode2000.pdf.

Federal National Gazetta of the Federal Democratic Republic of Ethiopia. (2004). *The (Revised) Criminal Code 414/2004.* Retrieved from http://www.ilo.org/dyn/natlex/docs/ELECTRONIC/70993/75092/F1429731028/ETH70993.pdf.

Feigelman, W., and Silverman, A. (1983). *Chosen Children: New Patterns of Adoption Relationships.* New York, NY: Praeger.

Ferguson, I., Lavalette, M., and Mooney, G. (2002). *Rethinking Welfare: A Critical Perspective.* London: Sage.

Fernald, L., Gertler, P., and Neufeld, L. (2008). Role of cash in conditional cash transfer programmes for child health, growth, and development: An analysis of Mexico's Oportunidades. *The Lancet*, 371, 828-37.

Fessler, A. (2007). *The Girls Who Went Away: The Hidden History of Women who Surrendered Children for Adoption in the Decades Before Roe v. Wade.* New York, NY: Penguin Group USA.

Fieser, E. (2009, December 23). Guatemala: A baby factory no longer? *Global Post.* Retrieved from http://www.globalpost.com/dispatch/the-americas/091222/guatemala-adoptions.

Fischer, G., Teshale, E., Miller, C., Schumann, C., Winter, K., Elson, F., and Perz, J. (2008). Hepatitis A among international adoptees and their contacts. *Clinical Infectious Diseases*, 47, 812-14.

Fiszbein, A. and Schady, N.R. (2009). *Conditional Cash Transfers: Reducing Present and Future Poverty.* Washington, D.C.: World Bank.

Fonseca, C. (2002). An unexpected reversal: Charting the course of international adoption in Brazil. *Adoption and Fostering*, 26(3), 28-39.

Fonseca, C. (2003). Patterns of shared parenthood among the Brazilian poor. *Social Text*, 21(1), 111-27.

Fonseca, C. (2009). Transnational connections and dissenting views: The evolution of child placement policies in Brazil. In D. Marre and L. Briggs (eds), *International Adoption: Global Inequalities and the Circulation of Children* (pp. 154-73). New York, NY: New York University Press.

France 24 International News. (2007a, October 27). *Sarkozy calls Chad President about 'Kidnapping.'* Retrieved from http://www.france24.com/france24Public/en/archives/news/world/20071029-chad-darfur-zoe-ark-association-members-held-sarkozy.php.

France 24 International News. (2007b, October 28). *Zoe's Ark Stranded in Chad.* Retrieved from http://www.france24.com/france24Public/en/archives/news/world/20071028-chad-darfur-zoe-ark-association-members-held.php.

France 24 International News. (2008, April 1). Zoe's Ark members released from jail. Retrieved from http://www.france24.com/en/20080401-zoes-ark-members-released-jail-chad-france.

France-Chad Agreement on Judicial Matters. (1978, June 15). Retrieved from http://untreaty.un.org/unts/1_60000/30/16/00058763.pdf.

Frank, D.A., Klass, P.E., Earls, F., and Eisenberg, L. (1996). Infants and young children in orphanages: One view from pediatrics and child psychiatry. *Pediatrics*, 97, 569-78.

Fravel, D.L., McRoy, R.G., and Grotevant, H.D. (2000). Birthmother perceptions of the psychologically present adopted child: Adoption openness and boundary ambiguity. *Family Relations*, 49, 425-33.

Freedom House. (2010). Countries at the crossroads-Guatemala. Retrieved from http://freedomhouse.org/template.cfm?page=139andedition=8.

French aid workers convicted of kidnapping may be pardoned by Chad President. (2008, March 7). *Web in France Magazine.* Retrieved from http://www.webinfrance.com/french-aid-workers-convicted-of-kidnapping-may-be-pardoned-by-chad-president-307.html.

French held over Chad 'adoptions.' (2007, October 26). *British Broadcasting Corporation.* Retrieved from http://news.bbc.co.uk/2/hi/7063324.stm.

Freundlich, M. (1998). Supply and demand: The forces shaping the future of infant adoption. *Adoption Quarterly*, 2(1), 13-46.

Freundlich, M. (2000a). *Adoption and Ethics: The Role of Race, Culture, and National Origin in Adoption.* Washington, D.C: Child Welfare League of America.

Freundlich, M. (2000b). Market forces: The issues in international adoption. In M. Freundlich (ed.), *Adoption and Ethics: The Role of Race, Culture, and*

National Origin in Adoption (pp. 37-66). Washington, DC: Child Welfare League of America.

Freundlich, M., Heffernan, M., and Jacobs, J. (2004). Interjurisdictional placement of children in foster care. *Child Welfare*, 83, 5-26.

Freundlich, M. and Lieberthal, J.K. (2000). *Korean Adoptees' Perception of International Adoption.* New York, NY: Evan B. Donaldson Adoption Institute. Retrieved from: http://www.adoptioninstitute.org/proed/korfindings.html.

Fronek, P. (2006). Global perspectives in Korean intercountry adoption. Asia Pacific *Journal of Social Work and Development*, 16(1), 21-31.

Fronek, P. and Cuthbert, D. (2012). The future of intercountry adoption: A paradigm shift for this century. *International Journal of Social Welfare*, 21(2), 215-24.

Fronek, P. and Tilse, C. (2010).Controversy and its implications for the practice of contemporary social work in intercountry adoptions: A Korean-Australian case study. *Australian Social Work*, 63, 445-59.

Frydman, M. and Lynn, R. (1989). The intelligence of Korean children adopted in Belgium. *Personality and Individual Differences*, 10, 1323-5.

Funes, M. (2010, January). *In the Name of the Salvadoran State, I Ask for Forgiveness (Number 342).* Retrieved from http://www.envio.org.ni/articulo/4142.

Gaetan, E.K. (2005). *Curative Politics and Institutional Legacies: The Impact of Foreign Assistance on Child Welfare and Healthcare Reform in Romania, 1990-2004.* (Doctoral Dissertation). Retrieved from http://www.lib.umd.edu/drum/bitstream/1903/3219/1/umi-umd-3045.pdf.

Gailey, C.W. (2010). *Blue-Ribbon Babies and Labors of Love: Race, Class, and Gender in U.S. Adoption Practice.* Austin, TX: University of Texas Press.

Garcia, M.L.T., and Fernandez, C.B. (2009). The care and shelter of children and adolescents in Brazil: Expressions of social issues. *Social Work and Society*, 7(1). Retrieved from http://www.socwork.net/2009/1/special_issue/garciafernandez.

Gaskell, S. (2010, January 30). American Baptists with 'Haitian orphan rescue mission' detained in Haiti for child trafficking. *New York Daily News*. Retrieved from http://articles.nydailynews.com/2010-01-31/news/27054975_1_haitian-children-laura-silsby-orphanage.

Geary, D.C. (2008). Evolution of fatherhood, In C.A. Salmon and T.K. Shackelford (eds), *Family Relationships: An Evolutionary Perspective* (pp. 115-44). New York, NY: Oxford University Press.

Geoghegan, A. (2009). Fly away children. *The Australian Broadcasting Corporation.* Retrieved from http://www.abc.net.au/foreign/content/2009/s2686908.htm.

Gibbons, J.L., Wilson, S.L., and Schnell, A.M. (2009). Foster parents as a critical link and resource in international adoptions from Guatemala. *Adoption Quarterly*, 12, 59-77.

Giberti, E. (2000). Excluded mothers: Birth mothers relinquishing their children. In P. Selman (ed.). *Intercountry Adoption: Developments, Trends and Perspectives* (pp. 458-66). London: British Agencies for Adoption and Fostering.

Gindis, B. (2005). Cognitive, language, and educational issues on children adopted from overseas orphanages. *Journal of Cognitive Education and Psychology*, 4, 290-314.

Glaser, G. (2004, July 4) Sending Black babies north. *The Sunday Oregonian*, p. L01.

Glennen, S. (2007). Predicting language outcome for internationally adopted children. *Journal of Speech, Language and Hearing Research*, 50, 529-48.

Glennen, S. and Masters, M.G. (2002). Typical and atypical language development in infants and toddlers adopted from Eastern Europe. *American Journal of Speech and Language Therapy*, 11, 417-33.

Global Overseas Adoptees' Link. (2001). *G.O.A.'L Guide to Living in Korea for Overseas Adopted Koreans.* Retrieved from http://goal.or.kr/eng/?slms=roomandlsms=1andsl=6andls=52.

Global Overseas Adoptees' Link. (2011). *Introduction.* Retrieved from http://goal.or.kr/eng/?slms=infoandlsms=1andsl=1andls=1.

Global Overseas Adoptees' Link. (2011, January). *Updated News! Dual Citizenship for Korean Adoptees.* Retrieved from http://goal.or.kr/eng/?slms=forandlsms=2andsl=5andls=1andquery=viewanduid=256.

Goddard, L.L. (1996). Transracial adoption: Unanswered theoretical and conceptual issues. *Journal of Black Psychology*, 22, 273-81.

Goedeke, S. and Payne, D. (2010). A qualitative study of New Zealand fertility counsellors' roles and practices regarding embryo donation. *Human Reproduction*, 35, 2821-8.

Goerge, R.M., Howard, E.C., Yu, D., and Radomsky, S. (1997). *Adoption, Disruption, and Displacement in the Child Welfare System, 1976-94.* Chicago, IL: University of Chicago, Chapin Hall Center for Children.

Goldberg, S. (2010, January 30). How NASCAR came to the rescue of Haiti orphans. *Time.* Retrieved from http://www.time.com/time/specials/packages/article/0,28804,1953379_1953494_1957885,00.html.

Goodman, A. (2007, November 2). Agencies: Most children in adoption dispute not Sudanese orphans. *CNN.* Retrieved from http://www.cnn.com/2007/WORLD/africa/11/01/chad.children.

Goodman, E. (2003, July 3). Cloe's first fourth. *Boston Globe*, p. A13.

Goodman, P. (2006, March 12). Stealing babies for adoption. *Washington Post,* p. A01.

Goodwin, M.B. (2010). *Baby Markets: Money and the New Politics of Creating Families.* New York, NY: Cambridge University Press.

Goody, E. (1982). *Parenthood and Social Reproduction.* Cambridge: Cambridge University Press.

Gough, I. and Wood, G. (2004). *Insecurity and Welfare Regimes in Asia, Africa and Latin America: Social Policy in Development Contexts.* Cambridge: Cambridge University Press.

Government of South Africa. (2006, June 19). Children's Act 38 of 2005. *Government Gazette*, 492. Retrieved from http://www.info.gov.za/view/DownloadFileAction?id=67892.

Graff, E.J. (2008, November 1). The lie we love. *Foreign Policy,* Retrieved from http://www.foreignpolicy.com/story/cms.php?story_id=4508andprint=1.

Graff, E.J. (2010, Summer). The baby business. *Democracy: A Journal of Ideas*, 17. Retrieved from http://www.democracyjournal.org/17/6757.php.

Green, D.M. (2010). The paradox of self-determination for marginalized individuals. *Social Work and Society*, 8(1). Retrieved from http://www.socwork.net/2010/1/green.

Greenhalgh, S. and Li, J. (1995). Engendering reproductive policy and practice in peasant China: For a feminist demography of reproduction. *Signs*, 20, 601-41.

Greenwell, F. (2006). The impact of child welfare reform on child abandonment and deinstitutionalization, Romania 1990-2000. *Annales de demographie historique,* 1(111), 133-57. Retrieved from http://www.cairn.info/revue-annales-de-demographie-historique-2006-1-page-133.htm.

Gresham, K., Nackerud, L., and Risler, E. (2004). Intercountry adoption from Guatemala and the United States: A comparative policy analysis. *Journal of Immigrant and Refugee Studies*, 1(3/4), 1-20.

Grice, H. (2005). Transracial adoption narratives: Prospects and perspectives. *Meridians: Feminism, Race, Transnationalism*, 5(2), 124-48.

Griffith, K. (1996). *New Zealand Adoption History and Practice, Social and Legal: 1840-1996.* Wellington, New Zealand: K.C. Griffith, MBA.

Gross, H. (1993). Open adoption: A research-based literature review and new data. *Child Welfare*, 72, 269-84.

Grotevant, H.D. (2009). Emotional Distance Regulation over the Life Course in Adoptive Kinship Networks. In G.M. Wrobel and E. Neil (eds), *International Advances in Adoption Research for Practice* (pp. 295-316). Chichester, West Sussex: Wiley-Blackwell.

Grotevant, H.D., Dunbar, N., Kohler, J.K., and Esau, A.L. (2000). Adoptive identity: How contexts within and beyond the family shape developmental pathways. *Family Relations*, 49, 379-87.

Grotevant, H.D., Wrobel, G.M., Von Korff, L., Skinner, B., Newell, J., Friese, S., and McRoy, R. (2007). Many faces of openness in adoption: Perspective of adopted adolescents and their parents. *Adoption Quarterly*, 10(3-4), 79-101.

Groves, M. (2009, November 11). Trafficking reports raise heart wrenching questions for adoptive parents. *Los Angeles Times.* Retrieved from http://www.latimes.com/news/local/la-me-china-adopt11-2009nov11,0,4189900,full.story.

Groza, V. (1999a). Adoptia copiilor in Romania: Continuare a unui studiu asupra familiilor care au adoptat copii romani [A follow up study of Romanian families who adopted Romanian children]. *Calitatea Vietii*, 10, 251-68.

Groza, V. (1999b). Institutionalization, behavior, and international adoption. *Journal of Immigrant Health*, 1(3), 133-43.

Groza, V. (2006). Adoption in India: Policies and experiences. *Social Service Review*, 80, 558-60.

Groza, V., Conley, A., and Bercea, F. (2003). A study of Romanian foster families in Bistrita Judet. *Calitatea Vietii*, 1, 1-16.

Groza, V. and Ileana, D. (1996). A follow-up study of adopted children from Romania. *Child and Adolescent Social Work Journal*, 13, 541-65.

Groza, V., Ileana, D., and Irwin, I. (1999). *A Peacock or a Crow? Stories, Interviews and Commentaries on Romanian Adoptions.* South Euclid, OH: Willes e-press.

Groza, V., Muntean, A. and Ungureanu, R. (2012). The adoptive family within the Romanian cultural context: An exploratory study. *Adoption Quarterly*, 15, 1-17.

Groza, V., Ryan, S.D., and Thomas, S. (2008). Institutionalization, Romanian adoptions and executive functioning. *Child and Adolescent Social Work Journal*. 25, 185-204.

Guerrant, D.I., Moore, S.R., Lima, A.A., Patrick, P.D., Schorling, J.B., and Guerrant, R.L. (1999). Association of early childhood diarrhea and cryptosporidiosis with impaired physical fitness and cognitive function four-seven years later in a poor urban community in northeast Brazil. *American Journal of Tropical Medicine and Hygiene*, 61, 707-13.

Gunnar, M.R., Bruce, J., and Grotevant, H.D. (2000). International adoption of institutionally reared children: Research and policy. *Development and Psychopathology*, 12, 677-93.

Gurman, S. and Schmitz, J. (2010, January 19). Rescue mission bringing Haitian orphans to Pittsburgh. *Pittsburgh Post Gazette.* Retrieved from http://www.post-gazette.com/pg/10019/1029290-455.stm.

Hague Conference on Private International Law. (1993, May 29). *The Hague Convention on Protection of Children and Co-operation in Respect of Intercountry Adoption.* Retrieved from www.hcch.net/index_en.php?act=conventions.pdfandcid=69.

Hague Conference on Private International Law. (2001). *Report and Conclusions of the Special Commission on the Practical Operation of the Hague Convention of 29 May 1993 on Protection of Children and Co-operation in Respect of Intercountry Adoption 28 November-1 December 2000.* Retrieved from http://www.hcch.net/upload/scrpt33e2000.pdf.

Hague Conference on Private International Law. (2007). *Report of a Fact Finding Mission to Guatemala in Relation to Intercountry Adoption.* Retrieved from www.hcch.net/upload/wop/mission_gt33e.pdf.

Hague Conference on Private International Law. (2008a, September 1). *Outline: Hague Intercountry Adoption Convention.* Retrieved from http://www.hcch.net/upload/outline33e.pdf.

Hague Conference on Private International Law. (2008b). *The Implementation and Operation of the 1993 Hague Intercountry Adoption Convention, Guide to Good Practice, Guide No.1.* Family Law. Bristol, UK: Author. Retrieved from www.hcch.net/upload/adoguide_e.pdf.

Hague Conference on Private International Law. (2010). *Draft Accreditation and Adoption Accredited Bodies: General Principles and Guide to Good Practice. Guide No. 2 under the Hague Convention of 29 May 1993 on Protection of Children and Co-operation in Respect of Intercountry Adoption.* Retrieved from http://www.hcch.net/upload/wop/adop2010_pd02e.pdf.

Hague Conference on Private International Law. (2011a). *Convention of 29 May 1993 on Protection of Children and Co-operation in Respect of Intercountry Adoption.* Retrieved from http://www.hcch.net/index_en.php?act=conventions.statusandcid=69.

Hague Conference on Private International Law. (2011b). *List of States that have Signed, Ratified or Acceded to the 1993 Hague Convention.* Retrieved from www.hcch.net/index_en.php?act=conventions.statusandcid=69.

Hague Conference on Private International Law. (2011c). *Status Table, Convention of 29 May 1993 on Protection of Children and Co-operation in Respect of Intercountry Adoption.* Retrieved from http://www.hcch.net/index_en.php?act=conventions.statusandcid=69.

Hansen, M.E. and Pollack, D. (2010). Transracial adoption of Black children. In M.B. Goodwin (ed.), *Baby Markets: Money and the New Politics of Creating Families.* Cambridge: Cambridge University Press.

Hao Thi Popp v. Lucas, 438. A.2d 755758 n.3 (Conn. 1980).

Harding, L.F. (1991). *Perspectives on Child Care Policy.* Essex, UK: Longman Group.

Hariyadi, M. (2005, January 3). Jakarta blocks tsunami orphan adoptions. *AsiaNews. It.* Retrieved from http://www.asianews.it/index.php?art=2246andl=en.

Harper, C.J., Pennell, J., and Weil, M. (2002). *Family Group Conferencing: Evaluation Guidelines.* Englewood, CO: American Humane Association.

Harris, P. (2008). *The Colours in Me: Writing and Poetry by Adopted Children and Young People.* London: British Agencies for Adoption and Fostering.

Harrison, L, Rubeiz, G., and Kochubey, A. (1996). Lapsele Oma Kodu [bringing abandoned children home]: A project from Tallinn, Estonia to reunite institutionalized children with families. *Scandanavian Journal of Social Welfare*, 5, 35-44.

Hart, A. and Luckock, B. (2004). *Developing Adoption Support and Therapy: New Approaches for Practice.* London: Jessica Kingsley.

Hawk, B.N. and McCall, R.B. (2011). Specific extreme behaviors of postinstitutionalized Russian adoptees. *Developmental Psychology*, 47, 732-8.

Hawkins, A., Beckett, C., Rutter, M., Castle, J., Colvert, E., Groothues, C., and Sonuga-Barke, E. (2007). Communicative openness about adoption and interest in contact in a sample of domestic and intercountry adolescent adoptees. *Adoption Quarterly*, 10(3-4), 131-56.

Hayes, P. and Kim, H. (2007). Openness in Korean adoptions: From family line to family life. *Adoption Quarterly*, 10(3-4), 53-78.

Hegre, H., Ellingsen, T., Gates, S., and Gleditsch, N.P. (2001). Toward a democratic civil peace? Democracy, political change, and civil war, 1816-1992. *American Political Science Review*, 95, 33-48.

Heilmann, J. (2008, January 28). *Zoe's Ark Aid Workers Get Eight Years in Prison in France.* Retrieved from Voice of America website: http://www.51voa.com/VOA_Standard_English/VOA_Standard_English_16763.html.

Heimsoth, D. and Laser, J.A. (2008) Transracial adoption: Expatriate parents living in China with their adopted Chinese children. *International Social Work*, 51, 651-68.

Heinlein, P. (2010a, December 14). *Under Pressure, Ethiopia Plans Crackdown on Baby Business.* Retrieved from Voice of America website: http://www.voanews.com/english/news/Under-Pressure-Ethiopia-Plans-Crackdown-on-Baby-Business-111848424.html.

Heinlein, P. (2010b, December 17). *Ethiopia Working with Child Advocacy Groups to Clean Up Adoptions.* Retrieved from Voice of America website: http://www.voanews.com/english/news/africa/Ethiopia-Working-with-Child-Advocacy-Groups-to-Clean-Up-Adoptions--112078034.html.

Heinlein, P. (2011a, February 11). *Ethiopia Revokes License of US Adoption Agency.* Retrieved from the Voice of America website: http://www.voanews.com/english/news/africa/Ethiopia-Revokes-License-of-US-Adoption-Agency-115950129.html.

Heinlein, P. (2011b, March 4). *Ethiopia to Cut Foreign Adoptions by up to 90 percent.* Retrieved from the Voice of America website: http://www.voanews.com/english/news/africa/-Ethiopia-to-Cut-Foreign-Adoptions-by-Up-to-90-Percent-117411843.html.

Hene, B. (1987). De utlandska adoptivbarnen och deras språkutveckling. [International adoptees and their language development]. *Sprins rapport 36.* Göteborg; Institutionen för Lingvistik, Göteborgs Universitet.

Herman, E. (n.d.). *The Adoption History Project.* University of Oregon. Retrieved from http://pages.uoregon.edu/adoption/.

Herrmann, K.J., Jr. and Kasper, B. (1992). International adoption: The exploitation of women and children. *Affilia*, 7(1), 45-58.

Hesketh, T. and Zhu, W. (2006). Abnormal sex ratios in human populations: Causes and consequences. *Proceedings of the National Academy of Sciences*, 103, 13271-5. Retrieved from http://www.pnas.org_cgi_doi_10.1073_pnas.0602203103.

Heying, S. (2010, February). *Guatemala's War Orphans: Thriving and Hope Despite Adversity.* Presented at the annual meeting of the Society for Cross-Cultural Research, Albuquerque, NM.

Hilborn, R. (2007, May 1). May 1: Nine new adoption rules start in China. *Family Helper.* Retrieved from http://www.familyhelper.net/news/070501chinarules.html.

Hilborn, R. (2010, January 31). Earthquake halts new adoptions in Haiti—Americans arrested at border. *Family Helper*. Retrieved from http://www.familyhelper.net/news/haiti.html.

Hjern, A. and Allebeck, P. (2002). Suicide in first- and second-generation immigrants in Sweden. A comparative study. *Social Psychiatry and Psychiatric Epidemiology*, 37, 423-9.

Hjern, A., Lindblad, F., and Vinnerljung, B. (2002). Suicide, psychiatric illness, and social maladjustment in intercountry adoptees in Sweden: A cohort study. *The Lancet*, 360, 443-8.

Hodges, J. and Tizard, B. (1989). IQ and behavioural adjustment of ex-institutional adolescents. *Journal of Child Psychology and Psychiatry*, 30, 53-75.

Hoelgaard, S. (1998). Cultural determinants of adoption policy: A Colombian case study. *International Journal of Law, Policy and the Family*, 12, 202-41.

Hofstede, G. (2001). *Culture's Consequences: Comparing Values, Behaviors, Institutions, and Organizations across Nations* (2nd ed.). Thousand Oaks, CA: Sage.

Högbacka, R. (2008). The quest for a child of one's own: Parents, markets and transnational adoption. *Journal of Comparative Family Studies*, 39, 311-30.

Högbacka, R. (2011). Exclusivity and inclusivity in transnational adoption. In R. Jallinoja and E. Widmer (eds), *Families and Kinship in Contemporary Europe: Rules and Practices of Relatedness* (pp. 129-44). New York, NY: Palgrave MacMillan.

Hoksbergen, R.A.C. (ed.). (1986). *Adoption in Worldwide Perspective. A Review of Programs, Policies and Legislation in 14 Countries.* Lisse: Swets and Zeitlinger.

Hoksbergen, R.A.C. (1991a). Intercountry adoption coming of age in the Netherlands: Basic issues, trends and developments. In H. Altstein and R.J. Simon (eds), *Intercountry adoption: A Multinational Perspective* (pp 141-58). New York, NY: Praeger.

Hoksbergen, R.A.C. (1991b). Understanding and preventing "failing adoptions." In E.D. Hibbs (ed.), *Adoption: International Perspectives* (pp. 265-78). Madison, CT: International University Press.

Hoksbergen, R.A.C. (2000). Changes in attitudes in three generations of adoptive parents. In P. Selman (ed.), *Intercountry Adoption: Development, Trends and Perspectives* (pp. 86-101). London: BAAF.

Hoksbergen, R.A.C., Juffer, F., and Waardenburg, B.C. (1987). *Adopted Children at Home and at School.* Lisse: Swets and Zeitlinger.

Hollinger, J.H. (2008). Intercountry adoption: Legal requirements and practical considerations. In J.H. Hollinger (ed.), *Adoption Law and Practice 1988-2008* (pp. 97-148). New York, NY: LexisNexis Matthew Bender.

Hollingsworth, L.D. (1998). Promoting same race adoption for children of colour. *Social Work*, 43, 104-14.

Hollingsworth, L.D. (1999). Symbolic interactionism, African American families, and the transracial adoption controversy. *Social Work*, 44, 443-54.

Hollingsworth, L.D. (2003). International adoption among families in the United States: Considerations of social justice. *Social Work*, 48, 209-19.

Hollingsworth, L.D. (2008). Commentary: Does the Hague Convention on Intercountry Adoption address the protection of adoptees' cultural identity? And should it? *Social Work*, 53, 377-9.

Holman, B. (2005, May 5). Warfare to welfare. *Community Care*, (1571), 32-3.

Hopgood, M. (2009). *Lucky Girl: A Memoir.* Chapel Hill, NC: Algonquin Books.

Horvitz, L.A. and Catherwood, C. (2006). *Encyclopedia of War Crimes and Genocide*. New York, NY: Infobase Publishing.

Hostetter, M.K., Iverson, S., Thomas, W., McKenzie, D., Dole, K., and Johnson, D.E. (1991). Medical evaluation of internationally adopted children. *The New England Journal of Medicine,* 325, 479-85.

Howard, J.A. and Smith, S.L. (2003). *After Adoption: The Needs of Adopted Youth.* Washington, DC: Child Welfare League of America.

Hrdy, S.B. (1999). *Mother Nature: A History of Mothers, Infants, and Natural Selection.* New York, NY: Pantheon.

Hrdy, S.B. (2008). Evolutionary context of human development: The cooperative breeding model. In C.A. Salmon and T.K. Shackelford (eds), *Family Relationships: An Evolutionary Perspective* (pp. 39-68). Oxford and New York, NY: Oxford University Press.

Hrdy, S.B. (2009). *Mothers and Others: The Evolutionary Origins of Mutual Understanding.* Cambridge, MA: Belknap Press.

Hua v. Scott, 405 N.E.2d 255 (Ohio 1980).

Huang, S. (1989). *The Spiral Road.* Boulder, CO: Westview Press.

Hübinette, T. (2004a). Demographic information and Korean adoption history. In E. Kim (Ed). *Guide to Korea for Overseas Adopted Koreans* (pp. 12-19, 25-47). Seoul: Overseas Koreans Foundation.

Hübinette, T. (2004b). The adopted Koreans and an identity in the third space. *Adoption and Fostering*, 28(1), 16-24.

Hübinette, T. (2006). *Comforting an Orphaned Nation: Representations of International Adoption and Adopted Koreans in Korean Popular Culture. Korean Studies.* Seoul: Jimoonda Publishing Company.

Hübinette, T. (2007a). Disembedded and free-floating bodies out-of-place and out-of-control: Examining the borderline existence of adopted Koreans. *Adoption and Culture*, 1, 129-62.

Hübinette, T. (2007b, March 3). Korea must stop overseas adoptions. *Korea Herald.* Retrieved from http://www.tobiashubinette.se/adoptionstop.pdf.

Hübinette, T. (2007c). Nationalism, subalternity, and the adopted Koreans. *Journal of Women's History*, 19(1), 117-22.

Hübinette, T. (2009). Adoption. In A. Iriye and P.Y. Saunier (eds), *The Palgrave Dictionary of Transnational History. From the Mid-19th Century to the Present Day* (pp. 11-13). Basingstoke: Palgrave Macmillan.

Hübinette, T. and Tigervall, C. (2008). *Adoption med förhinder: Samtal med adopterade och adoptivföräldrar om vardagsrasism och etnisk identitet* [Adoption with obstacles: Conversations with adoptees and adoptive parents on everyday racism and ethnic identity]. Tumba: Mångkulturellt centrum.

Huizinga, J. (2007, November 1). Chad adoption scandal embarrasses Paris. *Radio Netherlands.* Retrieved from http://www.radionetherlands.nl/currentaffairs/071101-chad-adoption.

Human Rights Watch. (1996). *Death by Default: A Policy of Fatal Neglect in China's State Orphanages.* New York, NY: Human Rights Watch.

Huynh Thi Anh v. Levi, 586 F.2d 625, (6th Cir. 1978).

Independent Group for International Adoption Analysis. (2002). *Re-organising the International Adoption and Child Protection System.* Bucharest: IGIAA. Retrieved from www.afaener.org/Rapport_FINAL_ang.doc.

Ingle, L. (2010, January 17). *Haiti Orphanages in Crisis.* Retrieved from Fox News website: http://onthescene.blogs.foxnews.com/2010/01/17/haiti-orphanages-in-crisis/.

Inter-American Commission on Human Rights. (2001). *Report N° 31/01, Case 12.132. Ernestina and Erlinda Serrano Cruz, El Salvador.* Retrieved from http://cidh.org/annualrep/2000eng/ChapterIII/Admissible/ElSalvador12.132.htm.

Intercountry Adoption Act of 2000. (2000). *Public Law 106-279.* Retrieved from http://coanet.org/files/hr2909.pdf.

International Korean Adoptee Associations. (2011). *Gathering News.* Retrieved from http://gathering.ikaa.info/en/page/351.

International Social Service. (2009). *Intercountry Adoption from Viet Nam; Findings and Recommendations of an Assessment.* Geneva: ISS. Retrieved from http://www.iss-ssi.org/2009/assets/files/news/vietnam%20report_ENG.pdf.

International Social Service. (n.d.). *Fact Sheet No. 19: The Adoptability of the Child: Objectives and Responsibilities.* Retrieved from http://www.iss-ssi.org/2009/assets/files/thematic-facts-sheet/eng/19.Child%20adoptability.pdf.

Irhammar, M. and Cederblad, M. (2000). Outcome of intercountry adoption in Sweden. In P. Selman (ed.), *Intercountry Adoption: Developments, Trends and Perspectives* (pp. 143-63). London: British Agencies for Adoption and Fostering.

Iwanek, M. (1987). *A Study of Open Adoption Placements.* Petone, New Zealand: Department of Social Welfare, New Zealand.

Iwanek, M. (1997). Adoption in New Zealand—Past, present and future. In K. Sprengers (ed.), *Adoption and Healing: Proceedings of the International*

Conference on Adoption and Healing (pp. 62-73). Wellington: New Zealand Adoption Education and Healing Trust.

Jackson, M.R. (1981). Perspectives on Romania's economic development in the 1980s, In D.N. Nelson (ed.), *Romania of the 1980s*. Boulder, CO: Westview.

Jacoby, W., Lataianu, G., and Lataianu, C.M. (2009). Success in slow motion: The Europeanization of Romanian child protection policy. *The Review of International Organizations*, 4, 111-33.

Jaffari-Bimmel, N., Juffer, F., Van IJzendoorn, M.H., Bakermans-Kranenburg, M.J., and Mooijaart, A. (2006). Social development from infancy to adolescence: Longitudinal and concurrent factors in an adoption sample. *Developmental Psychology*, 42, 1143-53.

Jaffe, E.D. (1991). Foreign adoptions in Israel: Private paths to parenthood. In H. Altstein and R.J. Simon (eds), *Intercountry Adoption: A Multinational Perspective* (pp. 161-79). New York, NY: Praeger.

James, S. (2011). What works in group care?—A structured review of treatment models for group homes and residential care. *Children and Youth Services Review*, 33, 308-21.

January, B. (2007). *Genocide: Modern Crimes against Humanity*. Minneapolis, MN: Twenty-First Century Books.

Jerng, M.C. (2010). *Claiming Others: Transracial Adoption and National Belonging*. Minneapolis, MN: University of Minnesota Press.

Joe, B. (1978). In defense of intercountry adoption. *Social Service Review*, 52, 1-20.

Johansson, S. and Nygren, O. (1991). The missing girls of China: A new demographic account. *Population and Development Review*, 17, 35-51.

Johns, S.E. and Belsky, J. (2008). Life transitions: Becoming a parent. In C.A. Salmon and T.K. Shackelford (eds), *Family Relationships: An Evolutionary Perspective* (pp. 71-90). Oxford and New York, NY: Oxford University Press.

Johnson, A. and Groze, V. (1993). The orphaned and institutionalized children of Romania. *Journal of Emotional and Behavioral Problems*, 2(4), 49-52.

Johnson, D.E., Guthrie, D., Smyke, A.T., Koga, S.F., Fox, N.A., and Zeanah, C.H. (2010). Growth and associations between auxology, caregiving environment, and cognition in socially deprived Romanian children randomized to foster vs ongoing institutional care. *Archives of Pediatrics and Medicine*, 164, 507-16.

Johnson, D.E., Miller, L.C., Iverson, S., Thomas, W., Franchino, B., Dole, K., and Hostetter, M.K. (1992). The health of children adopted from Romania. *Journal of the American Medical Association*, 268, 3446-51.

Johnson, K.A. (2002). Politics of international and domestic adoption in China. *Law and Society Review*, 36, 379-96.

Johnson, K.A. (2004). *Wanting a Daughter, Needing a Son. Abandonment, Adoption, and Orphanage Care in China*. St. Paul, MN: Yeong and Yeong Book Company.

Joint Council on International Children's Services. (2010, July). *Summary Report: A Six-month Update on the Humanitarian Parole Program for Haitian Children.* Alexandria, VA: JCICS.

Joint Council on International Children's Services. (n.d.). *Hague Adoption Convention.* Retrieved from http://www.jcics.org/Hague.htm.

Jolley, M.A. (2009). *A Heartbreaking Assignment.* The Australian Broadcasting Corporation. Retrieved from http://www.abc.net.au/foreign/content/2009/s2686187.htm.

Jones, M. (2007, October 28). Looking for their children's birthmothers. *New York Times Magazine.* Retrieved from http://www.njarch.org/images/Adoption%20Search%20NYTimes.pdf.

Joyce, K. (2011, December 12). How Ethiopia's Adoption Industry Dupes Families and Bullies Activists. *The Atlantic.* Retrieved from http://www.theatlantic.com/international/archive/2011/12/how-ethiopias-adoption-industry-dupes-families-and-bullies-activists/250296/.

Juffer, F. (2006). Children's awareness of adoption and their problem behavior in families with 7-year-old internationally adopted children. *Adoption Quarterly*, 9(2/3), 1-22.

Juffer, F., Bakermans-Kranenburg, M.J., and Van IJzendoorn, M.H. (2005). The importance of parenting in the development of disorganized attachment: Evidence from a preventive intervention study in adoptive families. *Journal of Child Psychology and Psychiatry*, 46, 263-74.

Juffer, F., Bakermans-Kranenburg, M.J., and Van IJzendoorn, M.H. (eds). (2008). *Promoting Positive Parenting: An Attachment-based Intervention.* New York, NY: Lawrence Erlbaum/Taylor and Francis.

Juffer, F., Palacios, J., LeMare, L., Sonuga-Barke, E.J.S., Tieman, W., Bakermans-Kranenburg, M.J., Vorria, P., Van IJzendoorn, M.H., and Verhulst, F.C. (2011). Development of adopted children with histories of early adversity. In R.B. McCall, M.H. Van IJzendoorn, F. Juffer, C.J. Groark, and V.K. Groza, Children without permanent parents: Research, practice and policy. *Monographs of the Society for Research in Child Development*, 76(4), 31-61.

Juffer, F. and Tieman, W. (2009). Being adopted: Internationally adopted children's interest and feelings. *International Social Work*, 52, 635-47.

Juffer, F. and Van IJzendoorn, M.H. (2005). Behavior problems and mental health referrals of international adoptees: A meta-analysis. *JAMA, The Journal of the American Medical Association*, 293, 2501-15.

Juffer, F. and Van IJzendoorn, M.H. (2007). Adoptees do not lack self-esteem: A meta-analysis of studies on self-esteem of transracial, international, and domestic adoptees. *Psychological Bulletin*, 133, 1067-83.

Juffer, F. and Van IJzendoorn, M.H. (2009). International adoption comes of age: Development of international adoptees from a longitudinal and meta-analytical perspective. In G.M. Wrobel and E. Neil (eds), *International Advances in Adoption Research for Practice* (pp. 169-92). London: Wiley.

Junhong, C. (2001). Prenatal sex determination and sex-selective abortion in rural central China. *Population and Development Review*, 2, 259-81.

Juntunen, C. (2009). *Both Ends Burning: My Story of Adopting Three Children from Haiti.* Parker, CO: Outskirts Press. Retrieved from http://bothendsburning.org.

Kane, S. (1993). The movement of children for international adoption: An epidemiological perspective. *The Social Science Journal*, 30, 323-39.

Kaplan, L.E. and Bryan, V. (2009). A conceptual framework for considering informed consent. *Journal of Social Work Values and Ethics.* Retrieved from http://www.socialworker.com/jswve/content/view/130/69/.

Kapstein, E.B. (2003). The baby trade. *Foreign Affairs*, 82(6), 115-25.

Kapstein, E.B. (2005, February 16). The orphans in the Tsunami's wake. Retrieved from the Foreign Affairs website: http://www.foreignaffairs.com/articles/64232/ethan-b-kapstein/the-orphans-in-the-tsunamis-wake.

Keil, T.J. and Andreescu, V. (1999). Fertility policy in Ceausescu's Romania. *Journal of Family History*, 24, 478-92.

Keller, A. (2010, November 1). *Whose Standards?* Retrieved from the Florida Trends website: http://www.floridatrend.com/print_article.asp?aID=53889.

Keller, H. and Chasiotis, A. (2008). Maternal investment. In C.A. Salmon and T.K. Shackelford (eds), *Family Relationships: An Evolutionary Perspective* (pp. 91-114). New York, NY: Oxford University Press.

Keystone, J.S. (2005). Travel-related hepatitis B: Risk factors and prevention using an accelerated vaccination schedule. *The American Journal of Medicine*, 118, 63-8.

Khabibullina, L. (2006, July). *Circulation of Russian Children in Europe (Case Study of Transnational Adoption of Children from Russia to Catalonia).* Paper presented at the Second International Conference on Adoption Research, Norwich. Retrieved from http://www.uea.ac.uk/swp/icar2/papers.htm#PS7.

Khan, I. (2009). *The Unheard Truth: Poverty and Human Rights.* New York, NY: Norton and Company.

Kideckel, D. (1993). *The Solitude of Collectivism: Romanian Villagers to the Revolution and Beyond.* Ithaca, NY: Cornell University Press.

Kim, E.J. (2000). Korean adoptee auto-ethnography: Refashioning self, family and finding community. *Visual Anthropology Review*, 16, 43-70.

Kim, E.J. (2004). Korean adoptees' role in the United States. In I.J. Kim (ed.), *Korean-Americans: Past, Present, and Future* (pp. 180-202). Elizabeth, NJ: Hollym.

Kim, E.J. (2010). *Adopted Territory: Transnational Korean Adoptees and the Politics of Nelonging.* Durham, NC: Duke University Press.

Kim, G.S., Suyemoto, K.L., and Turner, C.B. (2010). Sense of belonging, sense of exclusion, and racial and ethnic identities in Korean transracial adoptees. *Cultural Diversity and Ethnic Minority Psychology*, 2, 179-90.

Kim, J. and Staat, M.A. (2004). Acute care issues in internationally adopted children. *Clinical Pediatric Emergency Medicine*, 5, 130-42.

Kim, T., Shin, Y., and White-Traut, R. (2003). Multisensory intervention improves physical growth and illness rates in Korean orphaned newborn infants. *Research in Nursing and Health*, 26, 424-33.

Kimball, C.E. (2005). Barriers to the successful implementation of the Hague Convention on Protection of Children and Co-operation in Respect of Intercountry Adoption. *Denver Journal of International Law and Policy*, 33, 561-84.

Kirpalani, R. and Ng, C. (2011, August 5). *Missouri Couple Silent on Order to Return Adopted Daughter to Guatemala.* Retrieved from the ABC News website: http://abcnews.go.com/US/missouri-couple-silent-order-return-adopted-daughter-guatemala/story?id=14234379.

Kirton, D., Feast, J., and Howe, D. (2000). Searching, reunion and transracial adoption. *Adoption and Fostering*, 24(3), 6-18.

Klarberg, R. (2010). Hague accreditation: What does it mean for the practice of outbound intercountry adoption? *Judges' Page Newsletter*. Retrieved from http://www.casaforchildren.org/site/c.mtJSJ7MPIsE/b.5720901/k.DC28/Hague_Accreditation__Outbound_Intercountry_Adoption.htm.

Klein, C. (2003). *Cold War Orientalism: Asia in the Middlebrow Imagination, 1945-1961.* Berkeley, CA: University of California Press.

Kligman, G. (1995). Political demography: The banning of abortion in Ceauçescu's Romania. In F. Ginsburg and R. Rapp (eds), *Conceiving the new world order* (pp. 78-102). Los Angeles, CA: University of California Press.

Koh, F.M. (1981). *Oriental Children in American Homes: How Do They Adjust?* Minneapolis, MN: East West Press.

Kozinski, A. (1991). The dark lessons of utopia. *The University of Chicago Law Review*, 58, 575-94.

Kralnova, N. (2010, June 18). Adoption deal fast-forwarded for approval. Retrieved from the Moscow Times website: http://www.themoscowtimes.com/news/article/adoption-deal-fast-forwarded-for-approval/408511.html.

KRO Brandpunt. (2011). *Handel in kinderen* [Children for sale]. [Television series episode]. Retrieved from www.youtube.com/watch?v=QYpm3V0XFu8;www.youtube.com/watch?v=7M9ZQr4Ug08andfeature=related and www.youtube.com/watch?v=YAjGfSzKnB0.

Kuhn, C.M. and Schanberg, S.M. (1998). Responses to maternal separation: Mechanisms and mediators. *International Journal of Developmental Neuroscience*, 16, 261-70.

Kvifte-Andresen, I.L. (1992). Behavioral and school adjustment of 12-13 year old internationally adopted children in Norway. *Journal of Child Psychology and Psychiatry*, 33, 427-39.

Lal, B.B. (2001). Learning to do ethnic identity: The transracial/transethnic adoptive family as site and context. In D. Parker and M. Song (eds), *Rethinking "Mixed Race"* (pp. 154-72). London: Pluto Press.

Lalonde, R., Giguere, B., Fontaine, M., and Smith, A. (2007). Social dominance orientation and ideological asymmetry in relation to interracial dating and transracial adoption in Canada. *Journal of Cross-Cultural Psychology*, 38, 559-72.

Lammerant, I. and Hofstetter, M. (2007). *Adoption: At What Cost? For an Ethical Responsibility of Receiving Countries in Intercountry Adoption.* Lausanne: Terre des Hommes. Retrieved from www.crin.org/docs/Adoption_at_what_cost[1].pdf.

Landau, L.B. and Freemantle, I. (2010). Tactical cosmopolitanism and idioms of belonging: Insertion and self-exclusion in Johannesburg. *Journal of Ethnic and Migration Studies*, 36, 375-90.

Landrieu, M. and Inhofe, J. (2010, March 3). *New Approach Needed to Help World's Orphans.* Retrieved from the Washington Examiner website: http://washingtonexaminer.com/node/113276.

L'Arche de Zoé. Retrieved from http://www.archedezoe.fr/.

Latin American Institute for Education and Communication, and United Nations Children's Fund. (2000). *Adoption and the Rights of the Child in Guatemala.* Retrieved from http://poundpuplegacy.org/files/Guatemala-UNICEFILPECENG.pdf.

Laughlin, W. (2010a). Haiti's angel house: All 26 orphans survive the earthquake. *Causecast.* Retrieved from http://www.causecast.org/news_items/9554-haitis-angel-house-all-26-orphans-survive-the-earthquake.

Laughlin, W. (2010b). *Twenty-six Points of Light.* Retrieved from the Tonic website: http://www.tonic.com/article/angel-house-orphanage-miracle-adoption-in-haiti/.

Lee, J. and Wang, F. (2001). *One Quarter of Humanity: Malthusian Mythology and Chinese Realities, 1700-2000.* Cambridge, MA: Harvard University Press.

Lee, R.M. (2003). The transracial adoption paradox: History, research and counseling implications of cultural socialization. *The Counseling Psychologist*, 31, 711-44.

Lee, R.M., Grotevant, H.D., Hellerstedt, W.L., Gunnar, M.R., and the Minnesota International Adoption Project Team. (2006). Cultural socialization in families with internationally adopted children. *Journal of Family Psychology*, 20, 571-80.

Lee, R.M., Seol, K.O., Sung, M., and Miller, M.J. (2010). The behavioral development of Korean children in institutional care and international adoptive families. *Developmental Psychology*, 46, 468-78.

Leifsen, E. (2009). Adoption and the governing of child welfare in 20th Century Quito. *Journal of Latin American and Caribbean Anthropology*, 14, 68-91.

Leinaweaver, J.B. (2008). *The Circulation of Children: Kinship, Adoption, and Morality in Andean Peru.* Durham, NC: Duke University Press.

Leisinger, K.M. (2004). Overcoming poverty and respecting human rights: Ten points for serious consideration. *International Social Science Journal*, 180, 313-20.

Levitas, R. (2005). *The Inclusive Society? Social Exclusion and New Labour* (2nd ed.). Basingstoke: Palgrave Macmillan.

Levy-Shiff, R., Zoran, N., and Shulman, S. (1997). International and domestic adoption: Child, parents and family adjustment. *International Journal of Behavioral Development*, 20, 109-29.

Lien, N.M., Meyer, K.K., and Winick, M. (1977). Early malnutrition and "late" adoption: A study of their effects on the development of Korean orphans adopted into American families. *American Journal of Clinical Nutrition*, 30, 1734-9.

Lindblad, F., Dalen, M., Rasmussen, F., Vinnerljung, B., and Hjern, A. (2009). School performance of international adoptees better than expected from cognitive test results. *European Child and Adolescent Psychiatry*, 18, 301-8.

Lindblad, F., Hjern, A., and Vinnerljung, B. (2003). Intercountry adopted children as young adults: A Swedish cohort study. *American Journal of Orthopsychiatry*, 73, 190-202.

Lindblad, F., Ringbäck Weitoft, G., and Hjern, A. (2010). ADHD in international adoptees: A national cohort study. *European Child and Adolescent Psychiatry.* 19, 37- 44.

Linden, R.H. (1986). Socialist patrimonialism and the global economy: The case of Romania. *International Organization*, 40, 347-80.

Lister, R. (2003). *Citizenship: Feminist Perspectives*. New York, NY: New York University Press.

Liu, Y. (2010). Finding Family. *Beijing Review.* Retrieved from http://www.bjreview.com/life/txt/2010-08/02/content_288309.htm.

Llorca, J.C. (2010, November 12). U.N.-backed investigators shake up Guatemala. *Associated Press.* Retrieved from www.deseretnews.com/article/700081241/UN-backed-investigators-shake-up-Guatemala.html.

Logan, J. and Smith, C. (2005). Face-to-face contact post adoption: Views from the triangles. *British Journal of Social Work*, 35, 3-35.

Lombe, M. and Ochumbo, A. (2008). Sub-Saharan Africa's orphan crisis: Challenges and opportunities. *International Social Work*, 51, 682-98.

Ludbrook, R. (1990). *Adoption: Guide to Law and Practice.* Christchurch, New Zealand: Government Printing Office.

Lund, F. (2006). Gender and social security in South Africa. In V. Padayachee (ed.), The development decade? *Economic and Social Change in South Africa 1994-2004* (pp. 160-79). Cape Town: Human Sciences Research Council.

Maggiore, G., Caprai, S., Cerino, A., Silini, E., and Mondelli, M.U. (1998). Antibody-negative chronic hepatitis C virus infection in immunocompetent children. *Journal of Pediatrics*, 132, 1048-50.

Makiwane, M. B (2003). 'Response to paper 2.' In Human Sciences Research Council (ed.), *Fertility. Current South African Issues of Poverty, HIV/AIDS and Youth: Seminar Proceedings* (pp. 57-78). Cape Town: Human Sciences Research Council and Department of Social Development.

Mandalakas, A.M. and Starke, J.R. (2004). Tuberculosis screening in immigrant children. *The Pediatric Infectious Disease Journal*, 23, 71-2.

Manley, K.L. (2006). Birth parents: The forgotten members of the international adoption triad. *Capital University Law Review*, 35, 627-53.

Marinara, M. (2003). Cartography of adoption: Identity and difference beyond the politics of the comfort zone. *Review of Education, Pedagogy and Cultural Studies*, 25, 139-52.

Marini, A. and Gragnolati, M. (2003). *Malnutrition and Poverty in Guatemala.* Retrieved from http://ssrn.com/abstract=636329.

Martin, A. (2000a). The legacy of operation babylift, *Adoption Today*, 2(4). Retrieved from http://www.adoptvietnam.org/adoption/babylift.htm.

Martin, A. (2000b). An Interview with Cherie Martin, Operation Babylift: The last flights out of Saigon. Retrieved from http://www.comeunity.com/apv/babylift-clark.htm.

Maru, M.T. (2009, June 27). On international adoption of Ethiopian children. *The Reporter.* Retrieved from http://en.ethiopianreporter.com/index.php?option=com_contentandtask=viewandid=1282andItemid=1.

Maskew, T. (2004). Child trafficking and intercountry adoption: The Cambodian Experience. *Cumberland Law Review*, 35, 619-38.

Maskew, T. (2010, September). *Implementing your Recommendations: Best Practices for Maximum Impact.* Presented at the Intercountry Adoption Summit, Waterloo, Canada.

Mason, J. and Hood, S. (2011). Exploring issues of children as actors in social research. *Children and Youth Services Review*, 33, 490-95.

Masson, J. (2001). Intercountry adoption: A global problem or a global solution? *Journal of International Affairs*, 55, 141-66.

Maugham, B., Collishaw, S. and Pickles, A. (1998). School achievement and adult qualifications among adoptees: A longitudinal study. *Journal of Child Psychology and Psychiatry*, 39, 669-85.

Maury, F. (1999). *L'Adoption interracial* [Interracial adoption]. Paris: Éditions l'Harmattan.

Mazzei, P., Reyes, G., and Burnett III, J.H. (2010, February 18). *8 Church Workers Freed from Haitian Jail Land in Miami.* Retrieved from the Miami Herald website: http://www.miamiherald.com/2010/02/18/1485935/eight-accused-of-child-smuggling.html.

Mbonda, E.M. (2004). Poverty as a violation of human rights: Towards a right to non-poverty. *International Social Science Journal*, 56, 277-88.

McCall, J.N. (1999). Research on the psychological effects of orphan care: A critical review. In R.B. McKenzie (ed.), *Rethinking Orphanages for the 21st century* (pp. 127-50). Thousand Oaks, CA: Sage.

McDonald, S.C. (2002, April 4). *Baby Lift Memorial Service*. Retrieved from http://www.vietnambabylift.org/Memorial.html.

McGinnis, H. (2003). Adult Korean intercountry adoptees: A resource for adoption practice. *Columbia University Journal of Student Social Work*, 1, 8-14.

McGinnis, H. (2005). *Intercountry Adoption in Emergencies: The Tsunami Orphans*. New York, NY: The Evan B. Donaldson Adoption Institute. Retrieved from http://www.adoptioninstitute.org/publications.

McGinnis, H. (2006a). From the ashes of war: Lessons from 50 years of Korean international adoption. In R.A. Javier, A.L. Baden, F.A. Biafora, and A. Camacho-Gingerich (eds), *Handbook of Adoption: Implications for Researchers, Practitioners, and Families*. New York, NY: Sage Publications.

McGinnis, H. (2006b). The search for identity in adoption: Understanding the meaning of one's life. In J. MacLeod and S. Macrae (eds), *Adoption Parenting: Creating a Toolbox, Building Connections* (pp. 452-57). Warren, NJ: EMK Press.

McGinnis, H., Livingston Smith, S., Ryan, S.D., and Howard, J.A. (2009). *Beyond Culture Camp: Promoting Healthy Identity Formation in Adoption*. New York, NY: Evan B. Donaldson Adoption Institute.

McGuinness, T.M. and Pallansch, L. (2000). Competence of children adopted from the former Soviet Union. *Family Relations*, 49, 457-64.

McKenzie, R.B. (ed.) (1999). *Rethinking Orphanages for the 21st Century*. Thousand Oaks, CA: Sage.

McKinley, J.C., Jr., and Hamill, S.D. (2010, January 20). 53 Haitian orphans are airlifted to USA. *New York Times*. Retrieved from http://www.nytimes.com/2010/01/20/world/americas/20orphans.html.

McKinney, L. (2007). International adoption and the Hague Convention: Does implementation of the Convention protect the best interests of children? Whittier *Journal of Child and Family Advocacy*, 6, 361-75.

McRae, K.O. and Nikora, L.W. (2006). Whangai: Remembering, understanding and experiencing. *MAI Review*, 1, Intern Research Report 7.

McRoy, R.G. (1999). *Special Needs Adoption: Practice Issues*. New York, NY: Garland.

Meier, D.I. (1998). Loss and reclaimed lives: Cultural identity and place in Korean-American intercountry adoptees. (Unpublished doctoral dissertation), University of Minnesota, Minneapolis and St. Paul, MN.

Meier, D.I. (1999). Cultural identity and place in adult Korean-American intercountry adoptees. *Adoption Quarterly*, 3(1), 15-48.

Meier, P. and Zhang, X. (2008). Sold into adoption: The Hunan baby trafficking scandal exposes vulnerabilities in Chinese adoptions to the United States. *Cumberland Law Review*, 39, 87-130. Retrieved from http://www.ethicanet.org/MeierZhang/pdf.

Melone, T. (1976, June). Adoption and crisis in the third world: Thoughts on the future. *International Child Welfare Review*, 29, 20-25.

Mezmur, B. (2009a). From Angelina (to Madonna) to Zoe's Ark: What are the 'A-Z' lessons for intercountry adoptions in Africa? *International Journal of Law, Policy and the Family*, 23, 145-73.

Mezmur, B. (2009b). Intercountry adoption as a measure of last resort in Africa: Advancing the rights of a child rather than a right to a child. *Sur—International Journal on Human Rights,* 6(10), 83-104.

Mezmur, B. (2010, June). *The Sins of the Saviours: Trafficking in the Context of Intercountry Adoption from Africa.* Paper presented at the Special Commission of the Hague Conference on Private International Law. The Hague, Netherlands. Retrieved from www.hcch.net/upload/wop/adop2010id02e.pdf.

Midgley, J. (2007). Perspectives on globalization, social justice and welfare. Journal of *Sociology and Social Welfare*. 34(2), 17-36.

Miller, B., Fan, X., Cristensen, M., Grotevant, H.D., and van Dulmen, M. (2000). Comparisons of adopted and nonadopted adolescents in a large, nationally representative sample. *Child Development*, 71, 1458-73.

Miller, L.C. (2005a). *Handbook of International Adoption Medicine: A Guide for Physicians, Parents, and Providers.* New York, NY: Oxford University Press.

Miller, L.C. (2005b). International adoption: Infectious diseases issues. *Clinical Infectious Diseases*, 40, 286-93.

Miller, L.C. (ed.) (2006). *Precocious Puberty: Why Internationally Adopted Children are Affected.* Warren, NJ: EMK.

Miller, L.C., Chan, W., Comfort, K., and Tirella, L.G. (2005). Health of children adopted from Guatemala: Comparison of orphanage and foster care. *Pediatrics*, 115, 710-17.

Miller, L.C., Chan, W., Litvinova, A., Rubin, A., Tirella, L., and Cermak, S. (2007). Medical diagnoses and growth of children residing in Russian orphanages. *Acta Paediatrica*, 96, 1765-9.

Miller, L.C., Chan, W., Litvinova, A., Rubin, A., Comfort, K., Tirella, L., and Boston-Murmansk Orphanage Research Team. (2006). Fetal alcohol spectrum disorders in children residing in Russian orphanages: A phenotypic survey. *Alcoholism, Clinical and Experimental Research*, 30, 531-8.

Miller, L.C. and Hendrie, N.W. (2000). Health of children adopted from China. *Pediatrics*, 105, E76.

Miller, L.C., Kiernan, M.T., Mathers, M.I., and Klein-Gitelman, M. (1995). Developmental and nutritional status of internationally adopted children. *Archives of Pediatrics and Adolescent Medicine*, 149, 40-44.

Miller, L.C., Tseng, B., Tirella, L.G., Chan, W., and Feig, E. (2008). Health of children adopted from Ethiopia. *Maternal and Child Health Journal*, 12, 599-605.

Miller Llana, S. (2010, February 18). US missionaries: Lessons from Haiti adoption or 'child kidnapping' case. *Christian Science Monitor.* Retrieved from http://www.csmonitor.com/World/2010/0218/US-missionaries-Lessons-from-Haiti-adoption-or-child-kidnapping-case.

Millman, J. (2010, February 5). Haitians, parents defend arrested Americans. *Wall Street Journal.* Retrieved from http://online.wsj.com/article/SB100014240527487045332045750477204430451 94.html.

Millman, J., Ball, J., and Schoofs, M. (2010, February 3). Missionary stumbles on road to Haiti. *Wall Street Journal.* Retrieved from http://online.wsj.com/article/SB10001424052748703357104575045794048725562.html.

Ministerio de Gobernación Guatemala. (2010). *Acuerdo Gobernativo Número 102-2010: Reglamento de la Ley de Adopciones* [Government Accord Number 102-2010: Rules of Adoption Law]. Retrieved from http://www.cna.gob.gt/portal/doc/acuerdogubernativo1822010.pdf.

Modell, J. (1994). *Kinship with Strangers: Adoption and Interpretations of Kinship in American Cultures.* Los Angeles, CA: University of California Press.

Modell, J. (2002). *A Sealed and Secret Kinship: Policies and Practices in American Adoption.* New York, NY: Berghahn Books.

Morrison, L. (2004). Ceausescu's legacy: Family struggles and institutionalization of children in Romania. *Journal of Family History*, 29, 168-82.

Moskoff, W. (1980). Pronatalist policies in Romania. *Economic Development and Cultural Change*, 28, 597-614.

Mullender, A. (ed.). (1991a). *Open Adoption: The Philosophy and the Practice.* London: British Agencies for Adoption and Fostering.

Mullender, A. (1991b). *Adult Adoption Information in New Zealand.* In A. Mullender (ed.), *Open Adoption: The Philosophy and the Practice* (pp. 129-37). London: British Agencies for Adoption and Fostering.

Murakami, H., Kobayashi, J.M., Zhu, X., Li, Y., Wakai, S., and Chiba, Y. (2003). Risk of transmission of hepatitis B virus through childhood immunization in northwestern China. *Social Science and Medicine*, 57, 1821-32.

Mylien, N., Meyer, K.K., and Winick, M. (1977). Early malnutrition and "late" adoption: A study of their effects on the development of Korean orphans adopted into American families. *The American Journal of Clinical Nutrition*, 30, 1734-9.

Nalavany, B., Ryan, S., Howard, J., and Smith, S. (2008). Pre-adoptive child sexual abuse as a predictor of moves in care, adoption displacements, and inconsistent adoptive parent commitment. *Child Abuse and Neglect*, 32, 1084-8.

National Authority for the Protection of Child's Rights. (2006). *Child Welfare in Romania: The Story of a Reform Process.* Bucharest: NAPCR. Retrieved from http://www.copii.ro/publicatie2815.html?id=80.

National Authority for the Protection of Child's Rights. (2010). *Statistics of the Child Protection System, December 2010.* Retrieved from http://www.copii.ro/alte_categorii.html.

Negeri, D. (2006). *Guddifachaa Practice as Child Problem Intervention in Oromo Society: The Case of Ada'a Liban District.* (Unpublished master's thesis). Retrieved from http://etd.aau.edu.et/dspace/bitstream/123456789/2458/1/SOCIAL_11.pdf.

Neil, E. (2006). Coming to terms with the loss of a child: The feelings of birth parents and grandparents about adoption and post-adoption contact. *Adoption Quarterly*, 10(1), 1-23.

Neiss, M. and Rowe, D.C. (2000). Parental education and child's verbal IQ in adoptive and biological families in the national longitudinal study of adolescent health. *Behavior Genetics*, 30, 487-95.

Nelson, C.A., Zeanah, C.H., Fox, N.A., Marshall, P.J., Smyke, A.T., and Guthrie, D. (2007). Cognitive recovery in socially deprived young children: The Bucharest Early Intervention Project. *Science*, 318, 1937-40.

New Zealand Parliamentary Counsel Office. (2010). *Human Assisted Reproductive Technology Act 2004.* Retrieved from http://www.legislation.govt.nz/act/public/2004/0092/latest/whole.html.

Ngabonziza, D. (1991). Moral and political issues facing relinquishing countries. *Adoption and Fostering*, 15(4), 75-80.

Ngarmbassa, M. (2007, December 22). *Zoe's Ark Lied about Flight Plans, Chad Court Told.* Retrieved from http://www.reuters.com/article/africaCrisis/idUSL22220888.

Nguyen Da Yen, et al. v. Kissinger, 528 F.2d 1194 (9th Cir. 1975).

Noel, B. (2008, January 17). Kidnapped kids reunite with families in Guatemala. *MSNBC.* Retrieved from http://insidedateline.msnbc.msn.com/_news/2008/01/17/4374303-kidnapped-kids-reunite-with-family-in-guatemala.

Nokes, C., McGarvey, S.T., Shiue, L., Wu, G., Wu, H., Bundy, D.A., and Olds, G.R. (1999). Evidence for an improvement in cognitive function following treatment of Schistosoma Japonicum infection in Chinese primary school children. American *Journal of Tropical Medicine and Hygiene*, 60, 556-65.

Noordegraaf, M. van Ninjnattan, C., and Elders, E. (2009). Assessing parents for adoptive parenthood: Institutional reformulations of biographical notes. *Children and Youth Services Review*, 31, 89-96.

O'Connor, M.K. and Netting, F.E. (2009). *Organization Practice: A Guide to Understanding Human Service Organizations* (2nd ed.). Hoboken, NJ: Wiley.

Odenstad, A., Hjern, A., Lindblad, F., Rasmussen, F., Vinnerljung, B., and Dalen, M. (2008). Does age at adoption and geographic origin matter? A national cohort study of cognitive test performance in adult inter-country adoptees. *Psychological Medicine*, 38, 180314.

Office of the High Commissioner for Human Rights. (1986). *UN Declaration on the Social and Legal Principles Relating to the Protection and the Welfare of Children.* Retrieved from the United Nations website: http://www.un.org/documents/ga/res/41/a41r085.htm.

Office of the UN High Commissioner for Refugees. (n.d.). *Basic Facts.* Retrieved from the United Nations website: http://www.unhcr.se/en/Basics/basics_index_en.html.

O'Halloran, K. (2009). *The Politics of Adoption: International Perspectives on Law, Policy and Practice* (2nd ed.). New York, NY: Springer.

O'Keefe, K. (2007). The Intercountry Adoption Act of 2000: The United States' ratification of the Hague Convention on the Protection of Children, and its meager effect on international adoption. *Vanderbilt Journal of Transnational Law*, 40, 1611-16.

Oleke, C., Blystad, A., Moland, K.M., Rekdal, O.B., and Heggenhougen, K. (2006). The varying vulnerability of African orphans: The case of the Langi, northern Uganda. *Childhood*, 13, 267-84.

O'Loughlin, S. and O'Loughlin, M. (2011). *Social Work Skills with Children, Young People and Families.* Exeter, UK: Learning Matters Limited.

Olsen, L.J. (2003). Live or let die: Could intercountry adoption make the difference? *Penn State International Law Review*, 22, 483-525.

O'Neill, A. (2005, June 6). Why are American babies being adopted abroad? *People*, 63(22), Retrieved from http://www.people.com/people/archive/article/0,,20147746,00.html.

Onishi, N. (2008, October 9). Korea aims to end stigma of adoption and stop exporting babies. *New York Times*. Retrieved from http://www.nytimes.com/2008/10/09/world/asia/09iht-09adopt.16801435.html.

Oreskovic, J. and Maskew, T. (2008). Red thread or slender reed: Deconstructing Prof. Bartholet's mythology of international adoption. *Buffalo Human Rights Law Review*, 147, 71-128.

Osborne, M. (2010). *Helping Haiti's Most Vulnerable: Orphans in Crisis.* Retrieved from the Rainbow Kids website: http://www.rainbowkids.com/ArticleDetails.aspx?id=688.

Overseas Koreans Foundation. (2006). *International Korean Adoptees Resource Book: Statistics.* Retrieved from http://eng.korean.net/download/oaks/06_Statistics.pdf.

Overseas Koreans Foundation. (2011). *Stats on Adoptees: International Adoptions, 1953-2007.* Retrieved from http://eng.korean.net/knt/cms/EngCmsHtmlView.do?menuld=MKNTENG00310andpageld=1291627703852.

Oyserman, D., Coon, H.M., and Kemmelmeier, M. (2002). Rethinking individualism and collectivism: Evaluation of theoretical assumptions and meta-analyses. *Psychological Bulletin*, 128, 3-72.

Pacepa, I.M. (1990). *Red horizons: The True Story of Nicolae and Elena Ceausescus' Crimes, Lifestyle, and Corruption.* Washington, DC: Regnery Publishing, Inc.

Palacios, J. (2009). The ecology of adoption. In G.M. Wrobel and E. Neil (eds), *International Advances in Adoption Research for Practice* (pp. 71-94). Chichester, UK: Wiley-Blackwell.

Palacios, J. and Brodzinsky, D.M. (2005). Recent changes and future directions for adoption research. In D.M. Brodzinsky and J. Palacios (eds). *Psychological Issues in Adoption* (pp. 211-31). Westport, CT: Praeger.

Palacios, J. and Brodzinsky, D.M. (2010). Adoption research: Trends, topics, outcomes. *International Journal of Behavioral Development*, 34, 270-84.

Palacios, J., Román, M., Moreno, C. and Esperanza, L. (2009). Family context for emotional recovery in internationally adopted children. *International Social Work*, 52, 609-20.

Palacios, J. and Sánchez-Sandoval, Y. (2005). Beyond adopted-nonadopted comparisons. In D. Brodzinsky and J. Palacios (eds), *Psychological Issues in Adoption: Research and Practice* (pp. 117-44). Westport, CT: Praeger.

Palacios, J., Sánchez-Sandoval, Y., and León, E. (2005). Intercountry adoption disruption in Spain. *Adoption Quarterly*, 9(1), 35-55.

Palmer, J.D. (2001). Korean adopted young women: Gender bias, racial issues, and educational implications. In C.C. Park, A.L. Goodwin, and S.J. Lee (eds), *Research on the Education of Asian Pacific Americans* (pp. 177-204). Greenwich: Information Age Publishing Inc.

Palmer, J.D. (2010). *The Dance of Identities: Korean Adoptees and their Journey toward Empowerment.* Honolulu, HI: University of Hawaii Press.

Pande, A. (2009). Not an 'angel' not a 'whore': Surrogates as 'dirty' workers in India. *Indian Journal of Gender Studies*, 16, 141-73.

Pardasani, M., Chazin, R., and Fortinsky, L. (2010). The Orphans International Tanzania (OIT) family care model: Strengthening networks and empowering families. *Journal of HIV/AIDS and Social Services*, 9, 305-21.

Parents for Ethical Adoption Reform. (2010a, June). *PEAR's Response to "The Baby Business."* Retrieved from http://pear-now.blogspot.com/search?q=Paper.

Parents for Ethical Adoption Reform. (2010b). *Results of PEAR's Ethiopia Study.* Retrieved from http://pear-now.org/docs/PEAR-Ethiopia-Survey-Results.pdf.

Park, Y.S. (2008). Revisiting the welfare state system in Korea. *International Social Security Review*, 61(2). 3-19.

Park Nelson, K. (2007). Adoptees as "White Koreans": Identity, racial visibility and the politics of passing among Korean American adoptees. In K.P. Nelson, E. Kim, and L. Myong Petersen (eds), *Proceedings of the 1st International Korean Adoption Studies Research Symposium, 2007* (pp. 195-211). Seoul: International Korean Adoptee Associations' International Research Committee.

Parker, R. (2008). *Uprooted: The Shipment of Poor Children to Canada, 1867-1917.* Bristol: Policy Press.

Paulsen, C. and Merighi, J.R. (2009). Adoption preparedness, cultural engagement, and parental satisfaction in intercountry adoption. *Adoption Quarterly*, 12, 1-18.

Pérez, L.M. (2008). *Situation faced by Institutionalized Children and Adolescents in Shelters in Guatemala.* Guatemala City: USAID and Holt International Children's Services.

Perez, S. (2011). Guatemala court orders US couple to return allegedly stolen child. *MSNBC.* Retrieved from http://www.msnbc.msn.com/id/44014559/ns/world_news-americas/#.TkMR-WCHc78.

Perry, T.L. (1993). Transracial adoption controversy: An analysis of discourse and subordination. *Review of Law and Social Change*, 21, 33-108.

Perry, T.L. (1998). Transracial and international adoption: Mothers, hierarchy, race and feminist legal theory. *Yale Journal of Law and Feminism*, 10, 101-64.

Perry, T.L. (2006). Transracial adoption and gentrification: An essay on race, power, family and community. *Boston College Third World Law Journal*, 26, 25-60.

Pertman, A. (2011). *Adoption Nation* (2nd ed.). Boston, MA: The Harvard Common Press.

Pickering, L.K., Baker, C.J., Kimberlin, D.W., and Long, S.S. (eds). (2009). *Red Book: 2009 Report of the Committee on Infectious Dseases* (28th ed.). Elk Grove Village, IL: American Academy of Pediatrics.

Pollock, K.E. (2005). Early language growth in children adopted from China: Preliminary normative data. *Seminars in Speech and Language*, 26, 22-32.

Ponte, I.C., Wang, L.K., and Fan, S.P. (2010). Returning to China: The experience of adopted Chinese children and their parents. *Adoption Quarterly*, 13, 100-24.

Popkin, M. (2001). Building the rule of law in post-war El Salvador. In M. Studemeister (ed.), *El Salvador—Implementation of the Peace Accords.* Washington DC: United States Institute of Peace. Retrieved from http://permanent.access.gpo.gov/websites/usip/www.usip.org/pubs/peaceworks/pwks38.pdf.

Post, R. (2007). *Romania: For Export Only: The Untold Story of the Romanian Orphans.* Brussels: Eurocomment Diffusion SA.

Pound Pup Legacy. (n.d.). *Cambodia—Lauryn Galindo Case.* Retrieved from http://poundpuplegacy.org/node/22103.

Pratt Guterl, M. (2009). Josephine Baker's "*Rainbow Tribe:" Radical Motherhood in South of France. Journal of Women's History*, 21(4), 38-58.

Pro-Búsqueda. (2002). *El día mas esperado—Buscando a los niños desaparecidos de El Salvador* [The most awaited day—Searching for the 'disappeared' children of El Salvador] (2nd ed.). San Salvador, El Salvador: UCA Editors.

Pro-Búsqueda. (2004). *Historias para tener presente* [Stories to have present]. (2nd ed.). San Salvador, El Salvador: UCA Editors.

Pro-Búsqueda. (2009). *Adoption during the Armed Conflict in El Salvador and its Effect on the Right to Identity of the Disappeared Children.* El Salvador: Author.

Pro-Búsqueda. (2011a). ¿Qué podemos hacer? [What we can do?]. Retrieved from http://probusqueda.org.sv/%c2%bfbuscas-a-tu-familia-biologica/%c2%bfquepodemos-hacer-por-usted/.

Pro-Búsqueda. (2011b). *El habeas corpus en casos de niñas y niños desaparecidos* [Habeas Corpus in the case of the disappeared children]. Retrieved from http://probusqueda.org.sv/2009/12/28/el-habeas-corpus-en-casos-de-ninas-y-ninos-desaparecidos/.

Pro-Búsqueda. (2011c). *Inicia labores Comisión Nacional de Búsqueda de Niños Desaparecidos* [Pro-Búsqueda initiates the National Commission for the Search of Disappeared Children]. Retrieved from http://probusqueda.org.sv/2011/03/30/inicia-labores-comision-nacional-de-busqueda-de-ninos-desaparecidos/.

Pro-Búsqueda. (2011d). *Discurso 29 de Marzo Día de la Niñez Desaparecida Pronunciado por la Coordinadora General, Ester Alvarenga* [March 29 speech on the occasion of the Day of the Disappeared Children by the General Coordinator, Ester Alvarenga]. Retrieved from http://probusqueda.org.sv/2011/04/05/discurso-del-dia-de-la-ninez-desaparecida/.

Profile: Zoe's Ark. (2007, October 29). *British Broadcasting Corporation.* Retrieved from http://news.bbc.co.uk/2/hi/europe/7067374.stm.

Proos, L.A., Hofvander, Y., Wennqvist, K., and Tuvemo, T. (1992). A longitudinal study on anthropometric and clinical development of Indian children adopted in Sweden. II. Growth, morbidity and development during two years after arrival in Sweden. *Upsala Journal of Medical Sciences*, 97, 93-106.

Pruzan, V. (1977). *Født i utlandet—Adoptet i Danmark* [Born abroad-Adopted to Denmark]. Rapport 77. Copenhagen: Socialforskningsinstituttet.

Quiroz, P.A. (2007). *Adoption in a Color-blind Society.* Lanham, MD: Rowman and Littlefield.

Raitt, F.E. (2007). Hearing children in family law proceedings: Can judges make a difference? *Child and Family Law Quarterly*, 19(2), 1-20.

Randolph, T.H. and Holtzman, M. (2010). The role of heritage camps in identity development among Korean transnational adoptees: A relational dialectics approach. *Adoption Quarterly*, 13, 75-99.

Rastas, A. (2004). Racializing categorization among young people in Finland. *Young: Nordic Journal of Youth Research*, 13(2), 147-66.

Recuperación de la Memoria Histórica. (1999). *Guatemala: Never Again!* Guatemala City, Guatemala: Archdiocese of Guatemala.

Reilly, T. and Platz, P. (2003). Characteristics and challenges of families who adopt children with special needs: An empirical study. *Children and Youth Services Review*, 25, 781-803.

Reinoso, M., Juffer, F., and Tieman, W. (2012). Children's and parents' thoughts and feelings about adoption, birth culture identity and discrimination in families with internationally adopted children. *Child & Family Social Work.*

Riben, M. (2007). *The Stork Market: America's Multi-billion Dollar Unregulated Adoption Industry.* Dayton, NJ: Advocate.

Rivera, C., Bromfield, N., and Rotabi, K.S. (2009, April). *Sold into Sex, Servitude, and Adoption.* Presented at Virginia Commonwealth University, Richmond, VA.

Roberts, J.A., Pollock, K.E., Krakow, R., Price, J., Fulmer, K.C., and Wang, P. (2005). Language development in preschool-age children adopted from China. *Journal of Speech, Language, and Hearing Research*, 48, 93-107.

Roby, J.L. (2007). From rhetoric to best practice: Children's rights in intercountry adoption. *Children's Legal Rights Journal*, 27(3), 48-71.

Roby, J.L. and Ife, J. (2009). Human rights, politics and intercountry adoption: An examination of two sending countries. *International Social Work*, 52, 661-71.

Roby, J.L. and Matsumura, S. (2002). If I give you my child, aren't we family? A study of birthmothers participating in Marshall Islands—U.S. adoptions. *Adoption Quarterly*, 5(4), 7-31.

Roby, J.L. and Shaw, S.A. (2006). The African orphan crisis and international adoption, *Social Work*, 51, 199-210.

Roby, J.L., Wyatt, J., and Pettys, G. (2005). Openness in international adoptions: A study of U.S. parents who adopted children from the Marshall Islands. *Adoption Quarterly*, 8(3), 47-71.

Roche Jr., W.F. (2010, February 25). Haitian children in legal quagmire. *Pittsburgh Tribune-Review*. Retrieved from http://www.pittsburghlive.com/x/pittsburghtrib/news/specialreports/haitiearthquake/s_668850.html.

Rockel, J. and Ryburn, M. (1988). *Adoption today: Change and Choice in New Zealand.* Birkenhead, Auckland: Heinemann Reed.

Rollings, J. (2008). *Love Our Way: A Mother's Story.* Sydney: Harper Collins.

Rooth, D.O. (2002). Adopted children in the labour market: Discrimination or unobserved characteristics? *International Migration*, 40(1), 71-98.

Rørbech, M. (1989). *Mit land er Danmark. En undersøgelse af unge adopterede fra Asien, Afrika og Latinamerika* [My country is Denmark. A study of young adoptees from Asia, Africa and Latin America]. Copenhagen: Socialforskningsinstituttet.

Rosenberg, K.F. and Groze, V. (1997). The impact of secrecy and denial in adoption: Practice and treatment issues. *Families in Society*, 78, 522-30.

Rosenthal, J.A. (1993). Outcomes of adoption of children with special needs. *The Future of Children*, 3(1), 77-88.

Rosenthal, R. (1991). *Meta-analytic Procedures for Social Research.* Beverly Hills, CA: Sage.

Rosenthal, R. (1995). Writing meta-analytic reviews. *Psychological Bulletin*, 118, 183-92.

Rosnoblet, J.F. (2007, October 29). French Group says aimed to help Chad children. *Boston Globe.* Retrieved from http://www.reuters.com/article/worldNews/idUSL2952179420071029.

Rotabi, K.S. (2007). Adoption of Guatemalan children: Impending changes under The Hague Convention for international Adoption. *Social Work and Society News Magazine.* Retrieved from www.socmag.net/?p=171.

Rotabi, K.S. (2008). Intercountry adoption baby boom prompts new US standards. *Immigration Law Today*, 27(1), 12-19.

Rotabi, K.S. (2009, August 22). Guatemala City: Hunger protests amid allegations of child kidnapping and adoption fraud. *Social Work and Society News Magazine.* Retrieved from http://www.socmag.net/?p=540.

Rotabi, K.S. (2010a, April 13). Poor placement practices could close Russian adoptions. *The Legatum Institute.* Retrieved from http://www.legatum.com/newsdisplay.aspx?id=3826.

Rotabi, K.S. (2010b, June 8). From Guatemala to Ethiopia: Shifts in intercountry adoption leaves Ethiopia vulnerable for child sales and other unethical practices. *Social Work and Society News Magazine*. Retrieved from www.socmag.net/?p=615.

Rotabi, K.S. and Bergquist, K.J.S. (2010). Vulnerable children in the aftermath of Haiti's earthquake of 2010: A call for sound policy and processes to prevent international child sales and theft. *Journal of Global Social Work Practice*, 3(1). Retrieved from http://www.globalsocialwork.org/vol3no1/Rotabi.html.

Rotabi, K.S. and Bromfield, N.F. (in press). Intercountry adoption declines lead to new practices of global surrogacy in Guatemala : Global human rights concerns in the context of violence and the era of advanced fertility technology. *Affilia*. doi: 10.1177/0886109912444102.

Rotabi, K.S. and Bromfield, N.F. (2010, July 7). Will global surrogacy be regulated? [Web log post]. Retrieved from http://www.rhrealitycheck.org/blog/78418.

Rotabi, K.S. and Bunkers, K.M. (2008, November 29). Intercountry adoption reform based on the Hague Convention on Intercountry Adoption: An update on Guatemala in 2008. *Social Work and Society.* Retrieved from www.socmag.net/?tag=adoption.

Rotabi, K.S. and Gibbons, J.L. (2012). Does the Hague Convention on Intercountry Adoption adequately protect orphaned and vulnerable children and their families? *Journal of Child and Family Studies*, 21(1), 106-19.

Rotabi, K.S. and Heine, T.M. (2010). Commentary on Russian child adoption incidents: Implications for global policy and practice. *Journal of Global Social Work Practice*, 3(1), Retrieved from http://www.globalsocialwork.org/vol3no2/rotabi.html.

Rotabi, K.S. and Morris, A.W. (2007, July). Adoption of Guatemalan children: Impending changes under the Hague Convention for Intercountry Adoption. *Social Work and Society.* Retrieved from http://www.socmag.net/?p=171.

Rotabi, K.S., Morris, A.W., and Weil, M.O. (2008). International child adoption in a post-conflict society: A multi-systemic assessment of Guatemala. *Journal of Intergroup Relations,* 34(2), 9-41.

Rotabi, K.S., Pennell, J., Roby, J.L., and Bunkers, K.M. (2012). Family Group Conferencing as a culturally adaptable intervention: Reforming intercountry adoption in Guatemala. *International Social Work*, 55, 402-16.

Roth, M. (1999). Children's rights in Romania: Problems and progress. *Social Work in Europe,* 6(3), 30-37.

Rothman, B.K. (2005). *Weaving a Family: Untangling Race and Adoption.* Boston, MA: Beacon Press.

Rothman, J. and Sager, J.S. (1997). *Case Management: Integrating Individual and Community Practice.* Boston, MA: Allyn & Bacon.

Ruggiero, J.A. and Johnson, K. (2009). Implications for recent research on Eastern European adoptees for social work practice. *Child and Adolescent Social Work Journal*, 26, 485-504.

Rutter, M., Kreppner, J., O'Connor, T., and the ERA Study Team (2001). Specificity and the heterogeneity in children's responses to profound privation. *British Journal of Psychiatry Special Issues*, 179, 97-103.

Rutter, M., Beckett, C., Castle, J., Colvert, E., Kreppner, J., Mehta, M., and Sonuga-Barke, E. (2009). Effects of profound early institutional deprivation: An overview of findings from UK longitudinal study of Romanian adoptees. In G. M Wrobel and B. Neil (eds), *International Advances in Adoption Research for National Advances in Adoption Research for Practice* (pp. 147-67). UK: Wiley-Blackwell.

Ryan, A.S. (1983). Intercountry adoption and policy issues. *Journal of Children in Contemporary Society*, 15(3), 49-60.

Ryan, S. and Groza, V. (2004). Romanian adoptees: A cross-national comparison. *International Social Work*, 47, 53-79.

Rycus, J.S., Freundlich, M., Hughes, R.C., Keefer, B., and Oakes, E.J. (2006). Confronting barriers to adoption success. *Family Court Review*, 44, 210-30.

Rygvold, A.L. (1999). Better or worse? Intercountry adopted children's language. In A. Rygvold, M. Dalen, and B. Sætersdal (eds), *Mine—Yours—Ours and Theirs: Adoption, Changing Kinship and Family Patterns* (pp. 221-9). Oslo: University of Oslo.

Rygvold, A.L. (2009). Language development of internationally adopted four-year olds. In M. Dalen and A.L. Rygvold (eds), *International Adoptees—School Performance, Educational Attainment and Social Adjustment* (pp. 51-60). Oslo: University of Oslo.

Saclier, C. (2000). In the best interests of the child? In P. Selman (ed.), *Intercountry Adoption: Developments, Trends and Perspectives* (pp. 53-65). London: BAAF.

Said, E. (1979). *Orientalism.* New York, NY: Vintage Books.

Saiman, L., Aronson, J., Zhou, J., Gomez-Duarte, C., San Gabriel, P., Alonso, M., and Schulte, J. (2001). Prevalence of infectious diseases among internationally adopted children. *Pediatrics*, 108, 608-12.

Sancar, F.H. and Severcan, Y.C. (2010). In search of agency: Participation in a youth organization in Turkey. In B. Percy-Smith and N. Thomas (eds), *A Handbook of Children and Young People's Participation: Perspectives from Theory and Practice* (pp. 277-86). London: Routledge.

Sang-Hun, C. (2007). Group resists Korean stigma for unwed mothers. *New York Times.* Retrieved from www.nytimes.com/2009/10/08/world/asia/08mothers.html?pagewanted=print.

Sargent, S. (2003). Suspended animation: The implementation of the Hague Convention on Intercountry Adoption in Romania and United States. *Texas Wesleyan Law Review*, 10, 351-78.

Sarri, R., Baik, Y., and Bombyk, M. (1998). Goal displacement and dependency in South Korean-United States intercountry adoption. *Children and Youth Services Review*, 20, 87-114.

Scarr, S. (1992). Development theories for the 1990s: Development and individual differences. *Child Development*, 63, 1-19.

Schechter, M. (1960). Observations on adopted children. *Archives of General Psychiatry*, 3, 21-32.

Scheper- Hughes, N. (1992). *Death without Weeping: The Violence of Everyday Life in Brazil.* Los Angeles, CA: University of California Press.

Scherman, R. (2010a). A theoretical look at biculturalism in intercountry adoption. *Journal of Ethnic and Cultural Diversity in Social Work*, 19, 127-42.

Scherman, R. (2010b). Does adopted mean different? The developmental impact of adoption on children. In J. Low and P. Jose (eds), *Lifespan Development: New Zealand Perspectives* (2nd ed.; pp. 196-205). North Shore, New Zealand: Pearson Education.

Scherman, R. and Harre, N. (2004). Intercountry adoption of Eastern European children in New Zealand: Parents' attitudes toward the importance of culture. *Adoption and Fostering*, 28(3), 62-72.

Scherman, R. and Harré, N. (2008). The ethnic identification of same-race children in intercountry adoption. *Adoption Quarterly*, 11, 45-65.

Scherman, R. and Hawke, W. (2010, July). *Openness and intercountry adoption.* Paper presented at the Third International Conference on Adoption Research. Leiden, The Netherlands.

Schieber, B. (2010, November 19). Guatemala health survey shows improvement in important health indicators. *The Guatemala Times.* Retrieved from http://www.guatemala-times.com/news/guatemala/1274-guatemala-health-survey-shows-improvement-in-important-health-indicators.html.

Schlesinger, S. and Kinzer, S. (1999). *Bitter Fruit: The Story of the American Coup in Guatemala.* Cambridge, MA: Harvard University Press.

Schmidt, V. (2009). Orphan care in Russia. *Social Work and Society.* Retrieved from http://www.socwork.net/2009/1/special_issue/schmidt.

Schuster Institute for Investigative Journalism. (n.d.). *Capsule History of Adoption Issues in Cambodia.* Retrieved from http://www.brandeis.edu/investigate/gender/adoption/cambodia.html.

Schwekendiek, D., Kwon, J.S., and Jung, A.R. (2008). *A Study on Post-adoption Services for Overseas Adopted Koreans: Evidence from Worldwide Survey.* Seoul: International Korean Adoptee Service.

Seekings, J., and Nattrass, N. (2006). *Class, Race, and Inequality in South Africa.* South Africa: University of KwaZulu-Natal Press.

Seijo, L. (2008, August 17). Mejor padres de Guatemala [Better Guatemalan parents.] *Prensa Libre*, pp. 2-5.

Selinske, J., Naughton, D., Flanaghan, K., Fry, P., and Pickles, A. (2001). Ensuring the best interests of the child in intercountry adoption practice: Case studies from the United Kingdom and the United States. *Child Welfare*, 80, 656-67.

Selman, P. (2000). The demographic history of intercountry adoption. In P. Selman (ed.), *Intercountry Adoption* (pp. 107-42). London: British Agencies for Adoption and Fostering.

Selman, P. (2002). Intercountry adoption in the new millennium: The "quiet migration" revisited. *Population Research and Policy Review*, 21, 205-25.

Selman, P. (2006). Trends in intercountry adoption: Analysis of data from 20 receiving countries, 1998-2004. *Journal of Population Research*, 23, 183-204.

Selman, P. (2007). Intercountry adoption in the twenty-first century: An examination of the rise and fall of countries of origin. In K. Nelson, E. Kim, and M. Petersen (eds), *Proceedings of the First International Korean Adoption Studies Research Symposium* (pp. 55-75). Seoul: IKAA.

Selman, P. (2008). *The Movement of Children for Transnational Adoption.* London: The Globalization of Motherhood Symposium.

Selman, P. (2009a). From Bucharest to Beijing: Changes in countries sending children for international adoption 1990 to 2006. In G.M. Wrobel and E. Neil (eds), *International Advances in Adoption Research for Practice* (pp. 41-69). New York, NY: Wiley.

Selman, P. (2009b). Intercountry adoption: Research, policy and practice. In G. Schofield and J. Simmonds (eds), *The Child Placement Handbook: Research, Policy and Practice* (pp. 276-303). London: BAAF.

Selman, P. (2009c). Intercountry adoption in Europe 1998–2007: Patterns, trends and issues. In K. Rummery, I. Greener, and C. Holden (eds), *Social Policy Review 21: Analysis and Debate in Social Policy* (pp. 133-65). Bristol: Polity Press.

Selman, P. (2009d). The rise and fall of international adoption in the 21st century. *International Social Work*, 52, 575-94.

Selman, P. (2010a). Intercountry adoption in Europe 1998-2009: Patterns, trends and issues. *Adoption and Fostering*, 34(1), 4-19.

Selman, P. (2010b). Intercountry adoption as globalised motherhood. In W. Chavkin and J. Mather (eds). *The Globalisation of Motherhood: Deconstructions and Reconstructions of Biology and Care* (pp. 79-105). London: Routledge.

Selman, P. (2010c, July). *The Global Decline of Intercountry Adoption: Is this the Beginning of the End?* Paper presented at the 3rd International Conference on Adoption Research. Leiden, the Netherlands.

Selman, P. (2010d, August). *Transnational Adoption of Children from Asia in the Twenty-first century.* Paper presented at Inter-Asia Roundtable: Transnational Migration and Children in Asian Contexts. Singapore.

Selman, P. (2011) Intercountry adoption after the Haiti earthquake. Rescue or robbery? *Adoption and Fostering*, 35(4), 41-9.

Selman P. (2012) Global Trends in Intercountry Adoption: 2001-2010, *Adoption Advocate* no 44. Retrieved from https://www.adoptioncouncil.org/publications/adoption-advocate-no-44.html.

Selman, P. (in press). The rise and fall of intercountry adoption in the 21st century: Global trends from 2001 to 2010. In J.L. Gibbons and K.S. Rotabi (eds), *Intercountry Adoption: Policy, Practice, and Outcomes.* Farnham: Ashgate Publishing.

Selman P. (in press) The Global Decline of Intercountry Adoption: What lies ahead? *Social Policy and Society,* 11(4)

Selman, P., Moretti, E., and Brogi, F. (2009). *Statistical Profile of International Adoption in the European Union: Report from ChildONEurope to the European Parliament.* Florence: Istituto degli Innocenti.

Shawyer, J. (1979). *Death by Adoption.* Auckland, New Zealand: Cicada Press.

Shepard, C., Finelli, L., Bell, B., and Miller, J. (2004). Acute hepatitis B among children and adolescents -- United States 1990-2002. *Morbidity and Mortality Weekly Report*, 53, 1015-18.

Shiao, J.L. and Tuan, M. (2007). A sociological approach to race, identity, and Asian adoption. In K.J.S. Bergquist, M.E. Vonk, D.S. Kim and M.D. Feit (eds), *International Korean Adoption: A Fifty-year History of Policy and Practice* (pp. 155-70). Binghampton, NY: Haworth Press.

Shiao, J.L., Tuan, M., and Rienzi, M. (2004). Shifting the spotlight: Exploring race and culture in Korean-White adoptive families. *Race and Society*, 7, 1-16.

Shiu, A. (2001). Flexible production: International adoption, race, whiteness, *Jouvert*, 6, 1-24.

Siegal, E. (n.d.). *Archive for Florida DCF Category.* Retrieved from http://findingfernanda.com/category/investigations/florida-dcf/.

Siegal, E. (2011). *Finding Fernanda: Two mothers, One Child, and a Cross-Border Search for Truth.* Oakland, CA: Cathexis Press.

Simon, R.J. and Altstein, H. (1981). *Transracial Adoption: A Follow Up.* Lexington: Heath.

Simon, R.J. and Altstein, H. (1987). *Transracial Adoptees and their Families: A Study of Identity and Commitment.* New York, NY: Praeger.

Simon, R.J. and Altstein, H. (1996). The case for transracial adoption. *Children and Youth Services Review*, 18, 5-22.

Simon, R.J. and Altstein, H. (2002). *Adoption, Race, and Identity: From Infancy to Young Adulthood.* New Brunswick, NJ: Transaction Publishers.

Simon, R.J. and Roorda, R.M. (2000). *In their Own Voices: Transracial Adoptees tell their Stories.* New York, NY: Columbia University Press.

Simsek, Z., Erol, N., Oztop, D., and Munir, K. (2007). Prevalence and predictors of emotional and behavioral problems reported by teachers among institutionally reared children and adolescents in Turkish orphanages compared with community controls. *Children and Youth Services Review*, 29, 883-99.

Sindelar, D. (2005, January 7). Asia: Fears rise about plight of tsunami orphans. *RadioFreeEurope.* Retrieved from http://www.rferl.org/featuresarticle/2005/01/fdb625c6-2596-4d6e-8f35-54f74a0fd501.html.

Singer, P. (2002). *One World: The Ethics of Globalization* (2nd Ed.). New Haven, CT: Yale University Press.

Sloutsky, V.M. (1997). Institutional care and developmental outcomes of 6- and 7-year old children: A contextualist perspective. *International Journal of Behavioral Development*, 20, 131-51.

Smith, S.L. (2007). *Safeguarding the Rights and Well-being of Birthparents in the Adoption Process.* New York. NY: Evan B. Donaldson Adoption Institute.

Smith, S.L. and Howard, J.A. (1991). A comparative study of successful and disrupted adoptions. *Social Services Review*, 65, 248-65.

Smith, S.L., Howard, J.A., Garnier, P.C., and Ryan, S.D. (2006). Where are we now? A post-ASFA examination of adoption disruption. *Adoption Quarterly*, 9(4), 19-44.

Smith-Garcia, T. and Brown, J.S. (1989). The health of children adopted from India. *Journal of Community Health*, 14, 227-41.

Smolin, D.M. (2004). Intercountry adoption as child trafficking. *Valparaiso University Law Review*, 39, 281-325.

Smolin, D.M. (2005). The two faces of intercountry adoption: The significance of the Indian adoption scandals. *Seton Hall Law Review*, 35, 403-93.

Smolin, D.M. (2006). Child laundering: How the intercountry adoption system legitimizes and incentivizes the practices of buying, trafficking, kidnapping, and stealing children. *Wayne Law Review* 52(1), 113-200. Retrieved from http://works.bepress.com/david_smolin/1.

Smolin, D.M. (2007a). Child Laundering as exploitation: Applying anti-trafficking norms to intercountry adoption under the coming Hague regime. *Vermont Law Review*, 32, 1-55.

Smolin, D.M. (2007b). Intercountry adoption and poverty: A human rights analysis. *Capital Law Review*, 36, 413-53.

Smolin, D.M. (2010). Child laundering and the Hague Convention on Intercountry Adoption: The future and past of intercountry adoption. *University of Louisville Law Review*, 48, 441-98. Retrieved from http://works.bepress.com/david_smolin/8.

Smolin, D. (2011). The missing girls of China: Population policy, culture, gender, abortion, abandonment and adoption in East Asian perspective. *Cumberland Law Review*, 41, 1-65.

Sohr, K. (2006). Difficulties implementing the Hague Convention on the Protection of Children and Co-operation in Respect of Intercountry Adoption: A criticism of the proposed Ortega's Law and an advocacy for moderate adoption reform in Guatemala, *Pace International Law Review*, 18, 559-94.

Sokal, E.M., Van Collie, O., and Buts, J.P. (1995). Horizontal transmission of hepatitis B from children to adoptive parents. *Archives of Disease in Childhood*, 72, 191.

Solinger, R. (2002). *Beggars and Choosers: How the Politics of Choice Shapes Adoption, Abortion, and Welfare in the United States.* New York, NY: Hill and Wang.

Song, S.L. and Lee, R.M. (2009). The past and present cultural experiences of adopted Korean American adults. *Adoption Quarterly*, 12, 19-36.

Sonuga-Barke, E.J.S., Beckett, C., Kreppner, J., Castle, J., Colvert, E., Stevens, S., and Rutter, M. (2008). Is sub-nutrition necessary for a poor outcome following early institutional deprivation? *Developmental Medicine and Child Neurology*, 50, 664-71.

Sorosky, A., Baran, A., and Pannor, R. (1974). The reunion of adoptees and birth relatives. *Journal of Youth and Adolescence*, 3, 195-206.

SOS Children's Villages, and International Social Service. (2010). *Guidelines for the alternative care of children.* Retrieved from the United Nations website: www.iss-ssi.org/2009/assets/files/guidelines/guidelines%20launch%20paper.pdf.

South African Institute of Race Relations. (2006). *South Africa Survey 2004/2005*. Johannesburg: South African Institute of Race Relations.

South Korean Ministry for Health, Welfare and Family Affairs. (2009). *Support for Children in Need of Care*. Retrieved from http://english.mw.go.kr/front_eng/jc/sjc0107mn.jsp?PAR_MENU_ID=1003andMENU_ID=1003060101.

Sprenkles, R., Carrillo Hernandez, L., and Villacorta, C.E. (2001). *Lives Apart—Family Separation and Alternative Care Arrangements during El Salvador's Civil War*. Retrieved from Save the Children website: http://www.crin.org/docs/Lives%20Apart%20%96%20Family%20Separation%20and%0Alternative%20Care%20Arrangements%20during%20El%20Salvador%92s%20Civil20War.pdf.

St. Petersburg USA Orphanage Research Team. (2008). The effects of early social-emotional and relationship experience on the development of young orphanage children. *Monographs of the Society for Research in Child Development*, 73, 1-262.

Staat, M.A. (2002). Infectious disease issues in internationally adopted children. The *Pediatric Infectious Disease Journal*, 21, 257-8.

Stams, G.J.J.M., Juffer, F., Rispens, J., and Hoksbergen, R.A.C. (2000). The development and adjustment of 7-year old children adopted in infancy. *Journal of Child Psychology and Psychiatry*, 41, 1025-37.

Stams, G.J.J.M., Juffer, F., and Van IJzendoorn, M.H. (2002). Maternal sensitivity, infant attachment, and temperament predict adjustment in middle childhood: The case of adopted children and their biologically unrelated parents. *Developmental Psychology*, 38, 806-21.

Stanculescu, M. and Grigoras, V. (2009). *Rapid Assessment of the Social and Poverty Impacts of the Economic Crisis in Romania: Final Report*. Retrieved from United Nations Children's Fund website: http://www.unicef.org/romania/First_Stage_Report_Sentinel_Monitoring_System.pdf.

Stein, J.G. (2001). A call to end baby selling: Why the Hague Convention on Intercountry Adoption should be modified to include the consent provisions of the Uniform Adoption Act, A. *Thomas Jefferson Law Review*, 24, 39-82.

Steiner, M.W.R. (2007). Suzanne's story: A 'lost child' of El Salvador returns home. *Salem Statement*. Salem, MA: Salem State College.

Stoler, A.L. (2002). *Carnal Knowledge and Imperial Power: Race and the Intimate in Colonial Rule*. Berkeley, CA: University of California Press.

Stone, D. (2002). *Policy Paradox: The Art of Political Decision Making* (revised ed.), New York, NY: Norton.

Storsbergen, H.E., Juffer, F., Van Son, M.J.M., and 't Hart, H. (2010). Internationally adopted adults who did not suffer severe early deprivation: The role of appraisal of adoption. *Children and Youth Services Review*, 32, 191-7.

Streissguth, A.P., Barr, H.M., Sampson, P.D., and Bookstein, F.L. (1994). Prenatal alcohol and offspring development: The first fourteen years. *Drug and Alcohol Dependence*, 36, 89-99.

Studemeister, M.S. (2001). Introduction. In M.S. Studemeister (ed.), *El Salvador: Implementation of the Peace Accords*. Washington DC: United States Institute of Peace. Retrieved from http://www.dplf.org/uploads/1190927825.pdf.

Stuy, B. (2006, October 9). Hunan one year after: Part one [Web log message]. Retrieved from http://research-china.blogspot.com/2006/10/hunan-one-year-after-part-one.html.

Stuy, B. (2010, March 9). Information from Hunan: Thirteen case studies [Web log message]. Retrieved from http://research-china.blogspot.com/2010/03/information-from-hunan-thirteen-case.html.

Swartz, L. (2003). Fertility transition in South Africa and its impact on the four major racial groups. In Human Sciences Research Council (ed.), *Fertility. Current South African Issues of Poverty, HIV/AIDS and Youth: Seminar Proceedings* (pp. 7-26). Cape Town: Human Sciences Research Council and Department of Social Development.

Tabacaru, C.L. (1999). The reform in child welfare: A retrospective of 1998. *In the Interest of the Child*, 1(9), 1-2.

Tae-hoon, L. (2011, June 30). New law to restrict adoption by foreigners. *The Korean Times*, Retrieved from http://www.koreatimes.co.kr/www/news/nation/2011/06/116_89951.html.

Tan, T.X. and Marfo, K. (2006). Parental ratings of behavioral adjustment in two samples of adopted Chinese girls: Age-related versus socio-emotional correlates and predictors. *Journal of Applied Developmental Psychology*, 27, 14-30.

Tan, T.X. and Nakkula, M.J. (2004). White parents' attitudes towards their adopted Chinese daughters' ethnic identity. *Adoption Quarterly*, 7(4), 57-76.

Taylor, E. and Rogers, J.W. (2004). Early adversity and developmental disorders. *Journal of Child Psychology and Psychiatry*, 46, 451-67.

Taylor, E. and Sonuga-Barke, E.J. (2008). Disorders of attention and activity. In M. Rutter, D. Bishop, D., Pine, S., Scott, J. Stevenson, E. Taylor, and A. Thapar (eds), *Rutter's Child and Adolescent Psychiatry* (5th ed.; pp. 521-42). Oxford, UK: Blackwell.

Templeton, D., Smith, P., Rodgers, A., Conway, R., Carpenter, M., and McKinnon, J. (2010, January 19). Haitian orphans settle in: Rescue team discusses trip. *Pittsburgh Post-Gazette.* Retrieved from http://www.post-gazette.com/pg/10019/1029348-100.stm.

Terre des Hommes and United Nations Children's Fund (Co-producers), and Sylvain, S-A. (Director). (2010). Paper Orphans [Documentary film]. UK: Image Ark Pvt. LTD.

Terzieff, J. (2005, January 24). From tragedy to slavery. *AlterNet.* Retrieved from http://www.alternet.org/story/21030/.

Therborn, G. (2006). African families in a global context. In G. Therborn (ed.), *African Families in a Global Context* (pp. 17-48). Uppsala: Nordiska Afrikainstitutet.

Thoburn, J. (2007). Globalisation and child welfare: Some lessons from a cross-national study of children in out-of-home care. Norwich: University of East Anglia. Retrieved from https://www.uea.ac.uk/polopoly_fs/1.103398!globalisation%201108.pdf.

Thomas, A. and Mabusela, S. (1991). Foster care in Soweto, South Africa: Under assault from a politically hostile environment. *Child Welfare*, 70, 121-30.

Thomas, D. (2006). *Tsunami: Two Year Update.* Retrieved from the United Nations Children's Fund website: http://www.unicef.org/emerg/disasterinasia/index_37334.html.

Thomas, K.A. and Tessler, R.C. (2007). Bicultural socialization among adoptive families: Where there is a will, there is a way. *Journal of Family Issues*, 28, 1189-219.

Thompson, G. (2010a, February 23). Questions surface after Haitian airlift. *New York Times.* Retrieved from http://www.nytimes.com/2010/02/24/world/americas/24orphans.html.

Thompson, G. (2010b, August 3). After Haiti quake, the chaos of USA adoption. *New York Times.* Retrieved from http://www.nytimes.com/2010/08/04/world/americas/04adoption.html.

Thompson, N.S. (2004). Hague is enough? A call for more protective, uniform law guiding international adoptions. *Wisconsin International Law Journal*, 22, 444-5.

Tieman, W., Van der Ende, J., and Verhulst, F.C. (2005). Psychiatric disorders in young adult intercountry adoptees: An epidemiological study. *American Journal of Psychiatry*, 162, 592-8.

Tieman, W., Van der Ende, J., and Verhulst, F.C. (2008). Young adult international adoptees' search for birth parents. *Journal of Family Psychology*, 22, 678-87.

Tigervall, C. and Hübinette, T. (2010). Adoption with complications: Conversations with adoptees and adoptive parents on everyday racism and ethnic identity. *International Social Work*, 53, 489-509.

Townsend, L. (2003). Open adoption: A review of the literature with recommendations to adoption practitioners. *Journal of Child and Adolescent Mental Health*, 15, 1-11.

Trenka, J.J. (2003). *The Language of Blood: A Memoir.* Minneapolis, MN: Borealis Books.

Trenka, J.J. (2006, Aug 19). Children's Home Society and GOAL [Online forum comment 45511]. Retrieved from http://groups.yahoo.com/group/koreanadopteesworldwide.

Trenka, J.J. (2009). *Fugitive Provisions: An Adoptee's Return to Korea.* Minneapolis, MN: Graywolf Press.

Triseliotis, J. (1973). *In Search of Origins: The Experiences of Adopted People.* London: Routledge and Kegan Paul.

Triseliotis, J. (2000). Intercountry adoption: Global trade or global gift? *Adoption and Fostering*, 24(2), 45-54.

Triseliotis, J., Shireman, J., and Hundleby, M. (1997). *Adoption: Theory, Policy and Practice.* London: Cassell Wellington House.

Truth and Reconciliation for the Adoption Community of Korea. (2011). *About TRACK.* Retrieved from http://justicespeaking.wordpress.com/objective.

Tuan, M. and Shiao, J.L. (2011). *Choosing Ethnicity, Negotiating Race: Korean Adoptees in America.* New York, NY: Russell Sage Foundation.

Tutu, D. (2000). *No Future without Forgiveness.* New York, NY: Double Day.

United Adoptees International. (2010, January 6). Council of Europe Conference reveals itself as an adoption lobby network. *United Adoptees International News.* Retrieved from http://uai-news.blogspot.com/2010/01/council-of-europe-conference-reveals.htm.

UNAIDS. (2010). *Global Report: UNAIDS Report on the Global AIDS Epidemic.* Retrieved from the United Nations website: http://www.unaids.org/globalreport/documents/20101123_GlobalReport_full_en.pdf.

United in grief farmers lament loss of children 'stolen' by officials. (2006, March 21). *South China Morning Post*, p. 7.

United Nations. (1948a, December 9). *Convention on the Prevention and Punishment of the Crime of Genocide.* Retrieved from http://www.un-documents.net/cppcg.htm.

United Nations. (1948b). *The Universal Declaration of Human Rights.* Retrieved from http://www.un.org/en/documents/udhr/index.shtml.

United Nations. (2000). *Protocol to Prevent, Suppress, and Punish Trafficking in Persons, Especially Women and Children, Supplementing the United Nations Convention against Transnational Organized Crime.* Retrieved from http://www.uncjin.org/Documents/Conventions/dcatoc/final_documents_2/convention_%20traff_eng.pdf.

United Nations. (2009). *Guidelines for the Alternative Care of Children, Human Rights Council, Eleventh Session Resolution 11/7.* Retrieved from http://ap.ohchr.org/documents/E/HRC/resolutions/A_HRC_RES_11_7.pdf.

United Nations Children's Fund. (1999). Intercountry adoption. *Innocenti Digest 4.* Florence: UNICEF Innocenti Research Centre. Retrieved from http://www.unicef-irc.org/publications/102/.

United Nations Children's Fund. (2001). *A Decade of Transition: Regional Monitoring Report 8, The Monee Project, CEE/CIS/Baltics.* Florence, Italy: Innocenti Research Centre.

United Nations Children's Fund. (2003). Africa's orphaned generations. *United Nations.* Retrieved from http://www.unicef.org/sowc06/pdfs/africas_orphans.pdf.

United Nations Children's Fund. (2007a). *Children at Risk in Central and Eastern Europe: Perils and Promises, Regional Monitoring Report No. 4.* Florence, Italy: UNICEF International Child Development Centre.

United Nations Children's Fund. (2007b). *Tsunami Press Room.* Retrieved from http://www.unicef.org/media/media_24628.html.

United Nations Children's Fund. (2008a). *Haiti at a Glance.* Retrieved from http://www.unicef.org/infobycountry/haiti.html.

United Nations Children's Fund. (2008b). *Statistics on South Africa.* Retrieved from http://www.unicef.org/infobycountry/southafrica_statistics.html.

United Nations Children's Fund. (2010). *Children of Haiti: Progress, Gaps, and Plans in Humanitarian Action Supporting a Transformative Agenda for Children.* Retrieved from http://www.unicef.org/malaysia/Final_UNICEF_Haiti_90-Day_Report_April_2010_reduced_size.pdf.

United Nations Children's Fund. (n.d.) *UNICEF's Position on Intercountry Adoption.* Retrieved from www.unicef.org/media/media_41118.html.

United Nations Children's Fund and Terre des Hommes. (2008). *Adopting the Rights of the Child: A Study on Intercountry Adoption and its Influence on Child Protection in Nepal.* Kathmandu, Nepal: Terre des Hommes Foundation.

United Nations Children's Fund and United Nations Development Programme. (2007). *La Niñez Guatemalteca en Cifras: Compendio estadístico sobre las niñas, niños y adolescentes guatemaltecos* [Guatemalan childhood in numbers: Statistical compendium about Guatemalan girls, boys, and adolescents]. Guatemala: UNICEF.

United Nations Children's Fund and Vox Latina. (2008). *Resumen encuesta nacional: UNICEF sobre las adopciones en Guatemala* [Summary of a national survey: UNICEF about adoptions in Guatemala]. Retrieved from http://www.unicef.org.gt/1_recursos_unicefgua/estudios_opinion/estudios_opinion_2008/adopciones_pdf/resultados_encuesta_nacional_pdf/resumen_encuesta_nac_adopciones.pdf .

United Nations Committee on the Rights of the Child. (2009). *Concluding observations: Romania.* Retrieved from http://www2.ohchr.org/english/bodies/crc/docs/co/CRC-C-ROM-CO-4.pdf.

United Nations Convention on the Rights of the Child, Committee on the Rights of the Child. (2010). *Concluding Observations: Guatemala.* Retrieved from http://daccess-dds-ny.un.org/doc/UNDOC/GEN/G10/459/58/PDF/G1045958.pdf?OpenElement.

United Nations Development Programme. (2009). *Informe sobre desarrollo humano 2009. Superando barreras: Movilidad y desarrollo humano* [2009 Human development report: Overcoming barriers: Mobility and human development]. Retrieved from http://hdr.undp.org/en/media/HDR_2009_EN_Complete.pdf.

United Nations Development Programme. (2010). *International Human Development indicators.* Retrieved from http://hdr.undp.org/en/data/profiles/.

United Nations Economic and Social Council Commission on Human Rights. (2000). *Report of the Special Rapporteur on the Sale of Children, Child Prostitution and Child Pornography: Report on the mission to Guatemala of Ms. Ofelia Calcetas-Santos.* New York, NY: United Nations.

United Nations Treaty Collection. (2011a). *Status Table: Convention on the Rights of the Child.* Retrieved from http://treaties.un.org/Pages/ViewDetails.aspx?src=TREATYandmtdsg_no=IV-11andchapter=4andlang=en.

United Nations Treaty Collection. (2011b). *Status Table: Optional Protocol to the Convention on the Rights of the Child on the Sale of Children, Child Prostitution and Child Pornography.* Retrieved from http://treaties.un.org/Pages/ViewDetails.aspx?src=TREATYandmtdsg_no=IV-11-candchapter=4andlang=en.

US Agency for International Development. (1975). *Operation Babylift Report.* Retrieved from http://darkwing.uoregon.edu/~adoption/archive/AIDOBR.htm.

US Agency for International Development. (2005). *Cambodia Orphanage Survey*. Retrieved from http://pdf.usaid.gov/pdf_docs/PNADI624.pdf.

US Agency for International Development. (2010). *Frequently Asked Questions: Haiti's Orphans and Vulnerable Children.* Retrieved from http://www.usaid.gov/helphaiti/opcfaq.html.

US Citizenship and Immigration Services. (2001). *Information Sheet Regarding the Intercountry Adoption Act of 2000.* Retrieved from http://www.uscis.gov/portal/site/uscis/.

US Citizenship and Immigration Services. (2006). Issuance of Adoption Certificates and Custody Declarations in Hague Convention Adoption Cases" *Title 22 code of Federal Regulations Part 97*. Current as of February 9, 2012. Retrieved from http://ecfr.gpoaccess.gov/cgi/t/text/text-idx?c=ecfr&rgn=div5&view=text&node=22:1.0.1.10.52&idno=22.

US Citizenship and Immigration Services. (2009). *Hague Home Study Tip Sheet for Adoption Service Providers and Prospective Adoptive Parents*. Washington, DC: Department of Homeland Security, Citizenship and Immigration Services.

U.S. Department of Health and Human Services. (2010). *The Adoption and Foster Care Analysis and Reporting System Report: Preliminary FY 2009 Estimates as of July 2010.* Retrieved from http://www.acf.hhs.gov/programs/cb/stats_research/afcars/tar/report17.htm.

U.S. Department of Health and Human Services Administration for Children and Families. (n.d.). *Child Welfare Information Gateway.* Retrieved from www.childwelfare.gov/.

U.S. Department of State. (2008). *Summary of Irregularities in Adoptions in Vietnam.* Retrieved from http://vietnam.usembassy.gov/irreg_adoptions042508.html.

U.S. Department of State. (2010a). *2010 Adoption Statistics.* Retrieved from http://adoption.state.gov/about_us/statistics.php.

U.S. Department of State. (2010b). *FY 2010 Annual Report on Intercountry Adoptions.* Retrieved from http://adoption.state.gov/content/pdf/fy2010_annual_report.pdf.

U.S. Department of State (2010c). *Intercountry Adoption.* Retrieved from http://adoption.state.gov.

U.S. Department of State. (2010d). *Notice: Adoption Processing at the U.S. Embassy in Addis Ababa.* Retrieved from http://adoption.state.gov/country_information/country_specific_alerts_notices.php?alert_notice_type=noticesandalert_notice_file=ethiopia_4.

U.S. Department of State. (2011a). *Adoption Statistics from Ethiopia.* Retrieved from www. Adoption.state.gov/about_us/statistics.php.

U.S. Department of State. (2011b). *Cambodia: Notice Update of Status of Adoptions in Cambodia.* Retrieved from: http://adoption.state.gov/country_information/country_specific_alerts_notices.php?alert_notice_type=noticesandalert_notice_file=cambodia_1.

U.S. Department of State. (2011c). *Intercountry Adoption Statistics.* Retrieved from http://adoption.state.gov/about_us/statistics.php#

U.S. Department of State. (2011d, July). *FAQs: Bilateral Agreement with Russia.* Retrieved from http://adoption.state.gov/content/pdf/FAQs_re_Agreement_07_13_2011_FINAL2.pdf.

U.S. Department of State. (2011e). *FY 2011 Annual Report on Intercountry Adoptions.* Retrieved from http://adoption.state.gov/content/pdf/fy2011_annual_report.pdf.

U.S. Department of State. (n.d.a). *Accredited Adoption Providers.* Retrieved from http://www.adoption.state.gov/hague/agency4.php?q=0andq1=andq2=0andq4=0andq5=0anddirfld=01.

U.S. Department of State. (n.d.b). *Intercountry Adoption, Country Specific Information.* Retrieved from http://adoption.state.gov/about_us/statistics.php#

U.S. Department of State Bureau of Consular Affairs. (2008). *The Hague Convention on Intercountry Adoption: A Web-guide for State Authorities on Outgoing Adoption Cases from the United States to Another Convention Country.* Retrieved from http://adoption.state.gov/content/pdf/web_guide_state_authorities.pdf.

U.S. Department of State Bureau of Consular Affairs. (2009a). *The Hague Convention on Intercountry Adoption: A Guide to Outgoing Cases from the United States.* Retrieved from http://adoption.state.gov/content/pdf/OutgoingCasesFAQs.pdf.

U.S. Department of State Bureau of Consular Affairs. (2009b). *Outgoing Cases: Guidance on 22 CFR 96.54(a).* Retrieved from http://adoption.state.gov/hague_convention/outgoing_cases.php.

U.S. Department of State Bureau of Consular Affairs. (2011). *The Hague Convention on Intercountry Adoption: A guide to outgoing cases from the United States*. Updated December 2011. Retrieved from adoption.state.gov/content/pdf/OutgoingCasesFAQs_2011.pdf.

U.S. Department of State, Bureau of Consular Affairs. (n.d.). *Process Summary.* Retrieved from http://adoption.state.gov/hague_convention/adoptions_from_us/process.php.

U.S. District Court, Western District of Washington at Seattle. (2004). *Plea Agreement: United States of America v. Lauryn Galindo.* Retrieved from http://www.pear-now.org/reference/USvsGalindoPlea.pdf.

U.S. Government Accountability Office. (2005). *Foreign affairs: Agencies have Improved the Intercountry Adoption Process, but Further Enhancements are needed (Publication No. GAO-06-133).* Retrieved from http://www.gao.gov/new.items/d06133.pdf.

U.S. House of Representatives. (2006a, April 6). *Concerning the Government of Romania's Ban on Intercountry Adoptions and the Welfare of Orphaned or Abandoned Children in Romania. House Resolution 578.* Retrieved from http://thomas.loc.gov.

U.S. House of Representatives. (2006b). *Sexual Exploitation of Children over the Internet: Follow-up Issues to the Masha Allen adoption: Hearings before the Subcommittee on Oversight and Investigations of the Committee on Energy and Commerce of the House of Representatives, 109th Cong., Second Session.* Retrieved from http://frwebgate.access.gpo.gov/cgi-bin/getdoc.cgi?dbname=109_house_hearingsanddocid=f:31471.pdf.

U.S. Institute for Peace. (2001). *From Madness to Hope: The 12-year war in El Salvador: Report of the Commission on the Truth for El Salvador.* UN Security Council, Annex, S/25500, 1993, 5-8. Retrieved from http://www.usip.org/files/file/ElSalvador-Report.pdf.

Vadapalli, D.K. (2009). Barriers and challenges in accessing social transfers and role of social welfare services in improving targeting efficiency: A study of conditional cash transfers. *Vulnerable Children and Youth Studies*, 4, 41-54.

Valk, M.A. (1957). *Korean-American Children in American Adoptive Homes.* New York, NY: Child Welfare League of America.

Van den Dries, L., Juffer, F., Van IJzendoorn, M.H., and Bakermans-Kranenburg, M.J. (2009). Fostering security? A meta-analysis of attachment in adopted children. *Children and Youth Services Review*, 31, 410-21.

Van den Dries, L., Juffer, F., Van IJzendoorn, M.H., and Bakermans-Kranenburg, M.J. (2010). Infants' physical and cognitive development after international adoption from foster care or institutions in China. *Journal of Developmental and Behavioral Pediatrics*, 31, 144-50.

Van IJzendoorn, M.H., Bakermans-Kranenburg, M.J., and Juffer, F. (2007). Plasticity of growth in height, weight, and head circumference: Meta-analytic evidence of massive catch-up after international adoption. *Journal of Developmental and Behavioral Pediatrics*, 28, 334-43.

Van IJzendoorn, M.H., Caspers, K., Bakermans-Kranenburg, M.J., Beach, S.R.H., and Philibert, R. (2010). Methylation matters: Interaction between methylation density and serotonin transporter genotype predicts unresolved loss or trauma. *Biological Psychiatry*, 68, 405-7.

Van IJzendoorn, M.H. and Juffer, F. (2005). Adoption is a successful natural intervention enhancing adopted children's IQ and school performance. *Current Directions in Psychological Science*, 14, 326-30.

Van IJzendoorn, M.H. and Juffer, F. (2006). The Emanuel Miller Memorial Lecture 2006: Adoption as intervention: Meta-analytic evidence for massive catch-up and plasticity in physical, socio-emotional and cognitive development. *Journal of Child Psychology and Psychiatry*, 47, 1228-45.

Van IJzendoorn, M.H., Juffer, F., and Klein Poelhuis, C.W. (2005). Adoption and cognitive development: A meta-analytic comparison of adopted and non-adopted children's IQ and school performance. *Psychological Bulletin*, 131, 301-16.

Van IJzendoorn, M.H., Luijk, M.P.C.M., and Juffer, F. (2008). IQ of children growing up in children's homes: A meta-analysis on IQ delays in orphanages. *Merrill-Palmer Quarterly*, 54, 341-66.

Van IJzendoorn, M.H., Palacios, J., Sonuga-Barke, E.J.S., Gunnar, M.R., Vorria, P., McCall, R.B., LeMare. L., Bakermans-Kranenburg, M.J., Dobrova-Krol, N.A. and Juffer, F. (2011). Children in institutional care: Delayed development and resilience. In R.B. McCall, M.H. van IJzendoorn, F. Juffer, C.J. Groark, and V.K. Groza (eds), Children without permanent parents: Research, practice and policy. *Monographs of the Society for Research in Child Development*, 76(4), 8-30.

Van IJzendoorn, M.H., Schuengel, C., and Bakermans-Kranenburg, M.J. (1999). Disorganized attachment in early childhood: Meta-analysis of precursors, concomitants, and sequelae. *Development and Psychopathology*, 11, 225-49.

Van Loon, H. (2000). Foreword to P. Selman (ed.), *Intercountry Adoption: Development, Trends and Perspectives.* London: BAAF.

Van Schaik, R., Wolfs, T.F., and Geelen, S.P. (2009). Improved general health of international adoptees, but immunization status still insufficient. *European Journal of Pediatrics*, 168, 1101-6.

Van Schalkwyk, S. (2008). Increase in abandoned babies. *Mail and Guardian.* Retrieved from http://mg.co.za/article/2008-06-03-increase-in-abandoned-babies.

Varnis, S. (2001). Regulating the global adoption of children. *Society*, 38(2), 39-46.

Vedder, P., Boekaerts, M., and Seegers, G. (2005). Perceived social support and well being in school. The role of students' ethnicity. *Journal of Youth and Adolescence*, 34, 269-78.

Velzeboer, M., Ellsberg, M., Arcas, C.C., and Garcia-Moreno, C. (2003). *Violence against Women: The Health Sector Responds.* Washington, DC: Pan-American Health Organization.

Veneman, A. (2007, November 5). *Statement by UNICEF Executive Director Ann M. Veneman.* Retrieved from http://www.unicef.org/media/media_41689.html.

Verhulst, F.C., Althaus, M., and Verluis-den Bierman, H. (1990). Problem behavior in international adoptees: I. An epidemiological study. *Journal of American Academy of Child and Adolescent Psychiatry*, 29, 94-103.

Verhulst, F., Althaus, M., and Versluis-den Bieman, H. (1992). Damaging backgrounds: Later adjustment of international adoptees. *Journal of the American Academy of Child and Adolescent Psychiatry*, 31, 518-24.

Vinnerlung, B., Lindblad, F., Rasmussen, F., and Dalen, M. (2010). School performance at age 16 among international adoptees: A Swedish national cohort study. *International Social Work,* 53, 443-56.

Vite, S. and Boechat, H. (2008). *Commentary on the United Nations Convention on the Rights of the Child: Article 21, Adoption.* Leiden: Martinus Nijhoff Publishers.

Vivano, E., Cataldo, F., Accomando, S., Firenze, A., Valenti, R.M., and Romano, N. (2006). Immunization status of internationally adopted children in Italy. *Vaccine*, 24, 4138-43.

Volkman, T. (2003). Embodying Chinese culture: Transnational adoption in North America. *Social Text*, 21(1), 29-58.

Von Borczyskowski, A., Hjern, A., Lindblad, F., and Vinnerljung, B. (2006). Suicidal behaviour in national and international adult adoptees. *Social Psychiatry and Psychiatric Epidemiology*, 41(2), 95-102.

Vonk, M.E. and Massati, R.R. (2008). Factors related to transracial adoptive parents' levels of cultural competence. *Adoption Quarterly*, 11, 204-26.

Vorria, P., Papaligoura, Z., Dunn, J., Van IJzendoorn, M.H., Steele, H. and Sarafidou, Y. (2003). Early experiences and attachment relationships of Greek infants raised in residential group care. *Journal of Child Psychology and Psychiatry*, 44, 1-13.

Vorria, P., Papaligoura, Z., Sarafidou, J., Kopakaki, M., Dunn, J., Van IJzendoorn, M.H., and Kontopoulou, A. (2006). The development of adopted children after institutional care: A follow-up study. *Journal of Child Psychology and Psychiatry*, 47, 1246-53.

Wallace, S. (2003). International adoption: The most logical solution to the disparity between the numbers of orphaned and abandoned children in some countries and families and individuals wishing to adopt in others. *Arizona Journal of International and Comparative Law*, 20, 689-724.

Wallis, D., Russell, H.F., and Muenke, M. (2008). Genetics of attention deficit/hyperactivity disorders. *Journal of Pediatric Psychology*, 33, 1085-99.

Walsh, J.M. (1999). *Adoption and Agency: American Adoptions of Marshallese Children* Retrieved from the Republic of the Marshall Islands Central Adoption Authority website: http://www.rmicaa.com/walsh.pdf.

Warren, S.B. (1992). Lower threshold for referral for psychiatric treatment for adopted adolescents. *Journal for Child Psychology and Psychiatry*, 31, 512-17.

Watkins, M. (2005). Adoption and identity: Nomadic possibilities for re-conceiving the self. In K. Wegar (ed.), *Adoptive Families in a Diverse Society* (pp. 259-74). New Brunswick, NJ: Rutgers University Press.

Watkins, M. and Fisher, S. (1993). *Talking with Young Children about Adoption.* New Haven, CT: Yale University Press.

Webhank. (2011, February 19). Both Ends Burning Foundation launches shirt campaign to raise awareness of international adoption crisis [blog post]. Retrieved from http://bothendsburning.org/about-us/news/page/4/.

Wegar, K. (2006). *Adoptive Families in a Diverse Society.* Piscataway, NJ: Rutgers University Press.

Weil, R.H. (1984). International adoption: The quiet migration. *International Migration Review*, 18, 276-93.

Wekker, G., Åsberg, C., van der Tuin, I., and Frederiks, N. (2007). *"Je hebt een Kleur, maar je bent Nederlands." Identiteitsformaties van Geadopteerden van Kleur* ["I have a color, but I am Dutch." Identity formation among adoptees of color]. Universiteit Utrecht: Leerstoelgroep Gender Studies.

Welsh, J.A., Viana, A.G., Petrill, S.A., and Mathias, M.D. (2008). Ready to adopt: Characteristics and expectations of pre-adoptive families pursuing international adoptions. *Adoption Quarterly*, 11, 176-203.

White, J. (March, 2006). Journal entry: February 26, 2006, Coban, Guatemala. *Guatemalan Student Support Group Newsletter*, 4(1), 5. Retrieved from http://www.gssg-usa.org/pdfs/GSSGnewsVol4-1.pdf.

White, O. (1999). *Children of the French Empire: Miscegenation and Colonial society in French West Africa 1895-1960.* Oxford: Oxford University Press.

Wickes, K. and Slate, J. (1996). Transracial adoption of Koreans: A preliminary study of adjustment. *International Journal for the Advancement of Counselling*, 19, 187-95.

Wiley, M.O. and Baden, A.L. (2005). Birth parents in adoption: Research, practice, and counseling psychology. *The Counseling Psychologist*, 33, 13-50.

Williams, D. (2010, April 9). Unwanted boy sent back to Russia. *Sky News Online.* Retrieved from http://news.sky.com/skynews/Home/World-News/Adopted-Boy-Sent-Back-To-Russia-From-US-Artyom-Savelyev-Rejected-By-His-Adopted-Tennessee-Mother/Article/201004215598120.

Williams, I. (2003). *Not Quite/Just the Same/Different.* (MA Thesis). University of Technology. Retrieved from http://hdl.handle.net/2100/316.

Wilson, S.L. and Gibbons, J.L. (2005). Guatemalan perceptions of adoption. *International Social Work*, 48, 742-52.

Winick, M., Meyer, K.K., and Harris, R.C. (1975). Malnutrition and environmental enrichment by early adoption. *Science*, 190, 1173-5.

Witwer, P. and Rotabi, K.S. (2011, March). *What Do We Know about Intercountry Adoption Agencies in the Context of Changes under the Hague Convention on Intercountry Adoption?* Paper presented at the Fourth Conference on International Social Work, Los Angeles, CA.

Wolfgram, S.M. (2008). Openness in adoption: What we know so far--A critical review of the literature. *Social Work*, 53, 133-42.

Wolfs, R. (2008). *Adoption Conversations: What, When, and How to Tell.* London: British Association for Adoption and Fostering.

World Bank. (2002). *Guatemala: From Poverty to Child Work.* Retrieved from http://info.worldbank.org/etools/docs/library/76309/dc2002/proceedings/pdfppt/guatemalachild.pdf.

World Bank. (n.d.) *Country and Lending Groups.* Retrieved from http://data.worldbank.org/about/country-classifications/country-and-lending-groups.

World Health Organization. (2011). *World Health Organization's List of Countries.* Retrieved from http://www.who.int/country.

Wrobel, G.M., Kohler, J.K., Grotevant, H.D., and McRoy, R.G. (2003). The Family Adoption Communication (FAC) Model: Identifying pathways of adoption-related communication. *Adoption Quarterly*, 7(2), 53-84.

Xinran. (2010). *Message from an Unknown Birthmother: Stories of Loss and Love.* London: Chatto and Windus.

Yade, R. (2007, October 28). *Zoe's Ark Press Conference.* Retrieved from http://www.ambafrance-uk.org/Rama-Yade-s-press-conference-on.html.

Yanez, L. (2010, January 21). Injured Haitian children win humanitarian visas to the USA. *Miami Herald.* Retrieved from http://www.miamiherald.com/2010/01/21/1438810/injured-haitian-children-win-humanitarian.html#ixzz0ppx16Krp.

Yankoski, L. (2010). *Haitian Orphan Support: Update from Sister Linda Yankoski, Holy Family Institute.* Retrieved from http://www.hfi-pgh.org/Haiti.htm.

Yngvesson, B. (2002). Placing the "gift child" in transnational adoption. *Law and Society Review*, 36, 227-56.

Yngvesson, B. (2010). *Belonging in an Adopted World. Race, Identity, and Transnational Adoption.* Chicago, IL: The University of Chicago Press.

Zappala, M. and Johnson, C. (2009). A case for ethical intercountry adoption. *Adoption Advocate No. 11*, Retrieved from https://www.adoptioncouncil.org/publications/adoption-advocate-no11.html.

Zeanah, C.H., Egger, H.L., Smyke, A.T., Nelson, C.A., Fox, N.A., and Guthrie, D. (2009). Institutional rearing and psychiatric disorders in Romanian preschool children. *American Journal of Psychiatry*, 166, 777-85.

Zeanah, C.H., Smyke, A.T., Koga, S.F., Carlson, E., and The Bucharest Early Intervention Project Core Group. (2005). Attachment in institutionalized and community children in Romania. *Child Development*, 76, 1015-28.

Zermatten, J., (2010). *The Best Interests of the Child: Literal Analysis, Function and Implementation.* Sion, Switzerland: Institute Internationale des Droits de L'Enfant.

Zhang, L. (1999). *Mighty Opposites: From Dichotomies to Differences in the Comparative Study of China.* Palo Alto, CA: Stanford University Press.

Zhang, W. (2006). Child adoption in contemporary rural China. *Journal of Family Issues*, 27, 301-40.

Zhang, Y. and Lee, G.R. (2011). Intercountry versus transracial adoption: Analysis of adoptive parents' motivations and preferences in adoption. *Journal of Family Issues*, 32, 75-98.

Zigler, E. (1976). A developmental psychologist's view of Operation Babylift. *American Psychologist*, 31, 329-40.

Zimmer, Z. and Dayton, J. (2005). Older adults in sub-Saharan Africa living with children and grandchildren. *Population Studies*, 59, 295-312.

Index